The Renaissance of the Saints after Reform

The Renaissance of the Saints after Reform

GINA M. DI SALVO

Great Clarendon Street, Oxford, OX2 6DP,
United Kingdom

Oxford University Press is a department of the University of Oxford.
It furthers the University's objective of excellence in research, scholarship,
and education by publishing worldwide. Oxford is a registered trade mark of
Oxford University Press in the UK and in certain other countries

© Gina M. Di Salvo 2023

The moral rights of the author have been asserted

All rights reserved. No part of this publication may be reproduced, stored in
a retrieval system, or transmitted, in any form or by any means, without the
prior permission in writing of Oxford University Press, or as expressly permitted
by law, by licence or under terms agreed with the appropriate reprographics
rights organization. Enquiries concerning reproduction outside the scope of the
above should be sent to the Rights Department, Oxford University Press, at the
address above

You must not circulate this work in any other form
and you must impose this same condition on any acquirer

Published in the United States of America by Oxford University Press
198 Madison Avenue, New York, NY 10016, United States of America

British Library Cataloguing in Publication Data

Data available

Library of Congress Control Number: 2023935114

ISBN 978–0–19–286591–5

DOI: 10.1093/oso/9780192865915.001.0001

Printed and bound by
CPI Group (UK) Ltd, Croydon, CR0 4YY

Links to third party websites are provided by Oxford in good faith and
for information only. Oxford disclaims any responsibility for the materials
contained in any third party website referenced in this work.

For Jeffrey, forever

Acknowledgments

The first spark of this book began twenty years ago on the top floor of St. Michael's Hall on Shoe Lane in a conversation with Brenna Kearney about women's bodies in Shakespeare (her essay), on the one hand, and medieval English hagiography (my essay), on the other. *The Renaissance of the Saints after Reform* is a book about saints and drama and the relationship of the Middle Ages to the early modern period, but it is also a book wrought in friendship, scholarly community, and familial and institutional support. In the years that it took for questions about sanctity and performance to find their final form at Oxford University Press on Great Clarendon Street, less than a mile away from Shoe Lane, I have gathered much to be grateful for.

Over the course of this project, I benefited from the generosity of a number of scholars who shared work with me, offered feedback on my own, and advised me on how to proceed. I am most grateful to Julia Fawcett, Katie Goodland, Marissa Greenberg, Carissa Harris, Erika Lin, Julia Lupton, Dassia Posner, Kim Solga, Karen Winstead, Katie Zien, and Jay Zysk. Sarah Beckwith and John Parker provided specific, careful, and insightful suggestions on an earlier draft of the manuscript that helped to reshape the argument and expand the project.

I was fortunate to study with faculty who offered incredible guidance on my thinking and, especially, my writing. The arguments, analysis, organization, and methodology of this book are owed to the education I received from Katherine Jensen, Patrick Tuite, Chris Wheatley, and the late Stephen Wright; Nicholas Crowe, Nigel Frith, and Diana Wyatt; Richard Dutton and Chris Highley; and Tracy Davis, Kasey Evans, Jeff Masten, and Barbara Newman. My gratitude, as well, to the late John Feneley and Sandra Feneley, the late Alun Thornton Jones, and Mark Philpott for their dedication to introducing American students to study in Oxford. I hope this book is worthy of the alumni shelf at the Centre for Medieval and Renaissance Studies.

I pursued graduate study in an atmosphere of intellectual inspiration, rigor, and generosity. I imitated the best habits of my cohort until I became habituated to them myself. My gratitude to Ray Ball, Jason Bush, Gib Cima, Jen Schlueter, and Terry Schoone-Jongen; Sara Armstrong and Louise Edwards Neiman; and Christine Scippa Bhasin, David Calder, Adrian Curtin, La Donna Forsgren, Nathan Hedman, Carolina Hotchandani, Keith Byron Kirk, Shannon Fitzsimmons Moen, Jesse Njus, Sam O'Connell, Chris Shirley, Dan Smith, Kati Sweeney, and Paul Thelan. Their fellowship left an indelible mark on this project's formation and

I am fortunate that a number of them are now valued colleagues. My gratitude extends to the extraordinary collegiality of Gina Buccola, Megan Geigner, Martine Green-Rodgers, Jenny Kokai, John Kuhn, Danielle Rosvally, Jonathan Shandell, and Donovan Sherman. Erin McCarthy, Laura Lodewyck, and Carla Della Gatta give continual professional and personal support and I am grateful for their friendship. The brilliant Gianna Mosser deserves sainthood for her editorial expertise, culinary wisdom, and comradeship at every stage of this project.

This book exists at all because Josh Chambers-Letson, Theresa Coletti, and Harvey Young believed in my pursuit of an academic career when I doubted it myself. I am also fortunate to have had the best of advisors during both my MA and PhD work. I hope this book carries on some of the legacy of the late Tom Postlewait's historiographic precision and indefatigable line edits. And I hope that Will West sees himself in any part of this book that, even for a sentence, achieves a combination of intellectual curiosity and elegance.

I am grateful to Eleanor Collins, Jo Spillane, Nadine Kolz, and all the staff at Oxford University Press who have expertly handled this book and guided me through the process. The two anonymous reviewers for the press helped transform the manuscript into the book it was meant to become. Thanks are also due to Jessica Hinds-Bond, Philip Dines, Priyan Gopathy, and Liz Laurie for their editorial support. Chapter 3 revises some material previously published in "'A Virgine and a Martyr both': The Turn to Hagiography in Heywood's Reformation History Play." *Renaissance and Reformation* (2018): 133–67, DOI: https://doi.org/10.7202/1061917ar. A part of Chapter 4 appears in "Saints' Lives and Shoemakers' Holidays: The Gentle Craft and the Wells Cordwainers' Pageant of 1613." *Early Theatre* (2016): 119–38, DOI: https://doi.org/10.12745/et.19.2.2706.

The University of Tennessee provided the bulk of the research resources for this project. Most instrumental to my success was a 2018–19 Faculty Fellowship at the University of Tennessee Humanities Center. Other UTHC programs, including a manuscript workshop, a book proposal workshop, and a writing accountability group, were also critical. Professional development funds from the Department of Theatre and a Riggsby Travel Grant allowed me to access archival material at the Beinecke, the Folger, the Newberry, the Bodleian, the British Library, and the National Archives in Kew. I thank the kind librarians at these institutions, especially the ones at the Beinecke who welcomed me to the staff lounge when I needed a cup of tea and the ones at the National Archives who kept my materials for me when I did not adequately reserve them. The staff of the University of Tennessee libraries deserves special thanks for their continual support of all faculty, but especially those of us who required access to materials during the pandemic. My professional development funds also supported my participation in a Rare Book School program with the delightful David Scott Kastan that reinvigorated my research. The Maples conference fund enabled me to present research and receive feedback at professional conferences, including the American Society for Theatre Research, the International Congress of Medieval Studies at Kalamazoo, the Sewanee Medieval Colloquium, and the Shakespeare Association of America. A Paul L. Soper Professorship allowed me to absorb extra costs of caretaking during an extended family emergency. The Newberry Consortium for Renaissance Studies helped to fund my participation in a Periodization seminar and Periodization 2.0 Symposium, both at the Folger Institute. A Mellon-funded seminar in English Paleography with the incomparable Heather Wolfe oriented my archival research and taught me how to decipher it. The initial survey of saint plays—the backbone of this book—was conducted during a beautiful month at the Huntington Library supported by a W. M. Keck Foundation fellowship.

I benefit every day from working in a Department of Theatre with a dual mission of academic study and artistic practice. My colleagues and students in Theatre inspire me. More than once, what I wanted to say about saints and drama became clear in production meetings or rehearsal as the craft of theatre making was in process. Colleagues from other parts of the University of Tennessee, including the Humanities Center and Marco Institute, helped me to find my footing as an interdisciplinary scholar. Particular thanks are due to Kate Buckley, Katie Cunningham, Margaret Lazarus Dean, Mary Dzon, Sarah Eldridge, Amy Elias, Stan Garner, Jessi Grieser, Chris Hebert, Gregor Kalas, Dan Magilow, Chiara Mariani, Harrison Meadows, Lo Presser, Lauren Roark, Jay Rubenstein, Alan Rutenberg, and Ryan Windeknecht. This book found its way because Justin Arft, Sara Ritchey, Tina Shepardson, and Anthony Welch offered specific guidance at crucial moments. I found my way because Misty Anderson, Heather Hirschfeld, and Casey Sams offer spectacular mentorship. Their practical strategizing, artistic and intellectual generosity, and encouragement are vital to my success and well-being. Laura De Furio and Helene Sinnreich provide the rare sort of camaraderie and trust that every woman in academia wishes for.

During the writing of this book, my family forged a new life in Knoxville and we are sustained here by good friends and community. The DeBolt, De Furio-Partridge, Mayer, Presser, Santos-Sulman, and Sinnreich-Johnson families have shared birthdays, holidays, school closures, and pool snacks with us. On multiple occasions Julia Price welcomed my kids to join her own while she herself had work to complete. Mary Linda Schwarzbart's porch provided much needed conversation about contemporary art and religion when most other things were cancelled. My walks and texts with Karen Ferency and Briana Rosenbaum saw me through the hardest setbacks and most celebratory progress of the past few years. I strive to reciprocate all that they give to me. I could not have completed this book without the staff and teachers at the Arnstein JCC Preschool and Summer Camp and the Stanford Eisenberg Knoxville Jewish Day School. They have provided a joyful education and consistent care for my daughters so that it was possible for me to leave for research and to maintain focus while at home. An overhaul of Chapter 1 was completed during the summer of 2020 because Mary McGarr used her creative genius to build cardboard cities and play mermaids with my daughters. This book transformed from a first draft to a final manuscript during a worldwide pandemic. With my deepest thanks to scientists and healthcare workers, especially those local to Knoxville, there would be no book if I had not first survived.

Further afield, my steadfast friends make me a more generous thinker and make the act of disagreeing a pleasurable and often laughter-filled endeavor. My gratitude to Cristina Canning and Tara Logan; to Fr. Mark DeCelles, Lisa Hacker, Rich Igrassia, Vinny Lacey, Mark LeVota, Kristopher Mecholsky, Christine Neulieb, and Joseph Price; to Gates and Reed Brown, Shawn Carey, Kristen French, and Pat McKenney. And to Brenna Kearney, I owe you a few rounds and a proper meal the next time we walk from Little Clarendon to Great Clarendon and then do the long walk across the Port Meadow.

Although I can never thank them enough, *grazie mille* to my entire family for their love and support. My parents' travel habits, cultural interests, dedication to service, and educational pursuits encouraged me to not only pursue an academic life but to pursue a good life. My extended family shares in my success and also ensures—often with food—that I have a good life. I am also grateful to those who came before me and for the many intergenerational gifts and sacrifices that make my achievement possible. More recently, my family offered specific support for the undertaking of this project. My cousin, Shelley Esposito-Blomberg, and her family offered me warmth in their London home during a brisk week of research. My sister, Angie, used her Jedi focus to edit the manuscript. The absent errata are because of her; those that remain belong to me. Especial thanks are due to my mother, Diane Tremblay Booth, and mother-in-law, Marygaye Tinley, who care for me and my family when I cannot. I grieve that my father-in-law, Jeffrey Tinley, Sr., will not see this book in print, but it is a wonder that I had the good fortune in my life to know him and to know that he was proud of me. My daughters, Adeline and Bernadette, have made 100 books in the time it has taken for me to make this one. I have made this book, in part, because I delight in their every breath and desire to provide a happy life for them. Because children are honest art critics and don't couch their comments for the adult ego, their thoughts about the motives and shapes of angels also helped clarify the Epilogue. I have completed this book because I am completed by Jeffrey Tinley, Jr. In the beginning of time, a jealous god split our kind apart, but some of us—inexplicably and astonishingly—are reunited with our lost half. No angelic interventions are necessary to signify that this completion is a miracle.

Contents

Abbreviations	xi
Textual Conventions and Citations	xiii
Introduction: Against Iconoclasm	1
1. The Archives of Performance and Sacred Time	22
2. Devils in the Details	57
3. Acts of Translation	80
4. Old Legends of England	111
5. Devices of Virgin Martyrdom	137
Epilogue: Look Up, Look Up	168
Note to Appendices 1 and 2	180
Appendix 1: Chronological Table of Saint Plays	181
Appendix 2: Table of Saints in Liturgical Calendars	204
Bibliography	233
Index	250

Abbreviations

In citing works in the notes, short titles have generally been used. Works and terms frequently cited have been identified by the following abbreviations:

BCP	*Book of Common Prayer*
BSPR	Clifford Davidson. "British Saint Play Records." 2002. https://scholarworks.wmich.edu/early_drama/2/
Caxton, *Golden Legend*	Jacobus de Voragine. *Legenda aurea sanctorum, sive, Lombardica historia* [The Golden Legend] (London: William Caxton, 1483).
Digby Plays	*The Late Medieval Religious Plays of Bodleian MSS Digby 133 and e. Mus. 160*. Edited by Donald C. Baker, John L. Murphy, and Louis B. Hall, Jr. EETS o.s. 283. Oxford: Oxford University Press, 1982.
DTRB	Ian Lancashire. *Dramatic Texts and Records of Britain: A Chronological Topography to 1558*. Toronto: University of Toronto Press, 1984.
EETS	Early English Text Society
e.s.	Extra Series
Foxe 1570	John Foxe. *The ecclesiasticall history contaynyng the actes and monumentes of thynges passed in euery kynges tyme in this realme: especially in the Church of England* . . . 2 vols. Aldersgate: Iohn Daye, 1570.
JMEMS	*Journal of Medieval and Early Modern Studies*
LMS	Lord Mayor's Show
LPD	*Lost Play Database*. Edited by Roslyn L. Knutson, David McInnis, Matthew Steggle, and Misha Teramura. Washington, D. C.: Folger Shakespeare Library. https://lostplays.folger.edu/
MSC III	*A Calendar of Dramatic Records in the Books of Livery Companies of London, 1485–1640*. Edited by Jean Robertson and D. J. Gordon. Malone Society Collections. Vol. 3. Oxford, 1954.
MSC XI	*Records of Plays and Players in Norfolk and Suffolk, 1330–1642*. Edited by David Galloway and John Wasson. Malone Society Collections. Vol. 3. Oxford, 1980.
MSW	Midsummer's Watch
NCPF	*Non-cycle Plays and Fragments*. Edited by Norman Davis. EETS, s.s. 1 London: Oxford University Press, 1970.
o.s.	Original Series

PhilMus	*The Philological Museum.* Edited by Dana Sutton and Martin Wiggins. https://philological.cal.bham.ac.uk/
REED: Cheshire	*Records of Early English Drama: Cheshire Including Chester.* Edited by Elizabeth Baldwin, Lawrence M. Clopper, and David Mills. Toronto: University of Toronto Press, 2007.
REED: Coventry	*Records of Early English Drama: Coventry.* Edited by R. W. Ingram. Toronto: University of Toronto Press, 1981.
REED: CWG	*Records of Early English Drama: Cumberland, Westmoreland, Gloucestershire.* Edited by Audrey Douglas and Peter Greenfield. Toronto: University of Toronto Press, 1986.
REED: Devon	*Records of Early English Drama: Devon.* Edited by John Wasson. Toronto: University of Toronto Press, 1986.
REED: HereWor	*Records of Early English Drama: Hereford and Worcestershire.* Edited by David Klausner. Toronto: University of Toronto Press, 1990.
REED: Kent	*Records of Early English Drama: Kent, Diocese of Canterbury.* Edited by James M. Gibson. 3 vols. Toronto: University of Toronto Press, 2002.
REED: Lincolnshire	*Records of Early English Drama: Lincolnshire.* Edited by James Stokes. 2 vols. Toronto: University of Toronto Press, 2009.
REED: Norwich	*Records of Early English Drama: Norwich, 1540–1642.* Edited by David Galloway. Toronto: University of Toronto Press, 1984.
REED: Oxford	*Records of Early English Drama: Oxford.* Edited by John R. Elliot and Alan Nelson (university), Alexandra F. Johnston and Diana Wyatt (city). 2 vols. Toronto: University of Toronto Press, 2004.
REED: Shropshire	*Records of Early English Drama: Shropshire.* Edited by J. Alan B. Sommerset. 2 vols. Toronto: University of Toronto Press, 1994.
REED: Somerset	*Records of Early English Drama: Somerset, including Bath.* Edited by James Stokes. Toronto: University of Toronto Press, 1996.
REED: York	*Records of Early English Drama: York.* Edited by Alexandra F. Johnston and Margaret Rogerson. 2 vols. Toronto: University of Toronto Press, 1979.
SEL	*Studies in English Literature*
Wiggins	Wiggins, Martin, and Catherine Richardson, eds. *British Drama 1533–1642: A Catalogue.* 9 Vols. Oxford: Oxford University Press, 2012–19.

Textual Conventions and Citations

Unless otherwise noted, I have retained the early spelling when quoting directly from early manuscripts and printed books. Expansions of abbreviations are noted by italics and brackets.

William Caxton's edition of Jacobus de Voragine's *Golden Legend* uses Roman numerals instead of Latin alphabet letters or Arabic numerals, which are both more common in early modern printed books. For this reason, I include recto and verso in my citations of the signature (i.e., Cix recto, Civ verso).

For Shakespeare's plays, unless otherwise noted, such as when quoting directly from quarto or folio, I cite the Folger Digital Texts (Barbara Mowat et al., eds., *Shakespeare's Play, Sonnets, and Poems*, www.folgerdigitaltexts.org).

Introduction: Against Iconoclasm

Near the end of the play of St. Katherine, the saint's mother begs her to give "false promise" to the lustful Roman emperor, Maximian, so that he will preserve their lives.[1] Katherine, steadfast in her love for Christ, refuses. In response, Maximian orders his men to "Draw then that Curtain" and unveil a hideous spiked wheel (54). The tyrant revels in sadistic anticipation. Katherine's wheel has been designed so that her breasts will "feel / First the rough razings of the pointed steel," as she is ground to death (54). Katherine prays for deliverance—not from dying, but from being stripped naked in violation of her sacred modesty. The angel of God "*descends swiftly with a flaming Sword, and strikes at the Wheel, which breaks in pieces, then he ascends again*" (55). Soon after, Katherine is beheaded offstage, and a series of stabbings in the Roman palace ends with Maximian's death. At the end of the performance, the actor who played Maximian's daughter revived to deliver a final epilogue that brought down the house. The actor was Nell Gwyn, member of the King's Company at Drury Lane and mistress of Charles II. Gwyn offered a comedic farewell to the audience that played up the irony of her erotic celebrity in a play about Christian conversion and virgin martyrdom: "Here *Nelly* lies, who, through she liv'd a Slater'n, / Yet dy'd a Princess, acting in *S. Cathar'n*" (67). The year was 1669, and the play was *Tyrranick Love, or the Royal Martyr* by John Dryden. Dryden's St. Katherine play is, according to Gwyn's epilogue, a "godly out of fashion Play" (67). Such a description suggests an anachronistic resurrection of the medieval Catholic saint play—but it is not medieval theatre that inspired the playwright. Rather, the play adapts the early modern saint play into the heroic tragic style of the Restoration stage.

The term *early modern saint play* describes an impossible collision between the religious and theatrical categories of historical periodization. Whereas there is one term—*medieval*—to describe one thousand years of religious and aesthetic development before 1500, the terminology bifurcates in the subsequent period, with *Reformation* applying to religion, and *early modern* applying to theatre and drama. In England, saints belong to the Middle Ages, and theatre—even if called early modern—belongs to the Renaissance. When saints appear beyond their proper expiration date, they are considered for their religious meaning, often to

---

[1] John Dryden, *Tyrranick love, or The royal martyr* (London, 1670), 53. All subsequent in-text citations are from this edition.

the exclusion of other categories. Such is not the case on the Continent. To consider the Italian painter Artemisia Gentileschi's two portraits of St. Katherine of Alexandria, for example, is to arrive at a critical juncture of a canon of gendered violence and the experience of the self. In both portraits, Katherine appears in a red Renaissance gown and a crown, with one hand on the icon of her passion, the wooden wheel with metal spikes, and a martyr's palm in the other hand. In the earlier portrait (c.1616), which now hangs in the National Gallery, London, she wears a cloth tied around her hair in addition to the crown, and her eyes meet the viewer. In the later portrait (1619), part of the Ufizi Gallery collection in Florence, her gaze is heavenward. Both portraits were painted early in Gentileschi's career, just a few years after she was raped and, then, tortured during the trial of her rapist. Her scenes of virgin martyrs and biblical women, especially her three laborious and bloody scenes of Judith and Holofernes, stand apart from the stories of saints told by other artists of the time. Gentileschi used herself as the model for both of her St. Katherines, orienting them toward the world (X-rays reveal that the later portrait's saint began with the same orientation as the first, only belatedly looking heavenward). There are many more St. Katherines on the Continent, and every one of them is allowed a different story: sometimes about patronage, sometimes about violence, sometimes about the self, sometimes about the craft, and sometimes about history. But when St. Katherine appears in England in the same period, the interpretation of the saint is constrained to confessional sanctity.

The Renaissance of the Saints after Reform recovers the theatrical life of the saints. In doing so, it counters the established history of English theatre and religion. That history asserts that the lives of the saints were dramatized throughout the Middle Ages and that saint plays were an expression of the Catholicism that was prohibited during the national conversion to Protestantism in the sixteenth century. But the age of miracles was not yet past on the Shakespearean stage. The saint play as a medieval phenomenon reflects a culture deeply invested in the lives of the saints. The saint play as an early modern phenomenon reflects a culture struggling to resolve its inheritance of hagiography. In the rupture between those two eras, the English church separated itself from the cult of the saints, and saints disappeared from public view until they reappeared in the theatre. In its transfer to the stage, sanctity also transformed into a matter of theatricality.

Early modern saint plays document a post-Reformation culture committed to saints—but not all saints. Under Elizabeth I, certain ancient martyrs and medieval English saints returned to the liturgical calendar in the Book of Common Prayer. This limited inventory performed an initial de-Catholicization of these saints, but it did not recover their lives: the calendar provided a list rather than a legendary. The saints' presence in the *BCP* authorized the professional theatre to experiment with them—and the bare-bones nature of their inclusion meant that the theatre also took on the role of providing story and significance for them. A period of experimentation with saints and devils in the 1590s was then followed by unprecedented innovation. Shortly after the death of Elizabeth I in 1603, she reappeared on the public stage as a virgin martyr saint. The playwright Thomas Heywood utilized traditional hagiography to celebrate the victory of the Protestant Reformation and memorialize Elizabeth's religious suffering under the Catholic regime of Queen Mary. Heywood's *If You Know Not Me, You Know Nobody: Or, The Troubles of Queen Elizabeth* (c.1604), a blockbuster of its time and the main subject of chapter 3, is built on the tropes of medieval virgin martyr legends and includes a miraculous dumb show involving angels and devils. This play not only presented Elizabeth as a new protomartyr, thus further de-Catholicizing sanctity, but also determined how to represent sainthood in the theatre. In the plays that followed, saints emerged through scenes of supernatural activity as icons of English history and virgin martyrs.

The excavation of saint plays reconfigures the religious question through its aesthetic iterations. The Pope is Catholic, but St. Katherine might be something else. One of the most well-known examples of saintly enactment from the period is the portrait *Henrietta Maria as St. Catherine*. Composed around 1639, it depicts the Catholic queen consort of England and wife of King Charles I in a flowing red gown, her hand on that iconic spiked wooden wheel. The portrait was produced at a time of growing political division over the nature of the Crown's institutional policies on the English church. It would seem, then, that the choice to present the queen as the saint emphasized the steadfast Catholicism of the queen, performing her devotion, her queenship, and her association with conversion. But I want to suggest that it is the queen's own Catholicism that renders this particular St. Katherine as Catholic. That is, the performative Catholicism of the portrait is supplied primarily by the person of Henrietta-Maria, not the saint.

St. Katherine reappeared many times in the seventeenth century. In 1620, St. Katherine appeared in the "maine Pageant" of the Haberdashers' Lord Mayor's Show,

> attired in a snow white sattin gowne, in one hand she held a *booke*, and in the other a *sword* with the point downeward... her head circled with a crowne of *gold*, which did intimate her *princely* descent; and at her feet lay a broken *wheele*: round about fare her Attendants twelue maydes of honor gorgeously attired, each one bearin gin her hand a *siluer sheild*, vpon which were portrayed *Catherin Wheeles*, and within the *Motto to the Companies armes, Serue and obey*. Vnder these sate her seruants at worke, some carding *Wooll*, some *Spinning*; others *Knitting* capps....[2]

---

[2] John Squire, *Tes irenes trophaea* (London, 1620), B3r.

Katherine's appearance in this tableau was not a speaking role, but the guild patron was identifiable through the elaborate iconography, which linked her martyrological passion and instrument of torture to the Haberdashers' industry. She was given lines in three subsequent pageants celebrating the guild, composed by Heywood in 1631, 1632, and 1637. The saint identified herself in the 1631 pageant as, "I, Katherin, long since Sainted for true piety, / The Lady patronesse of this Society, / A queene, a Virgin, and a Martir."[3] The 1632 pageant repeated this combination of iconography and presentational direct address, but the 1637 pageant, written for a London that was now well familiar with Katherine, transformed her role accordingly. By 1637, the saint had become a known "Patronesse," who on "populous streets beene borne in state," but not yet "on the Waters."[4] Therefore, in the opening water show, Heywood scripted her to ride a scallop shell and offer verses in honor of the new Lord Mayor. Just as Gentileschi's St. Katherines tell a different story than those of Caravaggio, Raphael, and Bugiardini, among others, so, too, do the Haberdashers' St. Katherines materialize a different set of meanings than does Henrietta-Maria's portrait. That the foreign, French-born, Catholic queen sat as St. Katherine does not also define the patron saint of the longstanding London guild as her co-religionist. On the contrary, the Haberdashers' Katherine united English historical identity and virgin martyrdom, the two dominant modes of sainthood on the early modern stage. This new version of sainthood involved careful negotiation of the boundaries between a general, traditional hagiography, like the Haberdashers' St. Katherine pageants, and a particular, Catholic sanctity, like Henrietta-Maria's St. Katherine portrait.

"They say miracles are past"

This project began with doubt. A single sentence in a 2002 essay by Catherine Sanok contradicted an accepted matter of theatre and Reformation history: "Anne of Denmark, James I's queen, was honored with a pageant of St. Ursula on the occasion of her visit to Wells in 1613."[5] Since there shouldn't be saint plays after 1600, I tried to clarify the matter by seeking out the record of the St. Ursula pageant in *Records of Early English Drama: Somerset*, only to find that in addition to that saint, SS Crispin and Crispinian, Clement, George, and John the Baptist also appeared in the Wells pageants.[6] No one was punished for these "godly out of fashion" displays. Instead, there was cause for civic celebration and self-congratulation. At the time, I concluded that these pageants amounted

---

[3] Thomas Heywood, *London ius honorarium* (London, 1631), C2r.
[4] Thomas Heywood, *Londini Speculum: or Londons Mirror* (London, 1632), B3v.
[5] Catherine Sanok, "Performing Feminine Sanctity in Late Medieval England: Parish Guilds, Saints' Plays, and the *Second Nun's Tale*," *JMEMS* 32, no. 2 (2002): 294.
[6] *REED: Somerset*, I: 372–7.

to a singular, anomalous event unrepresentative and unconnected to any larger historical movement. An exceptional blip in the historical record does not overturn the established narrative; it often reinforces it. I set aside the matter of saint plays. But as I continued to study the medieval alongside the early modern, and the theatrical alongside the religious, I located sixteen saint plays produced between circa 1592 and circa 1640.[7] The renaissance of the saint play in professional drama coincided with a revival of saints in public pageantry that celebrated longstanding English institutions.

This book is indebted to the study of hagiography in medieval studies, as well as the broader fields of performance studies and theatre historiography, but it is situated primarily in early modern studies. When I first began to chase down saints, the religious turn was well underway and the most provocative work proposed theses of evacuation, secularization, iconoclasm, and displacement.[8] The saint plays vexed me. Were early modern saint plays evidence of a persistence of Catholicism-as-subversion? Were they the excesses of medieval religion that found a home in the secular and secularizing theatre? Or, maybe, they sustained a meta-iconoclastic Protestant perspective? Julia Reinhard Lupton cut an alternative pathway to religion through psychoanalytic consideration of how hagiographic forms constructed the Renaissance canon.[9] Later, after Ken Jackson and Arthur F. Marotti hailed the religious turn, Lupton welcomed others to address "questions concerning religion" through "the chance to return to theory, to concepts, concerns, and modes of reading that found worlds and cross contexts, born out of specific historical situations, traumas, and debates, but not reducible to them."[10] Lupton's work made inroads as Stephen Greenblatt set off a storm. Through

---

[7] I include the lost plays *Richard of Chichester, St. Christopher, St. George for England, Tragedy of Saint Albans*, and *England's First Happiness, or the Life of St. Austin*, alongside the extant plays *A Knack to Know A Knave, The Devil and His Dame, If You Know Not Me, You Know Nobody, A Shoemaker, A Gentleman, The Martyr'd Soldier, The Virgin Martyr, Two Noble Ladies*, and *The Converted Conjuror, Guy, Earl of Warwick, The Birth of Merlin, The Seven Champions of Christendom*, and *Saint Patrick for Ireland*. Other lost plays that may have contained saints include *Warlamchester, Conan, Prince of Cornwall, Diocletian, Judas, Pontius Pilate*, and *The She Saint*. See appendix 1.

[8] See Ken Jackson and Arthur F. Marotti's landmark essay "The Turn to Religion in Early Modern English Studies," *Criticism* 46, no. 1 (2004): 167–90. For evacuation, see Stephen Greenblatt, *Shakespearean Negotiations: The Circulation of Social Energy* (Berkeley: University of California Press, 1989) and *Hamlet in Purgatory* (Princeton, NJ: Princeton University Press, 2001); for secularization, see Anthony Dawson, "Shakespeare and Secular Performance," in *Shakespeare and the Cultures of Performance*, eds. Paul Yachnin and Patricia Badir (New York: Ashgate, 2008), 83–97; for iconoclasm, particularly as the theatre developed iconoclastic modes, see Huston Diehl, *Staging Reform, Reforming the Stage: Protestantism and Popular Theater in Early Modern England* (Ithaca, NY: Cornell University Press, 1997); and Michael O'Connell, *The Idolatrous Eye: Iconoclasm and Theater in Early-Modern England* (Oxford: Oxford University Press, 2000); and for displacement, see Regina Mara Schwartz, *Sacramental Poetics at the Dawn of Secularism: When God Left the World* (Stanford, CA: Stanford University Press, 2008).

[9] Julia Reinhard Lupton, *Afterlives of the Saints: Hagiography, Typology, and Renaissance Literature* (Stanford, CA: Stanford University Press, 1996).

[10] Julia Reinhard Lupton, "The Religious Turn (to Theory) in Shakespeare Studies," *English Language Notes* 44, no. 1 (2006): 146.

refuting his claims concerning the constrained capacities and capabilities of both drama and religion, scholars expanded the field of inquiry concerning theology and theatricality.[11] During the years that I built the chronological table of saint plays (appendix 1), the religious turn picked up momentum and incorporated a new spate of postrevisionist Reformation scholarship.[12] Early modern studies pivoted from "one-sided attempts to attribute to Shakespeare" and other dramatists "rigid religious identifications, affiliations, or sets of religious practices" to the exploration of "a wide range of religious beliefs, practices, and confessional positions."[13] The most recent work in this area treats texts and performances that register and refigure the complex representations, debates, and ambiguities of a multi-confessional society. An important undercurrent of Brian Walsh's study of the staging of intra-religious disagreements is that the theatre was keen to present individual religious confessions, such as Protestantism, as heterogenous.[14] Musa Gurnis, working from a revitalized cultural materialist paradigm, expands on heterogeneity, arguing that "early modern plays draw contradictory scraps of confessional practice together in powerful fantasies that reconfigure existing structures of religious thought and feeling."[15] Rather than relying on theologians, polemicists, and the statutes of church and state to define religious belief and affect, Gurnis unearths a set of archival records pertaining to the religious lives of playwrights and playgoers to show how they sustained a range of religious thinking in

---

[11] For generative refutations, I am thinking especially of Sarah Beckwith, "Stephen Greenblatt's Hamlet and the Forms of Oblivion," *JMEMS* 33, no. 2 (2003): 261–80; Elizabeth Williamson, *The Materiality of Religion in Early Modern English Drama* (Aldershot: Ashgate, 2009); and Holly Crawford Pickett, "Angels in England: Idolatry and Wonder at the Red Bull Playhouse," in *Thunder at the Playhouse: Proceedings from the Fourth Blackfriars Conference*, eds. Peter Kanelos and Matt Kozusko (Selingsgrove, PA: Susquehanna University Press, 2010), 175–99.

[12] See especially Eamon Duffy, *The Voices of Morebath* (New Haven, CT: Yale University Press, 2001); Ethan Shagan, *Popular Politics and the English Reformation* (Cambridge: Cambridge University Press, 2002); Alexandra Walsham, *The Reformation of the Landscape: Religion, Identity and Memory in Early Modern Britain and Ireland* (Oxford: Oxford University Press, 2011); Peter Marshall, "The Naming of Protestant England," *Past and Present* 214, no. 1 (2012): 87–128, and Margaret Aston, *Broken Idols of the English Reformation* (Cambridge: Cambridge University Press, 2015).

[13] David Loewenstein and Michael Witmore, *Shakespeare and Early Modern Religion*, eds. Loewenstein and Witmore (Cambridge: Cambridge University Press, 2015), 3. In addition, Kristen Poole and Beatrice Groves marked separate early departures. Poole recovered how Puritanism figured in literary and dramatic works; see Poole, *Radical Religion from Shakespeare to Milton: Figures of Nonconformity in Early Modern England* (Cambridge: Cambridge University Press, 2000). Groves opened up new productive avenues in showing how Shakespeare's plays reflect both the emphasis of the "Word" in Protestantism and iconography in Catholicism while also putting an end to biographically inflected readings as a means of addressing religion; see Groves, *Texts and Traditions: Religion in Shakespeare, 1592–1604* (Oxford: Oxford University Press, 2007). These studies anticipated and ushered in what James Mardock calls "the second wave" of the religious turn; see Mardock, "'Reformation in a Flood': The Religious Turn's Second Wave," in *Stages of Engagement: Drama and Religion in Post Reformation England*, eds. James D. Mardock and Kathryn R. McPherson (Pittsburgh, PA: Duquesne University Press, 2014), 9.

[14] Brian Walsh, *Unsettled Toleration: Religious Difference on the Shakespearean Stage* (Oxford: Oxford University Press, 2016).

[15] Musa Gurnis, *Mixed Faith, Shared Feeling: Theater in Post-Reformation London* (Philadelphia: University of Pennsylvania Press, 2018), 1.

the theatre unlike "their everyday religious orientations."[16] Walsh and Gurnis bring depth to their studies of how plays engage religion due, in part, to their expansive knowledge of the repertory. Both scholars demonstrate the necessity of considering plays like *The Puritan Widow* and *The Spanish Gypsy*, among many others, alongside the usual suspects of *Measure for Measure* and *A Game at Chess*. The juxtaposition of canonical drama with the noncanonical or straight-up ignored parts of the early modern dramatic archive also characterizes Jay Zysk's remarkable study of eucharistic semiotics. The diversity of dramatic texts from both the Middle Ages and the early modern period allows Zysk to uncover how controversies concerning sacramental theology did not disappear from view but remained in play across the Reformation divide.[17] Lupton's invitation to find the theory lurking in the work itself has combined with this more expansive study of the repertory to revolutionize the religious turn.

The Renaissance of the Saints after Reform, therefore, rests on the work of scholars who, over the last three decades, redefined the theatre of Shakespeare's time as a site of divergent and dynamic epistemologies of religion. Nearly all the early modern plays I address in this book can be interpreted individually through any number of religious perspectives, but when they are addressed as a group, the coherence of that interpretation starts to falter and crack. *If You Know Not Me, You Know Nobody* portrays the Protestant Reformation as a virgin martyr legend, *A Shoemaker, A Gentleman* reinserts the sort of medieval hagiographic material that its de-Catholicized source tale rejected as superstitious, and *The Virgin Martyr* presents both iconoclasm and the sorts of miracles that iconoclasts condemned. But I do not approach these plays as puzzles to be solved. I take as my starting point not an early modern theatre vexed by religion but an early modern theatre invested in dramatizing the vexing parts of religion. O. B. Hardison claims that "for better or worse, modern Western drama is the product of a Christian, not a pagan, culture."[18] While our theatres likely also reflect whatever Hardison means by "pagan" culture, his assertion about the role of Christianity in the development of theatre is a particular apt one for the study of medieval and, especially, early modern drama. That drama is a product of a Christian culture is frequently taken as a comfortable fact in medieval studies, but it can cause intellectual—or actual—squirming in early modern studies. Nonetheless, as John Parker emphasizes in a counter to some of Hardison's claims concerning "'the framework of medieval Christianity,'"

---

[16] Gurnis, *Mixed Faith*, 3.

[17] Jay Zysk, *Shadow and Substance: Eucharistic Controversy and English Drama across the Reformation Divide* (Notre Dame, IN: Notre Dame University Press, 2017). Two other notable works that address sacramental theology and early modern drama are Sarah Beckwith, *Shakespeare and the Grammar of Forgiveness* (Ithaca, NY: Cornell University Press, 2013); and Heather Hirschfeld, *The End of Satisfaction: Drama and Repentance in the Age of Shakespeare* (Ithaca, NY: Cornell University Press, 2013).

[18] O. B. Hardison, *Christian Rite and Christian Drama in the Middle Ages: Essays in the Origin and Early History of Modern Drama* (Baltimore: Johns Hopkins Press, 1969), x.

that framework and its culture "is no singular entity."[19] The divergent, non-static, variable, and, vexing parts of religion make for excellent theatre. Thank God Hamlet is in purgatory. Without religion, *Hamlet* is a boring play about late adolescent disdain for a parent's second marriage that ends with him stabbing Claudius in Act III. With it, the ontological and eschatological are confounding, irrational, and all too real. In the theatre, St. Patrick occupies the same imaginative landscape as Horatio's studies in Wittenberg. Theology demands choices *between*, whereas theatre plays with the balance of *both* while also dispensing with equilibrium. Mid-sixteenth-century reformers, as Jennifer Summit has shown, came up with a litmus test for the leftovers of monasticism that aimed to separate "'monuments to antiquity' from 'monuments to superstition,'" but the history of Western theatre *is* a monument to superstition.[20]

What Reformation iconoclasm targeted as a matter of theology the theatre exploits in its multiple registers of storytelling. As Zysk and Katherine Steele Brokaw write, the stage is "a worldly site in which the sacred is presented not as a set of doctrines or liturgical rubrics but as itself a hermeneutically fluid concept, one shaped, but not replaced, by the signifying patterns of a secular world."[21] This is why we weep when Lear drags his daughter's body across the stage. In scripting this scene, which invents the death of Cordelia as *pietà*, Shakespeare stuns audiences with the image of the Madonna with her dead child. It is a religious icon that cuts to the core not because of controversies concerning the cult of the Virgin Mary or the theology of salvation but because the repetition of the crucifixion in Christian culture provides myriad ad hoc rehearsals in maternal grief that *King Lear* performs in full. The miraculous Virgin is impotent to give her son life. She, like all grieving parents, is denied his resurrection except for her own salvation. Tragic irony lives in the Mariological. It need not be affirmed as theology to add depth to tragedy, but neither must it be denied. In a foundational essay on medieval drama and religious ritual, Sarah Beckwith considers the Croxton *Play of the Sacrament*, which centers on eucharistic doubting, and the "social and dramatic resources through which our belief is commanded."[22] She contends that the play refuses "to separate church, ritual and theatre," so that religious ritual proves "vital to the play's theatrical resources, but, it never forecloses the play's readings."[23] As Beckwith states, "the miracle in a miracle play is a purely theatrical event," but that does not mean that

---

[19] John Parker, "Who's Afraid of Darwin? Revisiting Chambers and Hardison. . .and Nietzsche." *JMEMS* 40 (2010): 14.

[20] Jennifer Summit, *Memory's Library: Medieval Books in Early Modern England* (Chicago: University of Chicago Press, 2008), 108–9.

[21] Jay Zysk and Katherine Steele Brokaw, introduction to *Sacred and Secular Transactions in the Age of Shakespeare*, eds. Jay Zysk and Katherine Steele Brokaw (Evanston, IL: Northwestern University Press, 2019), 17.

[22] Sarah Beckwith, "Ritual, Church and Theatre: Medieval Dramas of the Sacramental Body," in *Culture and History, 1350–1600: Essays on English Communities, Identities, and Writing*, ed. David Aers (Detroit: Wayne State University Press, 1992), 66.

[23] Beckwith, "Ritual, Church and Theatre," 80.

religious experience is absent or that religious experience is rigid.[24] In my assertion that early modern theatre transformed sainthood from a matter of theology to a matter of theatricality, I do not mean that sainthood had to be completely extracted from one realm to occupy another, as if there is some theatrical device that vacuums out God in the process of flying in angels and experimenting with pyrotechnics. I mean something far less controversial: the theatre utilized theatricality to produce sainthood at a time when sainthood was absent from most other areas of public life.

Saints are not scarce in early modern theatre, but they are in early modern studies. Two notable exceptions are Lupton's work on typography and saintlike characters "dying-in" to citizenship in early modern drama, and Alison A. Chapman's study of patron saints in early modern literature.[25] The saint plays in this book expand the scope of sainthood beyond the saintlike and established "Catholic" saints. Part of my task is to show how the theatre produced new saints and new models of sainthood. Martyrdom, a subject transformed by Reformation writers and ubiquitous in early modern England, has received much scholarly attention and is indispensable to my work, but here I aim to fill in the gap on saints.[26] The history of English theatre has frequently been constructed by binaries of presence and absence: the era of the sacred and the era of the secular, the era of saints and the era of *Hamlet*. But as Parker has succinctly and expertly put it, "medieval and renaissance drama are divided by what they share."[27] I not only locate saint plays beyond the Middle Ages, but also I offer close examinations of lesser known plays alongside those authored by Shakespeare and other canonical dramatists. Saint plays are introduced in Henslowe's theatres and then innovated at the Red Bull and the Cockpit, playhouses and companies far less studied than

---

[24] Beckwith, "Ritual, Church and Theatre," 68.

[25] Julia Lupton, *Citizen-Saints: Shakespeare and Political Theology* (Chicago: University of Chicago Press, 2005); and Alison A. Chapman, *Patrons and Patron Saints in Early Modern Literature* (London: Routledge, 2013). Lupton's *Citizen-Saints* conceptualizes hagiographical meaning in plays, such as *Antigone* and *Othello*, that do not feature saints. Chapman, by contrast, locates a variety of saints in Shakespeare, Jonson, Milton, Drayton, and Donne, and argues that early modern authors of various religious backgrounds utilized saints as figures that perform systems of patronage. Karen Bamford's *Sexual Violence on the Jacobean Stage* (New York: St. Martin's Press, 2000) explores how five saint plays of the Jacobean era "dramatize the sexual mythology of Christian hagiography" (58). The majority of the discussion of hagiography in drama centers on *The Virgin Martyr*. See chapter 6 for these. For two studies of how a cross-confessional set of writers approached the Virgin Mary, see Gary Waller, *The Virgin Mary in Late Medieval and Early Modern English Literature and Popular Culture* (Cambridge: Cambridge University Press, 2012); and Lilla Grindlay, *Queen of Heaven: The Assumption and Coronation of the Virgin in Early Modern English Writing* (Notre Dame, IN: Notre Dame University Press, 2009).

[26] In addition to numerous studies focusing on John Foxe, see Susannah Brietz Monta, *Martyrdom and Literature in Early Modern England* (Cambridge: Cambridge University Press, 2005); and Alice Dailey, *The English Martyr from Reformation to Revolution* (Notre Dame, IN: Notre Dame University Press, 2011). These two studies approach martyrdom cross-confessionally.

[27] John Parker, *Aesthetics of Antichrist: From Christian Drama to Christopher Marlowe* (Ithaca: Cornell University Press, 2007), viii.

those associated with Shakespeare.[28] Saint plays are the least canonical plays of the most canonical era of English drama, and their absence in scholarship has resulted in a history predicated on their absence. Rather than addressing the Shakespearean uses of saints and sanctity in a separate chapter, I incorporate them throughout in order to show how Shakespeare, too, responded to trends in staging sanctity.[29] Not only will this approach to the repertory better elucidate how theatrical representation developed through the collaborative—and competitive—nature of the professional theatre, but the brief excursions into the canon should also help readers better navigate the unfamiliar miracles.

In considering saint plays across the Reformation divide, I explore how performances excerpted, improvised, and reinvented aspects of iconography and *vitae*. I am especially concerned with how theatre portrayed miracles associated with virgin martyrdom and materialized saints associated with the history of the English church. This trans-Reformation approach to the study of saint plays works across the medieval/early modern divide in order to consider how religion offers a repository of forms of knowledge. As in Zysk's study of eucharistic semiotics, the Reformation accomplishes rupture, but it does not determine the direction of aesthetic formation across the sixteenth century. *The Renaissance of the Saints after Reform* is a book about saint plays, but it is not a book *only* about religion. Barbara Newman cautions that "living in a place as culturally saturated with religion as medieval Europe ... could not fail to color the imaginations not just of the devout, but also of ordinary Christians, or even those who were not pious at all. That does not mean, however, that every allusion to the sacred needs to be assessed at its full theological weight."[30] As early modern England, too, was a culture saturated with religion, I draw both direction and inspiration from the work of medieval scholars who have established that hagiography performs complex negotiations of gender, culture, theology, and nationhood.[31] Far from being

---

[28] For more on the Red Bull, Cockpit/Phoenix, Queen Anne's Men, and Prince Charles's Men, see Lucy Munro, "Governing the Pen to the Capacity of the Stage: Reading the Red Bull and Clerkenwell," *Early Theatre* 9, no. 2 (2006): 99-113; Marta Straznicky, "The Red Bull Repertory in Print, 1605-60," *Early Theatre* 9, no. 2 (2006): 144-56; Eleanor Collins, "Repertory and Riot: The Relocation of Plays from the Red Bull to the Cockpit Stage," *Early Theatre* 13, no. 2 (2010): 132-49; Mark Bayer, *Theatre, Community, and Civic Engagement in Jacobean London* (Iowa City: University of Iowa Press, 2011); and Eva Griffith, *A Jacobean Company and Its Playhouse: The Queen's Servants at The Red Bull Theatre, c. 1605–1619* (Cambridge: Cambridge University Press, 2013).

[29] In doing so, I follow Tom Rutter, who encourages consideration of the early modern repertory that is, an approach that "takes the acting company—rather than, say, the individual dramatists—as the subject of its inquiry," and enables a consideration of style and dramaturgy across plays that speak to one another. See Tom Rutter, "Repertory Studies: A Survey," *Shakespeare* 4, no. 3 (2008): 336. See also Roslyn Lander Knutson, *Playing Companies and Commerce in Shakespeare's Time* (Cambridge: Cambridge University Press, 2001).

[30] Barbara Newman, *Medieval Crossover: Reading the Secular against the Sacred* (Notre Dame, IN: Notre Dame University Press, 2013), 7.

[31] See especially Karen A. Winstead, *Virgin Martyrs: Legends of Sainthood in the Middle Ages* (Ithaca, NY: Cornell University Press, 1997) and *Fifteenth-Century Lives: Writing Sainthood in England*. ReFormations: Medieval and Early Modern Series (University of Notre Dame Press, 2020);

static icons of piety or icons of rupture, saints in early modern drama renegotiate the boundaries of religious confession as well as the relationship of the English present to the English past. In early modern drama and pageantry, saints enact an uninterrupted history of a continual ancient English Christianity from the time of St. Alban to that of the Tudors and the Stuarts. The study of hagiography and medieval theatre also reveals a long history of diverging from the perspectives and narratives of devotional culture in theatrical contexts.[32] Early modern theatre did not invent alternative hagiographies as a secularized concession to Protestantism. It continued a medieval practice of hagiographical adaptation and invention as it professionalized plays of miracles.

A word is needed on what this book is not. This book began as an archival project, but it is not, strictly speaking, a work of theatre history. It is a book about saints and drama that begins by addressing the development of saint plays in the medieval era. It then offers a narrow examination of the liturgical calendar in the *BCP* to explain how a coterie of specific saints remained in the fold when the rest were excised during the mid-sixteenth century. A major contribution of this project is the reevaluation of saints in two divergent histories—theatre and Reformation—and so I begin by placing first theatre history and then Reformation history at center stage. I begin here for all readers, but especially for those students and scholars of early modern studies and theatre studies who, I expect, will require a tour of the archives of medieval performance and sacred time in chapter 1 before venturing onto the saints of early modern stage. I expect that medievalists and scholars of the Reformation and religious change in the sixteenth century will be more familiar with the dynamic nature of hagiography, performance, sacred time, and iconoclasm. As I turn to the saint plays of the early modern era, in the second and third parts of the book, I let up on the history to provide more theoretically informed analysis. While I do not lose sight of historical context, the balance transfers to exploring the making and meaning of saints in early modern drama. It is my hope that the archive of early modern saint plays that I excavate in this book will inform future scholarship on discourses of sainthood in the larger culture of post-Reformation England as well as the performativity of sanctity across the medieval and early modern periods. I also hope that the work of this book encourages future scholarship concerned with repertoire and repertory. In my excavation of saints in early modern drama, I have organized this book as a chronological consideration

---

Theresa Coletti, *Mary Magdalene and the Drama of Saints: Theater, Gender, and Religion in Late Medieval England* (Philadelphia: University of Pennsylvania Press, 2004); Patricia Badir, *The Maudlin Impression: English Literary Images of Mary Magdalene, 1550–1700* (Notre Dame, IN: University of Notre Dame Press, 2009); and Catherine Sanok, *New Legends of England: Forms of Community in Late Medieval Saints' Lives* (Philadelphia: University of Pennsylvania Press, 2018).

[32] Maggie Solberg's work on the vulgar debates concerning the Virgin Mary's sexuality from medieval drama to Shakespeare is especially illustrative in this regard. See Solberg, *Virgin Whore* (Ithaca, NY: Cornell University Press, 2018).

of the major trends and innovations in staging saints. Other studies of saint plays—
or other understudied genres—might do well to take as an organizing principle
playwrights, playhouses, and/or play companies. There is certainly much more
work to be done from the standpoint of repertoire and repertory in the study of
early modern theatre and drama. However, the focus of this book is on sanctity as
it emerges in a number of relatively unknown early modern plays.

There are also some Catholic gaps in this project, and they, too, are by design.
I barely address the years of Marian England (1553–58) because, for the most
part, annual observances involving saintly theatricality that disappeared under
the Protestant kings Henry and Edward did not return under the Catholic Queen
Mary. Although the categories of the medieval and the Catholic are sometimes collapsed, the Marian church did not suddenly time travel to late medieval English
Christianity, circa 1500.[33] The subject of this book is also not the culture or literature of Counter-Reformation Catholicism. Occasionally, I address newer Catholic
vitae or the drama's depiction of Catholic figures, but I do not sustain an examination of seventeenth-century anglophone Catholic hagiography. Nor do I address
saints in the drama of the English Catholic colleges on the Continent. As with
Catholic hagiography, this subject deserves a separate study.[34] In service of future
scholarship, however, I do include the seminary plays in appendix 1, and Sarum
liturgical calendars printed during Mary's reign in appendix 2.

"And we have our / philosophical persons to make modern and familiar"

The saints I address in *The Renaissance of the Saints after Reform* are dramatic
saints formed from practices and trends of theatrical performance at least as much
as the narratives and tropes of devotional saints' lives. The St. Winifred who
appears in *A Shoemaker, A Gentleman* (c.1618) by William Rowley, which I address
in chapter 4, overlaps with the same saint in late medieval hagiography, but how
she emerged on the Red Bull stage is based on tropes and scenarios developed by
the theatre for showing sainthood. In certain ways, saint plays in the later Middle

---

[33] For a discussion of the erroneous collapsing of *medieval* with *Catholic*, see James Simpson, "The Reformation of Scholarship: A Reply to Debora Shuger," *JMEMS* 42, no. 2 (2012): 249–68.

[34] The content of the college plays somewhat reflects the Jacobean tragicomedies explored in chapter 4 that draw from religious and romance legends associated with English history. The plays also hew to a different structure. Rather than the double or triple plot employed by London profes-sional dramatists, the college plays feature a single-focused plot with comedic interludes between acts. This reflects the entertainments of the early sixteenth century as well as the expected presentation at Continental theatres. In addition, there are far fewer women characters, likely as a consequence of the ban on boys and men cross-dressing as women in seminary entertainments. The result is that while SS Alban and Thomas Becket receive dramatization, virgin martyrs are absent. Many of the plays are available in translation through Dana F. Sutton's online Philological Museum, http://www.philological.bham.ac.uk/library.html.

Ages and the early modern era mirror the development of written hagiography. Unlike modern accounts of history and biography, which value differentiation as a sign of reliability, hagiography values repetition as a discursive act of verification. If saints' lives seem like a mess of recurrent conversions, miracles, mortifications, sufferings, and deaths, it is because they are intended to. The repetition of tropes, motifs, and events communicates to readers or viewers that the subject is a saint. A miracle is described in a legend; a halo is there in the painting. You believe these signs even if you do not believe in saints.

Hagiography imagines sanctity as a radically singular phenomenon inasmuch as all sanctity imitates the life of Christ. Gregory of Tours (c.538–94) theorized this singularity through grammar, insisting that the singular *vita* should be used instead of the plural *vitae*: life of the saints (*vita sanctorum*). He wrote "that it is better to speak of the 'Life of the Fathers' rather than the 'Lives of the Fathers,' the more so since there is a diversity of merits and virtues among them, but the one life of the body sustains them all in this world."[35] But how is sanctity to be determined if saints' lives do not seem to actually imitate Christ's life, miracles, passion, crucifixion, and resurrection? It is easier to understand how St. Katherine imitates Christ in her persecution, torture, miracles, and dismembered assumption after her martyrdom than it is to see how St. Dunstan, an archbishop who died of natural causes on cathedrals grounds (and the subject of two plays addressed in chapter 2), similarly imitates Christ. Thomas Heffernan argues that sanctity is both authored and authorized by the community.[36] The production of sanctity depends on a community that interprets the actions of a person, whether witnessed or reported, to approximate the life and sacrifice of Christ. Hagiographers, in turn, develop and rely on rhetorical strategies to tell a story of sainthood. For this reason, saints' lives sometimes more readily resemble one another than they do the life of Christ. Although St. Agatha, for example, ultimately derives her sanctity from imitating Christ, her legend more immediately resembles the legend of St. Agnes. Both women aristocratic virgins were martyred under lustful Romans.

The lives of Aelred of Rievaulx and St. Guinefort offer two examples of how lives were crafted to imitate the death of Christ in the absence of miracles, torture, or Christian martyrdom. As Heffernan has shown, the twelfth-century monk Walter Daniel composed an account of his friend Aelred's death, at which he was present, on the pattern of Christ's passion and crucifixion, despite the fact that Aelred was neither tortured nor executed. The *Life of Aelred* narrates the death of a monk within the walls of an abbey. Monastic life—whether eremitic or in community—was already considered a "white martyrdom," metaphorically comparable to the "red martyrdom" of actual execution because of the vowed

---

[35] Gregory of Tours, *Life of the Fathers*, trans. Edward James (Liverpool: Liverpool University Press, 1991), 2.
[36] Thomas J. Heffernan, *Sacred Biography: Saints and Their Biographers in the Middle Ages* (Oxford: Oxford University Press, 1988), 16–18.

renunciation of the world and the turn to penance and prayer. Building on the background of the "white martyrdom," Walter connected Aelred's physical suffering to specific episodes of Christ's passion. In doing so, as Heffernan argues, Walter transformed Aelred's fairly uneventful death into a saintly one for medieval Christians, whose twelfth-century cultural, political, and religious context meant that they perceived it as *imitatio Christi*.[37] Sanctity relies on an imitation of Christ, but the form of this imitation varies across place, time, society, gender, and religious expression, and the reception and circulation of that life within the local or universal Christian community is what transforms it into the *life* of a saint.

The case of St. Guinefort elucidates how a local community might perceive sainthood and then, through social practices and storytelling techniques, produce a new saint—even when the venerated individual does not meet the church's requirements for sainthood (Guinefort was not a human at all, but a dog!). Guinefort was unjustly executed for the alleged death of an infant. Yet, Guinefort was innocent; he had saved the child from a snake attack. A shrine was set up in France with Guinefort's relics, and he became a local patron of infants. Despite the efforts of the church to dissuade the laity from venerating the canine, they maintained Guinefort's cult, telling his story, visiting his shrine, and asking for his intercession. That is, the people performed practices that transformed the dog into a saint, the same practices that recognized and maintained the sainthood of SS Mary Magdalene, Genevieve, and Crispin and Crispinian, other popular saints in France during the Middle Ages.[38] The local laity saw in St. Guinefort's death a Christlike sacrifice, just as Walter saw in Alered's death a Christlike suffering. The process of discursively transforming a life into the *life* of saint recalls the funerary and reliquary practices adopted in early Christianity to transform the body of a deceased Christian into a saint. Janel Mueller emphasizes the "agency of living Christians" involved in "the care and control of saints' bodies."[39] The ritual care and control of the body of the saint informs the care and control of the memory of the saint. Sainthood relies on a range of discursive tropes that create an idea of sainthood; a saint is then recognized by others when, based on their perspective of sainthood, they encounter it. In other words, you should know sainthood when you see it.

The challenge of this project was to locate—to encounter—saints in early modern drama. Early modern saint plays are rarely titled with the saint's name, and even when they are, the saint in the title might not represent what sort of sainthood is explored in the play (*Saint Patrick for Ireland* actually dramatizes the problem

---

[37] Heffernan, *Sacred Biography*, 16–18.
[38] See Jean-Claude Schmitt, *The Holy Greyhound: Guinefort, Healer of Children since the Thirteenth Century*, trans. Martin Thom (Cambridge: Cambridge University Press, 1983).
[39] Janel Mueller, "The Saints," in *Cultural Reformations: Medieval and Renaissance in Literary History*, eds. Brian Cummings and James Simpson (Oxford: Oxford University Press, 2010), 168. For Peter Brown's discussion of the radical transformation of mortuary and memorial practices during the rise of Christianity and the cult of the saints, see *The Cult of the Saints: Its Rise and Function in Latin Christianity* (Chicago: University of Chicago Press, 1981).

of knowing virgin martyrdom, as I show in chapter 5). Therefore, it was necessary to scan through extant plays in search of saints as well as records collections in case the titles of lost plays indicated that saints might have been involved in the plot.[40] Familiarity with medieval English saints' lives and the scholarship of non-dramatic hagiography proved essential to this task. The work of individual writers, such as John Lydgate and Osbern Bokenham, informed my research into the saints of the early modern stage as did the larger collections of saints' lives, such as the *South English Legendary* and, especially, William Caxton's edition of the *Golden Legend*. Throughout this book, I reference Caxton's late-fifteenth-century "englyshed" version of Jacobus de Voragine's *Legenda aurea* when I provide basic information about hagiographic narratives, themes, motifs, and iconography.[41] Rather than referencing modern translations of Jacobus's thirteenth-century Continental text, I cite Caxton's *Golden Legend* due to its particular archive of English sanctities, something that Judy Ann Ford has studied recently in extraordinary detail. As Ford writes, "Caxton followed the tradition of modifying the *Legenda aurea* not only through translation but also through the addition of individual saints' lives."[42] The difference between the two legendaries will be more familiar to readers from medieval and Reformation studies than to readers from theatre studies and early modern literary studies. The two texts reflect vast regional, temporal, and cultural differences. Caxton's version includes saints that circulated in English legendaries and manuscripts. A number of English saints, such as St. Winifred of Wales, did not originate with Jacobus and do not appear in Continental versions of the *Legenda aurea*. Furthermore, Caxton augmented popular saints' lives with later medieval legends that circulated in England and details of their local cults.[43] Ford explains that the "British material reveals an unusual emphasis on political history, particularly on the monarchy and expresses a national pride."[44] The "englyshed" status of the legends of the saints was as cultural as it was vernacular,

---

[40] Three digital resources were invaluable to my research: *Database of Early English Playbooks*, *The Lost Plays Database*, and *Early English Books Online*. Toward the end of the research phase of this project, Martin Wiggins and Catherine Richardson's *British Drama 1533–1642: A Catalogue* (Oxford: Oxford University Press, 2012–19) allowed me to verify that I had not missed any saints in professional drama.

[41] The translation conflated the French *Legende Dorée* "c" version, various native English saints legends, and a Latin version of the *Legenda aurea*, all of which derive from Jacobus's original thirteenth-century manuscript, the *South English Legendary*, or the *Gilte Legende*. A total of ten editions of the *Golden Legend* were published between 1483 and 1527. See Manfred Gorlach, *The South English Legendary, the Gilte Legende and Golden Legend* (Braunschweig, Technische Universitat Carolo-Wilhelmina. Institut fur Anglistik und Amerikanistik, 1972). The most common modern translation of Jacobus is the Ryan edition, see Jacobus de Voragine, *The Golden Legend: Readings on the Saints*, trans. William G. Ryan (Princeton: Princeton University Press, 1993).

[42] *The Printing History of William Caxton's Golden Legend* (London: Routledge, 2020), 8.

[43] As Winstead explains, Caxton's legendary is the most comprehensive version of the *Legenda aurea* "in Middle English, but it is not a *Legenda aurea* that Jacobus would have recognized. Of Caxton's 250 chapters, about 70 are not found in Jacobus's collection, and more than 40 are not found in either of the prior Middle English translations." *Fifteenth-Century Lives*, 133.

[44] Ford, 8.

which is something that the theatre, too, seized on when it produced new legends of the saints in the time of Shakespeare. Still, this type of research only yields known saints, like Dunstan and Winifred. In order to identify saints produced through the processes of theatricality, such as Elizabeth in *If You Know Now Me, You Know Nobody*, I had to be able to identify theatrical sainthood. That is, I had to be able to identify the repertoire of sanctity, the theatrical equivalent of devotional literature's *imitatio Christi*. The way in which early modern saint plays turn on a repertoire of sanctity mirrors the process of medieval hagiographers like Walter Daniel: they repeat tropes drawn from elsewhere and perfect them through experimentation.

Repertoire, as a theoretical concept, accounts for the epistemic capabilities of performance (*performance* being cultural practices that enact, construct, identify, form, reveal, transfer, and dissemble). Diana Taylor argues that repertoire "enacts embodied memory: performances, gestures, orality, movement, dance, singing—in short, all those acts usually thought of as ephemeral, nonreproducible knowledge."[45] Unlike the archive, with its "texts, documents, buildings, bones," repertoire "transmits live, embodied actions. As such, traditions are stored in the body, through various mnemonic methods, and transmitted 'live' in the here and now to a live audience. Forms handed down from the past are experienced as present. Although this may well describe the mechanics of spoken language, it also describes a dance recital or a religious festival."[46] The most vital part of Taylor's theory of repertoire is her claim that "live, embodied practices not based in linguistic or literary codes" ought to be recognized as an "important system of knowing and transmitting knowledge."[47] That is, repertoire is concerned with an ephemeral and culturally specific language, not of text, but of performance and performative practices. Yet, Taylor's theory sees an unbridgeable divide between the archive and the repertoire—between, say, a dramatic script and a marriage ceremony—because "the unchanging text" of a play "assures a stable signifier."[48]

Theatre scholars have refined theories concerning how repertoire works in (scripted) dramatic theatre, something that allows theatre historians to recover meaning of past performances. W. B. Worthen writes that "repertoire materializes the process of transmission—embodied practices such as reading, annotating, memorization, movement, gesture, acting—that produces both a sense of what the text is, and what we might be capable of saying with and through it in/as performance."[49] This observation reorients the relationship of the archive (text) to the repertoire (performance). Tracy C. Davis, furthermore, expands on

---

[45] Diana Taylor, *The Archive and the Repertoire: Performing Cultural Memories in the Americas* (Durham, NC: Duke University Press, 2003), 20.
[46] Taylor, *The Archive and the Repertoire*, 19 and 24.
[47] Taylor, *The Archive and the Repertoire*, 25 and 26.
[48] Taylor, *The Archive and the Repertoire*, 29.
[49] W. B. Worthen, "Antigone's Bones," *TDR: The Drama Review* 52, no. 3 (2008): 12.

repertoire's operative abilities to account for the dynamic between performer(s) and audiences. Arguing against Taylor's theorization of the transferal of repertoire from body of performer to body of performer, Davis defines repertoire as

> multiple circulating recombinative discourses of intelligibility that create a means by which audiences are habituated to understand one or more kinds of combinations of performative tropes and then recognise and interpret others that are unfamiliar, so that the new may be incorporated into repertoire. Thus repertoire—as a semiotic of showing and a phenomenology of experiencing—involves processes of reiteration, revision, citation and incorporation. It accounts for durable meanings, not as memory per se but in the improvisation of naming, which sustains intelligibility.[50]

The transfer of knowledge and memory in Davis's conceptualization of repertoire thus incorporates the audience, insisting that those who witness performances participate in their intelligibility. In *The Renaissance of the Saints after Reform*, I maintain that sainthood is signified through theatrical repertoire even as it differs from how saints are represented elsewhere. This is not a secularization, a rejection, or even a subversion of those other forms of sainthood; it is how the theatre intelligibly and legibly finds a solution to the problem of dramatizing a recognizable idea for audiences.[51]

By including audiences in the process of meaning-making and signification, theatrical repertoire accounts for how both new and old conventions are incorporated into intelligibility. A more fleshed-out example of the recovery of historical repertoire is found in Jonathan Gil Harris's work on the stage presence of tyrants in the second Henriad (Shakespeare's plays *Henry VI, Part 1, 2*, and *3*, and *Richard III*). Harris shows how Shakespeare materializes the performance of tyranny through the citation of older conventions.[52] Although tyranny, like sainthood, might take different—and perhaps more meaningful—forms in pamphlets, at the pulpit, and in political practice, the second Henriad constructed a repertoire to enact tyranny on the stage. Harris writes that the acting styles of certain characters

---

[50] Tracy C. Davis, "Nineteenth-Century Repertoire," *Nineteenth Century Theatre and Film* 36, no. 2 (2009): 7.

[51] In a fascinating article, Davis takes up the problem of how audiences knew they were encountering a mermaid when iconography and descriptions varied widely and, furthermore, the onstage and out-of-water creatures had the burden of showing they were yet "*of water*." See Tracy C. Davis, "How Do You Know a Mermaid When You See One? How Do You See a Mermaid When You Know One?" *Theatre Journal* 71, no. 3 (2019): 271.

[52] See Jonathan Gil Harris, *Untimely Matter in the Time of Shakespeare* (Philadelphia: University of Pennsylvania Press, 2009). Harris uses the term *intertheatricality* rather than repertoire, but his use of the term very much falls in line with W. B. Worthen's and Tracy C. Davis's ideas of theatrical repertoire, in that he is not concerned with the use of texts by audiences, but with the way the acting styles in the Second Henriad communicated past, present, East, and West to spectators. See also Gina Bloom, Anston Bosman, and William N. West, "Ophelia's Intertheatricality, or, How Performance is History," *Theatre Journal* 65 (2013): 165–82.

in Shakespeare's plays connected them to "a string of oriental despots," such as Cambyses, Tamburlaine, Herod, and Amurath.[53] These acting styles, which were derived from "the ranting tyrants of the late medieval cycle drama" and "the Marlovian-era bombast popularized by Edward Alleyn and the Admiral's Men," marked a character as a tyrant because their particular stage conventions cited an English repertoire of tyranny.[54] In the theatre, if Richard III acts like Herod, the processes of repertoire are the reason that audiences know that Richard assumes that particular manner. That is, they can interpret his actions as affecting a tyrant, rather than thinking that Richard has suddenly gone mad and become a specific character in a biblical play.

The pressures of recognizability in the theatre necessarily reduce a range of previous iterations of a thing to an essential core of dramatic performatives that fuse together as that thing. Saints are no different. They are produced through a reduction and recombination of essential parts. My approach is thus concerned not with belief or disbelief in saints through theatricalization but rather with the production and recognition of saints in the theatre, something that English theatre makers had been experimenting with well before the early modern era.

"Things supernatural and causeless"

I approach the presence of saints in early modern drama as an extension of the frameworks provided by the archives of medieval performance and sacred time. Therefore, chapter 1 offers a survey of medieval saint plays and the reforms of the liturgical calendar of the English church. The development of theatrical repertoire in the Middle Ages and the shifts in the catalog of saints in liturgical calendars not only formed the epistemology of sanctity on the early modern stage but also determined which saints and which types of saints were dramatized in the professional theatre. I show that saints were depicted in snippets and scenes of iconography, miracles, transformation, and romance and these performances frequently occurred as part of a sacred temporality. When saints did appear in dramatic form, a process of vernacular improvisation interpolated tropes from other established genres and miracles were used to validate claims of sanctity. In all cases, it was common for theatrical and paratheatrical events involving saints to veer from their devotional *vitae*. The second half of chapter 1 tracks the growth, iconoclasm, and limited return of saints in English liturgical calendars across the various reforms of the sixteenth century. Despite a contention with saints and sanctity as England underwent Protestant reform, the official inventory of sanctity in the English church made space for certain ancient martyrs and medieval English

[53] Harris, *Untimely Matter*, 67.
[54] Harris, *Untimely Matter*, 67–8.

saints. Chapter 1 is complemented by the book's two appendices. Appendix 1 presents a table of nearly three hundred theatrical events involving saints between circa 965 and 1669, and appendix 2 inventories saints in liturgical calendars across the sixteenth century. Rather than attempt the futile task of comprehensively studying each and every one of these events and liturgical changes, I offer these appendices to augment my analysis and facilitate future research.

The survey of saints in late medieval performance and sacred time, along with the recalibration of Reformation iconoclasm offered in chapter 1, enables a fresh consideration of the seemingly impossible reentrance of saints in early modern drama. Chapters 2 and 3 address the first Elizabethan and Jacobean experiments with saints. In chapter 2, I explore how two St. Dunstan plays from the Elizabethan period retain elements of the saint's medieval legend, while also creating a new type of saint that overlaps with popular magician characters. These plays conflate hagiographic narratives and associate sanctity with spectacular theatricality, two elements of medieval performance. At the end of the chapter, I address Shakespeare's history plays from the same era that offer a suspicious perspective on sainthood. The Elizabethan plays do not recover sanctity or stage the making of sainthood, but they do reintroduce English saints to an English public. An examination of *If You Know Not Me, You Know Nobody* (c.1604) by Thomas Heywood in chapter 3 serves as the turning point of the book. It closely follows Heywood's renaissance of the saint play through the staging of Queen Elizabeth's Reformation struggles as miraculous virgin martyrdom, which culminates in the production of a new theatrical *vita*. The final part of the chapter turns to two plays that operate according to Heywood's new terms of theatrical sanctity. The anonymous *St. Christopher* (1609) and *Henry VIII* (1613) by Shakespeare and John Fletcher both depict overtly Catholic figures. An examination of the legal documents related to *St. Christopher* reveals that the pro-recusant play utilized the same oppositional theatrics of Heywood's play to sanctify the faithful and demonize the heretics. By contrast, *Henry VIII* carefully navigates and somewhat distorts Heywood's conventions of sanctity in order to frame Katherine of Aragon as saintlike but not quite sanctified.

Chapters 4 and 5 focus on two clusters of saint plays that follow the authoritative pattern of Elizabeth's sanctity through iterations of English ecclesiastical history and spectacular virgin martyrdom, respectively. Chapter 4 addresses five plays that extend the late medieval amalgamation of romance and hagiography to Stuart tragicomedy. I explore how *Pericles, Prince of Tyre* by Shakespeare and George Wilkins introduces "itinerant sanctity" in the ancient Mediterranean and how four less canonical plays materialize sanctity at specific English and Welsh sites and thereby plot sainthood along a map of legendary shrines, cathedrals, and castles. These plays celebrate English saints of the soil and anchor the Stuart present to the sanctity of the ancient ecclesiastical past. Chapter 5 explores how four outrageous virgin martyr plays address the problem of knowing sainthood.

These plays all feature angelic apparitions to musical accompaniment, books as apotropaic devices, and the miraculous—and often pyrotechnic—destruction of devils. And, in their formulaic production of virgin martyrdom, they use rape as a test to validate sanctity. I extend my exploration of virgin martyrdom to the Restoration stage. In that period, Matthew Medbourne and John Dryden composed new plays about SS Cecilia and Katherine, respectively, that replicated much of the repertoire of sanctity without utilizing the device of rape perfected by the earlier plays. The violent miracles of Jacobean and Caroline virgin martyr plays function as a sort of canonization in the theatre that occurs without adjudication by theology or religious confession. Finally, I conclude with an Epilogue that considers the absences and provocations of miraculous illusion in the twelfth-century *Life of Christina of Markyate*, Lars von Trier's film *Breaking the Waves* (1996), and the two-part dramatic epic *Angels in America* (1991-2) by Tony Kushner.

In *All's Well That Ends Well* (c.1601–5), the French lord Lafew utters a small speech that seems to divide the Middle Ages from the Renaissance through the rupture of the Reformation and the turn to natural philosophy or science: "They say miracles are past, and we have our / philosophical persons to make modern and familiar / things supernatural and causeless" (2.3.1–3). Ironically, this speech occurs just as the play commences episodes of healing, pilgrimage, vowed celibacy, holy death, and a final reconciliatory reappearance. Of course, as many readers and audiences know, the play only offers the bits and pieces of hagiography without holding it together as a *vita* or staging miracles. That phrase—"the bits and pieces of hagiography"—might sound like broken shards, but that is only if iconoclasm is privileged over the capabilities and capacities of play. The irony of Lafew's speech extends to the enterprise of experimenting with hagiography in the theatre. The themes, motifs, and scenarios of the legends of the saints not only emerge in a saint-less comedy like *All's Well That Ends Well* but also they structure new versions of the saints in other plays, such as SS Alban and Amphiabel, Crispin and Crispinian, and Winifred and Hugh in the Jacobean tragicomedy *A Shoemaker, A Gentleman*. Shakespeare's play premiered as sainthood in early modern drama underwent a great transformation from ambiguous supernatural association and negotiated patronage to a renaissance of miraculous theatricality and sacred place-making.

The Renaissance of the Saints after Reform excavates the legends of the saints at a site long thought to be absent of sainthood: the theatre. Between 1592 to the close of the theatres in 1642, the professional stage produced a new English legendary in dramatic form. The saints who populate the legends of the stage include SS Alban and Amphiabel, Andrew, Anthony, Crispin and Crispinian, Cyprian and Justina, Dennis, Dorothy, Dunstan, George, Hugh, James, Patrick, Richard of Chichester, and Winifred. This legendary also includes those saints who do not appear as characters but whose legends or iconography are borrowed by other saintly characters: Agnes, Bridget, Cecilia, and the Virgin Mary. In addition, the following saints figure in other performances of the era: SS Andrew, Christopher, Clement, Dunstan, James, John the Baptist, Katherine, Ursula, and Swithin. It is an inconsistent legendary to be sure: the legends are of varying lengths and genres and they also range from the traditional to the almost de-sanctified. The inconsistency of the legendary reflects its creation, which occurred over time and through a process of collection rather than planned composition. Despite the inconsistency of the entries in this conceptual dramatic legendary or commonplace promptbook of saints, the saints of the early modern stage reflect, re-form, and renew late medieval forms of sainthood founded on English patronage and virgin martyrdom, as well as an emphasis on the miraculous drawn both from earlier hagiography and theatricality. As medieval performance gave way to Reformation iconoclasm, saints were directed to *exeunt omnes*, but as religion continued to reform, that iconoclasm gave way to the early modern stage and the saints made a miraculous reentrance.

1
The Archives of Performance and Sacred Time

The 1540s were a time of crisis for the medieval saint play, a time of abrupt and sudden scarcity. The London Midsummer's Watch pageants, which featured guild patrons and occurred annually on the eve of the Feast of John the Baptist (25 June), ceased their parade at this time. So, too, did the Hereford procession, which occurred annually on Corpus Christi, a movable feast in early summer. Despite the radical governmental and religious reforms of the era, some performance traditions involving saints continued to persist until Henry VIII, now Supreme Head of the church, put a more definitive stop to them. Specifically, he prohibited activities associated with the holidays of "saynct Nicholas. Saynct katheryn. Saynct Clement. the holy Innocents And such lyke chyldern be strangely dect and appareled to counturfett prystes/ bishops / And women."[1] The rituals of boy bishops, cross-dressing, and other costumed paratheatricality on the eves of feast days are the medieval precursors to our own costumed behaviors on Mardi Gras (the eve of Ash Wednesday) and Halloween (the eve of All Saints' Day). It is easy to overlook the significance of Henry's proclamation due to the carnivalesque nature of these events and also because they do not conform to the received idea of the saint play. Nonetheless, the proclamation is significant because it announced the great divorce of performance from sacred time.

The saint play as a medieval phenomenon reflects a culture deeply invested in the lives of the saints and also a culture steeped in modes of performance to mark time, occasion, and local and national identities. While the medieval saint play could take any number of theatrical and paratheatrical forms, the records indicate that performance activities coincided with holidays and feast days. From the *Quem quaeritis* ritual at Winchester cathedral during Easter in the late tenth century to the Bassingbourn St. George play on St. Margaret's Day 1511 to the continued carnivalesque costuming associated with St. Katherine's Day in the early years of the Reformation, the liturgical calendar served as the heartbeat of the medieval saint play. Saint plays developed as part of a sacred temporality. When that rhythm slowed and ceased, the medieval saint play came to an end. However, the story of sacred time and the saint play does not end in mid-sixteenth-century Reformation

---

[1] *REED: HereWor*, 539. The feast days are SS Clement (23 Nov), Katherine (25 Nov), Nicholas (6 Dec), and the Holy Innocents (28 Dec).

iconoclasm. The series of reforms to the calendar of saints in the English church between the Henrician and Elizabethan periods not only dismantled the medieval cult of the saints, but also shaped sainthood on the early modern stage. As I show in the second half of this chapter, additional reforms to the calendar returned certain ancient martyrs and medieval English saints to the calendar of the English church. I contend that the curation of the inventory of sainthood in the Book of Common Prayer authorized the return of some saints to the stage in the new era of professional drama. The saints in the *BCP* did not effect a resurrection of the medieval saint play. Those miracles were forever past. But the repertoire of medieval saint plays combined with that authoritative inventory of English sacred time to produce a new theatrical life of the saints.

The Archive of Saint Plays

The archive of saint plays does not conform to common definitions or received histories of English theatre and drama. Rarely does the archive cough up records or texts that indicate an event organized according to even the loosest practices of Western drama: saint plays were generally not plays in the modern or even early modern sense. Drama involves the taking on of characters and the acting out of a story with dialogue, whether it is organized by episode or plot. The archive is also marked by lacunae. With the exception of the biblical plays that contain saints, there are only twelve theatrical or paratheatrical events that we know to have represented the part or a whole of a saint's life circa 1375–1554. Not one of them is documented through both a dramatic text and a record of theatrical production. Set pieces, properties, and finances (but no surviving text) document a play on the martyrdom of St. George in Bassingbourn (1511), whereas the Digby *Mary Magdalene* (East Anglia, c.1500) survives within Bodleian MS Digby 133 without any records.[2] While scholars of medieval drama have debated the definition of the saint play, the field has made peace with the discrepancies between the large archive of performances involving saints and the few records of drama.

When I refer to the archive of saint plays, I do not refer to a physical library or center of scholarly activity that has collected, cataloged, and organized all of the remains of saint plays from England, Scotland, Wales, Cornwall, and

---

[2] Beyond the Bassingbourn St. George and the Digby *Mary Magdalene*, these include the "gamen" of Theophilus (documented by a prologue fragment) (Durham, c.1375–1425), the "ludum de sancto" of St. James produced in six parts (York, 1446), an annual play of St. George (Lydd, 1456–1534), a play of St. Lawrence (documented by the Ashmole fragment) (unknown, c.1475–1500), the Digby *Conversion of Saint Paul* (East Anglia, c.1500), *The Life of Saint Meriasek* (Cornwall, c.1500), *The Interlude of St. John the Evangelist* (London, c.1510–20), *John the Baptist's Preaching in the Wilderness* by John Bale (1538), *The Life and Repentaunce of Mary Magdalene* by Lewis Wager (c.1550–66), and a St. George play (York, 1554). Of the standalone plays, one is in Cornish (*Saint Meriasek*), and two are written by Protestant reformers (Bale and Wager).

Ireland (as well as English-sponsored, English-language, or English-witnessed performances elsewhere) between the Middle Ages and the early modern period. The archive of saint plays encompasses the disparate and far-flung records, texts, and fragments that document performances of saints, their lives, their feast days, or related observances. From various physical and digital locations, it is possible to excavate saint plays and consider them as a conceptual archive. The basic inventory of this archive forms appendix 1 which is a chronological list of nearly three hundred performances or texts circa 965–1686. This table overlaps with and expands on Clifford Davidson's list of British Saint Play Records and Lawrence Clopper's appendices in *Drama, Play, and Game*, but my primary organization is chronological rather than by saint or location.[3] By organizing the records chronologically I hope readers can easily view patterns and also note the lack of patterns. I also hope to galvanize scholars of theatre, religion, culture, and literature from both sides of the Reformation divide to delve deeper into what can only be addressed at surface level in this chapter. My table continues into the seventeenth century in order to chart the rise of saint plays in professional theatre and the changes and continuities in occasional performances, such as civic pageantry. The extant evidence derives from physical places such as libraries, as well as digitized collections. Many of the records have also been collected, edited, translated, and published in reference and bibliographic collections, such as the *Annals of English Drama 975–1700*, *British Drama, 1533–1642: A Catalogue*, Malone Society Collections (MSC), and the Records of Early English Drama (REED). Much of the archive elides the exact nature of the performances that occurred. For example, the documentation of the 1393 London "pley of seynt Katerine" offers nothing more than a date and the name of the saint that might have been commemorated through performance in some manner.[4] Other plays of St. Katherine in the archive range from monastic dialogues to a welcome pageant for Katherine of Aragon to a ludic holiday observation. For every record that indicates representation of some aspect of the saint's iconography or *vita*, another record exists that cautions against that interpretation. Without more context or records of similar events (what Clare Sponsler calls "analogous and related performances"), these plays remain in the archive as singular unknowns.[5]

---

[3] See Clifford Davidson, "British Saint Play Records: The Saint Plays and Pageants of Medieval Britain," *Early Drama, Art, and Music* 2 (2002). https://scholarworks.wmich.edu/early_drama/2/; and Lawrence M. Clopper, "Appendix 2," in *Drama, Play, and Game: English Festive Culture in the Medieval and Early Modern Period* (Chicago, Il: University of Chicago Press, 2001), 295–306. See also Sally-Beth MacLean, "Saints on Stage: An Analytical Survey of Dramatic Records in the West of England," *Early Theatre* 2 (1999): 45–62.

[4] *A Chronicle of London, from 1089 to 1483*, ed. Edward Tyrell and Nicholas H. Nicolas (London: Longman, Rees, Orme, Brown, and Green, 1827), 80.

[5] Claire Sponsler, "From Archive to Repertoire: *The Disguising at Hertford* and Performance Practices," in *Medieval Theatre Performance: Actors, Dancers, Automata and their Audiences*, eds. Philip Butterworth and Katie Normington (Suffolk, UK: D.S. Brewer, 2017), 29.

Early drama scholarship is rife with disagreement over the definition and frequency of the saint play, which was not necessarily a devotional event and often lacked clear indicators of religious devotion. In general, Davidson includes pageantry in the definition, interprets records of "ludus" and "play" to approximate dramatic form, and understands the saint play, "with its mixture of the sensational, spectacular, and emotionally stunning elements... tuned to the hearts of the spectators," to be part and parcel of medieval religious affective piety.[6] Davidson theorizes that the ubiquity of hagiographic iconography and relics provides evidence for the "natural attractiveness" of saintly theatricality among medieval people, and that the dearth of evidence for saint plays rests on the Reformation suppression and destruction of records and texts of performances.[7] This is a sanitized view of a culture—even a devotional culture—that sometimes produced mischievous amalgamations of the sacred and profane, a view that imposes an operational piety on premodern theatre makers and audiences.[8] Clopper, on the other hand, sees no reason why we should think that saint plays, in the sense of drama, were a common occurrence in the Middle Ages and argues that there were only six saint plays, one of which was written in Cornish.[9] A saint play, according to Clopper, must "refer to enactments that depict the *vita* of a saint or some momentous event in the saint's life" and "have a spoken script based on the *vita*."[10] What emerges from both Davidson's and Clopper's scholarship is too narrow a definition of the saint play (i.e., a dramatized representational narrative based on the saint's *vita*), regardless of whether the saint play existed in large numbers (Davidson) or was quite scarce (Clopper).

Alexandra F. Johnston has revisited some of Clopper's claims, especially concerning the *miracula* that developed in monastic contexts and mostly occurred on the eves of feast days. Clopper—whom, as Johnston notes, initially had access to "only ten of the now twenty-five REED collections"—consistently understands *miracula* as "monstrosities" or inverted play.[11] Pulling from the expanded REED,

---

[6] Clifford Davidson, "Saints in Play: English Theatre and Saints' Lives," in *Saints: Studies in Medieval Hagiography*, ed. Sandro Sticca (Binghamton, NY: Medieval and Renaissance Texts and Studies, 1996), 160.

[7] Clifford Davidson, "British Saint Play Records: Coping with Ambiguity," *Early Theatre* 2 (1999): 97.

[8] See Emma Maggie Solberg, *Virgin Whore* (Ithaca, NY: Cornell University Press, 2018); and Noah D. Guynn, *Pure Filth: Ethics, Politics, and Religion in Early French Farce* (Philadelphia, PA: University of Pennsylvania Press, 2019).

[9] Clopper recognizes the following events as saint plays: The annual St. George performance at Lydd, Kent (1456–1534), which had a "pley boke"; the Ashmole fragment, which might be a part of a St. Lawrence play; the East Anglian Digby *Conversion of Saint Paul* and *Mary Magdalene*; the Cornish *Life of Saint Meriasek*; and the 1554 performance of St. George at York. See Clopper, *Drama, Play, and Game*, 295–306.

[10] Clopper, 128n78.

[11] Alexandra F. Johnston,"Pleyes of Myracles," *English: Journal of the English Association* 64, no. 244 (2015): 21. https://doi.org/10.1093/english/efu035

Johnston demonstrates that records of *miracula* or play, even in monastic contexts in the thirteenth, fourteenth, and early fifteenth centuries, might actually refer to more straightforward dramatic activities, and that occurrences of carnivalesque performance *do not also preclude the production of more serious drama*.[12] Johnston's response to Clopper's interpretation of *miracula* also responds to Davidson, whose work tends to speculate on the side of religious devotion and dramatic form. For example, in reviewing a record for payment to a man "referenti Miraculum Sancti Cuthberti" at the Durham Benedictine Priory, Johnston notes that "referenti" can refer to returning something or to retelling or repeating. The "referenti" might not have been a play in the form of drama, but "it is possible that" the event was a "retelling of the legend of St. Cuthbert for the monks of Durham, either alone or with others, by recitation or by mimetic action."[13]

Johnston's review of the "referenti Miraculum Sancti Cuthberti" is key to understanding the saint play before the early modern era. Sometimes it took the form of mimetic practices, and sometimes it took other forms, more fluid or ludic. The lacunae and varied vocabulary of the archive is not a problem to be solved but embraced. Informed by my training in performance studies, I accept the imaginative labor of medieval playmakers as it has come down to me in its current archival form. I also accept the commonly understood terminology of earlier scholars and interpreters. In Maggie Solberg's survey of the historical nomenclature used to describe the biblical plays and pageants that are legibly understood by the field of early drama studies as York, Chester, N-Town/Hegge, and Towneley/Wakefield, she upsets much of the rationale used to argue for or against "the mysteries." Nonetheless, at the end of her essay, Solberg argues elegantly for the field to embrace the term:

> "Mystery" carries within itself the memory of conflicts between Christianity and paganism, Catholicism and Protestantism, and Whig amateur antiquarianism and modern professional academia. Calling the plays mysteries evokes this long history of conflict. Yet none of this unpleasant history makes the term inauthentic.[14]

My interpretation of the records at both the micro and macro level is informed by historiographical, hagiographic, and philological considerations, but I am far less interested in answering the question of exactly what sort of event occurred and what it ought to be called—is it a play or not a play?—and far more interested in how a culture of play and performance developed various means of representing, presenting, or enacting saints.

---

[12] See, for example, Johnston's discussion of the *miraculum* of St. Cuthbert at Durham in 1410–11 and the *clericis ludentibus miracula* of St. Nicholas in Gloucester in 1283. Johnston, "Pleyes of Myracles," 15–16, 20–21.

[13] Johnston, "Pleyes of Myracles," 20.

[14] Emma Maggie Solberg, "A History of 'The Mysteries.'" *Early Theatre* 19, no. 1 (2016): 30.

Show Time

As the first half of Appendix 1 makes clear, while the archive is spotty circa 965–1375, it offers substantial evidence of the development of a culture of performance that enacted sainthood through theatrical shorthand and sacred temporality. The archive also offers evidence of the saint play's early iconoclasts. The earliest recorded performances that involved saints or may have involved saints represented miracles associated with the life of Christ at liturgically appropriate times under the auspices of clergy and religious. For example, the *Quem quaeritis* ("Whom do you seek?") trope of the Easter liturgy directs the monks of Winchester Cathedral in exactly how they are to depict the three Marys approaching the angel at the empty tomb after the resurrection.[15] Other episodes of liturgically timed drama followed during Easter at Eynsham (1196), Norwich (c.1260), Lincoln (intermittently, 1308–91), and Barking Abbey (1363–76), on Christmas Eve at Lichfield Cathedral (late twelfth century), and on the Epiphany at Lincoln (1317–87). The association between saint plays and feast days also appears in William Fitz Stephen's late twelfth-century *A Description of London*. Fitz Stephen, a former clerical servant to Archbishop Thomas Becket, documented "holier plays wherein are shown forth the miracles wrought by Holy Confessors of the sufferings which glorified the constancy of the martyrs."[16] Although there is no indication of which saints and which sort of representation Fitz Stephen witnessed, he contrasts the secular theatre of ancient Rome with the more sacred London plays and, furthermore, associates the latter with holiday sports. These sports include cockfighting and ball games on Shrove Tuesday, horse contests on Sundays during Lent, "naval tourneys" on water in the weeks following Easter, physical contests on feast days in the summer, and hog-baiting on feast days. That Fitz Stephen associates "holier plays" with the sports rather than with other types of theatre suggests a category of sacred play.

An elite antitheatrical culture developed alongside the theatre during this early period. Ecclesiastical administrators sought to impose various boundaries between performance and religion. In the twelfth century, John of Salisbury praised the efforts of ancient actors and condemned contemporary performers for creating what he called dishonest shows ("spectacula inhonesta").[17] A contemporary, Aelred of Rievaulx, struggled to divide theatrical showiness from liturgical ceremony. Aelred complained of the "histrionic gestures" of the choir;

---

[15] Cathedral Statutes of Bishop Hugh de Nonant, Staffordshire, Lichfield, 1188–98, D&C A/2/3 f46v and f48v, Lincolnshire Archives, REED Online, https://ereed.library.utoronto.ca/records/staff-ridm55095472/

[16] William Fitz Stephen, *Norman London*. Trans. H. E. Butler with an essay by Frank Merry Stenton (New York: Italica Press, 1990), 56.

[17] Lancashire, *Dramatic Texts and Records of Britain: A Chronological Topography to 1558* (Toronto: University of Toronto Press, 1984), 200.

cathedral-goers, he said, "come, not to an oratory, but to a theatre [ad theatrum], not to pray, but to gawk."[18] This period also witnessed the development of paratheatrical activities that were, according to Clopper, "boisterous, sometimes parodic," and involved "the use of masks, torturers, and ragged costumes."[19] After the Fourth Lateran Council banned clerical attendance or involvement in secular *ludi*, local iterations of the prohibition were directed at feast days. In 1333, for example, Bishop John Grandisson of Exeter ordered the "Cathedral vicars choral not to perform scandalous plays on Holy Innocents day as accustomed."[20] Additionally, "ludos ineptos et noxios" on 25–8 December (Christmas through Holy Innocents) were banned in Exeter Cathedral and collegiate churches,[21] and as late as 1422, the Bishop of Hereford directed the nuns of Limebrook Priory to avoid "comyn wakes or fetes, spectacles, and other worldy vanytees, and specially on holy dayes" and engaging in "all maner of mynstrelseyes, enterludes, dawnsyng, or revelyng" at the Priory.[22]

The records pick up considerably after 1375, during which era the history of the saint play follows the general contours of the development of theatrical performance in England. This is the period in which the Wycliffite authors of the *Tretise of Miraclis Pleyinge* argue against the dramatic representation "of Crist and of hise seintis" because to take "the most precious werkis of God in pley and bourde" so is to "errith in the byleve, reversith Crist, and scornyth God."[23] Unlike earlier attacks on theatricality, this one does not cite vague performances associated with feast days, but rather names the "pley of Antichrist and of the Day of Dome," and "the pley of Cristis passioun," biblical plays that are documented from at least 1376 and are associated with the Feast of Corpus Christi.[24] The "Crist and … his seintis"—Christ and his saints—might therefore refer to saints such as the Virgin Mary, John the Baptist, and Mary Magdalene, all of whom appear in episodes of the life and resurrection of Christ.

The liturgical calendar set the rhythm of the saint play for the rest of the Middle Ages. As Catherine Sanok observes, our modern sense of the sacred and the secular distinguishes primarily between location—a church versus city hall—whereas

---

[18] Aelred of Rievaulx, *The Mirror of Charity: The Speculum Caritatis of St. Aelred of Rievaulx*, trans. Geoffrey Webb and Adrian Walker (London, A.R. Mowbray, 1962), 210 and 211.
[19] Clopper, *Drama, Play, and Game*, 71.
[20] Lancashire, *Dramatic Texts*, 655.
[21] Lancashire, *Dramatic Texts*, 671.
[22] Lancashire, *Dramatic Texts*, 845.
[23] *A Tretise of Miraclis Pleyinge*, ed. Clifford Davidson (Kalamazoo: MIP, 1993), 93. Composed between 1380 and 1425, much of the first part of the *Tretise* refutes arguments in favor of miracle plays. For example, in response to the argument that witnessing "the passioun of Crist and of his seintis" in "gamen and pley" effects devotion, worship, and conversion, the author asserts that audience response can only be feigned holiness because only an unconverted person could interpret such theatre as holy rather than sinful vanities. *Tretise*, 102.
[24] *Tretise*, 101–2.

medieval people experienced that division as "a category of time."[25] Many records attest to a performance tradition associated with saint's days. Yet, it should be emphasized that sacred time—and holiday time—provided *merely* a venue for performance. With few exceptions, such as the figuration of St. George on 23 April across England and St. Thomas Becket on the streets of Canterbury on 7 July, a saint's feast day did not necessarily serve as an occasion for representing that particular saint. The expectation that the person or *vita* of St. Edmund would be dramatized on the Feast of St. Edmund or that the martyrdom of St. Agnes was dramatized on the Feast of St. Agnes for the education and adoration of the faithful is not supported by extant evidence in the archives. In present day Anglo-American culture, saints appear in nativity plays at Christmastime, the figuration of St. Patrick appears on St. Patrick's Day, and Mary Magdalene and John the Baptist appear in passion plays around Easter. Medieval producers of saint plays did not have our modern sense of schedule. In the Middle Ages, nativity and passion plays occurred around the Feast of Corpus Christi in the early summer and the Eve of the Nativity of John the Baptist provided a venue for Midsummer's Watch pageants that featured a variety of saints and other figures.

The excavation of theatrical and paratheatrical practices that occurred on feast days and holidays ought to normalize records of events that are named for saints and yet lack saints as characters. Three notable examples are the 1409 Winchester "pley of synt agnes," the 1525/26 Shrewsbury "Saynct Katheryn is play," and "three plays acted in the Church" in Braintree, Essex in 1523, 1525, and 1534, respectively. The St. Agnes play was planned—though, due to a dispute and a robbery, never performed—for the day following the Translation of St. Swithin.[26] Producer Richard Syngere hired four actors to perform the roles of two knights, a tormenter, and a steward. Jane Cowling argues that this minimal cast was not enough "to enact the basics of the legend of St. Agnes": "there would have to have been another six or seven characters in the Winchester play."[27] Yet, what obligation is there to dramatically represent the legend? The remarkable thing about the character roles named in the record is that they are not particular to the legend of St. Agnes at all. They are the stock characters of execution/martyrdom. For example, "tres tormenters" accompany St. Katherine in the Hereford Corpus Christi procession, and four knights execute Thomas Becket in a London Midsummer's Watch pageant.[28]

---

[25] *New Legends of England: Forms of Community in Late Medieval Saints' Lives* (Philadelphia: University of Pennsylvania Press, 2018), 12.
[26] *Records of Early English Drama: Hampshire*, eds. Peter Greenfield and Jane Cowling. 2020. https://ereed.library.utoronto.ca/records/hamps-ridp245582192/
[27] Jane Cowling, "A Fifteenth-Century Saint Play in Winchester: Some Problems of Interpretation," *Medieval and Renaissance Drama in England* 13 (2001): 28.
[28] Similar references to tormenters surface in the Aberdeen pageants of SS Lawrence, Sebastian, and Stephen. Mill, *Mediaeval Plays*, 124–31. In Perth, St. Eramsus's executioners came with a cord to represent his disembowelment. Anna Jean Mill, "The Perth Hammermen's Play: A Scottish Garden of Eden," *Scottish Historical Review* 49 (1970): 146–53.

It is possible that these characters could have portrayed a portion or episode of the *vita* without an Agnes. Or, perhaps these characters formed a different type of performance altogether.

Records for the Shrewsbury St. Katherine play also includes characters and properties that do not belong to a distinct narrative: a lord of misrule, a minstrel, three heads of hair, two beards, a jester's head, gold and silver paper, gold foil, six dozen bells, and ample gunpowder.[29] The explosion implied by the gunpowder could easily be explained by the miraculous combustion of the saint's wheel of torture in her *vita*, but the accounts do not contain a payment for a wheel. Furthermore, as Clopper points out, "there is no expenditure for the saint herself."[30] Unlike the St. Agnes play, there is not even a group of executioners who may have talked of the saint's martyrdom. The characters and properties indicate a more spectacular version of ludic play traditionally associated with the feast of St. Katherine. Other Shrewsbury records attest to a variety of local performances practices and customs.[31] Although it remains unclear why this event was recorded as "Saynct Katheryn is play," two possibilities stand out: it may have occurred either on or near St. Katherine's Day, or the event may have been named through the general association between ludic play and the saint's feast day.

The parish church of St. Michael in Braintree produced "three plays acted in the Church": St. Swithin in 1523, St. Andrew in 1525, and "Placy Dacy, alias St Ewestacy" in 1534.[32] St. Michael's produced these plays as part of fundraisers, which also included the sale of food and drink, in order to support the upkeep of the building. There are no extant records of parish ales and theatrical entertainments before or after these dates and, unfortunately, the only additional information about these events is that they included "players garments" and "play-books."[33] However, the churchwardens accounts do include two dates for the plays. The St. Swithin play was performed "on a Wednesday" and the St. Andrew play was presented on "the Sunday before Relique Sunday," which occurred around Midsummer.[34] The Translation of St. Swithin fell on a Sunday in 1523 and the Feast of St. Andrew occurs annually on 30 November. The fact that the St. Swithin play took place around

---

[29] REED: *Shropshire*, 1:183–4.
[30] Clopper, *Drama, Play, and Game*, 129.
[31] These include processions in the post-Easter season and "sport or play" on Pentecost. In addition, in 1515–16, Shrewsbury held a "ludum et demonstracionem Martiriorum feliciane et Sabine," and in 1517–18 there was a "tres Reges colonie equitantibus in interludo." The martyrdom of SS Feliciana and Sabina and the riding of the Three Kings of Cologne are unique events that were not repeated. They also were recorded in specific Latin terminology that indicates dramatic representation. Shrewsbury also participated in Hocktide paratheatricals until at least 1549 as well as an event involving Robin Hood in 1552–53. Hocktide plays entailed women capturing men, tying them up, and releasing them for a ransom fee, which was usually donated to the parish. REED: *Shropshire*, 1:184; 1: 172 and 173; 1:202 and I:203.
[32] Philip Morant, *The History and Antiquities of the County of Essex. Compiled from the best and most ancient historians* (London, 1768), 2: 399.
[33] Morant, 2:399.
[34] E. K. Chambers, *The Medieval Stage* (Oxford, 1903) 2: 342.

Midsummer and that the occasions for these performances were church ales raises the possibility that all three performances may have occurred in the post-Easter festive season. Certainly, that time of holiday-making would have been appropriate for some version of the romance hero St. Eustace, who is known as Placidas before his conversion, to emerge in the sing-song trochaic tetrameter of the play.[35]

The relationship between performance and sacred time cautions against interpreting records one way or the other if they are only documented as "the play of St. X" or the "St. X's play." Although records of performance are especially frequent between Easter and St. Bartholomew's Day (spring through the end of August) and between St. Clement and the Holy Innocents (late November to late December), the calendar alone did not determine the type of performances that were observed locally. The Bristol plays on the eve of St. Katherine may or may not have included the saint or, like the St. George entertainment at the Paston household, which featured the saint alongside unlikely companions Robin Hood and the Sheriff of Nottingham, they may have contained the saint alongside other characters.[36] If the Digby *Mary Magdalene* existed in record rather than in manuscript, it might have been documented as "a Corpus Christi play" or "a play on John Baptist eve." Likewise, the Digby *Killing of the Children*, which dramatizes the slaughter of the innocents but begins with a dedication to St. Anne, could easily have been recorded as either "Holy Innocents play" or "St Anns play." Such names reflect a range of possibilities rather than indicating content and form. An innocents play or St. Anne play could mean a carnivalesque event, a play about the saint, or another play occurring on the eve of the feast day of St. Anne.

How to Do Things with Saints

Some of the most substantial records of how saints were represented theatrically are archived in the records of civic or royal pageants, processions, and other events that featured patron saints. These performances did not aim to educate audiences about saints' lives. Rather, they relied on popular and recognizable moments of action and transformation. What emerges from the archive are scenes and fleeting snippets of miracles, martyrdom, and, even, romance. While some occasions were more elaborate in their depiction of aspects of a saint's legend, pageants and entries featured basic and easily identifiable iconography. The occasional pageantry and processions surveyed here suggest that iconographic familiarity

---

[35] Eustace, a Roman soldier, sees a vision of the cross while hunting a stag. He converts to Christianity, travels on a long journey, and reunites with his family, only to be executed with them by a tyrant pagan persecutor. This record is one of many that Davidson and Clopper interpret differently. Davidson speculates that the play portrayed the saint's martyrdom to "excite devotion," and Clopper doubts it was a play due to the fact that it was performed in the church. See Davidson, "Middle English Saint Play," 37.

[36] See the discussion of St. George performances in the next section.

and easy theatricalization determined the portrayal of each saint. For example, the 1534 London Midsummer's Watch Drapers' pageant of St. Christopher called for the saint to appear with "Ihc [Christ] vpon the Xpofers shoulder," and the accounts also record payments "for the hyer of A blak heer & A blak berde for the heremyte."[37] Together, these details point to the episode in Christopher's story when he is converted by a hermit who instructs the tall and brawny saint to serve Christ by carrying Christians across a river. The pageant seems to have only reproduced this particularly iconic and identifiable moment from Christopher's larger legend, which includes episodes as wild man and eventual martyr. Guilds beyond London also featured saints in similar presentation, such as in the Corpus Christi processions at Ipswich, Aberdeen, and Perth.[38]

Saints were not represented for their own sake. Rather, they were tailored to suit various forms and functions. Secular events and sponsorship, furthermore, could include the miraculous, martyrological, and legendary moments of their patron saints' lives. In 1519, the Skinners presented a London Midsummer's Watch pageant of Thomas Becket. The records indicate that the story was portrayed in two parts—"the pageant prison for Gilbert Becket," and "a pageant for the Martyrdom of St. Thomas"—and the characters included Tracy, "Sowden," Jewess, Gaoler, and Gilbert Becket, in addition to the martyred saint.[39] The titles and character list suggest that multiple plot points were included in the festivities: the "Sowden," (Soldan/Sultan), Jewess, and Gaoler refer to the pagan emperor, princess, and jailer who took Gilbert hostage when he went on pilgrimage to the Holy Land; the character "Tracy" in the cast list refers to William de Tracy, one of Thomas's four assassins. The Skinners' 1535 pageant of St. John the Evangelist may have contained even more plot points than their Thomas Becket pageant. The records include the saint, an executioner, an angel, and a dragon.[40] This cast list suggests that the Skinners presented three parts of John's medieval *vita*: the saint's torture and miraculous preservation (the executioner), his angelic visitations in exile (the angel), and the demonic visions he received on Patmos, as included in the Book of Revelation (the dragon).[41]

---

[37] *MSC* III, 23–4.

[38] For the complete list of saints, see Appendix 1 as well as *MSC* XI, 170–83 and Anna Jean Mill, *Mediaeval Plays in Scotland* (1927; repr., New York: Benjamin Blom, 1969), 271–3. Corpus Christi is a moveable feast of the post-Easter season that occurs between the end of May and the end of June. Other festive days include Whitsun, or the Feast of Pentecost, which occurs on the Sunday seven weeks after Easter. A week later is Trinity Sunday, and the Thursday of that week is Corpus Christi, although it is now usually observed three days later, on Sunday.

[39] *MSC* III, 4. These pageants may have been silent tableaux rather than short plays. As Robertson and Gordon, the *MSC* III editors, note, the "only clear instance of actual speeches being delivered in a Midsummer Show is in 1541," when the Drapers' paid Thomas Stretton for instructing child actors' speeches. See *MSC* III, xxii, 32–4.

[40] *MSC* III, 19.

[41] The emperor Domician ordered that John "be brought to Rome / And made hym to be caste in to a fatte or tonne full of hote oylle … of which he yssued out by the helpe of god / more pure / and more fayr / without felyng of ony hete or chauffyng / than he entred in / After thys that themperour sawe /

Guild, parish, and civic bodies organized the celebration of England's patron saint across cities. The records pertaining to the 23 April celebrations of St. George in Norwich (1408–1550, and beyond), York (1502–58, not inclusive), and Morebath (1528–47) attest to the range of playing practices that could be utilized to depict a relatively stable set of recognizable iconography.[42] St. George performances generally evaded the depiction of the saint's martyrdom, in favor of portraying him as an English knight, often astride a horse, and with a dragon.[43] The 1554 records of the York pageant include a cast of a king, queen, and "may" [maiden], played by actors, and a dragon that was either a large puppet or stage property.[44] Sometimes, he also appeared with St. Margaret. Although Margaret slew her own dragon in her own legend, she could be substituted as George's maiden in theatrical contexts.[45] In addition to the national, heroic, and romance dimensions of the George story, ridings and pageants were sometimes combined with religious observances. At Norwich, the saint battled the dragon before the Guild of St. George attended mass. The pattern was repeated with a festive meal preceding a return "to the cathedral to pray for the soul of their founder, Henry V, and for all benefactors and departed brethren. On the day following came requiem mass and the office of *Dirige*."[46] At York, The Guild of SS Christopher and George sponsored an annual "Procession & rydyng," from the early sixteenth century until 1558.[47] The "auncient Custome" included "the Solempne procession" in which George rode through the city followed by the mayor and masters of the town and church with their wives.[48] Following the procession, "a messe with a sermon" was celebrated "at Saynt Georges Chapelle."[49] Seemingly the only exception to this general focus on the saint's knighthood to the exclusion of his martyrdom was the Bassingbourn St. George play, which occurred on St. Margaret's Day in 1511 and was financed by twenty-seven villages in Cambridgeshire and Hertfordshire. This play may have represented the full *vita* of St. George, including not just the dragon/maiden episode but also the martyrdom. In addition to a dragon, the properties include "iiij Fawchones and iiij tormentoures axes" which were made by John

---

that he cessed not to preche the cristen faith / he sent hym in exile / vnto an yle called pathmos / There was saynte Iohan allone / and was visited of angellis and gouerned / there wrote he by the reuelacion of lord thapocalypse / which conteyned the secretes of holy chyrche / and of the world to come." Caxton, *Golden Legend*, C verso.

[42] For other appearances of St. George, see Appendix 1.

[43] For more on the forms the dragon could take, including as models or semi-automatous properties, see Philip Butterworth, "Late Medieval Performing Dragons," *The Yearbook of English Studies* 43 (2013): 318–42.

[44] REED: *York*, 1:318–19. I have deduced this because the records indicate that the dragon was initially brought forth on a pageant wagon and required mending afterward.

[45] A 1521 Midsummer's Watch pageant in London included St. George defeating the dragon and presenting it to Margaret. See Lancashire, *Dramatic Texts*, 969.

[46] REED: *Norwich*, xxvii.

[47] REED: *York*, 1:311.

[48] REED: *York*, 1:310.

[49] REED: *York*, 1:310.

Good and painted by John Bocher.[50] Good, who was also a wheelwright, donated one other item that figures as a central device of torture in George's legend: "a Rymbyll of a whele."[51]

Coronation pageants featured patron saints, even after the Reformation. SS Edward the Confessor and George greeted Edward VI at the Cheap in his 1547 procession toward Westminster, and Andrew and George represented the unification of Scotland and England for James I's coronation pageant, co-written by Thomas Dekker and Ben Jonson, in 1604.[52] But the saints in these pageants were presented less spectacularly than were those in events arranged through civic auspices to greet royal visitors. For example, in 1456, the city of Coventry hired a pageant deviser, John Wedurby of Leicester, for an elaborate pageant in honor of Queen Margaret's visit. The processional pageant opened with Edward the Confessor and John the Evangelist, included biblical, historical, and mythological characters, such as King David, Alexander the Great, and King Arthur, and concluded with the queen's patron saint at the "Cundit yn the Crossechepyng was arrayed right weell with as mony Virgyns as myght be þervppon and there was made a grete dragon & seynt Marget Sleyng hym be myracull."[53] Following the miracle, Margaret offered a speech to the queen in the hopes that "ye be hertely welcum to þis cyte" (sentiments voiced by other characters as well).[54] Coventry took out the dragon for a second time when Margaret of Anjou's son, Prince Edward, visited the city in 1474. Edward's patron, Edward the Confessor, greeted the prince to musical accompaniment and a fountain running with wine, but the final pageant of Edward's entry into Coventry featured England's patron saint "vpon the Condite in the Croschepyng was seinte George Armed and a kynges doughter a fore hym with a lambe and the fader & the moder beyng in a toure a boven beholdyng seint George savyng theire doughter from the dragon."[55] Perhaps the most spectacular pageant of all is the one that greeted Charles V of Spain in 1522. After presenting England's guest with the usual mix of mythological and historical figures, the entry concluded with an elaborate Assumption pageant that, in

---

[50] See J. Charles Cox, *Churchwardens' Accounts: from the fourteenth century to the close of the seventeenth century* (London: Methuen, 1913), 271–3. Excerpts are also available in B. Hale Wortham, "The Churchwardens' Accounts of Bassingbourn," *The Antiquary* 7 (1883): 24–6.

[51] Cox, *Churchwardens' Accounts*, 271.

[52] See Robert Withington, *English Pageantry: An Historical Outline*, Vol. 1 (Cambridge, MA: Harvard University Press, 1918), 184–7, 222–3; Thomas Dekker and Ben Jonson, *The Magnificent Entertainment*, in *Jacobean Civic Pageants*, ed. Richard Dutton (Staffordshire, ENG: Keele University Press, 1995).

[53] *REED: Coventry*, 34. St. Margaret already had greeted the queen once before as part of her London pre-coronation pageant in 1445, but the saint had stood stately and spoke verses emphasizing "pees bitwixt Englande and Fraunce," rather than performing any miracles. See John Lydgate, "Appendix: *Margaret of Anjou's Entry into London, 1445*," in *Mummings and Entertainments*, ed. Claire Sponsler (Kalamazoo, MI: Medieval Institute Publications, 2010), 160–6. See also Gordon Kipling, "The London Pageants for Margaret of Anjou: A Medieval Script Restored," *Medieval English Theatre* 4 (1982): 5–27.

[54] *REED: Coventry*, 34.

[55] *REED: Coventry*, 54–5.

addition to depicting "the assumpcion of owr lady meruelous goodly conveyde by a vyce and a clowde openyng with Michael and Gabriel angellys knelyng ... with most swetyst musycke that cowed be devysede" also included George, John the Baptist, Edmund, Edward the Confessor, Dunstan, Thomas Becket, and Erkenwald.[56] The miracles and major events in the *vitae* of the English saints are absent, but the saints themselves appear in the dramatization of an end-of-life miracle for another saint.

Two other regular events took spectacular form: the City of Canterbury's annual Thomas Becket pageant (1505–38), and Lincoln Cathedral's Assumption pageant, which occurred every few years between 1459 and 1553. In Canterbury, the summer Watch procession and pageants were on 6 June, the eve of the Translation of Thomas Becket. In addition to the pageant of the famous martyr, the city also produced pageants of St. George, the Annunciation, the Nativity, and the Assumption. The Thomas pageant stands out in the records for its constant innovation. The pageant always included four knights, Thomas's head, and gunpowder, but in 1507, blood ("sanguine") began appearing among the properties.[57] Whether the saint was represented by an actor or an inanimate figure, the blood featured in the assassination. The producers increased their special effects in 1515, when "the [de]vyce of ye angell" was introduced.[58] The device likely raised and lowered—or vice versa—the angel after the murder in the cathedral. At its most sophisticated, the pageant depicted the martyrdom of the saint before an altar, included the dramatic effect of a blood spill, and sanctified him through the apparition of an angel.[59] The annual Lincoln Assumption pageant, which played in the nave of the cathedral on St. Anne's Day (26 July), featured an inanimate Virgin Mary. In the pageant, the Coronation and Assumption of the Virgin were accomplished through mechanical technology. The Mary was raised from the floor or a platform of the nave to the roof using a device that cost forty-seven shillings. The Porter of the Close, who was responsible for the care of the great clock, was also employed for the Assumption pageant (and, later, the star on Christmas Eve).[60]

One final aspect of pageantry is consistent across both civic events and royal occasions: saints were rarely presented in isolation. Saints were integrated into a

---

[56] Unlike most pageantry devised for royal entries, this one was repeated for the city of London, sans Charles, the following year. See Withington, *English Pageantry*, 1:174–9; Sydney Anglo, *Spectacle, Pageantry, and Early Tudor Policy*, 2nd ed. (Oxford: Clarendon Press, 1997), 201–2.
[57] *REED: Kent*, 1:102–6.
[58] *REED: Kent*, 1:113.
[59] The annual pageant, in its Tudor form, ended in 1538, the year that Henry VIII officially banned the cult of St. Thomas Becket, destroyed the Shrine at Canterbury Cathedral, and posthumously convicted the de-sanctified archbishop of treason.
[60] The Cathedral paid Sir Henry Botery "pro factura mediate coronacionis beate Marie" in 1482. *REED: Lincolnshire*, 1:24. It is assumed that the characters in the Christmas pageant were played by human actors because of an annual expense, referred to as a custom, of giving gifts to actors. It would have been odd for the cathedral officials to allot finances to replace the gloves on Mary, the angel, Elizabeth, and the two prophets year after year. See *REED: Lincolnshire*, 1:26–67. Also see Clopper, *Drama, Play, and Game*, 154–5, 302n28.

variety of other rituals and performances that ranged from liturgical and paraliturgical processions (such as the one on St. Anne's day that led to Lincoln Cathedral) to performances that depicted nonsacred subjects (such as historical and mythological figures) but that occurred during the same event. Medieval performances involving saints rarely afforded the perspective of the professional stage, in which one spectacle and/or narrative was presented at a time.

Vernacular Improvisation

The archive of saint plays offers few instances of scripted drama. Even so, it attests to a period of dramatic innovation, especially between roughly 1475 and 1525. In addition to the episodes of iconic figuration, martyrdom, and miracles discussed in the previous section, this period also witnessed the incorporation of existing theatrical strategies of staging sainthood into dramatic form. Darryll Grantley proposes that "the extensive transposition of motifs from one legend to another in the non-dramatic versions of the legends evolves a formulaic pattern within whose parameters a significant capacity for reshaping and invention exists, and this carried over into the drama."[61] This tendency characterizes English pageantry as well as earlier and later Continental experiments with saints and drama. For example, Hrotsvit's mid-tenth century *Dulcitius* is an adaption of the martyrdom of Agape, Chionia, and Irena through the tropes and scenario of Roman new comedy. In that play, the martyrdom is a jumping-off point, and the virgins land in the comedy of Terence and Plautus. The Roman masters are outwitted by the miracles associated with the lowly Christian virgins, and the repeated physical violence and buffoonery are coupled with mistaken identity. Later, in seventeenth-century Venice, nuns performed the conversion play *Saint Mary of Egypt* (*Santa Maria Egizziaca*) by Giacinto Cicognini, which presents the protagonist, an Eastern Magdalene figure, "in her pre-converted state: Saint Mary occupies the role of promiscuous prostitute for the first hundred (of 120) pages."[62] This particular comedy delayed the conversion episode until the end of the play in order to dramatize a not-yet-sainted life.

The dramatic flexibility of *Dulcitius* and *Saint Mary of Egypt* also characterizes the depiction of saints in English drama. While Davidson's primary mode of reconstructing saint plays relies heavily on devotional hagiography and religious iconography, the Digby *Mary Magdalene* (East Anglia, *c.*1500) and biblical plays depicting the Virgin Mary attest to an interest in dramatizing what is *not present* in

---

[61] Darryll Grantley, "Saints and Miracles," in *The Cambridge Companion to Medieval English Theatre*, eds. Richard Beadle and Alan J. Fletcher (Cambridge: Cambridge University Press, 2011), 270.

[62] Christine Scippa Bhasin, "Prostitutes, Nuns, Actresses: Breaking the Convent Wall in Seventeenth-Century Venice," *Theatre Journal* 66 (March 2014): 26.

the textual lives and narratives—like Mary Magdalene getting picked up in a bar.[63] What is present in these plays is the interpolation of dramatic tropes from established genres, such as comedy and psychomachia, erotic plotlines, and miracles that validate claims of sanctity.

The Digby *Mary Magdalene*, for which we have the surviving text but no records, is the most well-known medieval saint play. The play documents how East Anglian theatre makers imagined the life of the saint and staged miracles. Featuring a cast of nearly sixty characters and over two thousand lines of dialogue, it depicts both Mary's life in the Gospels and her legendary life as a miracle worker and *apostola apostolorum*. Throughout, the nature of holiness materializes through the actions of vice characters as well as miracles that verify sanctity and religious truth. Part 1 of the play opens as a martyrdom narrative, with the Inperator [Emperor] declaring "all swych to dye" that "percharsse of crystys incarnacyon."[64] Mary begins the play as a young castle-dwelling aristocrat. After her father's death, her castle is besieged by "þe dylfe, with þe seuen dedly synnes, a bad angyll an an good angyl" and "the prynse of dylles" who enters from "Helle ondyr-neth that stage"(SD 305 and SD 357).[65] This scene not only sets up Jesus's later exorcism of the seven devils but also provides a plot twist. In her grief, Mary allows Luxuria (Lust) to take her to a tavern in Jerusalem. There, Mary meets a gallant and goes home with him. Later, while she is resting in an arbor and waiting for when her next "lover wol apere," the Good Angel appears and rebukes her. She repents, resolves that she "xal porsue þe prophet," and confesses her sinfulness before Jesus while washing "þe feet of þe prophet with þe terres of hur yys, whypyng hem with hur herre" (II.607, SD 640). It is a love story: she trades her "valentynys," for Christ. Jesus accepts her, tells her to "vade In pace," and the "vij dellys . . . de-woyde from þe woman, and the bad angyll" returns to "hell with thondyr" (SD 691). Back in hell, Satan stomps mad over the failure of his minions; he punishes them and then sends them to set a house on fire. Pyrotechnics and sound effects abound in this play. The Digby *Mary Magdalene* does not depict the crucifixion and the harrowing of hell. Rather, it announces God's victory over Satan through a comical anti-Exsultet. A devil screams, "Owȝt ! Owȝt ! harrow I may crye and yelle, / for lost is all ower labor!" because Christ's passion has freed souls (SD 963–64).

In the second part of the play, the risen Christ sends Mary Magdalene to convert the king of Marseille and his subjects. Mary serves as a saintly preacher and companion of angels who fights the demonic powers of paganism. Like the devils

---

[63] See Clifford Davidson, "The Middle English Saint Play and Its Iconography," in *The Saint Play in Medieval Europe*, ed. Clifford Davidson (Kalamazoo, MI: Medieval Institute Publications, 1986), 31–122.

[64] "Mary Magdalene" in *Digby Plays* II.28–9. All subsequent in-text parenthetical citations come from this edition.

[65] Spelling is correct.

in the first part of the play, the pagan priest and his acolyte fulfill comedic roles. Their topsy-turvy liturgical proceedings include swearing by "mohvndes blod," and Latin gibberish (II.1175). After recounting the life of Christ to the king, Mary challenges the paganism of Marseille by praying in correct Latin. Her prayer effects miraculous destruction:

> Dominus, illuminacio mea, quem timebo!
> Dominus, protecctor vite mee, a quo trepedabo!
> Here xal þe mament tremyll and quake.
> Here xall comme a clowd frome hevene, and sette
> þe tempyl One a fyer, and þe prest and þe clerk
> xall synke.[66] (II.1553–54, SD 1554, SD 1562)

Just as the devils left Mary after her conversion, so, too, does the pagan priest disappear after the conversion of Marseille. But before the king converts, he demands miraculous intervention. He tells the saint that his "wyff and I together many yerys have byn, / and nevyr myth be conceyved wyth child."[67] As Mary prays, the king takes to his bed with his wife. Christ responds, "To Mary my lover," by sending an angel to the royal bedchamber. Soon after, the queen is "grett wyth chyld!" The play reinserts Mary's bodily knowledge from her preconversion life. Her past association with the erotic now enacts a miracle of Christian futurity. The rest of the play depicts a post-resurrection world absent of devils and paganism and full of romantic miracles and angelic visitations.

The Digby *Mary Magdalene* satisfies the received definition of the saint play. That is, it depicts the *vita* of the saint through conversions and miracles. But the way in which it improvises away from the *vita* through dramatic tropes and scenarios cannot be anticipated by source texts such as the *Golden Legend*. The creators of the play seem as interested in dramatizing what is not present in the *vita* as what is present. Outside of this play, Mary Magdalene's story is by tradition a conflation of the lives of three women mentioned in the New Testament coupled with a romance narrative of providential seafaring and miracles that resembles the Apollonius of Tyre legend.[68] None of these contexts tell us how the composite Mary Magdalene begins her initial downfall into sexual iniquity. The Digby *Mary Magdalene* understands that absence as a question, and it responds by situating her in a

---

[66] Spelling is correct.

[67] Theresa Coletti, ed., *The Digby Mary Magdalene Play*, TEAMS Middle English Texts (Kalamazoo, MI: Medieval Institute Publications, 2018), II:1566–7.

[68] Apollonius's narrative is echoed in the latter half of the king of Marseille episode in the Mary Magdalene legend (and appears as such in the Digby play). As in *Pericles*, which is addressed in chapter 5, the queen dies aboard a ship, and both her body and her baby are left on a Mediterranean island. In the Magdalene legend, the king and queen of Marseille are making pilgrimage to Rome when this occurs. On the return journey, the saint's prayers resurrect the queen—mirroring the raising of Lazarus and the resurrection of Christ—and the family, reunited, returns to Marseille to establish a Christian dynasty.

tavern. Where else? In the early twentieth century, Constantin Stanislavsky would name this practice of improvisation "the Magic If." It is a modern concept for actor training that gets along well with the imaginative practices of devotional meditations on the life of Christ, such as those of Pseudo Bonaventure. What if Mary Magdalene lost her beloved father? What if she responds to her grief through sex and drink? What if her period of sorrow and luxury is where she experiences spiritual awakening—literally, while napping in the arbor and awaiting her next lover? This is the medieval invention of the human. A century before Hamlet's mournful existential struggle premiered at the Globe in a play with its own supernatural tricks, the Digby play identified grief as a catalyst of spiritual transformation.

The practice of dramatizing what is not present in biblical or hagiographic stories surfaces in other late-medieval plays. For example, Noah's wife receives scant mention in Genesis, but she looms large in biblical plays. As Solberg writes, "The comedy of Noah's wife that we see in York, Chester, and Towneley reframes a cosmic struggle between good and evil as a domestic battle of the sexes."[69] The back-and-forth between spouses is less about two biblical figures than it is about the stock characters of household disharmony in a no-exit situation during worldwide annihilation. Perhaps recent memories of domestic isolation and quarantine during the plague in the 1390s helped fuel this situation-based comedy. Drama challenges the idea of what the sacred looks like in the Middle Ages. Though it might seem vulgar to post-Reformation Christians of all denominations, the devotional culture of late medieval England developed sacred subjects in profane episodes. Vernacular drama not only presented the sacred in the language of its audiences but also brought the miraculous down to earth through everyday scenarios.

Nowhere is this vernacular improvisation more present than in plays of the Virgin Mary. In the biblical plays, the Virgin gains new dimensions. She is Christ's mother and is frequently miraculous, but she is hardly ever the same Mary. She has moments of adoration and moments of maternal sorrow, most notably in the nativity scene at the end of the Towneley *Second Shepherd's Play* and in the York *Mortificacio Christi*, respectively. Elsewhere, however, she figures more as a young romance heroine caught up in a love triangle and challenged, repeatedly, to prove her chastity. Solberg points out that the N-Town marriage play of Mary and Joseph resembles farcical fabliaux in that the comedy turns on a May-December scenario with God as the cuckolding lover.[70] In that play, Joseph initially opposes his marriage to Mary, which is arranged by a miracle, because "an old man may nevyr thryff / With a yonge wyf."[71] The large age difference between Christ's parents is also present in the Chester *Annunciation/Nativity* play. In it,

---

[69] Solberg, *Virgin Whore*, 117–18.
[70] Solberg, 24–6.
[71] "Marriage of Mary and Joseph," *The N-Town Plays*, ed. Douglas Sugano (Kalamazoo: Medieval Institute Publications, 2006), ll. 278–9.

Joseph delivers a short monologue in which he thrice refers to himself as "ould" while demanding to know who impregnated Mary and also planning to divorce her.[72] Christina Fitzgerald characterizes Joseph's appearance in this play as "old, impotent, complaining, and anxious."[73] This is a recipe for cuckoldry. Joseph's age and his condemnation of his young bride's "velany" so offended the Protestant Christopher Goodman that he dispatched a complaint about the Chester Plays to the Archbishop of York in 1572.[74] Among other inventions, Goodman documented that "Ioseph chargeth his wife with open words, contrary to the Scriptures. Also he reprehendeth marriage betwixt a young person & an old."[75] Goodman's attack on how the Chester plays treat the problem—the dramatic conflict—of the Incarnation reveals a reformed sensibility that identifies the "Magic if" as scandalous rather than devotional.

In the N-Town Plays, the truth-claims concerning Mary's bodily and spiritual virginity after the conception and birth of Christ are settled by theatricality rather than by faith. In this regard, the plays resonate with the theme of doctrinal incredibility, which emerges frequently in medieval drama. As Steven Justice argues, doubt is frequently baked into medieval stories concerning miracles and religious doctrine.[76] In the Croxton *Play of the Sacrament*, for example, the impossibility of determining the truth of transubstantiation is resolved through antisemitic drama. The Jews view "The beleve of thes Cristen men ys false," that is, "For they beleve on a cake . . . that yt shuld be He that deyed upon the Rode."[77] The figure of the oppositional Jew is made to do the eucharistic doubting on behalf of a Christian community. As Justice observes, "[t]he protagonists of eucharistic miracles are often ignorant of eucharistic doctrine: young children, stupid peasants, Jews, lazy and ill-catechized Christians."[78] In the Croxton play, the Jews necessarily struggle to accept the official doctrine of the church and the epistemic conundrum of whether a wafer is the actual body of Christ is solved through special effects. Sarah Beckwith argues that "the very necessity to see what you believe is a testimony to the doubt which underlies the implicit logic of the miracle play."[79] The host bleeds when stabbed by the Jews, who then convert to Christianity after this miraculous proof. Stage blood is materially present and absolves the audience of supplying belief.

---

[72] "Marriage of Mary and Joseph," ll. 125, 134, 145.
[73] Christine M. Fitzgerald, *The Drama of Masculinity and Medieval English Guild Culture* (London: Palgrave Macmillan, 2007), 83.
[74] "Joseph's Doubt," in *The N-Town Plays*, ll. 103.
[75] REED: Cheshire, 1:147.
[76] See Steven Justice, "Eucharistic Miracle and Eucharistic Doubt," *JMEMS* 42, no. 2 (2012): 307–32.
[77] *Croxton Play of the Sacrament*, ed. John T. Sebastian (Kalamazoo: Medieval Institute Publications, 2012), ll. 199–200, 204
[78] Justice, "Eucharistic Miracle," 311.
[79] Sarah Beckwith, "Ritual, Church and Theatre: Medieval Dramas of the Sacramental Body" in *Culture and History, 1350–1600: Essays on English Communities, Identities, and Writing*, ed. David Aers (Detroit: Wayne State University Press, 1992), 68.

The drama of doctrinal doubt also characterizes depictions of the Virgin Mary. Nearly everyone seems to doubt the Virgin. Joseph, the religious court, a midwife, and onlookers all question her account of her child's conception and, by extension, her virginity and sanctity. At each juncture in the N-Town Plays, a miracle is produced to counteract that doubt. Mary's devotion to virginity is established in the *Marriage of Mary and Joseph*, in which she resists a decree that all girls who reach fourteen years of age must marry. She vows, instead, to "levyn ever in chastyté."[80] An angel intervenes and counsels Episcopus how to proceed: he should gather descendants of David in the Temple with plain rods or branches, and whichever one holds a branch that blooms is the rightful spouse of Mary. When the elderly Joseph's rod blooms, he also makes vows. He tells Mary that he will serve as "Her wardeyn and kepere," but "That in bedde we shul nevyr mete."[81] One context for Joseph's vow is his impotence, but another more important context is virgin martyr hagiography. While all virgin martyrs of medieval hagiography derive the authority of their vows of perpetual virginity from Christ's mother, the scenario of the *Marriage of Mary and Joseph* in the N-Town Plays imitates the legend of St. Cecilia. When the vowed virgin Cecilia is forced to marry, an angel intervenes and convinces her new husband, Valerian, to live a chaste marriage. Mary's next trial occurs when her husband accuses her of adultery after her belly begins to swell. He is incredulous when she and her maids tell him an angel announced that God impregnated her. Joseph rants, threatens, and cries woe—until another angel convinces him that his young bride speaks the truth.

In the N-Town Plays, the demands for Mary to prove her virginity continue throughout the rest of her life. After Mary gives birth to Christ, one of her midwives observes that she is "nott hurte of virgynité."[82] It is a wonder that the Virgin's breasts are "Ful of fayr mylke" while her hymen remains "undefiled."[83] The other midwife, Salome, cannot believe what she sees and "shal nevyr... but it preve / With hand towchynge."[84] Mary, therefore, instructs Salome to "Towch with youre hand and wele assay... Whethyr I be fowlyd or a clene may."[85] While this invitation sets up an episode of probing that will be repeated when her son, Christ, appears before St. Thomas in the play of *Cleophas and Luke; Appearance to Thomas*, to doubt Mary's virginity is a greater risk than to doubt the risen Christ. Salome's hand shrivels and is only restored when she repents of her doubting. This is a version of the curse-and-restore miracles that are more present in the lives of virgin martyrs, such as when St. Agnes's would-be-rapist is struck down and then restored by the saint's prayers. This pattern repeats itself yet again in the Assumption play. While angels

---

[80] "Marriage of Mary and Joseph," ll. 38
[81] "Marriage of Mary and Joseph," ll. 290, 295
[82] "Nativity" in *The N-Town Plays*, ll. 233.
[83] "Nativity" ll. 234, 241.
[84] "Nativity," ll. 246–7
[85] "Nativity," ll. 251, 253.

and saints welcome the Virgin to her heavenly home, Episcopus and his band of earthly deniers insult her and plan to steal her "bychyd body."[86] Solberg argues that "these detractors"—who appear frequently in virgin martyr hagiography— "seek to test the inviolability of the Virgin in the most rudimentary way possible: by means of violation."[87] A curse of sudden madness thwarts all but one detractor who manages to reach the Virgin's funeral bier. Like Salome, his hands are pained, and he is unable to free them until St. Peter intervenes, freeing the madman on condition of his conversion and subsequent evangelization of his fellow Jews. All who convert and are touched by a holy palm are also cured of their madness and pain. There is one holdout, however, who questions the "harlotys" who "Forsake oure lawe," and for him there is no restoration or salvation.[88] He belongs to the devils who storm in and rip him apart before returning to hell, an evisceration that anticipates the finale of *Doctor Faustus*.

In the N-Town Plays, Mary's virginal sanctity is doubted and proved through miraculous intervention. As drama, doubt or denial is a prelude to spectacular theatrical proof. It is iterative and instructs audiences to expect an escalation of miracles to adjudicate claims of incredulous sanctity. The theatricality of the virginity tests administered to the Virgin in the N-Town Plays inform the violent tests of virginity that appear in the virgin martyr plays examined in chapter 5.

Sacred Time

Throughout the centuries, the English liturgical calendar set the intervals of sacred time and also acted as an authoritative inventory of sainthood. In 1516, the king's printer, Richard Pynson, published *The Kalendre of the New Legende of England*, a vernacular adaptation of the Latin *Nova Legenda Anglie*. The *Kalendre* offered to readers who "vnderstande not the Laten tonge" abbreviated *vitae* of English saints.[89] Although the order of the brief legends was rendered alphabetically, from St. Adrian to St. Wulfstan, rather than by the feast days of the liturgical year, Pynson also writes that "þe pryncypall intent of this treatyse to be as a kalendre to shewe þe names of þe seyntes of theyr country & where they lye."[90] He goes on to explain the idea of the calendar in terms of its cultural genre: "eueryþynge in this treatyse is shortly touched more lyke to be a kalendre then a legend."[91] The *Kalendre*, in other words, figures as an inventory of native saints. Unlike other collections (including the *South English Legendary*) that include native and nonnative saints alike,

---

[86] "Assumption of Mary," in *The N-Town Plays*, ll. 396
[87] Solberg, *Virgin Whore*, 51–2.
[88] "Assumption of Mary," ll. 471
[89] *The Kalendre of the Newe Legende of Englande, edited from Pynson's 1516 edition*, ed. Manfred Görlach (Heidelberg: Universitätsverlag C. Winter, 1994), 46.
[90] *Kalendre of the Newe Legende*, 46.
[91] *Kalendre of the Newe Legende*, 46.

the *Kalendre* excludes even the most celebrated biblical, ancient, and medieval non-English saints. It is this idea of the calendar as a politically charged list of importance that informs my analysis of the changing liturgical calendars of the sixteenth century and, eventually, the remaining inventory of saints in Shakespeare's time.

As a means of organizing time, the calendar—whether past or present—exerts political, social, and cultural force. At present, the work week, weekend, and state holidays organize society and determine major cultural narratives. We might imagine our calendars as secular, but many public institutions in England, America, and Commonwealth countries continue to observe a calendar set by the post-Reformation Anglophone academic calendar. Even in the United States, where there is no official state religion, schoolchildren are released for a winter break that coincides with Christmas, while non-Protestant holidays organized around observance, fasting, rest, or familial gathering are largely ignored in the calendar: the Assumption, Rosh Hashanah, Yom Kippur, Diwali, Ash Wednesday, Nowruz, Eid al-Fitr. The Western weekend reflects the custom of a Saturday vigil and Sunday Sabbath, rather than the Islamic and Jewish division of the week. More importantly, how time is marked in the calendar also determines which stories and histories circulate into the future. More inhabitants of Anglophone countries can repeat narratives related to Santa Claus (but likely not as the intensely pious baby St. Nicholas who refused his mother's breast on Fridays) than they can St. Catherine of Sienna. The circulation of the *life* of Catherine is likely confined to Catholic communities with an historical presence of Italian immigrants. And the saints that remain recognizable in England and its former colonies likely have some sort of ancillary mechanism that propels their continued recognition: St. Crispin (Shakespeare), St. Patrick (Erin go Bragh), and St. George (patronage)—but also St. Pancras (the London train station). Little of the devotional lives of the saints are remembered through these performances, but certain saints remain in some form while others are lost to obscurity. For many readers, the saints in the calendars in Appendix 2 will be an introductory exercise.

An examination of the changes to the English liturgical calendar over the course of the sixteenth century refines our understanding of the extinction of saints in English drama, pointing not to a narrow history of iconoclasm but rather to the dynamism of sanctity and its epistemologies. So, of course, if the route of saints in drama is only tracked from the Digby *Mary Magdalene* through the Reformation *Life and Repentaunce of Mary Magdalene* by Lewis Wager and to a termination point at Shakespeare's demonization of La Pucelle (Joan of Arc) in *1 Henry VI*, which I address briefly at the end of chapter 2, then the perspective on saints in English drama will be one of iconoclasm and de-sanctification. But the joke of Joan of Arc in Shakespeare's play is that a witchy campground whore would make a claim to holy virginity. Her acutely anti-English status, alone, shuts her out of the English calendar on both sides of the Reformation divide: the French cult of Joan of Arc existed from the fifteenth century, but Catholics and Anglicans did not claim her as a saint until the twentieth century.[92] Although theologians and hagiographers will argue that sanctity is for all time, the historical entrances and exits of the saints point to the authority of an age as a significant factor of sainthood.[93]

Reformers of the mid-sixteenth century proclaimed that the saints were gone forever, never to return, and their voices were so loud that we have long believed them. The mere fact, then, of the appearance of St. Dunstan in *A Knack to Know a Knave* (1592) and *Devil and His Dame* (c.1600) in the Elizabethan period complicates our received account of religion and drama. But it is the calendar that provides a necessary corrective of time-bound analysis, showing Dunstan to be bound to the time of the English church at the beginning and end of the sixteenth century. St. Dunstan, the tenth-century Archbishop of Canterbury, can be considered a medieval Catholic saint, but he was not a *Roman* Catholic saint until John Bale and John Foxe promoted him to the office of the Lord Lieutenant of hell in the mid-sixteenth century and the English Roman Catholic calendar claimed him in 1599.[94] By the time St. Dunstan first appeared on the public stage in 1592, he had occupied his traditional space on 9 May in the calendar of the *BCP* since 1559, the second year of Elizabeth's reign. The place of Dunstan and other saints in the English calendar from the beginning of the Elizabethan era onward offers a counterbalance to the emphasis on the exacting iconoclasm of the mid-sixteenth century. The problem is not that iconoclasm is overemphasized. It is difficult to overemphasize the extent to which saints and the structures and practices that maintained them were torn down or converted into something else rather immediately. But that fervor did not last for all time, even if it did return in force during William Dowsing's university and parish visitations in the 1640s and when, later, Oliver Cromwell's armies ran their spikes through the stained glass windows of cathedrals during the Civil War. As Philip Schwyzer observes, "[t]he wave of iconoclasm that swept England in the early 1640s had to deal with two kinds of superstitious images and furnishings: those that had been newly introduced as innovations in the last 20 years and those which had survived from the period before the Reformation...."[95] The iconoclasm that was practiced as England

---

[92] The Tridentine church, which is not the medieval church, did not canonize Joan until 1920.

[93] Notably, St. Katherine of Alexandria was kicked out of the calendar in the era of Vatican II reforms on the basis that her *vitae* were fabulous ("non solum Passio S. Catherinae est omnino fabulosa"). Catholic Church, *Calendarium Romanum*. (Romae: Typis Polyglottis Vaticanis, 1969), 147. Like Thomas Cramer, Paul VI justified the need for revision because "the multiplication of feasts, vigils and octaves ... have often driven the faithful to particular devotions," whereas the new universal Calendar ... better reflects the universality of the Church. Paul VI, *Mysterii Paschalis* (Rome, Italy: St. Peter's, February 14, 1969) https://www.vatican.va/content/paul-vi/en/motu_proprio/documents/hf_p-vi_motu-proprio_19690214_mysterii-paschalis.html.

[94] See John Wilson, *The English Martyrologe* (Saint-Omer: English College Press, 1608).

[95] Philip Schwyzer "'Monuments of Our Indignation': John Milton and the Reception of Reformation Iconoclasm in the Seventeenth Century," in *Memory and the English Reformation*, ed. Alexandra Walsham et al. (Cambridge: Cambridge University Press, 2020), 238–54. 244.

became a Protestant nation did not become a settled matter of English Protestant practice, and the Elizabethan church dialed back some of the Edwardian reforms that had marked the end of the saints. There would have been far fewer religious images to break in the 1640s without the earlier Elizabethan authorization to conserve what had survived Edwardian iconoclasm as well as the refurbishing of images—including saints—that occurred under the early Stuarts.

The liturgical calendar is a site of orthodoxy. A review of English liturgical calendars over the course of the sixteenth century tells a story of evolving curation followed by periods of increase, absence, increase, and limited retention. A consideration of the calendar also places the quirks of sixteenth-century reform into a longer view of development and change. The reformed calendar not only charts the destructive forces of iconoclasm, but also contains an unarticulated theory of post-Reformation sanctity. As the 1559 column in appendix 2 shows, some medieval English saints were welcomed back into the fold of the *BCP*, and, despite their controversial status among Protestant polemical writers, there they remained.

That Catholicism was not the official religion in England by the time that purgatory surfaced in *Hamlet* elides the extent to which *Roman* Catholicism was always a somewhat foreign practice. Since the pre-conquest period, the English church had developed its own unique set of liturgical and paraliturgical customs. In the early sixteenth century, not only was the liturgy in York distinct from the liturgy in Rome, but also the liturgy of York remained distinct from the liturgies of Salisbury (Sarum) and Hereford. With these distinct liturgical traditions also came distinct observations in hagiography. St. Dunstan appears in certain medieval English liturgical calendars, but not Roman ones. The Roman use or variant, like the uses of Milan, Utrecht, Paris, and others, had its own calendar of saints, which often combined universal feast days (such as all of the Apostles), the Roman martyrology (such as SS Cecilia and Lawrence), and local or regional saints. Many of the saints restored to the *BCP* can be found in English and Welsh liturgical calendars between the tenth and sixteenth centuries but are absent from those on the Continent. Few Londoners would have cared about SS Zenon or Benoist, who appear in some French calendars from the late medieval period. And in Rome, why would anyone venerate SS Swithin or Etheldreda, whose relics anchored English cathedrals to their storied past? Their cults were as foreign as their names were unpronounceable.

Saints may be associated with the Middle Ages, but not all of those ages are associated with all saints. By the early sixteenth century, the saints of the Sarum, York, and Hereford calendars overlapped considerably. A national elevation of many regional saints occurred over the course of the fifteenth century. For example, in 1416, Sarum use adopted two feasts linked "to the glorious victory at Agincourt" on 25 October of the previous year: the feast of SS Crispin and Crispinian, but also the feast of the Translation of John of Beverley (formerly identified with only the use of York).⁹⁶ Of course, "That fought with us on Saint John of Beverley's day" has one more metrical foot than Shakespeare's speech and, unlike SS Crispin and Crispinian, he did not make it into the Elizabethan *BCP*. The saints of *Henry V's* great battle speeches—SS Crispin and George—are the legacy of the fifteenth-century nationalization of these saints and, eventually, the Elizabethan rehabilitation of them.

How the totality of pre-Reformation calendars and their saints intersected with lay religious practice can be observed through sermon collections, such as John Mirk's *Festial*. Collections of sermons document how more comprehensive legendaries could be and were used by priests throughout the liturgical year to curate the distribution of hagiography to the laity, who would not have been present for all the octaves, vigils, solemnities, and feasts that cathedrals and monasteries observed. Mirk, a late fourteenth-century Augustinian from Shropshire, produced sermons for other priests who were tasked with expounding on the thematic observance of the liturgical calendar without access to a personal or institutional library. Composed in Middle English, *Festial* survives in more than twice as many printed editions as the *Golden Legend* between 1483 and 1532. What is most striking about a comparison between the *Festial* and Sarum calendars in terms of its selection of saints is the scantness of the *Festial* inventory. For example, St. Dunstan's feast days are absent from Mirk, despite the fact that both the feast and the translation appear in other pre-Reformation calendars. This is because Mirk uses Dunstan's *vita* for a sermon on Candlemas, the Feast of the Purification of the Virgin, which would have been more widely observed than Dunstan's feast days in parish churches. As one of the exempla Mirk uses for the feast, he repeats an episode that frequently appears in the saint's life concerning his pregnant mother's own attendance at Candlemas. During Mass, "soddenly al þe candeles in þe chyrche veren que[yn]t and gret darkenes come wythal" but "þen come a fayre light from heuen and lyght þe candul þat Dounustannes modur bare in her hond, and so of hure al oþur tokon lyght."⁹⁷ Metaphorically, the rekindling of the candles promised the revival of religious devotion in England under Dunstan's archbishopric. Other saints of the Sarum calendar also appear in *Festial* on feast days other than their own, such as Edmund of Abingdon on Trinity Sunday. Like the civic and royal pageantry examined earlier, Mirk's selective list of both feast days and saints reflects a particular hierarchy of importance and lay popularity taken from the aggregate inventory of the entire medieval calendar.

---

⁹⁶ Richard W. Pfaff, *The Liturgy in Medieval England: A History* (Cambridge, MA: Cambridge University Press, 2009), 439.
⁹⁷ John Mirk, *A Critical Edition of John Mirk's Festial: Edited from British Library MS Cotton Claudius A.II*, Vol. 1 edited by Susan Powell, EETS o.s. 334 (Oxford: Oxford University Press, 2010), 1:14/119–23.

Iconoclastic Time

Under Henry VIII, even as saints were disinterred from the sites they made sacred and the cult of Thomas Becket was scraped from every possible surface, including the rubrics of liturgical books, the inventory of saints in the Sarum calendar actually grew in number. More saints from Continental calendars were imported, and nearly every day of the year was occupied with a saint (see Appendix 2). There was also a different distribution of saints. The pre-Reformation Sarum liturgy observed multiple feasts in a single day, but the Henrician and Marian versions of the Sarum calendar only observed one saint or feast per day. The force of this streamlining jettisoned John of Beverley from 25 October, the day more famously known as "St. Crispin's Day." In addition, the later Henrician Sarum calendar also exchanged the word *pope* for *bishop* next to certain saints (including Gregory and Linus), reflecting the Reformation rejection of papal authority over the English church.

The increase of saints in the calendars of service books during the years of the Henrician Reformation will be surprising to many readers. Yet, the Henrician Reformation was motivated by a consolidation and organization of religious capital, and the calendar posed little threat. The liturgical calendar, unlike the monasteries, did not monetize the power of purgatorial relief. The saints of the official liturgical calendar were allowed to grow in number, then, alongside iconoclastic processes in which saints were plucked from their shrines and stripped of their seasonal traditions. Even before Henry destroyed the cult of Thomas Becket in 1538, his more popular feast day (the Feast of the Translation on 7 July, not the commemoration of his martyrdom on 31 December) had been abolished because it conflicted with economic productivity. As Margaret Aston writes, "Parochial goodbyes to St. Thomas of Canterbury" started in 1536, after "the abolition of holy days that fell during the harvest season hit the feast of the translation"—an abolition that affected not just Thomas, but also Margaret (20 July), Mary Magdalene (22 July), Anne (26 July), and Lawrence (10 August).[98] The customs of performance associated with these and other feasts that formed the traditional festive season also ceased. And yet, the inventory of saints in the Sarum calendar would only dwindle by one: Thomas Becket.

A proclamation released in late 1538, just as the dissolution of the greater monasteries got underway, reflects the character of the Henrician Reformation. In it, the Crown regulated the publication and circulation of vernacular books, with special concern for unapproved "books of Scripture" and "false doctrine," especially those associated with Sacramentarianism and Anabapists.[99] Henry

---

[98] Margaret Aston, *Broken Idols of the English Reformation* (Cambridge: Cambridge University Press, 2015), 366

[99] "Henry VIII: November 1538 16," in *Letters and Papers, Foreign and Domestic, Henry VIII, Volume 13 Part 2, August–December 1538*, ed. James Gairdner (London: Her Majesty's Stationery Office, 1893), 353.

also prohibited priestly marriage and disputation of the eucharist, and retained traditional ceremonies associated with Good Friday, Corpus Christi, Candlemas, and the churching of women. And finally, the king devoted the final portion of the proclamation to eradicating the lasting problem of one meddlesome priest:

> Thos. Becket, sometimes abp. of Canterbury, shall no longer be named a saint as he was really a rebel who fled the realm to France and to the bp. of Rome to procure his abrogation of wholesome laws, and was slain upon a rescue made with resistance to those counselled him to leave his stubbornness. His pictures throughout the realm are to be plucked down and his feastival shall no longer be kept, and the services in his name shall be razed out of all books.[100]

As Helen L. Parish puts it, "[t]he campaign against Becket in the autumn of 1538 was unique."[101] Henry effectively produced the first authoritative use of anti-*vita*, an iconoclastic practice that can be traced from John Wycliffe to present social media. Janel Mueller traces the heterodox revamping "of the idea and vocabulary of 'sainthood'" from Wycliffe to Lollardy to Bale and Foxe and, finally, to seventeenth-century Puritans.[102] The radical redefinition of sainthood not only encompasses a rejection of traditional sainthood as "dubious," but also "regains its special charge of Pauline meaning and assumes new intensity within the Augustinian dichotomy of the earthly and heavenly cities."[103] Henry would never embrace this strain of radical saints, but in attacking the cult of Thomas Becket from his office as Supreme Head of the church he transformed iconoclasm, whether material or discursive, from heterodox to orthodox. The attack on a past Archbishop of Canterbury, even one infamous for his opposition to the king, opened the floodgates for future defamatory biographies. In 1537, John Bale composed the iconoclastic drama *De Traditione de Thomas Becket* as part of an effort to dismantle and discredit the cult of Thomas Becket. In September 1538, the shrine at Canterbury Cathedral was destroyed. Attempts to observe the Translation of Thomas Becket in Canterbury after the destruction of the shrine floundered. Beginning in 1537–38, the City Chamberlains' accounts refer to "bysshop Bekett" rather than St. Thomas (as was customary from 1504 to 1536).[104] The St. Thomas pageant cart was sold in 1539, a watch was observed without the pageant in 1541, and attempts to revive the pageant were short-lived.[105] And a number of

---

[100] "Henry VIII: November 1538 16," 354.
[101] Helen L. Parish, *Monks, Miracles and Magic: Reformation Representations of the Medieval Church* (London and New York: Routledge, 2005), 98. For details of the outlandish trial of Thomas Becket by the Crown in 1538, including the summons to appear in person, see pp. 96–7.
[102] Janel Mueller, "The Saints," in *Cultural Reformations: Medieval and Renaissance in Literary History*, ed. Brian Cummings and James Simpson (Oxford: Oxford University Press, 2010), 173.
[103] Janel Mueller, "The Saints," 174 and 175.
[104] *REED: Kent*, 1:147.
[105] *REED: Kent*, 1:152.

extant service books and devotional manuscripts suffered scraping or defacement, including Osborn Bokenham's unique verse *Legenda Aurea* (Advocates MS Fol.21r–26v). If there was a lasting test of political and religious orthodoxy, it was compliance with the eradication of Thomas of Canterbury. Even as Thomas Becket was scraped from liturgical books, however, the majority of those saints who were later removed under Edward's more coherent and radical reforms remained under Henry, their names intact in liturgical calendars, litanies, and, if applicable, pictorial representation.

Disfigurement

The authorized attack on Thomas Becket expanded to other holders of ecclesiastical office, especially those who were linked to the expansion of monasticism and the defense of the papacy. Under Edward, John Bale published *The Acts of English Votaries*, a two-part attack on hagiography, monasticism, and Catholicism that, in many ways, reads like a dystopic version of the *Kalendre of the Newe Legende of England*. The English saints of the soil, who are celebrated in traditional hagiography for their ties to an historical ecclesiastical tradition in England (and which form a subgroup of saint plays addressed in chapter 4), emerge as ridiculous and grotesque purveyors of monkery in *The Acts of English Votaries*. Textual iconoclasm does not disappear saints but disfigures them into a shameful parade of disorder and ugliness. Bale rereads English ecclesiastical history and saints' lives so that the legends of the English saints become evidence of the falsehood of Catholicism. Augustine (Austin) of Canterbury, the first Archbishop of England and the person who reestablished Christianity in England in the seventh century, is condemned for bringing a version of Christianity from Rome. While other reformers treat Augustine with reverence, Bale narrates that he "with his monkes" was sent from Rome to "prepare Antichrist a seate here in Englande."[106] Bale spares no saint.

Bale devotes more prose to St. Dunstan than to any other saint or churchman due to his role in the history of the English church. Late medieval hagiography celebrated Dunstan as a miracle worker and ecclesiastical reformer, and devotional literature included episodes of prophecy, visions, miracles, and pastoral work that marked Dunstan as a saint.[107] His *vita* frequently begins with the saint in utero on Candlemas, as in Mirk's homily for the Purification of the Virgin. As in the *Golden Legend*, Dunstan becomes a monk and, eventually, Abbot of Glastonbury Abbey, where he learns the craft of a smith. While he is working at his forge, the devil appears to him "in the liknes of a woman" to tempt him with "many nyce

---

[106] John Bale, *The first two partes of the actes or vnchast examples of the Englysh votaryes* (London, 1551), 25v.
[107] Representative lives are: *South English Legendary*, the *Gilte Legende*, William Caxton's "englyshed" *Golden Legend*, and Richard Pynson's *Kalendre of the Newe Legende of Englande*.

tysyllys,"[108] but he accurately perceives that she is "a wycked sprite / and anone caught hir by the nose wit a payre of tonges of yron brennyng" and made "the deuyl... to rore & crye."[109] Upon proving his holiness by overcoming the devil's seduction at the forge, Dunstan becomes a counselor to kings, and is later consecrated Archbishop of Canterbury under King Edgar. As head of the English church, he pursues a series of reforms, including the expulsion of lustful priests and the expansion of monastic life. The late medieval vernacular legends, such as those in Mirk and the *Kalendre*, emphasize Dunstan's advocacy for chastity rather than celibacy. In the *Kalendre*, for instance, the archbishop assigns a seven-year penance to King Edgar for the rape of a nun.[110] Among the miracles that feature regularly and prominently in later medieval *vitae* are several visions: one in which he sees his deceased parents in heaven, another in which he experiences angels singing the Kyrie Eleison, and yet another in which a harp accompanies his prayers, playing *Gaudete in Caelis* "wythout touchyng of ony honde that he could see."[111]

In Reformation polemic, Dunstan figures as the archnemesis of Christianity for the same acts that earlier illustrated his sanctity in fourteenth- and fifteenth-century devotional literature: the expulsion of married priests, the growth of monastic life, and his miracles. As Antonina Bevan Zlatar writes, when Protestants cited these same details, "these tales are made to underline, not the glory of the victorious saints, but their inherent ridiculousness."[112] Reading against the devotional paradigm, Bale recasts Dunstan as Satan's right-hand man: "Like as holye Iohan Baptyst by preaching repentaunce, prepared a playne pathaway to Christ... So ded thys vnholye Dunstane by sowynge of all superstycyons, make redye the waye to Satan."[113] Similarly, in the *Book of Martyrs* (first published in 1563), Foxe damned Dunstan for discharging "maryed Priestes and Chanans out of their houses, to plante Monkes in their celles," and he recounted the miracles of angelic singing and of the harp playing on its own as "the impudent and abhominable fictions of this Romish generation."[114] Parish characterizes this reframing of traditional sanctity as a "campaign of iconoclasm that reached beyond the physical remains and representations of the saints into the very nature of sainthood itself."[115] She goes on to

---

[108] Enticements or enticing tales.
[109] Caxton, *Golden Legend*, clxxii recto.
[110] The *South English Legendary* omits the episode of Edgar and the nun, who is sometimes identified as St. Wilfrida, mother of St. Edith. For more on the conflation of Edgar's multiple episodes of sexual pursuit and assault, see Kristen A. Fenton, *Gender, Nation, and Conquest in the Works of William Malmesbury* (Suffolk, UK: Boydell & Brewer, 2012), 71.
[111] Caxton, *Golden Legend*, clxxii verso. Neither of these visions are included in the *Kalendre*.
[112] Antonina Bevan Zlatar, *Reformation Fictions: Polemical Protestant Dialogues in Elizabethan England* (Oxford: Oxford University Press, 2011), 121
[113] Bale, *Englysh votaryes*, 72v.
[114] Foxe 1570, 1:199.
[115] Parish, *Monks, Miracles and Magic*, 83.

explain that Reformation polemicists "took apart the edifice of traditional hagiography and reassembled its component parts to present a new image of medieval sanctity."[116] Unlike material iconoclasm, which marred or disappeared representations of the saints, the image of medieval sanctity presented by Bale, Foxe, and others was both coherent and comprehensive. Saints—with their missing noses or heads—were not simply the sad losers in a new era of reform. Rather, they were powerful villains in an age-old battle between truth and falsehood. And yet, despite all the vitriol that was directed at St. Dunstan by reformers, he would be returned to the English calendar in 1559, along with some of his medieval ecclesiastical companions.

The project of the English Reformation was not just a de-papalization of the English church but also an alignment of practice among the many variations on the island. The consolidation of the English rites had begun in 1543, toward the end of the Henrician Reformation, with the adoption of the Latin Sarum rite. Under Edward, however, the Sarum rite lost its status as the official liturgy even as it served as the basis for the new vernacular liturgy. The pursuit of establishing a unformal repertoire of English worship and religious practice is explicit in the title of the primer published in 1547, the first year of Edward VI's kingship: *"The primer set furth by the Kinges maiestie his clergie, to be taught lerned, and red: and none other to be vsed thorowout all his dominions."*[117] The *Primer* announced the expectation of national orthopraxis. For the 1549 BCP, Cranmer was tasked with unearthing a more radical Protestant ideological and theological coherence from Henry's appropriation of monastic wealth and power, on the one hand, and traditional inclinations toward sacramentality and liturgy, on the other. In the preface, Cranmer directed his clergy to observe the one English liturgy over the many iterations of liturgy. They could not coexist: "where heretofore, there hath bene great diuersitie in saying & synging in churches w[ith]in this realme some following Salsbury vse, some Herford vse, some [the] vse of Bangor, some of Yorke, & some of Lincoln, now fro[m] he[n]ceforth all [the] whole realm shal haue but one vse."[118] Here, Cranmer divides time between a past of regional variation in church practice and a future age of national organization. Clergy were also directed to "not set further or extolle any Images, Reliques, or miracles," nor lure their flock "to the Pylgrimage of any sainct [saint] or ymage."[119] In addition to this attack on traditions, the regulation of religious uniformity demanded that Christians cease the performance of their own apotropaic practices such as the "ringynge of the holy Belles, or blessing with ye holy candel, to thintent, therby to . . . to driue awaye Deuilles," as well as the "keeping of priuate holy dayes, as Bakers, Brewers,

---

[116] Parish, *Monks, Miracles and Magic*, 83.
[117] Richard Grafton: London, 1547. Frontispiece.
[118] Church of England, *Book of Common Prayer* (1549), A3r.
[119] Church of England, *Iniunccions geue by the most excellent prince, Edward the sixte* (London: 1547), A3r.

Smithes, Shoomakers & suche other do."[120] Cranmer's aspirations for unification in the English liturgy were successful and, for a time, so was his stringent iconoclasm.

The 1549 calendar represents the smallest number of saint days in any liturgical calendar of the sixteenth century: all those saints were drawn from the New Testament, and even the most revered early church martyrs, such as Agnes and Katherine, were absent. But things began to change in 1552 when the Edwardian prayerbook reinserted three nonbiblical observances: St. George, Lammas Day, and St. Clement. A few years later, the original Edwardian injunctions against images, relics, and miracles were narrowly revised by the new Elizabethan church in 1559. In the directive against household images, paintings, "and other monumentes of fayned miracles, pilgrimages, ydolatry, or superstitcion," the word *saint* is now absent.[121] The saints' presence was no longer anathema. The chantries and pilgrimages would never return, as purgatory had been officially eradicated, but SS George and Clement would soon be joined by several other saints that had once populated the past "diuersitie" of Sarum, York, and Hereford.[122]

Re-curation

The reforms to the liturgical calendar in the sixteenth century overlap somewhat with the dissolution of monastic libraries and the creation of post-Reformation libraries. As Jennifer Summit's work on the subject has established, reformers sorted through the collections of England's monastic libraries, including books of hagiography and devotional literature, with a particular rubric: were the books "monuments of antiquity" or "monuments of superstition"?[123] The former could be preserved while the latter must be suppressed. The iconoclasm practiced against the medieval monastic library was not just a matter of destroying the suppressed "monuments of superstition." Anthologies were pulled apart, rebound, and sent off to new centers of research as the monasteries, themselves, came down and the monks were dismissed and dispersed. The iconoclastic reorganization of the "monuments of antiquity" into the Bodleian and other academic libraries also transformed secularity from an experience of the temporal to an experience of location. As Summit notes, "antiquarians removed saints from the church to the archive."[124] The sixteenth century un-collection of the monastic libraries and

---

[120] Church of England, *Iniunccions geue by the most excellent prince*, C2v.
[121] Church of England, *Ininctions geuen by the Quenes Maiestie* (London, 1559), C2v.
[122] Aston notes the rather inexplicable return of England's patron saint in the 1552 calendar: "The parliamentary session of Jan to April 1552 which passed the act of uniformity introducing the new Prayer Book also passed an act for the keeping of holy days and fasts days, which listed the appointed scriptural days. St George, unsurprisingly, was not on this list. But, peculiarly, the calendar of the 1552 Prayer Book, unlike that of 1549, *does* include St George's Day." *Broken Idols*, 414n199.
[123] *Memory's Library: Medieval Books in Early Modern England* (Chicago: University of Chicago Press, 2008), 108–9.
[124] *Memory's Library*, 156.

their limited re-collection in new locations highlights an overlooked aspect of iconoclasm that is especially apt for understanding the unexpected saints of the Elizabethan liturgical calendar: curation. Iconoclasm is frequently imagined as destruction—the breaking, the cracking, the fragmentation—whereas, as Summit shows, the Reformation undertook a great re-curation. The late medieval calendar organized all available items, taking up every single day of the calendar. In contrast, the curation of sainthood after the Reformation reflects a more modern exhibition of materials, determined as much by considered exclusion as by archeological survival. The Reformation, then, is not the era when the saints were destroyed but when the saints were carefully shelved.

In its early years, the Elizabethan church attempted to preserve existing monuments and to roll back some efforts of the Edwardian church. One site of that preservation was material culture. The shrines of many native saints had been destroyed during the dissolution, their remains scattered, confiscated, or hidden. Some abbeys and monasteries also had been destroyed, and their stones repurposed.[125] Seeking to bring such practices to an end, Elizabeth released a proclamation in 1560 "against defacers of monuments in churches." It denounced the "barbarous disorder" of individually empowered iconoclasm and called for necessary repairs and restoration.[126] It also addressed breaking or defacing "any image in glass windows in any church" or "any parcel of any monument, or tomb, or grave," especially those set up by "kings, princes, or noble estates of this realm," which explains the intact saints of Westminster Abbey and St. Winifred's Well in Wales.[127] But another site of preservation is the liturgical calendar. The Elizabethan 1559 *BCP* retains much of the minimalism of Edwardian prayer books, but it also includes instruction to fast before a few major feast days, such as Candlemas, and it reinserts a number of additional saints as black-letter days.[128] If the Elizabethan church was a compromise between Geneva and Rome, then the calendar represents a compromise between the Edwardian church and the pre-Henrician Sarum liturgy. Unlike the *Kalendre of the New Legende of England*, the liturgical calendar

---

[125] See Ethan Shagan, *Popular Politics and the English Reformation* (Cambridge: Cambridge University Press, 2003), especially Chapter 5, "Selling the sacred: Reformation and dissolution at the Abbey of Hailes," 162–96 and Chapter 7, "Resistance and Collaboration in the dissolution of the Chantries," 235–69.

[126] Edward Caldwell, ed., *Documentary annals of the reformed Church of England, 1546–1716*, 2 vols. (Oxford: Oxford University Press, 1844) 1: 289, 290.

[127] Caldwell, 1: 290. Notably, white washing superstitious images is absent from the list of prohibited iconoclasm. In the same year of William Shakespeare's birth, 1564, his father, John, was responsible for overseeing the whitewashing of certain images in the parish church. For more on these parish paintings, see Kate Giles, "Marking Time? A fifteenth-century liturgical calendar in the wall paintings of Pickering parish church, North Yorkshire," *Church Archaeology* 4 (2000): 42–51 and "Seeing and Believing: Visuality and Space in Pre-Modern England," *World Archaeology* 39, no. 4 (2007): 105–21.

[128] In the age of manuscript and in the early days of print, the rubrics (red letters) of the liturgical calendar highlighted the importance of major feast days. As the book was printed entirely in black ink, the *Book of Common Prayer* renders what was previously in red as italic typeface and the black-letter days as normal typeface.

in the *BCP* did not provide brief *vitae* or map out saints on the landscape of England, but it did curate an inventory of sacred time that included biblical, ancient, and native saints. There, it offered a place for an unspecified version of St. Dunstan and other saints that, nonetheless, rejected the anti-*vitae* iconoclasm of the polemicists.

The calendar of the Elizabethan *BCP* is a study in how the past reinserted itself into the present time. Those saints that did not derive their authority from the ancient martyrology of the Christian church are saints with extraordinary importance to the history of the English church: David, Chad, Bridget, Edward the Martyr, Richard of Chichester, Alphege, Dunstan, Augustine (Austin) of Canterbury, Translation of Edward the Martyr, Swithin, Translation of Edward the Confessor, Ethedreda (Audrey) of Ely, and Edmund the Martyr. Alec Ryrie notes that the theme of the Elizabethan addition of saints is "the link between English national and medieval sanctity."[129] With few exceptions, this is the calendar that remained through the seventeenth century.[130] What is notable about this set of saints is that they anticipate the late Elizabethan English Catholic interest in pre-conquest saints. As J. T. Rhodes observes, "The English reformers' obliteration of the English saints was lamented by English Catholics; rehabilitation of their national saints was important to them."[131] Yet, before English Catholics commenced their program of rehabilitation and were encouraged "to venerate their own national saints," the Elizabethan church created a coterie monument to English sanctity within the calendar in the *BCP*.[132] In contrast to both Foxe's *Book of Martyrs* and later Catholic martyrologies, such as John Wilson's *English Martyrologe* (1608), the *BCP* calendar excludes sixteenth-century martyrs. The saints of the 1559 calendar trace the history of the English church from its apostolic (SS John and Mary Magdalene) and ancient martyrological (SS Stephen and Katherine) origins through its pre-conquest forebearers (SS Swithin and Etheldreda) and, finally, to a lone high medieval administrator (St. Richard of Chichester). The saints also reflect the antiquarian impulse that Summit excavates in her work on libraries. Specifically, she finds that under Matthew Parker's archbishopric, "the post-Reformation library became a place of memory in content as well as form; those books deemed most worthy of preservation dealt with matters of national and ecclesiastical history, supplying the need for historical precedents to support

---

[129] Alec Ryrie, "The Liturgical Commemoration of the English Reformation, 1534–1625" in *Memory and the English Reformation*, ed. Alexandra Walsham et al. (Cambridge: Cambridge University Press, 2020), 422–38. 425.

[130] The exceptions included are the addition of the queen's birthday and coronation; the addition of Enarchus in 1604; the addition of monarchical nativities and ascension days; and the addition of Bede, Alban, Hugh, and Charles the Martyr in 1662, after the Restoration of the monarchy and the ascension of Charles II.

[131] J. T. Rhodes, "English Books of Martyrs and Saints of the Late Sixteenth and Early Seventeenth Centuries." *Recusant History* 22, no. 1 (1994): 10.

[132] "English Books of Martyrs and Saints of the Late Sixteenth and Early Seventeenth Centuries," 11.

the reformed state."[133] Much like the preserved books, the 1559 liturgical calendar preserves ancient martyrs, including virgin martyrs, and medieval saints who chart a distinctly English national ecclesiastical history. As I show in chapters 2–5, early modern drama produced saints primarily through an emphasis on English sanctity or the tropes of ancient virgin martyrdom, such as those that appear in the lives of SS Agnes, Agatha, Margaret, Cecilia, Katherine, and Lucy.

Foxe's outrage at Elizabethan religious compromise and its own reforms of the Edwardian Reformation can be felt in the opening pages of the second edition of the *Book of Martyrs* (1570). In the first edition of the *Book of Martyrs*, Foxe lauded Elizabeth as a second Constantine. The revised preface removes the opening dedication to the queen and, instead, trades it for a newly penned anti-litany. The betrayal over the return of some saints as the English church pursued the *via media* is palpable. Foxe narrates to his reader that after the era of Alban (the English protomartyr), Mellitus (the first Bishop of London), and Bede (author of the *Historia Ecclesiastica*), "corruption sprang forth here in England ... drowned in superstition and ceremonies" and names a responsible "swarme" of medieval monastic administrators. This list of infamy includes Dunstan, Chad, and Boniface, all of whom the Elizabethan church under the direction of Archbishop Parker, with his measured reverence for historical monuments to antiquity, restored to the liturgical calendar.[134]

Not that it would matter to Foxe, but if one of the Reformation challenges to the general cult of the saints is its damning association with the church of Rome, then the exoneration of a handful of medieval British-identified saints might have stemmed from their grounding on home soil. The reinstated saints represent royal persons, bishop-confessors, and important figures from the history of the English church (refer to appendix 2, 1559 column). Most of these saints—like Etheldreda and Swithin—had become saints through local veneration and translation of the relics to a shrine without the involvement of Rome. Between the eleventh and thirteenth centuries, the processes of sainthood would be transformed by the involvement and, eventually, the control of the papacy.[135] The canonization of Gilbert of Sempringham marked a turning point: between Gilbert's death in 1198 and his canonization by Innocent III in 1202, the papacy directed the process

---

[133] *Memory's Library*, 104.

[134] Foxe 1570, 1:5.

[135] Although Donald S. Prudlo notes "there is no record of Gregory VII canonizing *anyone*," his role in announcing miracles during the Roman Synod of 1078" caused a shift in the processes of sainthood by Gregory and his successors. *Certain Sainthood: Canonization and the Origins of Papal Infallibility in the Medieval Church* (Ithaca, NY: Cornell University Press, 2016), 25N34 (his emphasis); I. S. Robinson, *The Papacy, 1073–1198: Continuity and Innovation* (Cambridge: Cambridge University Press, 1990), 110. Andre Vauchez cites the late twelfth century as the time when "the papacy felt sufficiently sure of its rights to pronounce canonizations." *Sainthood in the Later Middle Ages*, trans. Jean Birrell (Cambridge: Cambridge University Press, 1997), 24.

from investigation to canonization.[136] Of the saints that were returned to the *BCP* under Elizabeth, only two enjoyed official canonization by the papacy: Edward the Confessor (d.1066, canonized 1161) and Richard of Chichester (d.1253, canonized 1262). Edward's case took the form of final validation by the papacy, whereas Richard's path to official sainthood occurred through the new process.[137] Edward and Richard are exceptions, and their Englishness offered a powerful counterweight to any association with Rome. Notably, there are no medieval saints from other nations in the *BCP* calendar.

The liturgical calendar is a curated inventory of sacred time. It presents a table without contents. These contents are located elsewhere: they might be cited in the text or illuminations of a breviary, if the calendar begins there, but they might also circulate in other forms, such as legendaries or poetry, or through performance cultures, such as pageantry or sermons. Because the liturgical calendar in the *BCP* lacks the narration of the *Kalendre*, the saints did not circulate as *lives*. Like the treasures of their former shrines, their lives were now up for grabs. Reformers, historians, pageant makers, and playwrights all appropriated them for their own purposes.

Along with facilitating a broader understanding of medieval saint plays, this examination of the liturgical calendar across the sixteenth century, especially through the Elizabethan period, offers a new framework through which to understand the appearance of saints in the professional drama between the 1590s and the 1630s. Not only were all saints not incompatible with the time of English Protestantism, but also not all revisions of saints' lives were a consequence of reformed iconoclasm. Certain saints were anathema to English Protestantism, such as Thomas Becket or papal saints, but other ancient and English saints had a role to play in post-Reformation culture. Nearly half a century after antiquarians took up the task of removing saints from the church to the archive, professional dramatists dusted them off and, starting with St. Dunstan, a subject of chapter 2, removed them once again to the public stage.

---

[136] Vauchez, *Sainthood in the Later Middle Ages*, 38. See also Michelle Light, "Evidence of Sanctity: Record-keeping and the Canonization at the Turn of the 13th Century," *Archivaria* 60 (2006): 105–23.

[137] For the full details of Richard's canonization, see David Jones, "The Cult of St. Richard of Chichester in the Middle Ages," *Sussex Archaeological Collections* 121 (1983): 79–86.

2
Devils in the Details

St. Dunstan begins the play alone. He enters the stage with appropriate accoutrements, that is, "*with his Beads, Book, and Crosier staff, &c.*" and then launches into a monologue that recounts his history as the tenth-century Archbishop of Canterbury.[1] The Prologue reintroduces Dunstan to audiences and uses the saint to conjure a particular era of the English past. The time of St. Dunstan is one in which the saint serves as "Chief Primate of the Holy *English* Church," expands monasticism, and develops a reputation as a miracle-worker and demon repeller according to "the golden Legend, / (That sacred Register of holy Saints)."[2] This play, known as *The Devil and his Dame* (c.1600) in Henslowe's diary and attributed to William Haughton, is the second of two extant Elizabethan plays that feature St. Dunstan. In the earlier Elizabethan St. Dunstan play, the anonymous *A Knack to Know a Knave* (1592), the stage directions do not call for that "*&c.*" of churchy trinkets, but that play also depicts Dunstan as a pious churchman and associates him with the supernatural through spectacular theatricality. The presence of St. Dunstan and this description of theatricality is at odds with the play's auspices and time period: the London professional stage at the turn of the seventeenth century. We would expect these plays to have been produced c.1500, the era of the Digby plays, not c.1600, the era of *Hamlet*. St. Dunstan might seem to be a figure of medieval Catholicism par excellence, but as I demonstrated in the previous chapter, he was not entirely incompatible with Elizabethan Protestantism, at least according to the *Book of Common Prayer*. The saint, along with a number of other Reformation-era exiles, had occupied a place in the English liturgical calendar since 1559.

Having addressed the history of the medieval saint play and saints in liturgical calendars in chapter 1, I now turn to saints in early modern drama. While Dunstan was reestablished as a saint in English culture through his inclusion in the calendar of the *BCP*, his lives ceased to circulate except in the infamy of reformed

---

[1] This first quote is taken directly from the 1662 duodecimo containing Haughton's *Grim the Collier of Croyden; Or, The Devil and his Dame: with The Devil and Saint Dunston*. The majority of quotes are taken from the edition prepared by William M. Baillie, which are also identifiable by act, scene, and line numbers. Occasionally, I quote directly from the duodecimo to preserve the original, albeit Restoration, archiving of playhouse repertoire. Here, I preserve the ampersand rather than the fully rendered et cetera to also preserve what might be theatrical shorthand. I.T. [William Haughton], "Grim the Collier of Croyden; Or, The Devil and his Dame: with The Devil and Saint Durston," in *Gratiae Theatrales, or, A Choice Ternary of English Plays* (London: Printed by R.D., 1662), G2r.
[2] William M. Baillie, *A Choice Ternary of English Plays: Gratiae Theatrales (1662)* (Binghamton, N.Y.: Medieval & Renaissance Texts & Studies, 1984), 1.1.7, 25–6.

anti-hagiography. On stage, Dunstan was not restored to his traditional glory, but neither was he depicted as a figure of religious corruption. *A Knack to Know a Knave* and *The Devil and His Dame* retain traditional elements of Dunstan's legend as they also formulate a new type of saint for the Elizabethan age. The new St. Dunstan has as much to do with the theatricality of Elizabethan magician characters as he does medieval hagiography. The St. Dunstan plays do not reproduce the traditional *vita* of the saint in dramatic form—but neither did most medieval saint plays. As such, the St. Dunstan plays' remixing of aspects of *vita* into new stories might be considered the end of Tudor experiments with saints and drama. *A Knack to Know a Knave* and *The Devil and His Dame* witness to a sustained interest in English saints and a continuation of the medieval theatrical depiction of saints with the supernatural. Although much overlooked by scholarship, these plays mark an important development in English drama and challenge the accepted history of an early modern theatre devoid of saints.

St. Dunstan lived many lives in the Elizabethan and Jacobean eras. At various turns, he emerged as a great Archbishop of Canterbury, the prime mover in the destruction of the English church, the administrative authority against monarchical lust, patron of smiths, and a conjuring monk who attracted supernatural activity. In this last role, he could either control or be upstaged by diabolical presences. As I addressed in chapter 1, Reformation polemic preserves St. Dunstan's reputation for miracle working albeit in the form of anti-*vita*. Helen L. Parish notes that the reformed "rejection of the miraculous powers of the medieval saints was certainly not a complete denial of the influence of the supernatural in the material world. What mattered was the source of that power. . . ."[3] In particular, "[t]he miracles of St. Dunstan were recast as diabolic wonders, worked in support of false doctrine and commemorated and celebrated by the congregation of Antichrist."[4] The morality play *A Knack to Know a Knave* and the city-country comedy *The Devil and His Dame* demonstrate how the theatre took up the variety of forms, associations, and aspects of saint plays and reinterpreted St. Dunstan through the developing repertory of Elizabethan drama. On stage, St. Dunstan is interpolated through traditional hagiography, Reformation theology and polemics, national history, and sixteenth-century stage magic. Both plays transform St. Dunstan from Christian saint into an Elizabethan stage saint. Christian sanctity centers on the imitation of Christ, as well as other saints, through a sequential series of acts that include conversion, evangelization, miracles, persecution, and martyrdom or monastic life. In the context of traditional hagiography, the episode of St. Dunstan overcoming the devil at his forge at Glastonbury mirrors Christ overcoming the temptations of Satan in the desert, as well as the many accounts of ancient saints defying or defeating devils, such as when St. Margaret of Antioch

---

[3] Parish, *Monks, Miracles and Magic*, 115.
[4] Parish, *Monks, Miracles and Magic*, 115.

causes the devil to disappear with the efficacious sign of the cross. An identifiable St. Dunstan materializes in both Elizabethan plays and he also retains his longstanding reputation as a chastity activist and marvel worker. Yet, the stage Dunstan no longer coheres around traditional religious sanctity.

The smoke and mirrors of the supernatural in these plays might seem religious or Catholic when, in actuality, the theatrics are a staple of the Elizabethan stage. As I show in the first half of this chapter, the stage life of St. Dunstan fragments and redistributes the saint so that he transforms into a holy conjuror in *A Knack to Know a Knave* and a barometer of demonic activity in *The Devil and His Dame*. In the second half of this chapter, I consider the theatricality of these plays in light of a longer history of English saint plays, both before and after the Reformation. What the St. Dunstan plays preserve in professional drama are two aspects of saints and performance that developed in the later Middle Ages: a practice of conflating, collapsing, and improvising on hagiographic narratives in performance and an association between sanctity and spectacular theatricality. I also address the depiction of saints and sanctity in the works of Shakespeare during the Elizabethan era and the return of patron saints to pageantry as the Elizabethan era transitioned to the Jacobean era. Shakespeare, like other playwrights, follows the trends in saints and drama. In such plays as *1* and *2 Henry VI*, Shakespeare ridicules the pretend performance of sanctity in his depiction of Joan of Arc and a blind man near St. Albans, respectively. There, he associates saints with devils and trickery. In contrast, the pageants featuring patron saints, such as SS Dunstan and Swithin, revitalize aspects of the saints' traditional legends.

Patron Conjuror

The apparent archaism of *A Knack to Know a Knave* masks the Elizabethan transformation of St. Dunstan from patron saint to patron conjuror. The play's dramaturgy cleaves to the conventions of moral drama, the medieval-identified genre that also flourished in English drama between 1558 and 1590.[5] The logics of moral drama drive the antagonism of virtues and vices in professional drama in such plays as *A Looking Glass for London and England* (c.1588) and, most famously, *The Tragical History of Doctor Faustus* (c.1589). In *A Knack to Know a Knave*, two morality plots intertwine. In the first plot, King Edgar appoints Honesty, a commoner, to root out the sin of greed that has overtaken England. Here, vice is personified by a bailiff and his four sons: a courtier, a priest, a cony-catcher, and a farmer, all of whom exploit their professions for material gain. King Edgar remains at court to hear pleas, along with his wise counselor, Dunstan. The king charges his courtier, Ethanwold, to arrange a marriage between himself and Alfrida. As

---

[5] Alan Dessen, *Johnson's Moral Comedy* (Evanston, Il: Northwestern University Press, 1971), 10.

it occurs in the pages of hagiography and history, the second plot unfolds as Ethanwold rejects his sovereign's command and marries Alfrida himself. In a conflation of two different legends of Edgar's lust, Ethanwold attempts to conceal his deceit by disguising Alfrida as a maidservant. When the deceit is discovered, the king vows "to be reuenged" on his courtier (F3v).[6] As the king shifts into the role of an additional vice character, Dunstan transforms into a second personification of virtue to oppose the king's lust. He also intervenes through supernatural means to prevent an adulterous murder. In the final scene of the play, the king forgives Ethanwold and Honesty delivers judicial sentences to the four vices for their sins against God and the Commonwealth.

Two episodes involving the devil in the play thematically distinguish the two moral plots from one another. Echoing *Doctor Faustus*, and earlier drama such as the N-Town *Assumption*, the first plot with Honesty features a devil who comes to claim the soul of the damned. In contrast, St. Dunstan transforms from a personification of good counsel to a priestly conjuror. The first devil that appears on stage does so in the Honesty plot and appears at the death of the Bailiff of Hexam. Notably, this entrance of the devil does not occur through conjuring and Dunstan is absent from this scene. As the bailiff lies on his deathbed, he and his sons perform the vice version of the *Ars moriendi*. Instead of repentance, a necessary turning point for salvation both before and after the Reformation, the bailiff advises his sons "to worke deceit" to "inrich thy selfe" and "care not what they say, / That bid you feare the fearfull Judgment day"(B2r). The bailiff's defiance concludes abruptly when he sees "pall Death," and is "damned to euer burning fyre" (B2r). Immediately after "He dyeth," the stage directions, which recall King Herod's final exit in some biblical plays, call for a demonic theatrical device to visibly mark the bailiff's exit from Earth and eternal entrance to hell: "Enter Deuil, and carie him away" (B3r). The bailiff's unrepentant death also lacks intervention by his priest son who does not read from his "book of exhortation" because he failed to bring it to his father's deathbed (B3r).[7] The priest, despite the pre-Reformation setting of the play, is not a derelict son of the old religion, but a hypocrite of the new faith of "Precisians" or Puritans (B2v).[8] But he certainly behaves like the derelict sons of the old religion, such as Chaucer's Pardoner. The religious talents of the priest in *A Knack to Know a Knave* lie with his skill at exploiting his particular realm of authority for financial gain, like his vice character brothers, rather than opposing

---

[6] *A Knack to Know a Knave* (London: Richard Iones, 1592). All subsequent in text parenthetical citations are from this edition.

[7] Although we might identify it as a medieval device, as John D. Cox writes, the device had been brought to London by Reformation dramatists who included "numerous instances of the devil carrying the Vice on his back in Protestant plays but also by the devil carrying the despairing and the wicked to hell in the graphic arts and in plays from before the Reformation, including Latin liturgical drama." *The Devil and the Sacred in English Drama, 1350–1642* (Cambridge: Cambridge University Press, 2001), 129. I address this in chapter 3.

[8] For more on the references to puritans, see Mary Grace Adkins Muse, "The Genesis of Dramatic Satire against the Puritan, as Illustrated in *A Knack to Know a Knave*." *RES* 22, no.86 (1946): 81–95.

the devil through the reading or, should he forget his book, the recitation of holy text.

The bailiff's death scene establishes the roles of the greedy brother vices and throws into relief the complex negotiation of traditional sanctity and Faustian incantation that occurs in the second scene with a devil. Without the first scene of the devil it would be difficult, if not impossible, to discern St. Dunstan's intervention as an act of holiness rather than damnable necromancy. In the penultimate sequence of the play, King Edgar intends to execute Ethanwold as retribution for marrying Alfrida. He also plans to wed her once she is widowed. As Edgar develops into a personification of wrath and lust, Dunstan shifts again, and performs as a virtue from the morality tradition. He exhorts his king to rethink his murder plan, lest he be "tearmed a foule Adulterer" (F3v). Edgar however, remains "resolued" to seek Ethanwold's death and rebukes his good counsel. Dunstan, therefore, switches tactics—as well as dramatic conventions—from "intreaties" to "Arte" (F3v). The art that Dunstan practices begins with a recitation of specific words in a specific order. That is, the sort of Latin phrase that transforms wine into blood, a sacramental office which Dunstan elsewhere enacts as a priest, or that translates the devil from hell to earth, a conjuration, which here, he performs as a stage saint.[9] With the utterance "Asmoroth, ascende, veni Asmoroth, Asmoroth veni," the play shifts its dramatic mode from *Mankind* to Marlowe as the words effect a supernatural stage direction: "Enter the Deuill" (F4r).

Within the play's structure, Dunstan's sequence with the devil repeats and revises two previous scenes associated with vice: the death of the Bailiff of Hexam and the deceitful dissembling of the kitchen maid as Alfrida. In contrast to the first appearance of a devil, in which the dying man and his sons were powerless against hell's claim, this devil is under Dunstan's control via his saintly efficacy. When Asmoroth refuses to reveal King Edgar's true intentions, the saint calls upon "heauen" and "the eternall liuing God / That keeps the Prince of darkness bound in chaines," to bend him to his will, and immediately the devil tells him that "the king doth mean to murther Ethanwold" (F4v). The devil's admission implies that as an inhabitant of the realm from which all vice emerges he has hellish foreknowledge of sins. Unlike the previous stage devil in *A Knack to Know a Knave*, this one does not haul a soul back to hell, but instead is made to stay on earth to prevent King Edgar's sins of lust and wrath. With the devil under his saintly control, Dunstan commands him to remain invisible until he conjures him again, commanding, "Veni Asmoroth," and making him appear in the guise of Ethanwold (G1v). This conjuration figures as a marvelously successful iteration of Ethanwold's own failed disguising of Alfrida as a maid. The king, under the influence of Dunstan's saintly

---

[9] For more on the performatives of conjuration and eucharistic consecration, see Jay Zysk, "Father Faustus? Confection and Conjuration in *Everyman* and *Doctor Faustus*," in *Shadow and Substance: Eucharistic Controversy and English Drama across the Reformation Divide* (Notre Dame, IN: University of Notre Dame Press, 2017), 119-54.

spell, experiences a sudden, inexplicable change of heart and agrees to a pardon. Only then does Dunstan release the devil, intoning, "Asmoroth away," upon which command Ethanwold returns unharmed (G1v). In contrast to the brother vices, the king ultimately turns away from vice, and ceases to exploit his office for personal gain. England is thus saved by the king's transformation from the vices of lust and murder to the virtues of "Honour" and "chastitie" (G2v).

Nevertheless the matter of Dunstan's "Arte" remains a troubling one. The king does not avoid mortal sin by overcoming temptation. Rather, Dunstan's conjuring prevents him from committing murder. This play derives its theatrical knowledge of conjuring from two other plays, *Friar Bacon and Friar Bungay* (c.1589) by Robert Green and *Doctor Faustus* (c.1592) by Christopher Marlowe. In these plays of scholar-magicians and devils, the art and consequences of conjuring form a consistent set of logics. In *Doctor Faustus*, Mephistopheles shape-shifts from an "ugly" shape to "an old Franciscan friar," the scholar calls him forth with the particular and memorable Latin phrase "Veni, veni, Mephistophile!," and the pair fly overnight from Germany to Rome, where they disrupt the Pope's banquet under the cloak of invisibility.[10] A similar set of marvels occur in *Friar Bacon and Friar Bungay*, a play that Lawrence Manley and Sally-Beth MacLean recognize as a likely influence upon *Knack* in its depiction of "erotic rivalry" and "magical intervention."[11] Like Faustus, Bacon's art is drawn from his study of "Magicke bookes" that "straine out Nigromancie" so that matter and knowledge can be translocated through time and space.[12] With a "motion" and "trance" Bacon enlists a devil to transport a woman from her kitchen to his study, sees events in other locations through a "glasse prospectiue," and, at one point, sends a muting spell through the magic glass to interrupt a wedding (B3r, B3v, H2r). Though these marvels often serve a comic function, *Doctor Faustus* and *Friar Bacon and Friar Bungay* explore a particular crux of conjuring that Andrew Sofer identifies as "the tension between conjuring as hocus-pocus and conjuring as black magic."[13] But conjuring, as the consequences bear out, is always black magic and requires abjuration. Famously, Faustus fails to repent and earns a demonic dismemberment in hell. But would his renunciation of the glamor of evil really have helped him avoid damnation? Yes, according to the expanded theatrical demonology of *Friar Bacon and Friar Bungay*. While Bacon eventually breaks his magic "christall," and finds redemption in "pure deuotion praying to my God," his servant continues to cavort with Bacon's demon and is "carried to hell on the Deuils backe" (H2r, H2v, Ir).

---

[10] Christopher Marlowe, *Doctor Faustus: A Two-Text Edition*, ed. David Scott Kastan (New York: W. W. Norton, 2004), 1.3.24, 1.3.25, 2.1.29.

[11] Lawrence Manley and Sally-Beth MacLean, *Lord Strange's Men and Their Plays* (New Haven, CT: Yale University Press, 2014), 100.

[12] Robert Greene, *The honorable historie of frier Bacon, and frier Bongay* (London, 1594), (B2r). All subsequent in text parenthetical citations come from this edition.

[13] Andrew Sofer, *Dark Matter: Invisibility in Drama, Theater, and Performance* (Ann Arbor, MI: University of Michigan Press, 2013), 25.

By way of contrast, in *Knack*, Dunstan does not repent of his "Arte," but neither does hell claim him.

The saint's particular use of Asmoroth in *A Knack to Know a Knave* stands apart from the art practiced by the scholar-magicians of the Elizabethan era. On the one hand, Dunstan performs like Faustus and Bacon in the translocation of the devil, the use of hell's creature as a mirror into Edgar's soul, and the performance of invisibility, shape-shifting, and sudden forgiveness. But, on the other hand, Dunstan retains a constant and exceptional control over the devil. As Manley and MacLean observe, Dunstan, Bacon, and Faustus are "primarily theatrical magicians," but the saint alone uses "theatrical illusion in the spiritual struggle of good against evil."[14] The use of magic at the end of *A Knack to Know a Knave* does not trigger Dunstan's damnation whereas, in the case of the titular character of *Doctor Faustus*, as Arthur F. Kinney explains, the play "charts the distance between his magical powers and his moral loss."[15] The moral cause is the thing that allows Dunstan to transform the "Arte" of conjuring from one of clear categorical vice to one of exemplary virtue. Scenes of conjuration in Elizabethan drama begin with explicit mention of "magic," and "necromancy," along with the devilish books that instruct how to enact them. Dunstan's interactions with Asmoroth are absent of the terms and properties of witchcraft. Blasphemy authorizes conjuration in *Friar Bacon and Friar Bungay* and calls up a demon to negotiate the contractual terms of leasing the devil's magic in *Doctor Faustus*. In contrast, Dunstan exhorts Edgar to inhabit forgiveness and chastity, virtues that belong to "heauen" and "the eternall liuing God" (*Knave*, F4r). Dunstan's intervention thus requires no repentance. Although the stage devil performs according to the supernatural logics of Elizabethan stage magic, the saint's control over the devil stems from the traditional aspects of his legendary fight with the devil at the forge. Having overcome the devil in the legend, Dunstan now intercedes as the king's patron saint and forces the devil to release his hold on Edgar's soul. If reformed accounts of the Dunstan legend de-sanctified the medieval abbot and archbishop because of his reputation as a marvel worker, then *A Knack to Know a Knave* re-sanctifies him through the dramatic conventions of Elizabethan demonology.

Magic and the Decline of Religion

Dunstan and demonic activity maintain a less straightforward relationship in *Grim, the Collier of Croydon, Or, The Devil and his Dame, with The Devil and Saint Dunston* by William Haughton. The play, which is recorded as "The Devil

---

[14] Manley and MacLean, *Lord Strange's Men*, 199
[15] Christopher Marlowe, "The Tragical History of Dr. Faustus," in *Renaissance Drama: An Anthology of Plays and Entertainments*, ed. Arthur F. Kinney, 2nd ed. (Malden, MA: Wiley-Blackwell, 2005), 195.

and His Dame," in Philip Henslowe's diary, is more aptly titled in its eventual publication. The three parts of the title identify the play's two interspersed plots and frame.[16] The play begins with a frame of St. Dunstan and a parliament of devils. There, Dunstan presents his traditional *vita* through a prologue speech, devils crowd the stage while he sleeps, and the archdevil dispatches Belphegor to earth with his servant, Akercock, to report back to hell on the true nature of women.[17] In London, Belphegor disguises himself as a Spanish doctor, Castiliano, and Akercock morphs into the English country devil, Robin Goodfellow. In the first plot, Castiliano interrupts a love triangle between Honorea, Musgrave, and Lacy, the suitor that Honorea's father prefers. St. Dunstan appears in the Castiliano plot, but the devil plays a far greater role. Deceit, disguising, shape-shifting, and a bed trick all occur so that Honorea is forced into a chaste marriage with Lacy and her adulterous maid weds Castiliano. In the subplot, Robin Goodfellow intervenes on behalf of Grim the Collier in a competition for Joan, a country maid. Cloaked in invisibility, Robin beats Grim's rival, Clack the Miller, and forces the lecherous Parson Short-hose to perform the marriage ceremony for Grim and Joan. At the end of the play, Castiliano, who has been deceived by his wife, returns to hell with horns on his head and reports that while his dame was unfaithful, some women are virtuous.

The medieval setting of *The Devil and His Dame* overlaps with that of *A Knack to Know a Knave*. Both plays are anchored to the world of medieval England by St. Dunstan, but the former play departs significantly from the latter in the depiction of the religious past. *A Knack to Know a Knave* casts Dunstan in the role of a virtue character who counsels the king as a religious authority. In contrast, *The Devil and His Dame* uses Dunstan to characterize the religion of the past "as superstitious, fool-hardy and credulous," the sort of polemic that Deanne Williams identifies as part of the Reformation invention of the medieval past.[18] The saint is not a learned bishop and administrator, but a Glastonbury monk with trinkets. Nonetheless, the play's comic medievalism does not also posit any future religious "evolution from medieval to modern, from Catholic to Protestant."[19] What *The Devil and His Dame* does offer is a chaotic demonology. As Stuart Clark has shown, demonology is a theory of "disorder by inversion."[20] That is, devils do things that are the inverted actions of Christian religion and follow the same logics. If Christians invoke the divine through utterance and sign, then so do demons and witches. If Christians have specified places, postures, vestments, and orders of ceremonies,

---

[16] Philip Henslowe, *Henslowe's Diary*, Vol. 1, ed. W. W. Greg (London: A. H. Bullen, 1904), 1: 121.

[17] For more on the Belphagor plot and Machiavelli's novel of the same name, as well as other source material, see Baillie's introduction to the play in *Gratiae Theatrales*, 173–200.

[18] Deanne Williams, "*Friar Bacon and Friar Bungay* and the Rhetoric of Temporality," in *Reading the Medieval in Early Modern England*, eds. Gordon McMullan and David Matthews (Cambridge: Cambridge University Press, 2007), 31–48.

[19] Williams, "*Friar Bacon and Friar Bungay*," 32.

[20] Stuart Clark, *Thinking with Demons: The Idea of Witchcraft in Early Modern Europe* (Oxford: Clarendon Press, 1997), 72.

then so do conjurors. Clark's assertion that "demonology in all its manifestations was not merely saturated with religious values; it was inconceivable without them," is located in the imagination of witches' Sabbaths and devils' parliaments.[21] There, these creatures behave according to the manner and logics of priests and cardinals. Early modern demonology imagines an organizational chart for hell. The devils in this play operate accordingly, but the fiends also disrupt the typical unidirectional opposition to and inversion of Christian values through their comical advocacy for chastity and fidelity.

In *The Devil and His Dame*, the devils upstage the saint and transform the oppositional cosmology between heaven and hell so that the devil's marvels eventually effect virtue. There is a medieval precedent for devils effecting good despite their evil intent. The devils of medieval plays are on the side of Caiphas, Annas, and the other unrepentant Jews who persecute Christ. Yet, at the same time, the crucifixion begets the harrowing of hell, the resurrection, the ascension, and universal salvation. This eventual Christian victory is the reason that the devil in the Digby *Mary Magdalene* stomps and screams. If *A Knack to Know a Knave* produces the paradox of a virtuous conjuring through the saint's summoning of the devil's magic to oppose vice, then *The Devil and His Dame* achieves the seemingly impossible with a devil who transforms into something akin to a saint.

The initial shift in the relationship between sanctity and demonic activity occurs over the course of the brief, action-packed frame. Dunstan begins as chorus and quickly transforms into a holy madman. Armed *"with his Beads, Book, and/ Crosier-staff, etc,"* the saint identifies himself as the "Abbot of *Glassenbury*" and the "Chief Primate of the Holy English Church" who "flourish'd in the reign of Seven great Kings" (SD 1.1.1, 1.1.31, 1.1.7, 1.1.11). Dunstan goes on to appeal to the authorities of traditional religion, arguing against those who "accuse me for a Conjurer, / By reason of those many miracles / Which Heaven for holy life endowed me with. / But who so looks into the golden Legend, / (That sacred Register of holy Saints) / Shall find me by the Pope-canoniz'd" (1.1.22–7). While other Elizabethan magician plays improvise on traditional religion's semiotics and logics, such as Faustus's inclusion of "Th'abbreviated names of holy saints" within his diabolical circle of spirit summoning, Dunstan's citation of the *Golden Legend* in concert with a fictional papal canonization is unprecedented (1.3.10). His monologue materializes an aggregate late medieval version of his *vita*. Dunstan then warns, "watch you, for Dunston dreams" and "*layeth him down to sleep*" (1.1.41, SD 1.1.42). His dream explodes across the stage in the form of *"the Devils Consistory*," complete with "Lightning and / Thunder" and the devils "Pluto, Minos, Æacus, Rhadamantus *set in Counsell, before them* Malbecco *his Ghost guarded with Furies*" (SD 1.1.1, 1.1.40). After the demonic counsel ends, devils swarm the stage again. The frame concludes with the saint enacting a nightmare from his legend

---

[21] Clark, *Thinking with Demons*, 437.

with comic – and demonic – alteration: "*It thunders and lightens; the Devils go forth* Dunston *rising, runneth about the Stage, laying about him with his Staff*" (SD 1.1.149). The saint twice demands "Sathan avaunt," the sort of un-conjuring words that ought to exorcize demons, but it has no effect against Belphegor who "to choose a Wife, is come from hell" (1.1.150, 1.1.153, 1.1.161). The frame thus sets up a world of supernatural activities, but one in which this saint cannot, as *A Knack to Know a Knave*'s saint did, contain and control the devil.

Dunstan's inability to control the devil in the frame is symptomatic of the inverted demonology of the play, which is reiterated when Castiliano upstages Dunstan's prayers with demonic magic. If the frame begins to pivot the relationship between the saint and the devil, then a central scene of their rival marvel-working completes this reorientation. The Earl of London, who hopes to arrange a marriage for his mute daughter, Honorea, sends for "holy *Dunston*" to restore her speech through intercessory prayers (1.2.27). The cure is the anticipated outcome since "Angels... tell to him the secrets of the Heavens" (1.2.36–7). Moreover, Dunstan attempts to restage the conditions of his famous miracle by hanging "*his Harp on the wall*" (SD 1.4.14). In the context of hagiography, the sudden playing of the suspended instrument indicates that Dunstan's prayers ought to effect a congruent production of sound from the mute Honorea. The saint calls upon "fasting prayer and religious works," a "solemn mass," "three sips of the holy Challice," and turning his "Beads with Aves and with Creeds" (1.4.44–7). The potential for subversion with staging these Catholic and superstitious practices evaporates when Castiliano appropriates Dunstan's own iconic companion. Through diabolical charms "Dunston's *Harp sounds on the wall*" and the saint is unable to "unbind the bonds" of Castiliano's magic to free his harp (1.4.53, 1.4.67). The devil, who is disguised as a Spanish doctor, then cures Honorea through a show of medicinal craft that involves straining "*the juyce of the Herb*" into a bowl of wine (1.4.92). Sensing the "secret mystery" of these spells, Dunstan lashes out at Castiliano and accuses him of sorcery. Thus, Dunstan continues in his role as holy madman, but, stripped of his marvelous efficacy, he becomes the fool.

What these two scenes together accomplish is the transformation of St. Dunstan into the tool and fool of the devil, but in such a way that deconstructs the expected demonology. As Bronwyn Johnston writes, the traditional "relationship between human and devil is... defined in terms of control, a question of whether the devil is an instrument of the human's magic or the human an instrument of the devil's malice."[22] The play retains the question of control, but it departs from this particular binary. Dunstan is rendered ineffective as a saint in order to demonstrate Castiliano's supernatural superiority. Whereas the theatricality of the devil usually offers a material measurement of supernatural activities, such as the

---

[22] Bronwyn Johnston, "Who the Devils is in Charge? Mastery and the Faustian Pact on the Early Modern Stage," in *Magical Transformations on the Early Modern English Stage*, eds. Lisa Hopkins and Helen Ostovich (Farnham, UK: Ashgate, 2014), 31.

state of a soul or the power of a magician, the saint's sudden apotropaic impotence in this scene affirms the power of the devil's magic. The play also reframes the matter of control through the depiction of the devil's magic as a force of virtue against malice. This inversion is not the accidental consequence of the devil doing evil that eventually effects good, as in the case of the crucifixion. Castiliano's charms cure the afflicted and enforce chastity because the saint is ineffective. In other words, the devil defeats Dunstan in order to replace him. Like the Dunstan of *A Knack to Know a Knave*, Castiliano is a creature of virtuous conjuring.

For the rest of the play, the devil and St. Dunstan work separately to ensure a chaste marriage between Honorea and Lacy, her father's preferred suitor. Honorea intends to continue her romance with young Musgrave despite her marriage to the older Earl. The love triangle is resolved not through St. Dunstan's virtuous counsel, but through Castiliano's magic. Disguised "like Musgrave," the Devil reproves her disregard for "the holy bond of marriage" and sends her "home ... to live / As chaste as Lucrece" (3.1.12, 26–7). Castiliano occupies the same role as virtue counselor that Dunstan did in Edgar's court. It works. When the real Musgrave asks the new bride "to renew the tenor of our loves," she steadfastly refuses due to "God's own work" (4.2.42, 47). Lacy interprets Honorea's turn to honesty as a "miracle," although it is the ironic result of the Devil's work (4.2.77). A final comedic scene on earth also turns on the problem of interpreting a seemingly miraculous intervention. Castiliano's wife and her lover frame him for murder by slipping Lacy a sleeping potion. Then, all of the other characters close in on Castiliano at the exact moment of his earthly expiration. Plunging toward his rightful home in the hell of the Rose or the Fortune, "*The Ground opens, and he falls down into it*" a sudden sight, again, that is pronounced as "God's judgement" by Dunstan (SD 5.2.71, 5.2.73). For a third and final time, the devil's magic succeeds in producing spectacular effects when spiritual efforts fail.

The subplot of the play features a provincial love triangle that, like the frame and main plot, also resolves through the magical intervention of a devil. Grim the Collier and Clack the Miller both desire to marry Joan, but Parson Shorthose plays the men against each other in order to have her himself. On Holy Rood Day, Akercock, who has transformed into Robin Goodfellow "in a suite of Leather / close to his body, his Face and Hands / coloured russet-colour, with a Flayle," recounts his own legends of English pastoral trickery (SD 4.1.1). He ends his soliloquy with resolve to defend Grim, "for long time ago / The Devil call'd the Collier like to like" (4.1.30–1). Therefore, when Joan and Grim gather nuts in the woods, a tradition on Holy Rood Day, the invisible Robin "beateth the Miller with a Flayle, and felleth him," and then "beateth the Priest with his Flayle" (SD 4.1.83, 89).[23] This bit of slapstick is repeated once more before Grim's rivals cease

---

[23] Although it is outside of the scope of this particular essay, the festive observation of Holy Rood Day in the subplot along with the comic fighting over Joan reflects the theatre's integration of "holiday traditions into the very semiotics of the medium," which Erika Lin has located in the anonymous 1593

their pursuit of Joan. When Robin later undoes his invisibility and reveals himself, Parson Short-hose responds in a way that parallels Dunstan's superstition in the main plot: he screams "benedicte!" and calls "for some holy-water." (5.1.62, 64). Nevertheless, Robin forces the priest to marry Grim and Joan. As in the main plot, the devil enforces an honest marriage and upsets the efforts of a churchman with magic.

The play concludes by returning to the frame with Dunstan as chorus. He narrates the transition from England to "the infernal Synod" with appropriate thunder and lightning at the devils' entrance and final exit (5.2.124). Castiliano/Belphegor returns "*like a Devil, with Horns on his head*," a new costume accessory (SD 5.3.2). Pluto decrees that all of hell's demons will wear horns in order to mitigate Belphegor's shame, "And in hell wee will make it Holy-day" (5.3.82). The archdevil's order mirrors the creation and evolution of commemorative traditions that occur in the imagined medieval world, especially in the subplot of Holy Rood Day. In this sense, *The Devil and His Dame* is a comic creation myth about the iconography of the Devil.[24] The holiday making is a final act of inversion. The devils mirror the celebration of the feast of the Holy Cross on earth through their own festal observance of the day they first wore horns. Notably, there is no mention of Dunstan's own "Holy-day," but that is because *The Devil and His Dame* has transformed from a play about St. Dunstan and the devils to a play about the devils and St. Dunstan.

St. Dunstan and the Archive of Saint Plays

A Knack to Know a Knave and *The Devil and His Dame* occupy a Janus-faced role in the history of saints and drama. In terms of their theatricality, the Elizabethan St. Dunstan plays mark the end of Tudor experiments with saints in performance and also stand as the immediate precursors to Jacobean and Caroline saint plays. Saints returned to the *BCP* in the early Elizabethan era, but the first record of a saint appearing in the professional commercial theatre did not occur until *A Knack to Know a Knave* premiered in 1592. The extant St. Dunstan plays document how early English performance practices involving saints transferred to professional dramatic form in two primary ways: marvelous theatricality involving devils and the production of alternative hagiographical narratives.

These two plays sustain the supernatural association between the devil and St. Dunstan through marvelous theatricality even as the oppositional dynamics

---

play, *George a Greene, the Pinner of Wakefield*. "Popular Festivity and the Early Modern Stage: The Case of *George a Greene*," *Theatre Journal* 61, no. 2 (2009): 295.

[24] For more on the mechanisms of holiday making in early modern drama, see Alison A. Chapman, "Whose Saint Crispin's Day Is It?: Shoemaking, Holiday Making, and the Politics of Memory in Early Modern England," *Renaissance Quarterly* 54, no. 4 (2001): 1467–94.

of saint and devil are deconstructed and reconfigured. In the Digby *Conversion of Saint Paul* (c.1500), a play that develops the sort of devil play that Elizabethan theatre riffs on, the opposition is clear.[25] The play begins with Saulus, as the apostle is known before his conversion, as a Jewish persecutor of Christians on his way to Damascus. The high priests Caypha and Anna have ordered him to "Constreyn all rebellys" (I.28, I.52). Devils do not appear on stage until Saulus converts to Christianity and rejects the evil of devils, Jews, and pagans. The conversion occurs through special effects: "Here commyth a seruent with gret tempest, and / saule faulyth down of hys horse : that done, godhed / spekyth in heuyn" (II. SD 182). God rebukes Saulus, he repents, is baptized, and devils appear as the new Christian undergoes his own persecution. In fact, the justice of Caypha and Anna is twinned with demonic pursuits in the play.[26] Immediately after the priests declare that they will force him to "repent hys Rebellyous treytory," the devils Belyall and Mercury enter. Belyall appears "with thunder and fyre" and Mercury follows him "with a fyeryng, commyng in hast, cryeng and roryng" (SD 411, SD 432). Interestingly, there is evidence that Belyall and Mercury, with their devilish pyrotechnics, did not appear in *The Conversion of Saint Paul* until a mid-sixteenth century revival of the play.[27] Their brief scene reveals that Caypha and Anna are not just an earthly judiciary, but have been placed in their positions as the devil's prelates "to persew and put downe, by powre ryall / thorow the sytyes of damaske and liba, / All soch as do worship the hye god supernall" (420–2). When they learn that their plans have been foiled because Saulus "now ys baptysyd" and having "soch grace he hath opteyned / that ondowtyd hys fayth from hym can-not fade," the two devils can do "non other but crye," which they do on cue (461–3, 468).[28] These cries reprise the noises made by Mercury at his entrance. Like the two high priests, the two devils plot their revenge against Saulus and end their scene vanishing "away with a fyrye flame and a tempest" (SD 502). Despite the plans of both the Jews and the devils, an antisemitic cooperative that reflects the demonology I addressed earlier in this chapter, Saulus becomes a Christian missionary. Yet, before Saulus returns to face his judges, an angel warns him that "The princes of Iues entende sertayn / To

---

[25] Donald C. Baker, John L. Murphy, and Louis B. Hall, Jr., eds., "The Conversion of Saint Paul," in *The Late Medieval Religious Plays of Bodleian MSS Digby 133 and e. Mus.160.* EETS o.s. 283 (Oxford: Oxford University Press, 1982). All subsequent in text parenthetical citations are from this edition.

[26] Heather Hill-Vasquez argues that the play and its staging of devils, in particular, "could support alternative theologies. In the hands of a shrewd Protestant sponsor, the *Saint Paul* can become an effective proto-reformist play, undergoing and demonstrating a process of change from the old to the new faith." See *Sacred Players: The Politics of Response in the Middle English Religious Drama*, (Washington, D.C.: The Catholic University of America Press, 2007), 54; and "The Possibilities of Performance: A Reformation Sponsorship for the Digby *Conversion of St. Paul*," *Research Opportunities in Renaissance Drama* 22 (1997): 2–20.

[27] Donald C. Baker and John L. Murphy, "MS. Digby 133: Scribes, Dates, and Early History," *Research Opportunities in Renaissance Drama* 10 (1967): 153–66. See also, John Coldewey, "The Digby Play and the Chelmsford Records," *Research Opportunities in Renaissance Drama* 18 (1975): 103–21.

[28] The stage directions to 468 read "Here thei shal rore and crye."

put yow to deth" and tells him to flee (III. 637–8). The play concludes with Paul journeying toward Jerusalem.

The Digby *Conversion of Saint Paul* follows the same three-part structure as *Mary Magdalene*: devils attack saints to tempt and oppose their conversion, the defeat of the devils verifies Christian transformation, and the appearance of angels signifies sanctity.[29] In these two plays, the pyrotechnic devils and angelic apparitions are a means of metaphysical validation. While the devilish special effects may have not appeared in *The Conversion of Saint Paul* until the 1550s, the opposition in the play functions in a similar fashion to the devils in *Mary Magdalene* as well as in the N-Town Plays. In contrast, the Elizabethan St. Dunstan plays do not utilize supernatural theatricality as part of this same system. In fact, the professional stage would not revive this medieval demonic theatricality until Heywood's *If You Know Not Me, You Know Nobody*, which I examine in chapter 3. *A Knack to Know a Knave* and *The Devil and His Dame* rely on the saint's proximity to demonic activity on stage to sustain an association between saints and the supernatural in drama. Moreover, the Elizabethan appearance of the devil as a supernatural force occurs in a time in which the depiction of the Trinity-as-supernatural is no longer possible. In the biblical plays, such as York, N-Town, and Chester, God and Christ appear as well as the devils. But on the iconoclastic professional stage, the devil supplies the bulk of the supernatural. Rather than devils opposing conversion, holy acts, and penance, the spectacular demonism simply appears alongside St. Dunstan to mark sainthood. Iconography and theatricality remain, even as the narrative of the traditional legend transforms variously.

St. Dunstan likely stood on the Elizabethan stage because he came with a legend involving a devil. The conventions of the theatre then determined how to stage St. Dunstan. In doing so, the St. Dunstan plays continue an English tradition of producing alternative lives of the saints in theatrical performance. From the fourteenth through sixteenth centuries, English theatre-makers produced pageants that depicted saints outside of devotional contexts, alongside other figures, and within new or altered narratives. Notably, these theatrical events did not cohere around the saint's *vita*. Therefore, the Elizabethan plays create new legends of St. Dunstan at least as much as they de-sanctify traditional hagiography.

A Knack to Know a Knave and *The Devil and His Dame* continue the late medieval English practice of excerpting iconography and episodes from saints'

---

[29] For more on the dramaturgy and theatricality of the Digby plays, see Sarah Salih, "Staging Conversion: The Digby Saint Plays and The Book of Margery Kempe," in *Gender and Holiness: Men, Women and Saints in Late Medieval Europe*, eds. Samantha J. E. Riches and Sarah Salih (London: Routledge, 2002), 121–34; Chester N. Scoville, "The Hood and the Basket: Image and Word in the Digby *Conversion of St. Paul*," *Research Opportunities in Renaissance Drama* 41 (2002): 157–67; Victor I. Scherb, "Frame Structure in *The Conversion of St. Paul*," *Comparative Drama* 26, no. 2 (1992): 124–39; Theresa Coletti, "The Design of the Digby Play of *Mary Magdalene*," *Studies in Philology* 76 (1979): 313–33; and Glynne Wickham, "The Staging of Saint Plays in England," in *The Medieval Drama*, ed. Sandra Sticco (Albany, NY: State University of New York Press, 1972), 99–119.

lives and producing alternative hagiographies within the context of theatrical performance. In pageantry, saints often performed beyond the narratives of their traditional lives as encountered in devotional literature. Saints appeared in other pageants alongside mythological and historical figures, and sometimes pageant makers repurposed both their legends and iconography. To recall from chapter 1, the 1522 London pageants for Charles V of Spain concluded with an Assumption pageant featuring the Virgin Mary along with SS George, John the Baptist, Edmund, Edward the Confessor, Dunstan, Thomas Becket, and Erkenwald. No account of the end of the Virgin Mary's life includes these other saints, but the pageant makers cast important English patrons in the miracle. Furthermore, this pageant occurred after a variety of other tableaux that did not include saints: Jason, Medea, and the golden fleece on Tower Bridge, the coronation of Charlemagne at a conduit, and ancient kings at another conduit. Other examples of alternative hagiography include the convergences of SS Margaret and George in pageantry due to their shared iconic antagonist. Between 1408 and 1550, Margaret rode alongside George in Norwich and in some years she played George's maiden.[30] A 1521 Midsummer's Watch pageant in London included St. George defeating the dragon and then presenting it to Margaret.[31] This romanticization of the legends of SS Margaret and George is particularly apt for considering the alternative legends of St. Dunstan that emerged in Elizabethan drama. In Margaret's *vita*, she slays her dragon after bursting out of its belly as part of her imprisonment and martyrdom. In George's *vita*, he slays the beast to save a maiden in an episode that occurs before enduring torture and martyrdom. These two lives, which were distinct in devotional literature, were transformed in theatrical conflation and improvisation. These pageants not only place Margaret at a central event of George's life, but also reinvent George and Margaret as romance heroes and, most notably, diminish Margaret's status as a saint in her own right. Recast as the maiden in these pageants, she no longer performs as the central agent and exemplar of virgin martyrdom. The longer history of saint plays cautions against ascribing a Reformation secularization to the Elizabethan transformation of St. Dunstan. On the contrary, when professional dramatists altered, adapted, and romanticized the Dunstan legend so that he appears alongside Honesty and Asmoroth in King Edgar's court and clowns with devils as they create hell's "holy-day," they resurrected a practice of medieval theatre.

---

[30] REED: *Norwich*, 4–30.
[31] Ian Lancashire, *Dramatic Texts and Records of Britain: A Chronological Topography to 1558* (Toronto: University of Toronto Press, 1984), 969.

Patron Fakes in Early Shakespeare

The post-*Faustian* era of theatre opened up a space for the theatre to reconsider religion and the supernatural, including the performance of saints and sanctity. In addition to St. Dunstan, a number of saints lived on in Elizabethan drama either through the actual representation of the saint or through the citation of associated hagiographical cultural practices and traditions. The revitalization of native saints in the calendar of the *BCP* and in new dramatic legends represents the post-Reformation inheritance of what Catherine Sanok identifies as a "fascination with native saints in the fifteenth century that can be explained as a response to a growing crisis in the central forms with which English history and identity had been represented."[32] Between the premieres of the two St. Dunstan plays, another play featuring a medieval English bishop appeared. Henslowe's diary records that *Richard the Confessor* was performed by Sussex's Men two times in January of 1594.[33] As Matthew Steggle argues, this lost play likely depicts some aspect of or association with Richard of Chichester, the saint whose shrine drew pilgrims to Chichester Cathedral until its destruction during the dissolution of the monasteries. Richard is one of the saints who returned to the liturgical calendar when Dunstan did.[34] Two other lost plays, *Warlamchester* (c.1594) and *Diocletian* (c.1594), may have portrayed St. Alban and other ancient martyrs. Additionally, St. Winifred's Well appears in *John a Kent, John a Cumber* (c.1590) by Anthony Munday, and SS Crispin and George are famously invoked in *Henry V* (c.1599) as is St. Hugh in *Shoemaker's Holiday* (c.1599). Many of these saints, who were either English or important to the English, appear again in the Jacobean period. The martyrdom of St. Alban forms a subplot of *A Shoemaker, A Gentleman* (c.1618) by William Rowley, a play that also features SS Crispin, Winifred, and Hugh as heroes and Diocletian as a Roman persecutor.

But the repeated invocation of saints in *Henry V* represents a shift in Shakespeare's representation of saints and sanctity from his earlier history plays: *2 Henry VI* (c.1591), *Richard III* (c.1592), and *1 Henry VI* (c.1592). While these plays mostly focus on the machinations, murders, and battles associated with the Wars of the Roses, occasional subplots or scenes address saints or sanctity. The skeptical derision in these early plays stands in stark contrast to the moments of hagiographical wonder that appear in *Pericles, Prince of Tyre* (1608) and *Henry VIII* (1613). The repertory of saints and sacred spaces in professional drama in the 1590s and 1600s

---

[32] Catherine Sanok "Good King Henry and the Genealogy of Shakespeare's First History Plays," *Journal of Medieval and Early Modern Studies* 40, no.1 (2010): 42. https://doi.org/10.1215/10829636-2009-013

[33] Philip Henslowe, *Henslowe's Diary*, ed. R. A. Foakes, 2nd ed. (Cambridge: Cambridge University Press, 2002), 20.

[34] See Matthew Steggle, "Richard the Confessor (1593)," *Digital Humanities and the Lost Drama of Early Modern England: Ten Case Studies* (Farnham: Ashgate, 2015), 43–60.

likely influenced Shakespeare's hagiographical turn, as his playwriting practice repeatedly seized on trends in the theatre and reproduced them with refinement. In his early career, however, Shakespeare cautioned skepticism when it came to sanctity. Later plays, such as *Measure for Measure* (1604) and *The Winter's Tale* (1610) treat the problem of discerning *being* from *seeming*, but in the beginning, there were only repeated exploits of seeming saintly in English history.

Whereas St. Dunstan conjures the devil for good in *A Knack to Know a Knave*, and the location of St. Winifred's Well offers a fitting backdrop to medieval magic in *John a Kent, John a Cumber*, the depiction of miraculous intervention on English soil in *2 Henry VI* is, in fact, a fraudulent performance.[35] Early in the play, the king and his party are near St. Albans, the site of the English protomartyr's execution and shrine at the abbey. They are interrupted by the announcement of a miracle in which "a blind man at Saint Alban's shrine ... hath received his sight" (2.1.70-1). The blind man testifies that he was "called / A hundred times and oftener in my sleep / By good Saint Alban" to make pilgrimage to the shrine in order to be cured (2.1.97-9). The pilgrimage is strenuous because the man is also lame. The Duke of Gloucester suspects deceit and calls on St. Alban to also "restore this cripple to his legs again" (2.1.147). As Lindsey Row-Heyveld writes, Shakespeare's version of this episode of the cured blind man, which is first found in Thomas More's *A Dialogue Concerning Heresies* and later in Foxe's *Book of Martyrs*, invents the lameness and emphasizes Gloucester's skepticism.[36] The Duke calls for a beadle to restore the man's legs with his whip and the violent intercession produces "A miracle!" when the charlatan pilgrim runs off to escape (SD 2.1.165). A similar show of sanctity occurs in *Richard III*. Between removing Lord Hastings and plotting the deaths of his young nephews, Richard pauses his political matters for an interlude of piety. Stage managed by the Duke of Buckingham, Richard is cast in a show of sham sanctity before the citizens of London in a bid for the support of his kingship. Buckingham directs him to "get a prayer book in your hand / And stand between two churchmen," and feign humble refusal of requests to take the Crown (3.7.48-9). Richard is within so that when he is discovered by London "with two right reverend fathers, / Divinely bent to meditation" his audience witnesses "his holy exercise" (3.7.62-3, 65). This medieval virtue signaling does the trick. The Lord Mayor is convinced by the presence of the "Two props of virtue" who stand on either side of Richard and the prayer book in his hand (3.7.99). By the end of the scene the gathered crowd says "Amen," to "Richard, England's worthy king" (3.7.243, 242). The utterance is a mistaken prayer for the vice character

---

[35] Indeed, the episodes of false shows of sanctity in the Henry VI plays, with the charlatan pilgrim at St. Albans and Joan of Arc, might exist to contrast with a residual cult of Henry VI. See Sanok for the way in which the Henry VI plays present "the afterlife of a saint's cult." Sanok, "Good King Henry," 38.

[36] Lindsey Row-Heyveld, "'The lying'st knave in Christendom': The Development of Disability in the False Miracle of St. Alban's," *Disability Studies Quarterly* 29, no. 4 (2009). https://dsq-sds.org/article/view/994/1178.

who impersonates the habitus of a holy man. In both *2 Henry VI* and *Richard III*, then, these episodes warn against pretend sanctity on English soil in the fifteenth century, a century known for making and solidifying the place of native saints in the wider culture.

The depiction of Joan of Arc in *1 Henry VI* presents yet another version of false sanctity, but it is a more complex one. Even if the English know that the French "Pucelle" is no saint, the saint herself is confused over the matter. Joan's understanding of sanctity is stuck in a pre-Reformation epistemology in which the supernatural and the Marian determine the nature of sainthood. Moreover, Joan's worldview reflects a transnational Christendom in which the Pope and the saintly might adjudicate claims of national sovereignty. But the rules of the game have changed since Joan's death in 1431. *1 Henry VI* presents the story of the Maid of Orleans through the perspective of Elizabethan Protestant historiography. Joan's reception of divine messages concerning the war between the House of Valois and Henry VI contradict the English Crown's claim to French land. If the rubric of popular sainthood at the end of the Elizabethan era requires pride in an ancient English ecclesiastical tradition or, at the very least, not contradicting it, then Joan fails this test. Her opposition to the rightful English rule of France is as unsaintly as Thomas Becket's loyalty to Rome.

Joan, who is called "Pucelle or Puzel," the virgin or the whore, appears throughout the play (1.4.107). Before audiences meet her, however, they witness the funeral procession of Henry V. English nobles stand by and denounce the French for their "Conjurers and sorcerers, that, afraid of him, / By magic verses have contrived his end" (1.1.26–7). Messages are delivered that indicate English defeat: the French have won a series of battles, taken Talbot prisoner at the Siege of Orleans, and crowned the Dauphin Charles the new King of France. By the end of this opening, the English vow to light "Bonfires in France . . . To keep our great Saint George's feast withal" (1.1.156–67). The citation of St. George's Day is a small detail, but it is one that pits English sanctity and nationhood against false sainthood and, by extension, French statehood. The celebration of England's patron saint—with bonfires—also predicts the end of the heretical French puzzle at the stake.

Joan is every unnatural opposite to the English. She is a devotee of the Virgin Mary and physically overcomes the Dauphin. Edward Burns argues that "Joan Puzel parallels Spenser's female warrior Britomart," the allegorical embodiment of Elizabeth I in the *Faerie Queene* inasmuch as "the woman warrior . . . is an agent of confusion."[37] Yet whereas Britomart's unique physical abilities can be explained by a divinely bestowed gift in a fantasy world, Joan claims that "Christ's mother helps me; else I were too weak" (1.2.108). Joan more readily resembles Radigund, the emasculating virgin who leads a band of warrior maidens and captures,

---

[37] Edward Burns, introduction to *Henry VI, Part 1* by William Shakespeare, ed. Edward Burns, Arden Shakespeare Third Series (London: Arden Shakespeare, 2004), 31–2.

starves, and forcefully cross-dresses the knight Artegal in Book V of the *Faerie Queene*. Spenser's Radigund, like her namesake medieval saint, embodies a pre-Reformation feminine sanctity that rejects a sexual subjectivity defined by the presence and control of men, including and especially, husband and king. She lives like an unruly nun in that she operates beyond the containment of the cloister. In the wider world, the unnatural Radigund wreaks havoc on the orderly masculine body by violently transforming men into her own image. Joan's special relationship to the Virgin Mary, who she attempts and fails to imitate, associates her with Catholicism. As Maggie Solberg writes, "the historical Joan of Arc . . . received her visions from Saint Margaret, Saint Catherine of Alexandria, and the archangel Michael," but "early modern English polemicists preferred to insist that Joan had named the Virgin Mary as her primary source of otherworldly inspiration."[38] In the Elizabethan period, Joan's original intercessors who also appear in the *BCP* were not identifiable icons of Catholicism. That role was better performed by "the papist idol of the Madonna."[39]

Unlike the Dauphin, the English Lord Talbot always interprets Joan as unnatural and disorderly. He calls into question her saintly status by cursing her as "Devil or devil's dam" and "witch" (1.5.5–6). She is the false version of what she and the French claim that she is. The enemies of England interpret the Maid of Orleans as "a holy prophetess," a descriptor that also links Joan to Elizabeth Barton, the Holy Maid of Kent (1.4.102). Barton was executed in 1534 for treason after her visions challenged the Crown. As the Reformation commenced, her visions turned from an acceptable range of late-medieval mysticism—Marian piety, pilgrimages, repentance—to the Henry VIII's assured death if the king divorced his wife and broke with Rome. When early reformers, such as William Tyndale and Thomas Cranmer, rejected Barton's prophesies, they not only did so on political grounds, but also because they interpreted them as diabolical in nature.[40] This is exactly how Talbot, the chivalric representative of the English who eventually dies by French hands, sees Joan. He describes her as "that witch, that damned sorceress" who "hath wrought . . . hellish mischief" (3.2.38–9). The Dauphin asks Joan to "enchant. . .with thy words" the Duke of Burgundy who has fought for Henry's claim to France (3.3.40). Joan does not offer spells, but rather speaks of France's grief and wounds. Nonetheless, when Burgundy experiences a rather quick change of heart to fight on the side of the Dauphin, he wonders if "she hath bewitched me with her words" (3.3.58). The play sets up a problem: Joan claims that the Virgin

---

[38] Emma Maggie Solberg, *Virgin Whore* (Ithaca, NY: Cornell University Press, 2018), 160.

[39] Solberg, 160. The misogyny associated with this version of Joan, Patrick Ryan argues, is also steeped in "Protestant apocalyptic ideology" that divides the world between England and "England's Roman Catholic foes" and associates Joan with the Whore of Babylon. "Shakespeare's Joan and the Great Whore of Babylon." *Renaissance and Reformation* 28, no. 4 (2004): 55.

[40] See James Simpson, "1534–1550s: Texts," in *The Cambridge Companion to Medieval English Mysticism*, eds. Samuel Fanous and Vincent Gillespie (Cambridge: Cambridge University Press, 2011), 249–64.

Mary counsels her, but the sources of her visions and powers are necromantic. But neither the Virgin Mary nor cavorting with the devil will resolve the puzzle. The play is clear on this by the end. Just prior to a final skirmish during the French defeat of the English, Joan enters the stage alone and calls to her supernatural aids. They are not saints or angels, but "charming spells" and "choice spirits" who appear in the guise of "*Fiends*" to "*Thunder*" (5.3.2–3, SD 5.3.4, SD 5.3.7). She offers her "body, soul, and all," but she is an ineffective barterer with demons (5.3.43). Unlike St. Dunstan in *A Knack to Know a Knave*, she cannot control a devil, nor does she seek to do so for the cause of virtue. The English capture her and condemn her to the stake for her sorcery. At the last minute, the virgin pleads her belly and is roundly mocked as "the holy maid with child," the bastard version of the Annunciation, before naming two separate men as the father of her child (5.3.65). Philippa Shepherd has compared English and French versions of the life of Joan of Arc and notes that whereas Fronton Du Duc's *The Tragic History of La Pucelle of Domremy* (1580) "is very interested in La Pucelle's trial and charges," Shakespeare offers "no real trial scene."[41] In place of a trial, the audience views Joan attempting to conjure demons and to save her body from burning by impugning her reputation as a virgin. Unlike the virgin martyrs Katherine and Margaret, whom the historical Joan named in her trial as her intercessors, Shakespeare's dramatic version of the Pucelle refuses to go to her death like a saint. Albert Tricomi, who interprets *1 Henry VI* as an "inverted saints play," points out that Joan also fails to imitate the "reported steadfastness and calm" of the sixteenth-century Protestant martyrs lauded by Foxe in the *Book of Martyrs*.[42] Instead, she is dragged to the stake as a sad pretender to sainthood, a failed witch and confused "puzel." In Shakespeare's later works, he would continue to play with sanctity in terms of the virginal and the Marian, but that sanctity would not emerge so readily identifiable as papist or anti-English.

Common Saints

The late Elizabethan experiments with saints in performance navigate various aspects of historical, religious, and cultural authority. In this period of time, it remained paramount for theatricalized saints—that were depicted as saints and not as charlatans or mistaken foreign heretics—to patronize the history of the English church. A final authorizing gesture for saints in performance occurred at the end of this era. In the summer of 1602, the queen visited Harefield estate,

---

[41] Philippa Sheppard, "The Puzzle or Pucelle or Pussel: Shakespeare's Joan of Arc Compared with Two Antecedents," in *Renaissance Medievalisms*, ed. Konrad Eisenbichler (Toronto: Centre for Reformation and Renaissance Studies, 2009), 205.

[42] "Joan la Pucelle and the Inverted Saints Play in *1 Henry VI*," *Renaissance and Reformation* 25, no. 2 (2001): 24.

home of Alice and Thomas Egerton. There, Elizabeth's hosts welcomed her to their country estate with a traditional entertainment. Of the five pageants that were presented to Elizabeth between 31 July and 2 August, the third amounted to a petition of pardon—not of the hosts, but of St. Swithin. During the queen's visit, Harefield had suffered inclement weather.[43] Tradition held St. Swithin was the cause: it had rained two weeks earlier on St. Swithin's Day (15 July according to the Sarum calendar as well as the *BCP*), and according to the folklore, rain on that day meant forty more days of inclement weather. "The Petition of St. Swithin," also referred to as "The humble peticion of a giltles sainte," begins with verses recounting Elizabeth's heavenly origins ("Saintes and Angells ... did smile att your faire birth"), before a single heavenly inhabitant makes amends:

> Onelie poore *St. Swithin* nowe
> Dothe heare you blame this cloudie browe
> But that poore Sainte devoutlie sweares
> Yt is but a tradition vaine
> That his much weepeinge causethe raine
> For saintes in heauen shed no teares.[44]

The pageant presented for Elizabeth retains traditional associations with St. Swithin even as he is cast in the role of messenger. In addition to serving a similar function to Punxsutawney Phil (the forecasting groundhog), Swithin was a ninth-century bishop of Winchester whose cult grew when St. Dunstan arranged for the translation of his relics a century later.[45] As Archbishop of Canterbury, Dunstan revered Swithin for his association with monasticism and chastity. Swithin's most famous miracle involves a defense of chastity, which is cited in the pageant verses to Elizabeth: "If saintes could weepe, had wepte as much / As when hee did the Ladye Leade, That did on burning iron treade."[46] These lines refer to the trial of Queen Emma, mother of St. Edward the Confessor. According to the legend, Emma underwent trial by ordeal to prove her innocence

---

[43] In her analysis of late Elizabethan country house entertainments, Elizabeth Zemon Kolkovich argues that certain estates "focused more on showing off than on providing charitable service," and Harefield proved no exception. Kolkovich estimates that the queen's brief visit cost the estate slightly more than their annual expenses. The St. Swithin pageant served as a preamble for giving the queen two extraordinarily expensive gowns, one with embroidered rainbows and the other with rubies and pearls. Elizabeth Zeman Kolkovich, *The Elizabethan Country House Entertainment: Print, Performance, and Gender* (Cambridge: Cambridge University Press, 2016), 90 and 111. https://doi.org/10.1017/CBO9781316460818

[44] Elizabeth Goldring et. al., eds., *John Nichols's The Progresses and Public Processions of Queen Elizabeth I: A New Edition of the Early Modern Sources* (Oxford: Oxford University Press, 2014), 4: 185.

[45] Swithin is unique in that the feast of his translation is his only feast day in the liturgical calendar. Typically, the commemoration of the translation of a saint's relics are observed in addition to the day of their death. The case of Swithin is different because his cult was created, in part, through the translation of his relics.

[46] Goldring, *John Nichols's Progresses and Public Processions*, 4:185.

against accusations of an adulterous affair with the bishop of Winchester. Through Swithin's intercession, Emma proved her chastity by walking barefoot over nine burning ploughshares of iron.

Like Dunstan and Richard, Swithin is an English saint, a medieval bishop, and a returnee to the liturgical calendar in the *BCP*. Furthermore, he is associated with a legend of English monarchy and romance. His life and miracles circulated in both medieval legendaries and in defamed form in Reformation polemic. Even though Swithin's part in the pageant derived from his association with a folk explanation for bad weather, it is significant that an aspect of the saint's traditional patronage—rain and drought—was enacted before Elizabeth. Furthermore, the verses invoked the miraculous proof of a past English queen's true chastity, an appropriate motif for the Virgin Queen. Like *Henry V*, this pageant revitalized a legend of a patron saint and celebrated the association of sainthood with the history of the English monarchy. In doing so, it thoroughly rejected the reformers' version of Swithin.

The late Elizabethan encounter with Swithin is the first recorded royal entertainment to include a saint—albeit a saint of absent presence—since Edward VI's coronation pageant in 1547. It would be followed, two years later, by the appearance of SS George and Andrew in King James' coronation pageant. The careful reintroduction of saints in royal pageantry in a time of established Protestantism likely played a role in the reintroduction of saints in other pageantry. The first saint to return to the London streets for a civic occasion was none other than St. Dunstan. Before the saint served as the arch-patron of hell in the writings of Foxe and Bale, he had figured as the patron of smiths. It is the latter role that he reprised when, in 1611, Anthony Munday cast Dunstan in a Lord Mayor's Show that celebrated the inauguration of a Goldsmith as the mayor of London. The series of figures in Munday's pageant include the famous medieval Goldsmith mayor Nicholas de Farndone, English kings, ancient Greek heroes, and personifications of gold and silver, all of which honor the history of the livery company. At the conclusion of the pageant, "learned *Dunstane*, who beeing Byshop of *Worcester*, *London*, and Arch-Byshop of *Canterbury*" and who "had no little delight in the Arte of Cold-Smithery ... shewes himselfe now (as then) acting that profession."[47] Dunstan materializes at his forge and, notably, without his demon because the conventions of civic pageantry emphasize his status as patron saint through a shared craft. As an icon "now (as then)" of the Goldsmiths, Dunstan serves to anchor the company within a longer English history.

The Entertainment at Harefield would not be the last encounter between Elizabeth and sainthood. In the following chapter, I turn to a play that represented the late queen as a saint. *If You Know Not Me, You Know Nobody* (c.1604) by Thomas Heywood rehabilitated virgin martyrdom for the English by explicitly separating it from the Marian and the Catholic. Heywood drew on both Foxe's

---

[47] Anthony Munday, *Chruso-thriambos. The triumphes of GOLDE*. (London: W. Iaggard, 1611), B1r.

narrative of Elizabeth's persecution during the reign of Mary I and a tradition of sanctity derived from both pre-Reformation hagiography and medieval theatricality. A general sorting of sanctity occurred between the pretend virgin martyr Joan in *1 Henry VI* and the true virgin martyr Elizabeth in *If You Know Not Me, You Know Nobody*. Just as Shakespeare gave Joan the task of imitating the Catholic-identified Virgin Mary instead of the martial St. Michael and the virgin martyrs SS Katherine and Margaret, Heywood had his Protestant virgin queen imitate the ancient virgin martyrs as her Catholic persecutors associated themselves with the Marian—both the queen and the saint. Without the dramatic downfall of Shakespeare's Joan, there might have been no rise of Heywood's Elizabeth.

3
Acts of Translation

When saints first returned to public view in Elizabethan playhouses and pageantry, they did so without performing their lives. As I showed in chapter 2, St. Dunstan appears with his iconic devil, but the plays do not represent his life and miracles as set down by either his medieval hagiographers or his Reformation detractors. The structure and tropes of saints' lives are absent from the initial theatrical experiments with saints as dramatic characters. The performance of *vita*, the life of a saint, did not occur until after the end of the Elizabethan era when, in an unprecedented turn of events, the playwright Thomas Heywood scripted the religious struggles of Queen Elizabeth into the *life* of a virgin martyr saint. *If You Know Not Me, You Know Nobody* (c.1604) innovated the English saint play and set the terms of sanctity for the rest of the early modern period. The saint is no longer a subplot character, a villain, or a pageant device. The saint of Heywood's play is the virgin martyr protagonist in a story of suffering, martyrdom, heavenly coronation, and the triumph of Protestantism in England. In this chapter, I demonstrate how the play's portrayal of Elizabeth as the new English protomartyr reauthorized sainthood as a theatrical subject. Whereas the liturgical calendar of the Elizabethan church authorized the theatre to welcome back certain saints to the stage, Heywood's sanctification of Elizabeth as a virgin martyr restored the performative abilities of theatre to produce saints.

Despite its understudied status, *If You Know Not Me, You Know Nobody* was the first notable play of the Jacobean era and a blockbuster of its time.[1] The unexpected achievement of the play is its recovery of medieval "Catholic" hagiography for

---

[1] The complete title of the play is *If You Know Not Me, You Know Nobody, Part 1, or the Troubles of Queen Elizabeth*. Unlike the first play, its sequel, *If You Know Not Me, You Know Nobody, Part 2, The Building of The Royal Exchange* (c.1606) features the queen in only three scenes and devotes the majority of its stage time to clever urban-dwelling merchants and guildsmen. Nathaniel Butter published part one in 1605, 1606, 1608, 1610, 1613, 1623, 1632, and 1639 and part two in 1606, 1609, 1623, and 1633. Butter transferred both plays to Miles Flesher in 1639, although there is no record of Flesher's subsequent publication of either play. As John Watkins observes, "no other seventeenth century writer devoted so many individual works to the Queen of famous memory." *Representing Elizabeth in Stuart England: Literature, History, Sovereignty* (Cambridge: Cambridge University Press, 2002), 37. Heywood authored *Gunaikeion* (1624, revised in 1640) and *England's Elizabeth* (1631), both of which offer the life of Elizabeth in prose, and may have authored *The Life and Death of Queen Elizabeth* (1639), a verse version. Georgiana Ziegler offers an analytical review of these works in "England's Saviour: Elizabeth I in the Writings of Thomas Heywood," *Renaissance Papers* (1980): 29–37. *If You Know Not Me, You Know Nobody* may have premiered at the Curtain, where the Queen's Servants were in residence until they moved into the Red Bull in 1605, where it then played. See Eva Griffith, *A Jacobean Company and Its Playhouse: The Queen's Servants at The Red Bull Theatre, (c. 1605–1619)* (Cambridge: Cambridge University Press, 2013), 49N53.

The Renaissance of the Saints after Reform. Gina M. Di Salvo, Oxford University Press. © Gina M. Di Salvo (2023).
DOI: 10.1093/oso/9780192865915.003.0004

post-Reformation audiences. It not only navigates epistemologies of both medieval Catholic and Reformation Protestant devotional literatures, but also it develops a specific set of theatrical actions to enact sanctity. With the premiere of the play, I propose, the theatre performed an act of translation, in two senses, that renegotiate the boundaries of religion. In the first sense, *If You Know Not Me, You Know Nobody* circulated as a work of vernacular hagiography in as much as the play presents the history of Elizabeth and the English Reformation as *vita*. Prevalent in medieval studies, vernacular theology explains how theology circulated beyond official ecclesiastical Latin spaces and writings in Middle English, or other vernacular, literature, and practices. As Nicholas Watson argues, "Not only do vernacular texts derive material from an array of Latin systems of thought, they generate their own systems."[2] Thus, for Watson, the Middle English poem *Piers Plowman* proposes a theology of universal salvation and, for Theresa Coletti, the Digby *Mary Magdalene*, the N-Town Mary Play, and the Chester *Antichrist* all "produce complex intersections of dramatic form and religious ideology."[3] In the absence of an ecclesiastical office that organized sainthood, the theatre undertook the activity of articulating sainthood from both medieval devotional paradigms and the most basic tenants of Protestant theology and practice. This act of translation, from the conventions of saints' lives and the dogma of the reformed church, offered a new version of sanctity in a space of vernacular practice, the public playhouse. *If You Know Not Me, You Know Nobody* performs translation in another sense as well, one that is less about the act of translation in terms of language—from the high to the common and from the written to the performed—and more about translation as an act of relocation and revival. In religious terms, translation is the ritual transferal of a saint's physical remains or relics from one location to another. Translation usually occurs after the saint attains renown due to patronage or miraculous intervention on behalf of the faithful. The act also involves a disinterment from a modest location to a reinterment at a more prominent shrine, such as in a cathedral. Translation frequently revives, adjusts, and, even, expands the particular sainthood of the saint. Through translation, the saint's cult is renewed and takes on new meaning. This play, then, can be understood as the early Jacobean cultural event that oversaw the translation of sainthood from the medieval cathedral to the early modern playhouse. In the case of Heywood's dramatic *vita* of Elizabeth, sainthood was translated from a matter of theology to a matter of theatricality—but without an evacuation of theological matter.

Heywood drew on the account of Elizabeth's persecution in John Foxe's *Book of Martyrs*, but the play performs against the tropes of Protestant martyrdom. Elizabeth's progression in *If You Know Not Me, You Know Nobody* is patterned

---

[2] Nicholas Watson, "Visions of Inclusion: Universal Salvation and Vernacular Theology in Pre-Reformation England," *Journal of Medieval and Early Modern Studies* 27 (1997): 146.

[3] Theresa Coletti, *Mary Magdalene and the Drama of Saints: Theater, Gender, and Religion in Late Medieval England* (Philadelphia, PA: University of Pennsylvania Press, 2013), 4.

on the narrative sequence and tropes of virgin martyr hagiography. Whereas the actual life of the historical Elizabeth I more easily aligns with the life and themes of the Virgin Mary as depicted in medieval drama—that is, a persecuted perpetual virgin who dies in old age rather than by martyrdom—Heywood structured Elizabeth's stage sanctity on virgin martyrdom. The play, however, presents two notable obstacles to virgin martyrdom. Elizabeth is neither a vowed religious virgin nor is she executed. I contend that these apparent exceptions to virgin martyrdom are not exceptions at all. Instead of staging the events of vowed virginity and martyrdom explicitly, the play communicates them implicitly through theatrical episodes that allude to virgin martyrdom. The turning point of the play is a miraculous dumb show that features demonic Catholic clergy opposed by Protestant angels. Heywood's particular use of hagiography and miraculous theatricality would influence the depiction of saints for the next three decades. But Heywood's new terms of sanctity more immediately emerge, through inversion and distortion, in two other plays that premiered shortly after *If You Know Not Me, You Know Nobody*. The anonymous *St. Christopher* (1609), a lost play performed for recusant audiences in Yorkshire, and *Henry VIII* (1613) by John Fletcher and William Shakespeare both depict Catholic figures according to the conventions of Jacobean stage sanctity. Along with *If You Know Not Me, You Know Nobody*, these two subsequent plays offer a guide to the unarticulated orthodoxy of saints and sanctity in this new Stuart era. I contend that theatrical sanctity rests on the repetitions of conventions inherited from medieval hagiography and theatricality as well as aligning with or, at the very least, not against the English church. *St. Christopher* boldly violates those terms and *Henry VIII* witnesses to a sophisticated circumvention of them.

A Virgin and a Martyr Both

It is surprising that the virulently anti-Catholic narrative of Elizabeth's account of suffering under the regime of her half-sister Queen Mary, "The miraculous preseruation of Lady Elizabeth, now Queene of England" from Foxe's *Book of Martyrs* could be translated into a virgin martyr play.[4] Foxe constructed the suffering of Protestants under Mary to mirror the ten great persecutions of the early Church, especially the worst of them, The Tenth Persecution, under Diocletian and Maximian.[5] Heywood adapts the sequence of events and dialogue in Foxe and champions Elizabeth, Protestantism, and the English Bible as the protagonists of

---

[4] This narrative first appears in the 1563 edition of *A&M*, although the title of the episode does not appear until the 1570 edition. For an expanded discussion of *If You Know Not Me, You Know Nobody*, see Gina M. Di Salvo, "'A Virgine and a Martyr both': The Turn to Hagiography in Heywood's Reformation History Play," *Renaissance and Reformation* (2018): 133–67.

[5] These historical Roman emperors, frequent antagonists in medieval hagiography and in the early pages of Foxe, reappear as stock tyrants in the Jacobean and Caroline tragicomedies and virgin martyr plays addressed in chapters 4 and 5.

the English Reformation, but he does not reproduce this history as Foxean martyrology.[6] Instead, *If You Know Not Me, You Know Nobody* takes up the oppositional dynamics of Foxe's anti-Catholic paradigm and grafts them onto the structure of medieval virgin martyr hagiography. The play recovers hagiography for a broad Protestantism and, through its dramatization of key events of the Reformation, marks the boundary between where that broad Protestantism ends and where it is incapable of absorbing, accommodating, or even, converting traditional religion from its pre-Reformation form to the Jacobean present. There are limits to translation.

If You Know Not Me, You Know Nobody presents a general Protestantism at odds and only at odds with a particular mid-sixteenth century Catholicism. Heywood's play iterates the divide between the Catholic and the Protestant as sharply defined in terms of religious confession and perfectly vague in terms of doctrinal definition. Unlike *When You See Me, You Know Me*, which, Brian Walsh argues, reminded "audiences of the Lutheran origins of the English Reformation," Heywood's play refuses to define its Protestantism beyond opposition to Catholic tyranny and an affirmative belief in the vernacular Bible.[7] *If You Know Not Me, You Know Nobody* entered the stage at a crucial moment in English theatrical, religious, and political history. Written between the Hampton Court Conference, in which theologians entertained broadening the parameters of English Protestantism to include Catholic and Puritan elements, and the Powder Plot, the aftermath of which witnessed a concerted and violent suppression of Counter-Reformation Catholicism, Heywood's early Jacobean play widens the imagination of previous Reformation-era plays and follows Henry's Protestant daughter into a virgin martyr legend. The effect of the vague yet clearly identifiable stage Protestantism is the creation of a broad church that is so inclusive that its particular confession need not be named even once in the play. Like the Catholicism that need not be named until the advent of the Protestant Reformation, it imagines itself as universal English Christianity. The marked category, the particular here, is Catholicism. In scripting the recently departed Virgin Queen as the martyr whose struggle refounded the Church of England, Heywood brings together a narrative of Protestant triumph through the perspective of *vita*.

---

[6] The relationship between the play and Foxe has been interpreted variously. Mark Bayer understands the play to be "in dialogue" with the *Book of Martyrs*. "Staging Foxe at the Fortune and the Red Bull," *Renaissance and Reformation* 27 (2003): 68; Teresa Grant describes Heywood's dramatization as a "supra-Foxian glorification of Elizabeth." "Drama Queen: Staging Elizabeth in *If You Know Not Me You Know Nobody*," in *The Myth of Elizabeth*, eds. Susan Doran and Thomas S. Freeman (New York, NY: Pagrave MacMillan, 2003), 129; Marsha S. Robinson sees the play as an "appropriation of Foxe's historiographic vision," *Writing the Reformation: Acts and Monuments and the Jacobean History Play* (Aldershot, UK: Ashgate, 2002), xvi.

[7] Brian Walsh, *Unsettled Toleration: Religious Difference on the Shakespearean Stage* (Oxford: Oxford University Press, 2016), 12.

Heywood's Elizabeth lives and metaphorically dies within the structure of medieval virgin martyr hagiography. According to Karen Winstead, there are a series of "standard ingredients" in the *vitae* of early Christian martyrs: "the saint refuses to participate in pagan sacrifices, debates her antagonist, affirms the fundamental tenets of Christianity, destroys idols, performs miracles, and endures excruciating torments."[8] The lives of virgin martyrs include "a preoccupation with gender and sexuality" that is absent "from those of their male counterparts," an aspect that materializes through sexual violence and the virgin's status as *sponsa Christi*.[9] Medieval English virgin martyr legends, such as those of SS Agnes, Agatha, Cecilia, Katherine, and Margaret, unfold in a six-part narrative trajectory that lines up with Winstead's definition: (1) A virgin martyr is a young Christian aristocratic woman who proclaims her faith and opposes false religion; (2) She is interrogated on her beliefs and debates a Roman official; (3) She rejects the sexual advances of that official, because she has vowed her virginity to Christ; (4) She is tortured and jailed for her refusal to give up her religion, her virginity, or both; (5) Spectacular miracles thwart attempts to rape or kill her; and (6) She is finally executed and ascends to Christ, her heavenly spouse. In scripting Elizabeth as a virgin martyr, Heywood generated a paradigm of sanctity that resembled medieval models more than a Foxean one.

The difference between medieval collections of saints' lives and Foxe's *Book of Martyrs* is not that the former contains virgin martyrs, like St. Katherine of Alexandria, and the latter contains Protestant martyrs, like Anne Askew, but that medieval writers and editors included details that Foxe omits and disparages in his account of the same ancient martyrs. In the early pages of the *Book of Martyrs* that recount the persecutions under Diocletian and Maximian Foxe takes aim at miracles and vowed virginity but is not against Christian exemplarity. Before Foxe addresses St. Katherine, he complains that "stories of Saintes haue bene poudered and sawsed wyth dyuers vntrue additions and fabulous inuentions of men ... of a superstitious deuotion" that "almost nothyng remaineth in them simple & vncorrupte."[10] This is especially true "of good Katherine" who "in her lyfe was great holines, in her knowledge excellencie, in her death constancie."[11] Foxe rejects the

---

[8] *Virgin Martyrs: Legends of Sainthood in Late Medieval England* (Ithaca: Cornell University Press, 1997), 5. For more on the wide circulation of virgin martyr hagiography in medieval England, see Jocelyn Wogan-Browne, *Saints' Lives and Women's Literary Culture, c. 1150–1300: Virginity and Its Authorizations* (Oxford: Oxford University Press, 2001); and Catherine Sanok, *Her Life Historical: Exemplarity and Female Saints' Lives in Late Medieval England* (Philadelphia: University of Pennsylvania Press, 2007). For more particular virgin martyr cults in England, see Katherine J. Lewis, *The Cult of St. Katherine of Alexandria in Late Medieval England* (Rochester: Boydell Press, 2000); Jacqueline Jenkins and Katherine J. Lewis, eds., *St. Katherine of Alexandria: Texts and Contexts in Western Medieval* (Turnhout, BE: Brepols, 2003); and Juliana Dresvina, *A Maid with a Dragon: The Cult of St. Margaret of Antioch in Medieval England* (Oxford: Oxford University Press, 2016).
[9] Winstead, *Virgin Martyrs*, 6.
[10] Foxe 1570, 132.
[11] Foxe 1570, 132.

"straunge fictions" of Katherine's mystical marriage to the infant Christ, a hallmark of her late medieval English *vitae*, and revises the legend of St. Agnes so that God does not intervene with a miracle when she is stripped naked.[12] In the entries on SS Agnes and Cecilia, Foxe deemphasizes their vows of virginity, writing that Agnes was "yong & not maryable" and denies that Cecilia's guardian "Angell . . . was the keeper of her virginity."[13] Foxe explains that fantastical miracles are offensive, "because they haue no grou[n]d vpon any aunciA[n]t or graue authors, but taken out of certayne newe Ledgends," a likely reference to medieval collections of saints' lives, such as the *Golden Legend*.[14] As Megan Hickerson has shown, even when early Christian women saints are praised for their virginity in authoritative ancient sources, the Foxean account "depriveleges the virginity so valued in them, establishing his own ideal of female sainthood, of which it is no longer a condition."[15] Thus, in ancient and medieval collections of saints' lives, "Agnes is a virgin martyr; in Foxe's she is a martyr who happens to be a virgin."[16]

Heywood's play removes the wedge that Foxe drove between virgins and martyrs. A comparative reading of medieval hagiography and *If You Know Not Me, You Know Nobody* reveals that Heywood structured Elizabeth's sanctity on virgin martyrdom. The legends begin with the establishment of Christian character through evangelization, prayers, vows of virginity, charitable works, and acts of iconoclasm. Additionally, the virgin's holiness emerges within a persecuting regime headed by a tyrant who, like St. Agnes's Roman provost "was moche glad" to hear "that she was crysten [...] by cause to haue power on her."[17] Heywood situates Elizabeth similarly, but the play splits the tyrant over two parts. Queen Mary gives the orders and Stephen Gardiner, Bishop of Winchester, actively plots against Elizabeth. The play opens to the aftermath of the Protestant rebellion at the beginning of Mary's reign.[18] Winchester argues that Elizabeth is guilty of treason because, "She is a fauorite of [...] heritiques," and suggests that Mary execute her sister to preserve a Catholic England (A4v).[19] The queen is so determined in her program of religious persecution that she charges Winchester to "Take you[r] Comission to examine her/ Of all supposed Crimes," and exits "to our Nuptials" (B3v). In actuality, the historic Mary granted Elizabeth a reprieve from inquiry and imprisonment

---

[12] Foxe 1570, 131.
[13] Foxe 1570, 85, 131.
[14] Foxe 1570, 85.
[15] Megan Hickerson, *Making Women Martyrs in Tudor England* (New York: Palgrave Macmillan, 2005), 117.
[16] Hickerson, *Making Women Martyrs*, 117.
[17] Caxton, *Golden Legend*, cxxr recto.
[18] The events dramatized in the play begin during late February or early March of 1554. Eight months before, in July of 1553, Mary's supporters crushed the Duke of Northumberland's rebellion and forced Jane Grey to abdicate. Mary spared Jane's life until her father, Henry Grey, Duke of Suffolk, joined the Wyatt Rebellion in January of 1554.
[19] Thomas Heywood, *If you knovv not me, you know no bodie; or, The troubles of Queene Elizabeth* (London, 1605). All subsequent in-text parenthetical citations are from this edition.

to attend her wedding to Philip of Spain, but Heywood reverses historical fact in order to set the stage with a Catholic tyrant and a Protestant martyr.

In hagiography, virgin martyrs undergo interrogation and debate adversaries, a part of *vitae* in which saints often display rhetorical skill, proclaim Christianity, and reject false religion. Elizabeth fulfills this part of the narrative. In Foxe, she is questioned for her role in "*Wiates* conspiracie," but the play renders the interrogation as a hagiographical event rather than a political one.[20] Before the commission begins, Elizabeth prayerfully bids farewell to her tearful household, consoling them with her piety and charity.

> Eliz: My Innocence yet makes my hart as light
> As my front's heauie: all that heauen sends is welcome
> Gentlemen diuide these few crownes amongst you,
> I am now a prisoner; and shall want nothing,
> I haue some friends about her maiesty,
> That are prouiding for mee all things; all things;
> I, euen my graue; and being possest of that,
> I shall need nothing: weepe not I pray,
> Rather you should reioyce:
> If I miscarry in this enterprise and ask you why,
> A Virgine and a Martyr both I dy. (B4r–v)

This soliloquy instructs audiences to interpret Elizabeth within a particular pattern of sanctity. She proclaims herself a Christian who accepts God's charge to her, offers her worldly riches for charity, locates her current episode of martyrdom ("I am now a prisoner"), and, finally, foreshadows her own death and categorizes it as virgin martyrdom. In welcoming troubles and rejoicing in suffering, Elizabeth mirrors medieval virgin martyrs at similar moments in their *vitae*. For example, when St. Agatha is arrested, she "wente also gladly and with as good wyll as she had ben prayd to goon to a weddyng."[21] Elizabeth's moment of meta-hagiography anticipates a particular series of episodes: interrogation, torture and imprisonment, miracles, execution, and heavenly coronation. The phrasing of "A Virgine and a Martyr both," registers a unique martyrological paradigm that promises to bridge the divide between medieval and Reformation exemplars of Christian sacrifice.

During the debate against Mary's counselors, Elizabeth performs like a saint. Surrounded by sitting men while "*shee kneeles*," Heywood's virgin martyr controls the scene, manipulates meaning, and reveals the injustice of her sham trial (C1r). In responding to the twinned charges of heresy and treason against the Roman state, virgins rarely answer directly and prefer to manipulate the tenor

---

[20] Foxe, 1570, 1587.
[21] Caxton, *Golden Legend*, cxxxv verso.

of questioning to exhibit better rhetorical abilities than their pagan enemies.[22] Elizabeth avoids responding to the commissioners' questions in either the direct affirmative or negative. Instead, when Winchester demands that the princess incriminate herself and "submit, vnto her highness," she glosses his strategy on "Hauing nothing wheron you can accuse me, / Do seeke to haue myself, my self betray" (C1r). Winchester tires of her word play and demands that she "ansere briefly to these treasons," and the Constable confirms what we already know, that "the Queen must here you sing another song" (C1v). Elizabeth seizes on a single word to redirect the judicial proceeding toward a confirmation of her sanctity, "One day in quiers of Angels I shall singe," and, as her interrogators exit the trial, she offers a final prayer, "as my hart is knowne to thee most pure, / Grant mee release, or patience to endure" (C1v). As in the preceding soliloquy, this couplet limits the scope of historical action to a saint play.

Torture and imprisonment form the next part of virgin martyrdom. The steadfast suffering of the virgin is coupled with miraculous healings, angelic visitations, or the intervention of a vengeful God. Saints' lives entail notoriously grotesque tortures. Hooks of iron that "rende and drawe [...] flessh to the bones" are common as is being stripped, hung up, beaten, and burned.[23] Miracles thwart and counteract the effects of devised punishments, a form of divine intervention that sanctifies the virgin and punishes or embarrasses her Roman persecutors. In the legend of St. Margaret, her tormenters set her tortured body in water so that the elemental properties add to her suffering, but the saint does not suffer. Instead, once she is immersed, the virgin prays, "I besech the my lord that thys water may be to me the fonte of baptysme in to euer lastyng lyf / And anon there was herde grete thondre / and a douue descended from heuen and sette a golden crowne on her hede."[24] This miracle imitates Christ's baptism in order to emphasize Margaret's holiness. In addition to sites of torture, prison is an important location of devotion and miraculous restoration. There, Christ sends a starving Katherine "a whyte dowue whiche fedde her with mete celastyal" and Margaret counteracts an attack of "the fende" with "the signe of the crosse."[25] Divine intervention also takes the form of vengeance. Throughout virgin martyr hagiography, Roman officials and onlookers experience sudden death through earthquakes, explosions, and combustions.

In the play, Elizabeth is not physically tortured herself. Instead, the Constable of the Tower emerges as a sadistic jailer who attempts to cause her physical and

---

[22] For an examination of rhetoric in virgin martyr hagiography, see Maud Burnett McInerney, *Eloquent Virgins: From Thecla to Joan of Arc* (New York, NY: Palgrave Macmillan, 2002). Additionally, Jocelyn Wogan-Browne describes the debate between a virgin and her tyrant as a "combat contest not of strength, but of meanings." *Saints' Lives and Women's Literary Culture*, 106.

[23] Caxton, *Golden Legend*, ccxv verso.

[24] Caxton, *Golden Legend*, ccxv verso.

[25] Caxton, ccclxxxviii verso, ccxv recto.

spiritual suffering. As an agent of Winchester, he refuses her a chair, rescinds the "the priuiledge [...] to ope / Her windowes, casements to receiue the ayre," and obstructs servants from bringing her dinner (C4r, C4v, D1r.). Swearing to "vex her," the Constable fantasizes, "that I could but draine her harts deare blood, Oh it would feede me, do my soule much good" (D2v). During Elizabeth's imprisonment, the Constable pursues torture by proxy. Heywood adapts an episode from Foxe that features a young boy threatened with whipping for bringing flowers to the princess. Foxe, who valued facts over motifs, records that a three-year-old boy brought "her grace floures, which likewise he did to other prisoners."[26] When the boy is accused of serving as a go-between for Elizabeth and Earl of Devonshire, her jailers tell him,

> thou shalt be whipped if thou come any more to the Lady Elizabeth, or the Lord Courtney [...] Whereupon the childes father was commaunded to permit the boy no more to come vp into theyr chambers. The next daye, as her grace was walking in the garden, the childe peeping in at a hole in the doore, cried vnto her, saying: mistres, I can bring you no more flowers.[27]

The play excises the context of political conspiracy, no other prisoners are mentioned, and when the boy gives a nosegay to Elizabeth, the Constable seizes him and orders his men to "take him away, / Let him be soundly whipt I charge you" (D3v). The Foxean version presents an array of unique examples of Catholic cruelty and Protestant suffering, but Heywood performs the work of a hagiographer in revising the episodes of Elizabeth's trials to mirror virgin martyrdom.

Preserving Miracles

The way in which *If You Know Not Me, You Know Nobody* diverges from Foxe's report of events can be explained as dramatic license up until this point in the narrative. In staging Elizabeth's trial, imprisonment, and torture by proxy, Heywood has not yet quit the martyrological paradigm of the *Book of Martyrs* for the *Golden Legend*. But he goes there in the second half of the play when he continues to translate Foxe's "The Miraculous Preservation" so that *If You Know Not Me, You Know Nobody* preserves and revitalizes the miracles of hagiography. Virgin martyrdom emerges more obviously as Elizabeth imitates both Christ and the virgins of medieval legends.

When Elizabeth is transferred from the Tower to the custody of Sir Henry Bedingfeld[28], a Catholic who regards Elizabeth as "the Queenes enemy," she defines her

---

[26] Foxe 1570, 2:2291.
[27] Foxe, 2:2291.
[28] The historical Sir Henry Bedingfeld or Bedingfield is rendered as "Beningfeild" throughout Heywood's play. I retain the quarto's spelling when quoting directly from the play.

own suffering as sharing in Christ's sacrifice (E1r). Specifically, she tells the English people who witness her sad progress, "tanquam Ovis," which Foxe glosses in his marginalia as "like a shepe to the slaughter" and Heywood has a common character translate to the audience as the versified "like to a sheep, that's to the slaughter's led" (E1r).[29] This reference to the paschal image of the lamb of God (*agnus Dei*) serves a similar function as the detail of a dove descending from heaven during St. Margaret's tortuous bath. The saints are sanctified in their imitation of Christ and onlookers witness to this. It is important that those who are audience to Elizabeth's suffering are not a few elite members of the English aristocracy, but that they represent the social body of England. Elizabeth's religious suffering figures as a national sacred struggle.

In dramatizing the Virgin Queen's ascent to the throne as *vita*, Heywood dropped Elizabeth's historic cult of virginity for the virgin martyrdom perfected by medieval hagiographers. Representational practices of Elizabeth shifted in the 1580s when the unmarried queen aged beyond the possibility of producing an heir, causing anxiety about royal succession. Between the early 1580s and 1603, the year of Elizabeth's death, her problematic maidenhood was fashioned into a mark of exceptional monarchical divinity.[30] In portraiture and literature, as many critics have established, the image of Elizabeth appropriated the terms and metaphors associated with Christian virginity and sacrifice, including that of the Virgin Mary. Like Christ's mother, Elizabeth enjoyed the glory of a life of perpetual virginity that did not end in martyrdom. But Heywood's play emphatically divides Elizabeth's virginal sanctity from association with the Virgin Mary inasmuch as *If You Know Not Me, You Know Nobody* associates the Virgin Mary with Catholicism and Elizabeth with the cause of the Protestant Reformation.

Traditional sainthood separates virgins, even virgin queens, from virgin martyrs. Holy virginity relies on a rejection of all other suitors in favor of an erotic spiritual relationship with Christ the Lover. In St. Agnes's rejection of a Roman pagan official, she speaks of her "louer" who "I haue gyuen my faith / To hym I haue comanded my herte / whan I loue hym thenne am I chaste / and whan I touche hym thene am I pure and clene / And whan I take hym thenne am I a virgyne / Thys is the loue of my god."[31] Agnes does not explain her status as virgin as the absence of bodily sexual activity, but articulates it as something that she becomes

---

[29] Foxe 1570, 2:2292.

[30] Roy Strong categorizes the presentational portraiture of the Elizabethan era as "neo-Gothic," rather than Renaissance. See *The Cult of Elizabeth: Elizabethan Portraiture and Pageantry* (Berkeley and Los Angeles, CA: University of California Press, 1977), 47. See also, Philippa Berry, *Of Chastity and Power: Elizabethan Literature and the Unmarried Queen* (London: Routledge, 1989); Susan Doran, "Virginity, Divinity and Power: The Portraits of Elizabeth," in *The Myth of Elizabeth*, eds. Susan Doran and Thomas S. Freeman (New York, NY: Pagrave MacMillan, 2003), 171–199; Catherine Loomis, *The Death of Queen Elizabeth I: Remembering and Reconstructing the Virgin Queen* (New York: Palgrave Macmillan, 2010); Louis Montrose, *The Subject of Elizabeth: Authority, Gender, and Representation* (Chicago: University of Chicago Press, 2006); and, especially, Helen Hackett, *Virgin Mother, Maiden Queen: Elizabeth I and the Cult of the Virgin Mary (New York, NY: St. Martin's Press, 1995)*.

[31] Caxton, *Golden Legend*, cxix verso.

through spousal love. Put differently, one might be born a virgin, but one becomes a virgin martyr. As the brides of Christ, virgin martyrs experience metaphysical marriage ceremonies and receive visions of heaven.[32] These miracles verify that the saints have knowledge of an eternal life as *sponsa Christi* after earthly martyrdom.

Two dreams in *If You Know Not Me, You Know Nobody* signal that Elizabeth has progressed from unmarried princess to *sponsa Christi* and her "crown of martyrdom" is imminent. Heywood's virgin fears that the immediate future "Wilbe my graue" (F2v) and then experiences a premonitory nightmare in which "she herself was cast into a dungeon, / Where enemyes enuiron'd her about, / Offering their weapons to her naked brest" (F4v). Clarentia (Clarity), her handmade, receives her own dream that complements and concludes Elizabeth's nightmare of political execution with a virginal vision

> of weddings, and of flowers,
> Me thought I was within the finest garden,
> That euer mortall eie did yet behould,
> The strayght me thought some of the cheife were pickt
> To dresse the bride, O'twas the rarest show,
> To see the bride goe smiling longst the streets,
> As if she went to happynes eternall. (F4v)

The two dreams, together, narrate the sequence of virgin martyrdom from an earthly violent death to a heavenly consummation. The interpretation of the execution and nuptial imagery is further constricted to martyrdom when another trusted servant hears of them in sequence and responds, "O most vnhappy dreame" (F4v). The traditional virginity that Foxe "de-privileges" is re-privileged as a sanctifying aspect of Elizabeth's metaphorical martyrdom, which is soon completed as her enemies are vanquished and she receives her crown.

Heywood combines hagiographic allusion with theatrics to canonize Elizabeth. The hagiographic dramaturgy of the play relies as much on a series of highly theatrical pageants as it does the narrative structure of saints' lives and *sponsa Christi* motifs to transform Elizabeth's story into a metaphysical struggle.[33] The symbolic system at work embraces a miraculous theatricality derived from late medieval

---

[32] When threatened with torment, Dorothy replies that "I am al redy to suffre it / for the loue of my spouse Ihesu cryste / In whose gardyn ful of delyces I haue gadred roses spyces and apples." Caxton, *Golden Legend*, ccclxxxvi verso. In Katherine's legend, the saint is taken up to a celestial hall of virgins, angels, and heavenly music. There, the infant Christ "espoused hir / in ioynyng hym self to hir by spirituel maryage." Caxton, *Golden Legend*, ccclxxix recto.

[33] Heywood's play resurfaced on the Restoration stage, where the extensive pageantry proved too much for Samuel Pepys in 1667. His diary entry describes "the most ridiculous" play as extending its pageantry to also include a milkmaid who sings "a song to Elizabeth." *Diary of Samuel Pepys VIII*, eds. Robert Latham and William G. Matthews (Berkeley and Los Angeles, CA: University of California Press, 2000), 388. The milkmaid was likely a later addition supplied by a part in *England's Elizabeth* in which the imprisoned princess desires the life of a milkmaid.

devotional culture as well as Reformation iconography anchored by demonic Catholic clerics and the vernacular Bible. These seemingly disparate elements of religious knowledge fuse together to form a complete cycle of virgin martyrdom and create a saint play for the Jacobean public.

The stage business that identifies Elizabeth as a Protestant involves a vernacular Bible. In a pivotal moment before Elizabeth enters her prison chamber in the Tower, she instructs her handmaid, "Clarentia, reach my book," and then she turns back to the Constable once she holds it and says, "now leade me where you please / From sight of day; or in a dungeon; I shall see to pray" (C4v). The book, which remains with Elizabeth throughout the play, fortifies her and repels her foes. The Constable declares that he desires to

> Lay her in a dungeon where her eyes
> Should not haue light to read her prayer booke,
> So would I danger both her soule and body
> Cause she an alyen is to vs catholiques. (D2r)

The identification of Elizabeth's property as a "prayer booke" is a purposeful misdirection. She uses the text for prayer, but its content is ambiguous.[34] It is later revealed to be a vernacular Bible. The representation of Elizabeth's passion with that icon of the Reformation transfers to the stage a tradition of Protestant martyrology and book culture in order to present the opposition between Protestantism and Catholicism primarily through visual differentiation and theatrical form. For Foxe and other reformers, the reading body and textual piety functioned as a symbol of Protestant faith. As John King observes, reformers imagined themselves as scriptural readers in direct opposition to a Catholicism that favored nontextual devotional practices over literate piety.[35] In *If You Know Not Me, You Know Nobody*, the Bible signals Elizabeth's steadfast Protestantism as it also becomes her theatrical and spiritual defense against the devil characters. Heywood creates his angels and devils especially through blocking and stage action. Much of the work that renders historical events as hagiographical episodes occurs through theatricality.

At the center of the play are three dumb shows that translate Reformation history into necessary episodes of *vita*. The first dumb show occurs during Elizabeth's captivity in the Tower. After the Constable seizes her dinner and orders her

---

[34] The Foxean version records that "she called to her Gentlewoman for her booke, desiryng God not to suffer her to build her foundation vpon the sandes, but vpon the rocke," but the Constable does not oppose the book. Foxe 1570, 2:2290. There is extensive detail about the Constable's dishonorable cruelty, but that conflict centers on Elizabeth's diet.

[35] John N. King, *Foxe's Book of Martyrs and Early Modern Print Culture* (Cambridge: Cambridge University Press, 2006), 182. See also James Simpson, *Burning to Read: English Fundamentalism and Its Reformation Opponents* (Cambridge, MA: Harvard University Press, 2007).

92   THE RENAISSANCE OF THE SAINTS AFTER REFORM

confined to her cell, Sussex and Howard petition the queen to give Elizabeth leave to walk the gardens:

> *A dumb show.*
> Enter six with torches.
> *Tame* and *Shandoyse*, bare-headed, *Phillip* and
> *Mary* after them: then *Winchester, Beningfeild*, and
> *Attendants:* at the other dore, *Sussex* & *Howard*,
> *Sussex* deliuers a peticion to the King, the King
> Receiues it, shewes it to the Queene, she shewes
> It to *Winchester* and to *Beningfeild*: they storme, the
> King whispers to *Sussex*, and raises him & *Howard*,
> Giues them a piticion, they take their leaues and
> Depart, the King whispers a little to the Queene.
> *Exeunt.* (D1v)

Dumb shows depict necessary plot points through soundless fast-paced action rather than dialogue. It is not important to know the exact words uttered by the diabolical team of Winchester and Bedingfeld. The gist of their reaction is that Sussex and Howard's petition has foiled their plot and it pains them that Elizabeth will not remain in harsh conditions. The court scene also reminds spectators that although the Constable serves as the nearest vehicle of torment, the first mover in the Catholic scheme is Winchester. Here, Winchester and Bedingfeld become reassociated with the cause of evil through oppositional blocking. In the next dumb show, the most important one of the play, the blocking repeats and the action transitions from mortal opposition to metaphysical attack.

Property Divisions

The central miraculous dumb show of the virgin martyr, her spiritual protectors, and her demonic opposition occurs immediately after dramatic focus returns to her companion stage property, the vernacular Bible. As soon as Elizabeth arrives at Woodstock, "*Beningfeild takes a book and looks / into it*" and asks, "soft what book's this"? (E3v). The text was first referred to as "a prayer book" by the Constable, but only after watching Elizabeth carry it back and forth across the stage as she progressed from one prison to another does Heywood identify it. Bedingfeld here exclaims, "Marry a God. What's here an English bible? [...] Sanctum Maria pardon this prophanation of my heart" (E3v–E4r).[36] The Bible functions

---

[36] This scene does not appear in Foxe, although Heywood adapts the prayer to the Virgin Mary from a digression in Foxe's narrative that is included for "refreshing the reader," a goat that wandered past

symbolically and efficaciously as both a property of Protestantism and spiritual fortification. As James Kearney has shown, the depiction of reading on stage "is the way to both salvation and damnation. Both conversion and apostasy," as in *Doctor Faustus*, "are time and again the consequences of an encounter with text."[37] The Bible maintains Elizabeth's steadfastness and it decodes forms of Catholicism. In the previous encounter with it, the Constable reacted with cruelty and, here, the new jailor proves superstitious and calls for holy water to cleanse himself of Protestant impurity as he prays to the Virgin—the other one, the Catholic one. The book marks a boundary between hagiography predicated on an imitation of Christ, in the case of Elizabeth, and prayer to the Virgin Mary, in the case of Bedingfeld. As the play enacts the sainthood of Elizabeth, it recovers hagiography, namely virgin martyrdom, for Protestantism and through the business with the vernacular Bible it emphatically rejects the Catholic cult of the Virgin Mary.

In the central miraculous dumb show of the play, the Bible counteracts demonic Catholicism. While Elizabeth sleeps at Woodstock, music plays and then the following choreographed action occurs:

> A *dumb show*.
> Enter *Winchester, Constable, Barwick*, and *Fryars*;
> at the other dore 2. *Angels*: the *Fryar* steps to her,
> Offering to kill her: the *Angels* driues them back.
> *Exeunt*. The *Angel* opens the Bible, and puts it in
> Her hand as she sleepes; *Exeunt Angels, she wakes*. (E3v)

This dumb show is a necessary sanctifying miracle. It is also foundational to the translation of literary holiness to theatrical virgin martyrdom. This spectacle builds on the preceding dumb show of the petition and materializes the opposition between Elizabeth and her foes as part of the ongoing battle between God and the devil through the introduction of two angels, two friars, and the demon-repelling properties of the Bible.[38] In its production of a miracle, the dumb show

---

the many security measures on Bedingfeld's estate. When Elizabeth asks a servant to leave the goat, he replies "no by saint Mary (if it like your grace) will I not: for I can not tell whether he be one of the Queenes frendes or no," and takes it to Bedingfeld. Heywood retains the "saint Mary" as code for Catholicism. Foxe 1570, 2:2293.

[37] James Kearney, *The Incarnate Text: Imagining the Book in Reformation England* (Philadelphia, PA: University of Pennsylvania Press, 2009), 142.

[38] The verse that the angel opens the Bible to is "Whoso putteth his trust in the Lord,/Shall not be confounded" from Proverbs 29:25 (D4r). It also appears in *The Song of the Three Holy Children* in the apocrypha. The 1568 Parker Bible translates it as "for there is no confusion vnto the[m] that put their trust in thee" and the 1611 King James Bible as "for they shall not bee confounded that put their truth in thee." Dieter Mehl finds the story, which is another telling of Shadrach, Meshach, and Abednego from the *Book of Daniel*, to give "added force to the miracle" of the dumb show because "the future Queen is symbolically placed in the same situation as the three children in the 'burning fiery furnace' and by divine intervention comes out of the flames like a victorious martyr." "The Late Queen on the Public Stage: Thomas Heywood's *If You Know Not Me You Know Nobody*, Parts I and II," in *Queen Elizabeth I: Past and Present*, ed. Christa Jansohn (Münster, DE: Lit Verlag 2004), 158.

re-forms medieval theatricality as well as Reformation iconography. The scene navigates a history of religious performance in its popular forms, but it does not privilege the reformed imagination over and above a theatrical tradition of staging sanctity that can be traced from fifteenth-century plays and pageantry to the early seventeenth-century *When You See Me, You Know Me*, the Reformation history play that preceded this one. The dumb show of Elizabeth, her book, angels, and "demons," turns the history of English theatre back onto itself through a series of revisions and re-formations. It spins through various iterations of religious knowledge in/as theatre that are not of the past, as Kurt Schreyer has cautioned, but were first produced in specific eras, for specific audiences, and are experienced by the future audiences through particular historical and historiographical relationships to those theatrical pasts.[39] With a final revision to a key scene of *When You See Me, You Know Me*, the momentary dumb show ultimately shoots back into the Jacobean present.

The miraculous dumb show in *If You Know Not Me, You Know Nobody* materializes a tradition of theatrical sanctification that underwent strict revision by mid-sixteenth-century reformers. Reformation dramatists used theatre to address issues of doctrine, advocate for Protestant reforms, and attack the Catholic church. These plays not only demonized Catholic clergy, but also they banished angels.[40] Stage devils continued to appear in Reformation drama in order to "enact whatever opposed individual well-being and the sacramental community," as John Cox demonstrates.[41] However, the utilization of angels to depict the opposite side of things, that is, the support of individual well-being and the sacramental community, dropped out of theatre in the mid-sixteenth-century and appeared rarely in the drama of the professional theatre in the later sixteenth century.[42] *Doctor Faustus* is a notable exception.

The Reformation playwrights John Bale and Lewis Wager depicted sanctity without staging martyrdom or miracles as they appeared in earlier plays and

---

[39] In his study of the Chester Banns and Shakespeare's plays, Schreyer theorizes a performance of "synchronic diachrony," to explain how the post-Reformation Chester Cycle "distinguishes the present time of performance from the city's Catholic past.... Diachronic change is in this way the guarantor of synchronic contact with the past." *Shakespeare's Medieval Craft: Remnants of the Mysteries on the London Stage* (Ithaca, NY: Cornell University Press, 2014), 2, 7.

[40] Peter Womack categorizes traditional hagiography into "four possible gests: conversion, martyrdom, miracle, and withdrawal from the world," and notes that "Lewis Wager's Protestant dramatization of the Mary Magdalen legend (1566) drops both the miraculous story and the eventual sanctification in the wilderness, leaving what is essentially a play about conversion." "Shakespeare and the Sea of Stories," *Journal of Medieval and Early Modern Studies* 29 (1999): 182.

[41] John D. Cox, *The Devil and the Sacred in English Drama, 1350–1642* (Cambridge: Cambridge University Press, 2001), 2.

[42] Previous to the dumb show in *If You Know Not Me, You Know Nobody*, angels appeared in *Three Lords of London* by Robert Wilson, *A Looking-Glass for London and England* (1590) by Robert Greene and Thomas Lodge, and *Doctor Faustus* (1592) by Christopher Marlowe. For the rare use of angels in professional drama, see Holly Crawford Pickett, "Angels in England: Idolatry and Wonder at the Red Bull Playhouse," in *Thunder at the Playhouse: Proceedings from the Fourth Blackfriars Conference*, eds. Peter Kanelos and Matt Kozusko (Selingsgrove, PA: Susquehanna University Press, 2010), 175–99.

pageantry. Bale's *King Johan* (1538) is the earliest text to create a stage martyr through a reformist perspective. In the early thirteenth century, Pope Innocent III excommunicated the king and placed England under interdict. John eventually submitted to the papacy and died shortly thereafter. Drawing on William Tyndale's *Obedience of a Christen Man* (1528), Bale depicted John as a true Christian king who, along with Widow England, is besieged by the regicidal papal minions, Sedition and Dissimulation. The most theatrical sequence of the play stages John's martyrdom. The king's sanctity is defined less through his own actions than through his victimization by demonic monks. On a suicide mission that involves ritual magic, Dissimulation embodies "the malyce of the clergye" as he collects "the poyson of a toade" for two cups of ale, one for himself and one for the king.[43] Convinced that he will ascend to "paradyse" without "that whoreson purgatory," Dissimulation receives advanced absolution from Sedition for the planned regicide.[44] Bale's iconic monk-devil also appears in Foxe's account of King John in the *Book of Martyrs*, in the prose as well as six woodcuts. Two central illustrations show the dead king and the scene of his murder. These two panels are surrounded by four other scenes that depict seditious religious practices: two monks pray over the dead assassin monk, a requiem Mass for the soul of the assassin monk, the assassin monk mixes the poison, and, finally, the monk is absolved by another with accompanied speech of "Ego absoluo te&c," as in *King Johan*. Bale's choice to embody devils in the guise of Catholic clergy transferred to Foxe's woodcuts and through the Foxean imagination of the English Reformation to Heywood's play.

In Wager's *The Life and Repentaunce of Mary Magdalene*, the repentant sinner must overcome the temptations of luxury, sensuality, and vanity, all of which can be understood as the demons of papist practice. The title character, like the reforming church, must rid herself of excess in order to progress from sinner to saint. When the vain Magdalene first appears on stage she does so "triflyng with her garments," an outward sign of her inward excess but the play lacks the romance subplots, miracles, angels, and demons in the saint's medieval legends.[45] The seven deadly sins are exorcised out of her by Christ, but this miracle is performed without the spectacular theatricality of angels and devils at the castle in the Digby *Mary Magdalene*. Reformation dramaturgy located sinfulness not only in Catholicism but also in miraculous staging. Therefore, Wager staged Mary's battle against sin through morality play characters whose assaults on her soul were confined to tactics of courtly seduction rather than otherworldly feats. Katherine Gillen finds that, as a playwright, Bale, "endeavored to distinguish his productions from Catholic miracle plays by creating a theatre of signs (rather than miracles) that accorded

---

[43] John Bale, *King Johan* (London: Printed for the Malone Society by J. Johnson at the Oxford University Press, 1931), lines 2010, 2168.
[44] Bale, *King Johan*, 2039–40.
[45] Lewis Wager, *A new enterlude, neuer before this tyme imprinted, entreating of the life and repentaunce of Marie Magdalene* (London, 1566), sig. A4r.

with Protestant understandings of sacramental representation."[46] The same can be said for Wager. The demonic action of the monks in *King Johan* and the morality play exorcism in the *Life and Repentaunce* present outward signs of damnation and salvation, but they are—and were designed to be—categorically different from the miracles that attend Mary Magdalene in the Digby play.

The demonology of *If You Know Not Me, You Know Nobody* can be traced to *King Johan* as well as to Reformation iconography. Bale revised the repertoire of earlier theatrical demons to identify "traditional religion itself with the devil," notably in the guise of monks and cardinals who serve the arch-enemy of the true Church, the Pope.[47] Marsha S. Robinson notes that Winchester is depicted as the maniacal pursuer of Protestants across Reformation history plays, including the anonymous *Thomas Lord Cromwell* (c.1600), *The Famous History of Sir Thomas Wyatt* (1602) by Thomas Dekker and John Webster, *When You See Me, You Know Me* (1604) by Samuel Rowley, and *The Duchess of Suffolk* (1624) by Thomas Drue.[48] Reformation demonology, therefore, explains Heywood's choice to depict Stephen Gardiner, Bishop of Winchester as *Cardinal* Winchester. Although Gardiner is cast as the archvillain of the Marian age in the *Book of Martyrs*, Foxe never refers to him as "Cardinal," because he never achieved that position and died as the *Bishop* of Winchester. A bishop might be a Protestant or a Catholic, but only Catholic clergy are friars, monks, or cardinals. In creating Winchester a cardinal, Heywood translated the villain of the *Book of Martyrs* into the devil of his saint play.

Heywood's drama with the book in the dumb show also cites and revises the division between Catholicism and Protestantism as represented by the character of Queen Mary in two previous history plays, *The Famous History of Sir Thomas Wyatt* and *When You See Me, You Know Me*. *Sir Thomas Wyatt* begins just as Edward VI is dying and depicts the brief monarchy of Lady Jane Grey, the Wyatt rebellion, and the eventual execution of Jane, her husband, and Thomas after Mary ascends to the throne. Mary's first entrance at the beginning of this play impacts the shape of Elizabeth's Protestant sanctity in Heywood's play. The stage directions instruct, "*Enter Queene Mary with a Prayer Booke in her / hand, like a Nun*," and Dekker and Webster script Mary's first lines to clearly communicate her cloister-like religiosity, "Thus like a Nun, not like a Princesse borne.... Their seuerall pleasures: all their pride and honour, / I haue forsaken for a rich prayer

---

[46] See Katherine Gillen, "Authorial Anxieties and Theatrical Instability in John Bale's Biblical Plays and Shakespeare and Wilkins' *Pericles, Prince of Tyre*," in *Stages of Engagement: Drama and Religion in Post Reformation England*, eds. James D. Mardock and Kathryn R. McPherson (Pittsburgh, PA: Duquesne University Press, 2014), 174.

[47] Cox, *The Devil and the Sacred*, 84–5. In Bale's *The Temptation of Our Lord* (1538), Satan appears in the habit of a monk.

[48] Robinson, *Writing the Reformation*, 16.

Booke" (A4r–v).⁴⁹ Moments later, Sir Henry Bedingfeld enters and announces, "Your Brother King is dead, / And you the catholicke Queene must now succeede" (A4v). It is the only part of the play that names a particular religious confession, but Mary "like a Nun," along with Winchester restores Catholicism to England. The play does not reference saints, except in one aspect. During the Kentish rebellion, led by Wyatt, the two sides both invoke St. George to their separate causes in an almost Hegelian tragic iteration of Shakespeare's *Henry V* speech at Agincourt. As the troops charge, Wyatt invokes, "Saint George for England, Wiat for poore Kent, / Blood lost in Countries quarrel, is nobly spent," and on the side of the Crown, the Duke of Norfolk prays, "God and Saint George, this day fight on our side, / While thus we tame a desperate Rebels pride" (D4v, E1v).

The orthodoxy of England's patron saint also surfaces in *When You See Me, You Know Me*, a play that produces a complex view of the Henrician Reformation. St. George is invoked five times by Charles Brandon and Henry VIII, and when the king plans the ceremonial meeting with the Holy Roman Emperor, Charles V, he includes the icon of the patron saint in the order of the procession, "And with our George and our coller of estate, / Present him with the order of the Garter" (K2v).⁵⁰ The Englishness of St. George is contrasted in the play by the Catholicism of the general cult of the saints, again, through association with Queen Mary.

The status of saints also informs the confessional differences between Mary and Elizabeth at a crucial moment in *When You See Me, You Know Me*, a part of the play that Heywood cites in the angelic dumb show. When Edward VI receives correspondence from his sisters, their confessional differences materialize through traditional and reformed positions toward intercessory prayer. Mary's letter begins, "The blessed Mother of thy redeemer, with all the Angels & / holy Saints be intermissers to preserue thee of Idolatrie, to invocate the Saints for helpe," but Edward resolves to "pray / For preseruation . . . Without the helpe of Saint or cerimonie" (I1r). In contrast, Elizabeth's letter encourages the young prince to "Be dedicate to God onely," and "to shun Idolatrie, / Heaven send thee life to inherite thy election"(I1r). As Walsh argues, the theatrical opposition between the bad Catholic letter and the good Protestant letter exhibits a "clever adaptation of the morality play trope of dueling influences competing for a protagonist's soul."⁵¹ Heywood draws on this trope in the miraculous dumb show, but he revises it so that angels and demons actually materialize. This revision responds to the antecedent of Edward with the letters in Rowley's play by taking the angels out

---

[49] Thomas Dekker and John Webster, *The famous history of Sir Thomas VVyat* (London: Printed by E A for Thomas Archer, 1607). All subsequent in-text parenthetical citations are from this edition. Teresa Grant has observed that "[d]evout women of either branch of Christianity, relying on their prayer-book or bible, became representative in early Jacobean drama for chastity and goodness." Grant, "Drama Queen," 125.

[50] Samuel Rowley, *VVhen you see me, you know mee* (London, 1605). All subsequent in-text parenthetical citations are from this edition.

[51] Walsh, *Unsettled Toleration*, 149.

of Mary's Catholic letter and reassigning them to Elizabeth, the Protestant virgin martyr with the unmediated word of God. What is remarkable about the appearance of the heavenly beings is, as Astrid Stilma argues, that "angels are not really needed on stage" to show the opposition between metaphysical good and evil because the stage devil alone functions as "an agent of order."[52] Indeed, order already is established in *If You Know Not Me, You Know Nobody* through Winchester, the Constable, and Bedingfeld's Catholic opposition to Elizabeth and the Bible. What the dumb show clarifies through the appearance of the friars on the Catholic side, the demons developed by Reformation visual culture, and the angels on Elizabeth's side, is that the play represents a spiritual struggle in which God intervenes with a miracle to sanctify the virgin martyr. The miracle on stage can be understood as allegorical or as efficacious. Its ambiguity, accomplished by the lack of verbal reference to doctrinal definitions that are present in other Reformation-era plays, allows it to be interpreted as both. What is not ambiguous, however, is the confessional identity of the miracle. It is a Protestant.

The Ascension of the Saint Play

Following the dumb show, the play completes Elizabeth's theatrical *vita* through additional pageantry that presents martyrdom, divine retribution, and heavenly coronation, the final parts of virgin martyrdom. Saints are preserved as devils and tyrants are struck down. This sequence occurs in the play's third and final dumb show. After Elizabeth's handmaid, Clarentia, relates the dreams of assassination and *sponsa Christi* imagery, the scene abruptly ends and the one that follows is a funeral procession intended to be understood as the foreshadowed martyrdom.

> Enter, A dumb show: six Torches.
> *Sussex* bearing the Crowne, *Howard* bearing the
> Scepter, the *Constable* the Mace, *Tame* the Purse,
> *Shandoyse* the Sword, *Phillip* and *Mary*; after them
> The *Cardinall Poole, Beningfeild* & *Attendants: Phil-*
> *lip* and *Mary* confers; he takes leaue, and *Exit.*
> Nobles bring him to the dore, and returne; she
> Fales in a swound; they comfort her; a dead march.
> Enter foure with the herse of *Winchester*, with
> The Scepter and Purse lying on it, the *Queen* takes
> The Scepter and Mace, and giues it *Cardinall Poole*; a
> Sennet, and *Exeunt Omnes, preter Sussex.* (G1r)

---

[52] Astrid Stilma, "Angels, Demons and Political Action in Two Early Jacobean History Plays," *Critical Survey* 23, no. 2 (2011): 23.

Building on premonitions of martyrdom, Mary's swoon and the funeral march indicate the death of the virgin martyr. Instead, God has intervened vengefully. The end of the dumb show communicates that Winchester has died and his office is transferred to Cardinal Poole. More news follows. Cardinal Poole, Winchester's "more base" replacement, and the queen also take ill and soon die (G1r). Yet, Elizabeth is "still preseru'd, and still her foes do fall" (G1r). The sudden deaths, like the preceding dumb show of the good book, demonstrate the power of God and Christianity over the devil and Catholicism.

The final scene of the play depicts Elizabeth's ascension to the throne of England and this event structurally parallels martyrdom and ascension to heaven in *vitae*. Two contrasting coronation pageants bookend the plot of the play, those of Mary and Elizabeth, respectively. Mary's first entrance at the beginning of the play occurs in a small coronation pageant that precedes her tyrannical assumption of the throne and Elizabeth's arrest.

> *Enter Tame bearing the purse: Shandoyse the Mace: Howard*
> *The Septer; Sussex the Crowne: then the Queene, after her*
> *The Cardinall, Sentlow, Gage, and attendants.* (A3v)

Mary's pageant contains the necessary elements of a royal procession, but Elizabeth's upstages hers:

> *A Sennet. Enter 4. Trumpetors: after them Sargeant Trumpeter with a Mace, after him Purse-bearer,* Sussex *with Crown,* Howard *the scepter,* Cõstable *with the Cap of mayntenãce,* Shandoyse *with the Sword,* Tame *with the Coller and a* George, *foure Men bearing vp her trayne, six gentle-men* Pensioners, *the* Queene *takes state.* (G3r)

The second coronation pageant dwarfs Mary's and exchanges the patron devil of Catholicism, Winchester, for the patron saint of England. Among Elizabeth's royal accoutrements is an object missing from Mary's procession—the "George" carried by Tame. The Protestant virgin martyr is on the side of St. George and other acceptable saints. Elizabeth's final sanctification in the play occurs when she is reunited with the companion of her passion. The Mayor of London presents the new Virgin Queen with the English Bible, and she receives it by identifying herself with the formerly captive corpus:

> This booke that hath so long conceald it selfe,
> So long shutvp, so long hid; now Lords see,
> We here vnclapse, for euer it is free:
> Who lookes for ioy, let him this booke adore. (G4r)

In this final speech, Elizabeth moves from a symbiotic relationship with the book to conflating her story of sanctity with the icon of the Reformation. According to Elizabeth Williamson, the staging of the coronation pageant at the end of the play "reminds its audience that Elizabeth's public image, which was based on Protestant ideals about the immateriality of faith, was very much rooted in physical gestures and in the Bible itself as a material object."[53] As a martyr, Elizabeth suffered for and protected the book. The book, in turn, remained her fellow sufferer and also functioned as a miraculous shield against demonic forces that aimed to destroy Elizabeth and English Protestantism.

A Catholic Interlude up North

Shortly after *If You Know Not Me, You Know Nobody* premiered in London, another saint play popped up in Yorkshire. On 7 July 1614, Sir John Yorke of Nidderdale and members of his household were found guilty of hosting a seditious interlude and "fined and imprisoned for a scandalous play acted in favour of Popery."[54] Thus was the conclusion of the lengthy trial that centered on a performance of *St. Christopher* at Gouthwaite Hall, Sir John's home, during the post-Christmas season of 1609.[55] *St. Christopher*, a lost play, is unique in the study of saint plays not only due to its association with Catholic recusancy but also because the play retains much of the late medieval legend of the saint. Yet, the play's association with sedition did not stem from the part of the play that featured the *vita* of St. Christopher. The parts of the play that triggered the multi-year legal investigation are the ones that reiterated and flipped the oppositional terms of sanctity in *If You Know Not Me, You Know Nobody* and did so through overt theological disagreement. *St. Christopher* contained an interlude that featured a disputation of religion, something that had been illegal since the early Elizabethan era when "The Queen's majesty straightly forbid all manner [of] interludes to be played ... wherein either matters of religion or of the governance of the estate of the commonweal shall be handled or treated."[56] For the Jacobean government, the inclusion of the St. Christopher legend was not controversial. The government

---

[53] Elizabeth Williamson, *The Materiality of Religion in Early Modern English Drama* (Farnham, UK: Ashgate, 2009), 167.
[54] *Calendar of State Papers Domestic: James I, 1611–18*, ed. Mary Anne Everett Green (London: Her Majesty's Stationery Office, 1858), 242.
[55] Legal proceedings began in 1611 and did not end until the final depositions were taken in 1614 and a verdict delivered. A number of witnesses place the play during twelfth night, although a close servant of Sir John testifies that *St. Christopher* occurred nearer to Candlemas. The Christmas season could last from the Epiphany until Candlemas or even Shrove Tuesday. See The National Archive (TNA): STAC 8/19/10 Fol. 24.
[56] Paul L. Hughes and James F. Larkin, C.S.V., eds., *Tudor Royal Proclamations, Vol. II: The Later Tudors (1553–1587)* (New Haven, CT: Yale University Press, 1969), 115–116.

seized on the religious nonconformity of the play's hosts and, especially, on the use of theatre as theological subversion in the debate episode.

St. Christopher circulates in the study of Shakespeare due to the repertory of the acting troupe that performed the play. The Simpsons were not a London company of actors, but they also were not amateurs as Siobhan Keenan has established.[57] The Yorkshire troupe specialized in recent romance-inflected drama produced at the Globe, Blackfriars, and the Red Bull.[58] Although there is no extant text of *St. Christopher*, the other three plays—*The Travels of Three English Brothers*, "Kinge Lere," and *Pericles*—were published between 1605 and 1608 and available in quarto. Paul Whitfield White notes that *St. Christopher* "drew extensively on the 'green world' of folk customs and medieval romance."[59] While the three other plays do not all feature a green world, they do retain elements of romance. The lesser known play, *The Travels of Three English Brothers* (1607) John Day, William Rowley, and George Wilkins, follows the Sherley brothers on their separate passages through the Mediterranean and the Ottoman Empire.[60] The play mixes Elizabethan clowning, a Venetian Jew, the torture of a Christian by Muslims, battle scenes, and concludes in a reconciliatory mode. The chorus, Fame, ends the play with a monologue that situates each of the three brothers in Spain, Persia, and England, respectively. As Fame speaks, he "*giues to each a prospectiue glasse*" through which "*they / seeme to see one another, and offer to em- / brace at which Fame parts them.*"[61] The legal documents do not name the author of "Kinge Lere," but both the anonymous Elizabethan play and Shakespeare's version were available, the former having been published in 1605 and the latter in 1606.[62] If the Simpsons chose the play based on a preference for medieval religious aesthetics then there are arguments for both versions. On the one hand, the *pietà* of Cordelia and Lear in Shakespeare's version momentarily materializes grief through an icon of Marian religious affect. On the other hand, as Douglas Arrell argues, the earlier *King Leir*, with its "references to various Catholic beliefs and practices, including prayer beads, purgatory, pilgrimage, nuns and cloisters, blessing oneself

---

[57] Siobhan Keenan, "The Simpsons Players of Jacobean Yorkshire and the Professional Stage," *Theatre Notebook* 67 (2013): 16–35.

[58] Part of the troupe's defense of playing without license was that the plays came from published books purchased in London.

[59] Paul Whitfield White, *Drama and Religion in English Provincial Society, 1485–1660* (Cambridge: Cambridge University Press, 2008), 130.

[60] The play was entered into the Stationer's Register on 29 June 1607, and the quarto was printed by George Eld for John Wright. Although the Queen Anne's Men were associated with the Red Bull theatre, the Stationer's Register attribution assigns the play to The Curtain.

[61] George Wilkins, John Day, and William Rowley, *The trauailes of the three English brothers* [. . .] (London: John Wright, 1607), H4v.

[62] *The True Chronicle of King Leir*, part of the Queen's Men's repertory, was first entered into the Stationer's Register in 1594, although no quarto from that period survives. It was, again, entered on 8 May 1605, and shortly thereafter printed by Simon Stafford for John Wright. Q1 of Shakespeare's *Lear* was entered into the Stationer's Register on 26 November 1607, and printed by Nicholas Okes for Nathaniel Butter in 1608. "Kinge Lere" is mentioned in the deposition of William Harrison, TNA STAC 8/19/10, Fol. 29.

(making the sign of the cross) and swearing by Mary and the saints," is also a likely contender.[63] The final play, *Pericles, Prince of Tyre*, by Wilkins and Shakespeare, was published in 1609. Whether by design or accident, all four plays—the two possibilities for their "King Leare," *Three English Brothers*, and *Pericles*—indicate that the Simpsons specialized in a repertory of romantic wandering due to the accidents of fortune or God, something that *St. Christopher* featured as well.[64]

The late medieval English legend of St. Christopher is a two-part narrative in which a story of romance precedes post-conversion acts of sanctity.[65] This legend remained well known even after the Reformation. For example, a few years after the trial a Jacobean anti-Catholic tract reproduced it as an example of the fabulous use of the sign of the cross as an apotropaic gesture in saints' lives:

> Saint *Christopher* being a Giant of twelue cubits in height, determined with himselfe to serue none but the greatest King in the world: and therefore being in seruice to a great King, he spied him crossing himselfe against the Diuell: wherefore perceiuing that he was afraid of the Diuell, he went to serue him as one greater then the former, and perceiuing that the Diuell auoyded the sight of a crosse, he asked him, why he did so? to whom the Diuell answered, that there was a man called Christ which was hanged on the Crosse, in feare of whom, as oft as he saw the signe of the Crosse he fled from it, for which cause Saint *Christopher* perceiuing that Christ was a greater King, renounced the Deuill, and betooke himselfe to the seruice of Christ, and was called *Christopher*, whereas before his name was *Reprobus*.[66]

In the next episode, the newly christened giant becomes a holy hermit who helps travelers across a river. A child appears and asks Christopher to bear him across the water, but "the child was heuy as leed," and the saint fears he will drown, but he prevails.[67] The child is revealed to be Christ. Christopher then travels to Lycia where the city leaders "supposed that he had be a fool," but he proves an excellent evangelist and converts the Lycians before suffering martyrdom.[68] The English St. Christopher legend, like the St. George legend, begins as a romance and then transforms into a martyrdom as the saint changes locations. In the Thornton

---

[63] Douglas Arrell, "*King Leir* at Gowthwaite Hall," *Medieval & Renaissance Drama in England* 25 (2012): 88. An additional consideration is the fact that both *The Travels of Three English Brothers* and *King Leir* could have been purchased at John Wright's shop.

[64] *Pericles* was entered in the Stationers' Register on 20 May 1608, and printed by William White and Thomas Creede for Henry Gosson in early 1609, which would mean a recent acquisition for the Simpsons. The play is also mentioned by Harrison in his deposition. TNA STAC 8/10/10, Fol. 29.

[65] Versions of the legend appear in the *Early South English Legendary*, the *Gilte Legende*, and the *Golden Legend*.

[66] Thomas Beard, *A retractiue from the Romish religion* (London: printed by William Stansby, 1616), 435–6.

[67] Caxton, *Golden Legend*, ccxxvi recto.

[68] Caxton, *Golden Legend*, ccxxvi recto.

Manuscript *Vita Sancti Cristofori*, a unique Middle English life of the saint that is grouped with romances rather than devotional literature, the saint performs as he does in other medieval legends with the added characteristic of wandering the sorts of landscapes that are populated by folk figures. The Thornton life narrates that "he wandirde Este & Weste, / Thorgh wyldirnes and whilde forest, / Many a mountayne & many a valaye."[69] In fact, this wandering through wild forests occurs twice between his different stages of conversion, first to find the devil and then to find Christ, the sort of pattern of repetition welcomed by dramatic form.

Although the documents associated with *Attorney General v. Yorke* are far less concerned with the saint than they are with the defamation of the church and seditious behavior, the testimony of witnesses and the accused reveal that *St. Christopher* represented the legend of the saint and merged it with folklore. The play began with "Raphabus a wilde man appearlled all in greene, with a greene Garland about his head that neither feared God nor the Diuell," but would serve the greatest power.[70] Reprobus is sometimes accompanied on stage by a servant/fool "who in Jeasteinge manner made sporte to the people."[71] He pledges to Lucifer's service. A hermit approaches Reprobus but cannot convert him and leaves. Lucifer returns to the stage with Reprobus and then the hermit also enters dressed as a doctor of divinity, "attired with a gown" as well as a "Cornerd Capp on his head,& a Crosse of wood on his shoulder."[72] At the sight of the cross, Lucifer shrinks back and admits that he fears not the cross, "but the Adored Jewe thereupon executed w∧ch was his enemie."[73] The hermit then says to Reprobus, "yo∧u may see what vertue there is in this Crosse."[74] Two separate witnesses, one who was in the audience at Gouthwaite and another at an earlier performance at Ellerbeck, testified that a dispute occurred between a Green Man and another character with "a Cornerd capp & a blacke gowne and a Cross on his shoulder."[75] Lucifer's defeat converts Reprobus and the conversion, in turn, causes Lucifer to go "away casteing fire about."[76] The hermit returns, gives Reprobus penance, and an angel appears who christens him Christopher. After that, "Rephabus ... carried Christ over the water."[77]

The use of the traditional St. Christopher legend in the play reflects a revitalization of medieval English hagiography. The version of the legend captured

---

[69] Carl Horstmann, ed., "Vita Sancti Cristofori," in *Altenglische Legenden, Neue Folge* (Heilbronn: Henniger,1881), 454–66, lines 12-14. The life is also available in *The Thornton manuscript (Lincoln Cathedral Ms. 91)*, comp. Robert Thornton, Facsimile of the original manuscript printed by Derek Brewer and A.E.B. Owen (New York: British Book Centre 1975), fol. 122b.
[70] TNA STAC 8/19/10, Fol.6.
[71] TNA STAC 8/19/10, Fol.6.
[72] TNA STAC 8/19/10, Fol.6.
[73] TNA STAC 8/19/10, Fol.6.
[74] TNA STAC 8/19/10, Fol.11.
[75] TNA STAC 8/19/10, Fol. 10, Fol. 11.
[76] TNA STAC 8/19/10, Fol.6.
[77] TNA STAC 8/19/10, Fol.1.

by the Thornton manuscript informs the Green Man or wild man figuration of Reprobus at the beginning of the play. In chapter 2, I argued that the St. Dunstan plays continue a tradition of juxtaposing sacred and folk figures, such as Dunstan and Robin Goodfellow, and conflating romance and hagiography in theatrical contexts, such as the pageants that cast St. Margaret as St. George's helpless maiden. Whatever the origins of the *St. Christopher* play are, whether it began as a parish play, as Paul Whitfield White suspects, or if it was devised by the Simpsons, the way the play materializes a folk figure with the saint reflects available models of staging saints in drama and pageantry.[78] This use of medieval hagiography stands in contrast to Counter-Reformation Catholic versions of saints' lives that excised romance and reverted to more ancient formulations of martyrdom. In the late sixteenth-century Spanish *Golden Legend*, which was translated into English and smuggled onto the island, the *vita* of Christopher begins at the end of the medieval English version: Christopher is a successful evangelist whose preaching effects conversions and, consequently, earns him persecution from the tyrannical pagan king of Lycia; the saint remains steadfast against sexual seduction, idolatry, and torture, before being tied to a tree and shot with arrows, an ordeal he survives before his final beheading.[79] There is no wandering.

St. Christopher was not a Catholic saint play. Its conversion to Catholicism occurred when it played in Catholic households and the Simpsons introduced "a disputation" between a Catholic priest and a minister of the Church of England that "toucheth of matters of religion wherein he that plaied the Englishe minister was ou[er]come."[80] As described by deponent William Symonds, the interlude began "After Rephabus had carried Christ over the water," which suggests that the interlude was appended to the end of the play.[81] In fact, two separate deponents describe the evening's entertainment as "two playes or Interludes acted and played."[82] As actors and other witnesses later testified, the Simpsons performed *St. Christopher* "open in town" and at Protestant houses, but they only performed the priest-and-minister bit for Catholic households.[83] Gouthwaite Hall was notorious

---

[78] White writes that the play may have begun as "part of the revels tradition of the Simpsons' own home parish of Egton and retained in their repertory after they upgraded from parish players to a noble-household sponsored troupe." *Drama and Religion in English Provincial Society, 1485–1660*, 153. Phebe Jensen wonders if they might be derived from the efforts of educated, lay Catholics "making a concerted effort to re-create late medieval dramatic culture," like the Stonyhurst Pageants, "Recusancy, Festivity, and Community: The Simpsons at Gowlthwaite Hall," *Reformation* 6 (2002): 93.

[79] Alonso de Villegas, *Flos Sanctorum* (Saint-Omer, 1621), 499–502. Although the Flos Sanctorum *life* of Christopher did not appear in English until 1628, it appeared in the original Spanish version in the late sixteenth century. I cite it here to demonstrate the difference between Continental Catholic hagiography and the medieval English legend's tendency toward romance.

[80] TNA STAC 8/19/10, Fol. 131.

[81] TNA STAC 8/19/10, Fol. 1.

[82] TNA STAC 8/19/10, Fol. 24, Fol. 50.

[83] TNA STAC 8/19/10, Fol. 1. Actor Richard Simpson testified that St. Christopher was "a printed booke" and the troupe claimed they only performed plays that were performed on the public professional stages and published. The actors also defended their performance at Gouthwaite by repeatedly denying that the interlude between the minister and the priest occurred at all. TNA STAC 8/19/10, Fol. 24, Fol. 29.

for its Catholicism. Although the persecution of Catholics had diminished since the executions of priests and priest-hiders in the late Elizabethan era and would not fully restart until the aftermath of the Powder Plot, the surveillance and punishment of Yorkshire recusants was underway prior to late 1605.[84] Fines, confiscations, and, even, executions of lay Catholics occurred.[85] Witnesses described Sir John as "popishly affected" and that Dame Julian, his wife, was a recusant in the true sense of the word. She remained absent from church on Sunday and holy days. Some deponents also testified that the Yorkes' servants and tenants were similarly "backwards in Religion and popishly affected" and that Catholic vestments and service books could be found on the estate.[86]

For the audiences at Gouthwaite and other Catholic households, the performance did not conclude with the episode of St. Christopher carrying the Christ child. Instead, after *St. Christopher* ended, an afterpiece of Yorkshire Catholic agitprop began. A priest and minister enter, dispute, and then exit. A conjuror comes out and calls up a devil with the words, "Ho! Telryon! Ascende!"[87] The conjuror, who behaves like an Elizabethan magician, then sends the devil Telryon to his master in hell to bid him to return. The conjuror continues performing magic until Telryon reenters with Lucifer and "his trayne" of other devils to a "flaunt of fyre."[88] The conjuror speaks with the prince of hell and then they exit the stage. The priest and minister return with the priest besting the minister in a theological discussion. The minister holds a Bible as defense of his theology and the priest deems it insufficient; in the priest's defense, he has the cross, likely repurposed from the hermit in *St. Christopher*.[89] As Williamson has established, crosses and crucifixes appeared in other early modern plays and their status and meanings shifted in performance.[90] The cross became a Catholic means of defense when the priest used it as a weapon against the Bible-toting minister. This part of the interlude, then, recodes as Catholic the previous scene of universal Christian conversion in the St. Christopher legend. During the debate, a fool "claps the English minister on the shoulder and mocked him . . . and said, Well, thou must away anon!"[91] After this, "the devells with thundering and lightning and with great noyse compassed the minister about and carryed him away as it were to hel."[92] The audience at Gouthwaite cheered the minister's final exit.[93] An angel enters, takes the priest's

---

[84] Edward Peacock, ed., *A List of the Roman Catholics in the County of York in 1604* (London, 1872).
[85] Thomas Welbourne and John Fulthering were executed at York on 1 August and William Brown was executed at Ripon on 5 September. In 1608, unrelated to the Powder Plot, the priest Matthew Flathers was executed at York on 21 March. See Charles Dodd, *Dodd's Church History of England, From the Commencement of the Sixteenth Century to the Revolution in 1688* (New York, 1841), 179–80.
[86] TNA STAC 8/19/10, Fol. 10.
[87] TNA STAC 8/19/10, Fol. 1.
[88] TNA STAC 8/19/10, Fol. 1.
[89] TNA STAC 8/19/10, Fol. 17.
[90] Elizabeth Williamson, "Persistence and Adaptation: Staging the Cross at Home and Abroad," in *The Materiality of Religion in Early Modern English Drama* (New York: Routledge, 2009), 109–48.
[91] TNA STAC 8/19/10, Fol. 12.
[92] TNA STAC 8/19/10, Fol. 1.
[93] TNA STAC 8/19/10, Fol. 12.

hand, and leads him off stage, possibly to musical accompaniment. Like the dumb show in *If You Know Not Me, You Know Nobody*, this play stages its religious victory through a scene of opposites—virtue and vice, Catholic and Protestant, and angel and devil—with a Bible.

Attorney General v. Yorke offers some useful distinctions concerning saints, theatre, and religious controversy in the Jacobean era. The terms of religion and the theatre were not one and the same as they had been for reformers in the previous century. John Murphy argues that the dramatization of the St. Christopher legend "challenges the very heart of the reformer's condemnation of the miraculous faith and ... the kind of dramatic action which the reformers sought to expunge from the clerkly drama."[94] Likewise, Phebe Jensen writes that, "this play is Catholic in genre and topic. It is a saint's play, named *Saint Christopher* ... and based on the account of that saint in *The Golden Legend*."[95] But the categories of religious and political orthodoxy had shifted since the mid-sixteenth century and not all saints aligned with Catholicism. The content of the play is less subversively Catholic in the context of the inclusion of SS Dunstan, Richard of Chichester, and Swithin in late Elizabethan plays and pageantry. The Reprobus/Rephabus episode, with its wild man figure, would not have been out of place in a subplot of a Lord Admiral's Men magian play in the 1590s. Furthermore, between 1609 and 1614, Crown investigators did not take issue with the St. Christopher portion of *St. Christopher*. As Jensen also cautions, the "representing of saints and Catholic practices" in drama "may be more upsetting to modern scholars who have internalized a model of Protestant iconoclasm than it was to most Jacobean Protestants."[96] The St. Christopher legend was appropriate for public audiences, whereas the Catholic play—that is, the seditious interlude of the minister, the priest, and the vernacular Bible—enacted a moral drama organized by the values of a marginalized and persecuted community. The same Bible that sanctifies Elizabeth in *If You Know Not Me, You Know Nobody* was translated into an object of theological ridicule before a hostile audience. The interlude, then, can be understood as a particular Yorkshire Catholic response to the more general claims of religion for all England in Heywood's virgin martyr play.

Our Lady of the Blackfriars

In 1613, Katherine of Aragon defended herself and her marriage at Blackfriars. It was a repeat performance—and the outcome of her pleading had not changed since her first appearance at Blackfriars in 1529. *Henry VIII* concerns the political and religious changes of 1528-36, including the divorce and death of Katherine

---

[94] John L. Murphy, *Darkness and Devils: Exorcism and King Lear* (Athens, OH: Ohio University Press, 1984), 112.
[95] Jenson, "Recusancy, Festivity, and Community," 90.
[96] Jensen, "Recusancy, Festivity, and Community," 96.

of Aragon, the marriage and coronation of Anne Boleyn, and the birth of her daughter, the "maiden phoenix" Elizabeth I.[97] Henry's divorce proceedings were held at Blackfriars, the former Dominican priory. There, Katherine famously pleaded with Henry to acknowledge her virginity upon marriage and the truth of their union. And then she exited the court, refusing to come back when summoned. When Shakespeare and Fletcher dramatized this court scene, they gave Katherine a versified version of the historical speech that ends with her rejection of the court's authority concerning the ecclesiastical status of her marriage. Katherine's exit is the mic drop of the Reformation history play. The speech echoes the Virgin Mary against her doubters in medieval biblical plays and it also revises Hermione's wifely pleas at the beginning of *The Winter's Tale* into legal and theological protest. As *Henry VIII* continues and Katherine nears her death, she experiences a vision of "a blessed troop . . . whose bright faces / Cast thousand beams upon me" that recalls the dumb show in *If You Know Not Me, You Know Nobody* (4.2.96–8). Among the plays of Shakespeare and Fletcher, *Henry VIII* is notable for its extensive stage directions and depictions of ceremonies. What is remarkable about Katherine's role in *Henry VIII*, however, is how her death offers a miraculous moment within a play that otherwise rejects the signals of hagiography that translate the life of a person into the *vita* of a saint.

Henry VIII refracts the Jacobean saint play. Shakespeare and Fletcher's play is built on the theatricality of *If You Know Not Me, You Know Nobody*, but it is iconoclastic in that it presents a *vita* in fragments: there is a conversion (baptism), a persecution and trial, a death, and two coronations, but they occur out of order and are distributed across three queens. In Act 2 and Act 3, Katherine undergoes trial and persecution; in Act 4, Anne is crowned at Westminster Abbey and Katherine receives a coronation vision and dies; and, in Act 5, Elizabeth is baptized. Katherine is described as "Saint-like" at her trial, Anne is seen to pray "Saint-like" at her coronation, and Elizabeth is promised a blessed life at her baptism that will only end when "the Saints must haue her".[98] Is it possible that a Catholic, a Lutheran, and an English Protestant can all be so close to saints? The matter is not cleared up by the antagonists who normally orient the dramatic belligerents of virtue and vice. Whereas the Catholics in *If You Know Not Me, You Know Nobody* form a demonic bloc against the virgin martyr and her angels, no such congruent opposition surfaces in the religiously complex *Henry VIII*. There are evil cardinals, to be sure. From the beginning, Cardinal Wolsey and Queen Katherine are at odds. She opposes his exploitative taxation policies on behalf of the English people, and he hounds her to submit to the divorce. Wolsey's sidekick is Cardinal Campeius, known to London audiences as a vice character in *The Whore*

---

[97] Elizabeth was born in 1533 and Katherine died in 1536, but the play rearranges the chronology of these and other events. Katherine dies in Act 3 and Elizabeth is christened in the final scene of Act 5.
[98] *Mr. William Shakespeare's Comedies, Histories, & Tragedies* (London, 1623), 217, 225, and 232. Subsequent in-text paranthetical citations are noted by F.

of Babylon (1607) by Thomas Dekker. The Catholic queen identifies the pretend holiness of the clergy and fears that the "two reverend cardinal virtues" are actually "cardinal sins" (3.1.117–18). By the end of the play, Stephen Gardiner, Bishop of Winchester and stock villain of the Reformation, targets Thomas Cranmer, the reformed Archbishop of Canterbury. The opposition between Winchester and Cranmer works, but Katherine's main devil, Wolsey, is a co-religionist whose downfall also hinges on loyalty to the Pope.

Nonetheless, *If You Know Not Me, You Know Nobody* is essential to the "Saintlike" portrait of Katherine. As Amy Appleford notes, Heywood's play is the "most important intertext" for understanding "Katherine's masquelike dying vision in her private chamber."[99] After Katherine's trial, she retreats with her household to Kimbolton Castle, where her "soul grows sad with troubles" (3.1.1). Her two loyal companions, Griffith and Patience, mirror Elizabeth's servants, Gage and Clarentia. They also offer good counsel. As she ails, Katherine asks Griffith to describe Wolsey's unexpected death, which he does, and she responds by speaking ill of the dead. The play repeatedly represents Katherine as the virtue against the Cardinal's vice, but she falters in her charity toward her departed foe, whom, Griffith tells her, died "full of repentance" (4.2.31). Katherine—who is now styled as Katherine and not Queen in the Folio—catalogs his sins:

> His own opinion was his law. I' th' presence
> He would say untruths, and be ever double
> Both in his words and meaning. He was never,
> But where he meant to ruin, pitiful.
> His promises were, as he then was, mighty,
> But his performance, as he is now, nothing.
> Of his own body he was ill, and gave
> The clergy ill example. (4.2.41–8)

Katherine's account of vice is met by Griffith's recounting of Wolsey's scholarship, wisdom, support of university life, and that at his end, "he died fearing God" (4.2.75). This moves her to confess, "Whom I most hated living, thou hast made me, / With thy religious truth and modesty, / Now in his ashes honor. Peace be with him!" (4.2.80–3). Once reconciled, Katherine tires and experiences a heavenly pageant unlike any other in Shakespeare or Fletcher. It recalls the miraculous dumb show in *If You Know Not Me, You Know Nobody*, but it also lacks the allegorical opposition between heaven and hell. This scene, as "Sad and solemne Musicke" plays, offers only heaven:

---

[99] Amy Appleford, "Shakespeare's Katherine of Aragon: Last Medieval Queen, First Recusant Martyr," *Journal of Medieval and Early Modern Studies* 40 (2010): 154, 155.

The Vision

Enter solemnely tripping one after another, sixe Personages, clad in white Robes, wearing on their heades Garlands of Bayes, and golden Vizards on their faces, Branches of Bayes or Palme in their hands. They first Conge vnto her, then Dance: and at certain Changes, the first two hold a spare Garland ouer her Head, at which the other foure make reuerend Curtsies. Then the two that held the Garland, deliuer the same to the other next two; who obserue the same order in their Changes, and holding the Garland ouer her head. Which done, they deliuer the same Garland to the last two: who likewise obserue the same Order. At which (as it were by inspiration) she makes (in her sleepe) signes of reioycing, and holdeth vp her hands to heauen. And so, in their Dancing vanish, carry the Garland with them (F 226).

Even as this vision cites the miracle in *If You Know Not Me, You Know Nobody*, it does not sanctify in the same way. Katherine's vision is of heavenly coronation, the sort that the Virgin Mary receives in baroque pageants and portraiture in Spain and Italy. In those saturated heavenly scenes, the Virgin is frequently surrounded by a choir of angels above the clouds. Although it is anachronistic, *Henry VIII* imagines a pre-Reformation Spanish Catholic queen within the aesthetics of contemporary Counter-Reformation Spanish Catholicism. The conceit of this baroque aesthetic is that truth resides just beyond the veil or the façade of human encounter. Katherine is both the sole recipient of and sole witness to this ceremony. From her own particular religious perspective, it revises what appears to be a sad unqueened death at Kimbolton into a true vision of heavenly coronation. At the same time, the vision lacks the martyrological antagonism present in the other dumb show. Furthermore, the two coronations in Act 4 of *Henry VIII* are not presented as moral or mortal opposition. Scene One depicts a conversation between three gentlemen Londoners who describe Anne Boleyn's coronation and then the royal procession passes over the stage. Scene Two depicts Katherine with Griffith and Patience at Kimbolton with the heavenly vision. At the earthly coronation, Anne "Cast her fair eyes to heaven and prayed devoutly," just as Katherine does in the heavenly coronation according to the detailed choreography (4.1.101). There is no stark contrast between vice and virtue, heaven and hell. Instead, there is a heavenly consolation awaiting the decrowned dowager queen.

In Heywood's play, the angelic miracle not only sanctified the virgin martyr for her suffering, but also it validated the truth of her cause, that is, of the Protestant Reformation. Katherine's vision is the result of a more personal holiness. The vision does not come from suffering under Wolsey's persecution of her for her religion. Rather, it affirms the truth of her claim at court—that she had not consummated her first marriage—and rewards her for being reconciled with her former earthly opponent. Katherine is not on her way to sainthood but is on pilgrimage for a good death following the prescriptions of the *ars moriendi*. She is saintlike in suffering the excruciating shame of the outcast wife and mustering the will to recognize the merits of the late Cardinal, but she is no martyr. As St. Augustine articulated and Reformation and Counter-Reformation writers repeated, it is not the suffering, but the cause that determines the martyr. Shakespeare and Fletcher's angels, therefore, operate within the bounds of theatrical orthodoxy. They valorize Katherine for her saintlike qualities, but they do not sanctify her for a religious cause. This sort of fragmentation between the saintlike subject and religious truth assigns a holy death to the dowager queen of the old faith while the play also celebrates the coronation of a Lutheran queen and the glorious reign of the Protestant "virgin, / A most unspotted lily" (5.4.69–70). Instead of a singular, unified religious truth, all is true in fragments.

There would be no Catholic saints on the early modern stage—at least not *only* Catholic saints. The inclusion or exclusion of saints in public life hinged on a continuum within English Protestantism, but the saints that signaled Catholicism exhausted the liberality of religious compromise. For example, Thomas Becket was a clear sign not of choosing Rome over Geneva, but of choosing Rome over Canterbury. In chapter 1, as part of the examination of the liturgical calendar in service books in the sixteenth century, I discussed how a test of political and religious orthodoxy was the excision of Becket from the calendar, the litany, and prayers. Other saints remained or returned while Becket was banished. Saints in the theatre functioned similarly in the Elizabethan era. Saints could be mocked, marked off limits, invoked, or fully represented, but their sanctity, however strictly or loosely associated with a version of *imitatio Christi* and Christianity, must not align with Rome over Canterbury. Therefore, St. Christopher can still achieve sainthood while Katherine of Aragon must settle for saintlike.

If You Know Not Me, You Know Nobody relies on a theatrical language of sanctity born of a combination and negotiation of medieval hagiography and Protestant martyrology. Yet, this innovation somewhat obscures the play's religious, social, and political performativity. The play does not recover an established saint. Rather, it composes a theatrical *vita*. The play's presentation of the story of Elizabeth's persecution and triumph through its particular means of hagiographical theatricality enacts sanctity. In doing so, it also offered instruction to other playwrights in how to present new legends of the saints on stage. Just as the *vita* of St. Agnes frequently served as a template of sainthood for other virgin martyrs, Heywood's *life* of Elizabeth, with its angels, devils, books, and miracles, set the terms of theatrical sainthood for the rest of the era. In chapters 4 and 5, I address two clusters of saint plays that follow the pattern of Elizabeth's sanctity in dramatic iterations of English ecclesiastical history and spectacular virgin martyrdom.

4
Old Legends of England

In the legends of the saints, Christ sometimes appears in unrecognizable forms. The tall and brawny St. Christopher carries a small child across the river only to find that he is actually Christ, and, at the end of the martyrdom of St. Dorothy, the Christ child brings the unbelieving Theophilus a basket of heavenly fruit and converts him on the spot. Typologically, the disguised Christ in the legends of the saints mirrors the hidden encounters with the risen Christ in the Gospels. After the resurrection, Christ does not resemble his old form to either Mary Magdalene at the tomb or to Cleophas on the road to Emmaus. Mary addresses him as the gardener and Cleophas thinks he is a traveling stranger. There is confusion over the nature of his shape in this new era. In his wandering and momentary appearances, Christ is not as readily identifiable as he was before. The problem of identifying the resurrected Christ in changed shapes and in new scenarios reflects the transformations of the saints in Jacobean and Caroline tragicomedies. In those plays, the Middle English literary amalgamation of romance and hagiography make new appearances on the Stuart stage.

The saints in *A Shoemaker, A Gentleman* (c.1618) and *The Birth of Merlin* (c.1622) both by William Rowley, *The Tragical History of Guy of Warwick* (c.1620) attributed to John Day and Thomas Dekker, and the *Seven Champions of Christendom* (c.1635) by John Kirke retain little of their original sacred *vitae*. Instead, the saints in these plays appear in the subplots of tragicomic romances. SS Winifred, Hugh, Crispin and Crispinian, and Alban and Amphiabel (*Shoemaker*), Anselm (*Merlin*), Guy (*Guy*), and George, Andrew, David, Patrick, Dennis, James, and Anthony (*Champions*) are anchored to the pre-Reformation landscape of England and Wales through miracles, monuments, or patron saint status. Many of these saints belong to the old legend of England, that is, the native or naturalized saints who populated the liturgical calendar and legendaries as the Middle Ages came to a close. As Catherine Sanok has shown, the fifteenth century is the point at which English saints began to appear in legends with distinctively English lives.[1] Defined by Karen Winstead as "the golden age of hagiography," fifteenth-century saints' lives can also be characterized by "the valuing of social and family life, the attention to female spirituality, and the privileging of Christian education

---

[1] Catherine Sanok, *New Legends of England: Forms of Community in Late Medieval Saints' Lives* (University of Pennsylvania Press, 2018).

and intellectualism.[2] The saints I address in this chapter represent the inheritance of that fifteenth-century project of elevating English sainthood in new vernacular legends. Yet, the saints have been hidden in the plain sight of extant early modern drama for some time now because their sacred shapes are altered. The exact episodes of conversion, evangelization, miracles, and martyrdom from their Latin and Middle English *vitae* are absent from these plays. The identification of these saints is not a matter of faith, but of perspective. When these plays are approached as a group and viewed from the perspective of medieval romance and the theatrical conventions of sanctity, then these tragicomedies can be seen to excavate the old legends of England.

In this chapter, I explore itinerant sanctity, a type of dramatic sanctity that emerges in the cluster of plays addressed here. These tragicomedies reflect two practices of late medieval English hagiography: the merging of hagiography with romance and fixing saints along the map of England. Before I turn to the dramatization of certain native saints, I first demonstrate how the medieval mix of hagiography and romance operates in the more familiar *Pericles, Prince of Tyre* by William Shakespeare and George Wilkins. In the play, Gower frames the story as appropriate for "holy days," Marina enacts virgin martyrdom, and the hagiographical and typological episodes of the play take place across the ports and islands of the Mediterranean. As the play moves between hagiography and romance, it also limns a particular geographical space. These twinned tendencies—wandering between genres and plotting sanctity along a map—also characterize the dramaturgy of the three Jacobean tragicomedies set in ancient Britain. In *A Shoemaker, A Gentleman*, Winifred converts Hugh near St. Winifred's Well in Wales, Crispin and Crispinian practice shoemaking in Kent, and Alban and Amphiabel die together at Verulamium, the Roman city that predated St. Alban's. In *Guy of Warwick*, the title character leaves England to go on Crusade and then returns home to live out his life as a penitential hermit near Warwick Castle. In *The Birth of Merlin*, which is set in various English and Welsh locations, Anselm defeats the devil and the Saxons and then becomes the first Bishop of Winchester. While the saints of these plays do not reiterate traditional *vitae* and are adapted to suit a stage version of sanctity, they all perform acts of conversion, penance, miracles, or martyrdom along the topography of England and Wales. These three Jacobean plays put forth new theatrical versions of native-identified saints at the time that patron saints, such as George, Andrew, and Katherine, were more frequently returning to public pageantry in London and elsewhere.

A Shoemaker, A Gentleman, Guy of Warwick, and *The Birth of Merlin* reflect the antiquarian impulse concerning saints that Jennifer Summit has studied in regard to the making of the Renaissance library. By the later sixteenth and early

---

[2] *Fifteenth-Century Lives: Writing Sainthood in England.* ReFormations: Medieval and Early Modern Series (University of Notre Dame Press, 2020), 1 and 8.

seventeenth centuries, antiquarians, such as Robert Cotton and William Camden, attempted "to remake the archive of saints in a self-conscious effort to transform the sources of superstition into new sources of British historiography."[3] As antiquarians took up the task of gleaning the historiographical from the hagiographical, the tragicomedies celebrated English and Welsh saints by embracing both the historiographical and the hagiographical. In the final part of this chapter, I address *The Seven Champions of Christendom* by John Kirke. Led by St. George, the saints in this play are nearly unrecognizable when compared to their original legends. However, their status as patrons of a collective western Christendom (England, Scotland, Wales, Ireland, Spain, France, and Italy) who crusade against monsters and pagans reclaims a medieval map of sacred geography. Notably, that past map lacks the religious divisions between a Protestant England and the Catholic countries in the Stuart present. Even as these plays variously produce new legends of old saints, they affix those saints to geographic points in the legendary past. In doing so, they also affix a national orthodoxy to these saints who stand as patrons of an unbroken English ecclesiastical tradition against the foreign intrusion of a false and newly invented Counter-Reformation sanctity.

Anthologizing Romance and "Holy Days" in *Pericles*

The first Jacobean play to exhibit the dramaturgy of itinerant sanctity is *Pericles*. Although the play wanders around sites of the ancient Mediterranean rather than ancient Britain, an examination of the momentary interpolation of hagiographic tropes is instructive for understanding how itinerant sanctity functions in the other tragicomedies. Earlier critics disparaged *Pericles* for its episodic structure and genre mixing. Ben Jonson famously described it as "scraps out of every dish raked forth into the common tub." Jonson's complaint about the composition of Shakespeare and Wilkins's tragicomedy, however, reflects the organization of medieval romances and saints' lives. These two genres were not only bound together in manuscript collections; they also sometimes converged. Although *Pericles* materializes a world of classical pantheism, the play flirts with hagiographical tropes and the source tale, the Apollonius of Tyre narrative, overlaps with the legend of Mary Magdalene in its various forms, including the Digby play.[4] Here, I explore how *Pericles* instructs audiences to receive the hagiographical romance before enacting temporary sanctity in a number of episodes.

---

[3] Summit, *Memory's Library*, 159.
[4] For more on the overlap between Gower's *Confessio Amantis* and Shakespeare and Wilkins's *Pericles, Prince of Tyre*, see Elizabeth Archibald, *Apollonius of Tyre: Medieval and Renaissance Themes and Variations* (Woodbridge, UK: Boydell & Brewer, 1991). For more on the Digby *Mary Magdalene* and *Pericles*, see Peter Womack, "Shakespeare and the Sea of Stories," *Journal of Medieval and Early Modern Studies* 29 (1999): 169–87; and Joanne M. Rochester, "Space and Staging in the Digby *Mary Magdalen* and *Pericles, Prince of Tyre*," *Early Theatre* 13, no. 2 (2010): 43–62.

The play begins with the medieval poet John Gower offering a medieval frame for the romance of the ancient Mediterranean. The historical Gower composed his own version of the story of Apollonius of Tyre in Book VII of *Confessio Amantis* (c.1390), a verse anthology like *The Canterbury Tales* and *The Decameron*. As the chorus in *Pericles*, the poet does not outright cite his own text, but rather conjures the past circulation of the Apollonius narrative in both performance and reading cultures. The ghostly Gower recites in the meter of witches and fairies rather than the standard blank verse of *Henry V*'s chorus. He begins:

> To sing a Song that old was sung
> From ashes auntient Gower is come,
> Assuming mans infirmities
> To glad your eare, and please your eyes:
> It hath been sung at Feastiuals,
> On Ember eues, and Holydayes:
> And Lords and Ladyes in their liues,
> Haue red it for restoratiues.[5]

Since Edmund Malone, editors have emended "Holydayes" to "holy ales," a category of festivity invented by a preference for end rhyme and the dissolution of the liturgical calendar. Church ales were festive fundraising efforts that continued into the early seventeenth century, but "holy ales" are absent from the historical record. The context of *Pericles*' past circulation, Gower implies, is important for its present reception. In the past, the story circulated as part of a communal repertoire of performance. He names occasions of performance associated with the pre-Reformation liturgical year: festivals, the eves of Ember Days—the quarterly periods of three days of fasting and prayer—and holy days or holidays. As discussed in chapter 1, the eves of feast days were a traditional time to enact saint plays whether they took the form of drama or embraced a more dynamic sense of play, such as the custom of boy bishops on the Eve of St. Nicholas or the 1525/26 Shrewsbury St. Katherine's Play that featured an explosion but no saint. Festive occasions invited improvisation on saints' lives and iconography. Occasionally, these alternative and romance iterations of saints' lives occurred in Shakespeare's time, such as when St. George rode alongside St. Andrew to celebrate the symbolic unification of England and Scotland in James I's 1604 coronation pageant in London and when St. George saved the daughter of the Egyptian king from a fiery dragon in the Mercers' pageant in Wells in June of 1607. Gower's chorus also implies that the Apollonius tale, and stories like it, were not out of place in liturgical time. On the contrary, it was appropriate material alongside a festive or solemn observation.

[5] William Shakespeare, *The Late, and Much Admired Play, Called Pericles, Prince of Tyre* [. . .] (London: Henry Gosson 1609), A2r.

Romance offers expansive possibilities for masculine holiness. Celibate or sexually active, mendicant or martial, the Christian heroes of romance are vocationally fluid in their pursuit of heaven. Middle English vernacular romance, such as the Apollonius legend in *Confessio Amantis*, most frequently treated "tales of knightly adventure and love together, linking the masculine, battlefield world of the *chanson de geste* with the increasing upper-class interest in what we would now call 'romantic love.'"[6] This type of chivalry characterizes popular medieval romances such as Arthur and Merlin, Havelok the Dane, Bevis of Hampton, King Horn, Sir Isumbras, and Guy of Warwick. These stories depict knightly missions of rightful vengeance and defense, battles to Christianize in England, Wales, and the East, geographic wandering, revelations of secret identities, and supernatural obstacles and interventions.[7] While these narratives reflect Christian concerns and their supernatural elements focus on the "body of the hero" as "the slate upon which the truth of God's will is indelibly and infallibly written," the protagonist knights are secular men who are as concerned with the pursuit of marriage as they are with holy quests.[8] Unlike the majority of saints' lives, including martial saints such as SS Christopher and George, holiness in romance does not depend upon permanent celibacy as a sign of Christian conversion or conviction. Many of the central figures of these romances beget children. Holiness in romance, moreover, occurs within its overall structure of determined mission and uncontrollable fortune. As Alison Wiggins explains, "every romance involves a journey or quest of some kind. This may be an exile, banishment, separation, seeking of fortune, abduction, abandonment, or a crusade."[9] Some romances, like *Pericles*, involve a combination of these scenarios.

By citing the circulation of the Apollonius tale as part of a reading practice, the ghostly poet materializes not only his own collection of stories but also anthologies of legends. In medieval England, romance heroes and saints kept company in story collections, such as *The Canterbury Tales*, as well as in multi-authored manuscript collections. In notable medieval manuscripts, such as Bodleian MS Laud Misc 108, The Lincoln Thornton Manuscript, and the Auchinleck Manuscript, romances are compiled with saints' lives and devotional literature. In Laud Misc 108, an early *South English Legendary* is followed by a handful of additional texts including *Havelok the Dane* and *King Horn*. The Lincoln Thornton Manuscript groups the

---

[6] Ronald B. Herzman, Graham Drake, and Eve Salisbury, eds., *Four Romances of England: King Horn, Havelok the Dane, Bevis of Hampton, Athelston* (Kalamazoo, MI: Medieval Institute Publications, 1999), 2.
[7] As Helen Cooper writes, romance proved useful "in the various nationalist agendas for 'the writing of England,' since many of the romances were native stories that asserted the value and vitality of English originary legends and narrative traditions." *The English Romance in Time: Transforming Motifs from Geoffrey of Monmouth to the Death of Shakespeare* (Oxford: Oxford University Press, 2004), 6.
[8] Herzman et al., *Four Romances of England*, 7.
[9] Alison Wiggins, ed., *Stanzaic Guy of Warwick* (Kalamazoo, MI: Medieval Institute Publications, 2004), 8.

chivalric *Vita Sancti Cristofori* in a romance section of the manuscript along with Arthurian romances and *Sir Isumbras*. Devotional and hagiographical works, such as Richard Rolle's commentaries, the *Mirror of St. Edmund*, and a *Life of St. John the Evangelist* follow in another section. Finally, The Auchinleck Manuscript compiles the lives of SS Margaret, Katherine, Mary Magdalene, and the Assumption of Mary along with *Sir Bevis of Hampton*, *Arthur and Merlin*, and three versions of the legend of Guy of Warwick. These collections of stories featured hagiography, romance, and hagiographical romance. Barbara Newman notes that this last category fused when hagiography "crossed the language barrier" from Latin to the vernacular, from the sacred to the common.[10] The borrowing from and, in Newman's term, "convergence" of these genres occurred so seamlessly and frequently that "vernacular saints' lives freely introduced romance elements, while romance heroes were made to teeter on the brink of sainthood."[11]

The Middle English practice of anthologizing—or what Seth Lerer calls the medieval "anthologistic impulse"—wherein hagiography converges with romance resurrects the "restorative" aspects of the saintly moments in *Pericles*.[12] *Pericles* does not present the lives of saints, but in between the Mediterranean storms, seafaring, and separations, Pericles, Thaisa, and Marina enact hagiographical tropes as a strategy toward eventual reunion. In romance, as in hagiography, the fortune of the sea is never just a series of chance encounters with unpredictable weather systems. The episodes in *Pericles* do not follow the structure of *vita*. Rather, they present excerpts of hagiography for part of an episode or even just a moment.

Both Thaisa and her daughter draw on virgin martyrdom in order to solve imminent challenges. After Thaisa meets Pericles and chooses him over the five other knights who gallantly strut through the court in Tarsus, her father must dismiss the other suitors. The lie he tells is a hagiographical one. The king says that Thaisa "for this twelvemonth, she'll not undertake / A married life" and instead "she'll wear Diana's livery," something that she has "vowed / And on her virgin honor, will not break it" (2.5.3–4, 9, 10–11). Here, the play introduces hagiography as a momentary strategy for transformation. The king's lie recalls the legend of St. Ursula who requests a reprieve of three years before she marries her own prince. During that time, she travels on a ship with eleven-thousand virginal companions who are martyred before they are able to return home to Britain. As Sanok notes, the legend of St. Ursula is "a narrative of marriage turned martyrdom."[13] Thaisa, another princess subject to the fortunes of the sea, performs the reverse: a narrative of martyrdom turned marital.

---

[10] Barbara Newman, *Medieval Crossover: Reading the Secular Against the Sacred* (Notre Dame, IN: University of Notre Dame Press, 2013), 37.
[11] Newman, *Medieval Crossover*, 37.
[12] Seth Lerer, "Medieval English Literature and the Idea of the Anthology," *PMLA* 118, no. 5 (2003): 1263.
[13] Sanok, *New Legends of England*, 241.

The virgin martyrdom that is introduced briefly in the episode of Thaisa and the knights repeats in a different iteration when Marina, in her misfortune, is sent to the brothel. Before she sets foot in there, however, she prays "If fires be hot, knives sharp, or waters deep, / Untied I still my virgin knot will keep. / Diana aid my purpose!" (4.3.151–3). Soon, Marina, who has vowed virginity while in the brothel, converts her would-be rapists. Having heard "divinity preached there," they leave swearing off "bawdy houses" and planning to "go hear the vestals sing" (4.5.4, 6). Like the virgin martyrs of medieval legends—and particularly St. Agnes who, in Caxton's edition of the *Golden Legend* "made she of the bordel her oratorye"— Marina converts those who endanger her virginity.[14] That her virginity is the source of her power is confirmed to us by the frustrated Bawd who orders, "Bolt, take her away, use her at thy pleasure, / crack the glass of her virginity, and make the rest / maleable" (4.6.148–50). Marina counters with a prayer to the gods, which Bawd interprets as conjuring in imitation of the persecutors of virgin martyrs in saints' legends. When no intercession occurs, Marina drops the virgin martyr act and takes up honest work outside of the brothel. Her vow of virginity and her brief play with virgin martyrdom is complete and she returns to her station as an honorable trafficked, pirated, orphan princess without an island kingdom.

Pericles takes place in what Peter Womack calls "the sea of stories" between romance and hagiography. The sudden wrecks, arrivals, and encounters determined by the sea are devices of fortune and providence.[15] To recall, Pericles travels from Antioch back to Tyre and sets out again to escape the murderous plans of the incestuous King Antioch. His ship wrecks at Tarsus, but the sea coughs up his rusty armor so that he can perform in the courtly pageantry with the other knights and woo the princess. The introduction of the miraculous in the play is usually identified as Cerimon's resuscitation of Thaisa at Ephesus. However, unlike in the Mary Magdalene legend, the raising of Thaisa is an ambiguous event rather than a verifiably miraculous one. Cerimon observes Thaisa's body in the coffin, saying, "look how fresh she looks. / They were too rough, that threw her in the sea," implying that she was not actually dead (3.2.91–2). Citing a tale of a dead Egyptian "Who was by good appliance recovered," the physician calls for fire and violin music (3.2.98). When Thaisa revives, he pronounces that "nature awakes a warm breath / Out of her" (3.2.105–6). I am not arguing that the episode does not recall the Magdalene legend, the raising of Lazarus, or the other stories of revival and resurrection in saints' lives. Certainly, it does. But, at this point, the play remains ambiguous about the typological and the miraculous.

When miraculous intercession is introduced late in the play during the episode of Marina and Pericles' reunion, it happens suddenly and almost without precedent. In an otherwise unnecessary scene that occurs just after Pericles has arrived

---

[14] Caxton, *Golden Legend*, cxx recto.
[15] Peter Womack, "Shakespeare and the Sea of Stories," *Journal of Medieval and Early Modern Studies* 29 (1999): 169–87.

at Tarsus, a courtier back in Tyre delivers news of the incestuous King Antiochus's death by intervention of the gods:

> When he was seated in a chariot of
> An inestimable value, and his daughter with him,
> A fire from heaven came and shriveled up
> Those bodies... (2.4.6–10)

This sudden, divine fire lays the groundwork for the sudden, small miracles that occur later in the play when Marina and Pericles are reunited aboard the ship near Myteline and Pericles receives a visit or vision from the Marian-seeming goddess, Diana. To recall, Pericles has spent the majority of the play as a penitent wanderer, a role he took up after Marina's foster parents told him that she died. He wears a sackcloth, grows his hair, and remains celibate. His celibacy, like Thaisa's, is not permanent. The mendicant-like wandering is a necessary condition for providential reunification. As a temporary vow, it serves to preclude remarriage. The use of religious wandering to extend a scenario of dramatic conflict also occurs in *All's Well That Ends Well* (*c.*1601–05) when Helena takes up a "sainted vow" to go on pilgrimage to the shrine of "Saint Jacques le Grand" at Santiago de Compostela because "Ambitious love hath so in me offended" (3.4.7, 3.5.36, 3.4.5). After the ordeal in the brothel, Marina is called aboard Pericles' ship to comfort the grieving man. When she tells him, "My name is Marina," his grief increases and he cries, "O, I am mocked / And thou by some incensed god sent hither / To make the world to laugh at me!" (5.1.164–6). His grief dissolves once she recounts her story, the effect of which is to restore Pericles to himself. He calls for his robes to return to his princely state and prays, "O heavens blesse my girle" (5.1.257). There are no stage directions in the quarto, but the dialogue indicates that "the Musicke of the Spheres" plays suddenly (Quarto, I1v). At first, only Pericles can hear the sound of supernatural affirmation, but soon the rest of the cast also shares in the miraculous soundscape in order to verify that it is real. Unlike the violin at Thaisa's awakening, there are no instruments present. Rather, like the music in the central angelic miracle of *If You Know Not Me, You Know Nobody*, this music, which causes a "thick slumber," plays on its own (5.1.268). While Pericles sleeps, the Marian-figure Diana descends and orders the recently united father and daughter to her temple at Ephesus, the site of the final reunification with Thaisa. Like Pericles and Marina, Thaisa also has taken on a temporary type of religious life in substitution for fulfilling a familial role. She had become a vestal nun, but she quits playing with monastic holiness in order to sail from Ephesus and return to her role as wife and mother.

The postmedieval quality of *Pericles* maps its hagiographical episodes on top of major sites associated with early Christianity and martyrdom. As Lucy Munro points out, "the classical setting of the narrative and the medieval ambience of Gower's choruses" combine with "anachronistic references to religious social customs" drawn from medieval and early modern England.[16] The play presents a version of the ancient Mediterranean from the perspective of an English tradition of saints' lives and romance legends. Shakespeare first dramatized this ancient Christianized seascape early in his career in *Comedy of Errors*, a play that converts Plautus's comedy *Menaechmi* from the pagan context of the Roman imagination to one that also embraces post-Pauline Christianity. George Parks summarizes Shakespeare's reorientation of the story:

> When Shakespeare came to adapt Plautus' *Menaechmi* to the English stage, he was obliged to find another setting for the action than the original Epidamnus, which would mean nothing to his audience. He shifted the setting to Ephesus, and then had to devise a complete new map for the play. In Plautus, the hunt for the lost brother (which ended in Epidamnus) had traversed the Italian region, from the Adriatic to Spain; now the hunt was shifted eastward to the Greek region, from Sicily to Asia Minor.[17]

Whereas Epidamnus might be received, at best, as a generic city of the ancient Mediterranean, Jacobean audiences understood Ephesus as a site of Christian syncretization and transformation. The city previously known for its dedication to Diana became renowned for its association with the Virgin Mary. In relocating the play's resolution of brotherly reunification to Ephesus, as John Parker shows, Shakespeare exploits the hagiographical resonances of the legendary site of the Virgin Mary's final days.[18] In the play, Diana's temple becomes a priory headed by an Abbess whose intervention brings about a happy resolution.

The geography of *Comedy of Errors* evokes a particular religious meaning that is repeated in *Pericles*. The central conflict of *Pericles*—the separation of the new family—resembles the king of Marseille episode in the legend of Mary Magdalene, in which the formerly pagan king loses his wife in childbirth while sailing to Jerusalem on pilgrimage and is miraculously reunited with both wife and child upon his return. The travels of Pericles, Thaisa, and Marina, moreover, limn a geographic space associated with the post-resurrection travels of the Apostles and other saints in medieval legends. As Sarah Beckwith writes, "romance is the form that systematically converts chance into providence."[19] The fortunes of the sea take

---

[16] *Archaic Style in English Literature, 1590–1674* (Cambridge: Cambridge University Press, 2013), 96, 98.

[17] George Parks, "Shakespeare's Map for *The Comedy of Errors*," *The Journal of English and Germanic Philology* 39 (1940): 93.

[18] John Parker, "Holy Adultery: Marriage in *The Comedy of Errors, The Merchant of Venice*, and *The Merry Wives of Windsor*," in *The Oxford Handbook of Shakespearean Comedy*, ed. Heather Hirschfeld (Oxford: Oxford University Press, 2018), 493. See also F. Elizabeth Hart, "'Great is Diana' of Shakespeare's Ephesus," *Studies in English Literature, 1500–1900* 43, no. 2 (2003): 347–74.

[19] Sarah Beckwith, *Shakespeare and the Grammar of Forgiveness* (Ithaca, NY: Cornell University Press, 2011), 92.

the family across the Roman world of Tyre, Ephesus, Antioch, and Tarsus, which, to medieval and early modern Christians, were recognizable sites associated with the conversion and subsequent preaching of St. Paul. In addition, Shakespeare and Wilkins's transformation of Apollonius's wife and daughter from Gower's source tale to their play rechristens them from Lucina and Tharsia to Thaisa and Marina, respectively. Both SS Thais and Marina can be found in the *Golden Legend*, although they are less well known in Western Christianity. In Eastern hagiography, Thais is a Magdalene figure like Mary of Egypt, a repentant sinner and desert contemplative. It is appropriate that a St. Thais figure would remove herself from the world as a "votive" for a Marian-styled deity. And although Marina is named for the place of her birth, her name-saint is known in the West as Margaret of Antioch, the popular virgin martyr who typologically enacts the story of Jonah and the whale when she bursts forth from the belly of the demon with the sign of the cross.

These moments of hagiographical tropes and the larger hagiographic resonances achieved through mapping and naming do not create saints as does the Digby *Mary Magdalene* or Heywood's *If You Know Not Me, You Know Nobody*. In fact, as Julia Reinhard Lupton urges us to consider in her extraordinary exploration of messianism and dwelling in *Pericles*, the play does not demand sacrifices. On the contrary, *Pericles*, like other late plays, moves "from a *sacrificial economy* (where persons and things get killed, destroyed, or consumed in order to renew the social body) to a *votive economy*, which strives to maintain multiple historical moments and possibilities within a fluid dramatic-symbolic space."[20] But *Pericles* also rejects the distortion of sainthood into "saint-like" that characterizes the approach to hagiography in *Henry VIII*. Rather, *Pericles* embraces the hagiographically fluid performances developed by the devotional culture in the Middle Ages "on festivals, ember eves, and holy days." That is, a virgin martyr at one moment can become a romance heroine and lover in the next. It is a transfiguration that reflects Marina at the Globe and Blackfriars as much as it does St. Margaret in medieval pageantry.

Saints of the Soil in *A Shoemaker, A Gentleman*

Saints appear more explicitly in *A Shoemaker, A Gentleman* than they do in *Pericles*. Like *Guy of Warwick* and *The Birth of Merlin*, this saint play occurs in a mythic English past. In all three plays, romance heroes are reborn as saints through the interpolation of hagiographical tropes. As in *Pericles*, *A Shoemaker, A Gentleman* enacts a wandering sanctity not bound to theology but to site-specific acts of monastic withdrawal, virginity, miracles, and martyrdom. The sites in the

---

[20] *Shakespeare Dwelling: Designs for the Theater of Life.* (Chicago: University of Chicago Press, 2018), 151.

play belong to a mythic landscape that combines legends of English and Welsh saints from the medieval period and sets them further in the past. SS Winifred and Hugh, Crispin and Crispinian, Alban and Amphiabel inhabit altered lives during the Roman occupation and persecution, an authoritative period for traditionalists and reformers alike.[21] The holiness of the ancient English church is connected to the Stuart present through recognizable places and monuments that have weathered and witnessed time all the while remaining part of a single, unbroken tradition. This English sanctity and its attendant theatricality recovers native saints for secular audiences.

William Rowley crafted his saint play by adapting the stories of SS Winifred and Hugh and Crispin and Crispinian from Thomas Deloney's prose narrative *The Gentle Craft* and adding a third pair of saints to the mix, SS Alban and Amphiabel, England's protomartyrs. While Deloney secularized these legendary saints into romance heroes, Rowley's play re-sacralized them through the insertion of hagiographical tropes into the new narratives. As Alison A. Chapman shows through an exploration of the association between shoemakers and early modern holiday-making, the legend of SS Crispin and Crispinian was flexible, perhaps uniquely so, in this period.[22] None of the saints in *A Shoemaker, A Gentleman* materialize their exact medieval *vitae*, but the adapted saints do enact tropes of conversion, persecution, virginity, miracles, and martyrdom and they do so in specific parts of England and Wales. In this play, the brother shoemakers hide from Roman persecutors in a cordwainer's shop in Kent, Winifred lives and dies as a miraculous body near her shrine in Wales, and Alban and Amphiabel are martyred at the site in Hertfordshire named for Alban.

The context of Christian persecution coupled with the celebration of English shoemakers produces a history in which England is and has long been a Christian nation. *A Shoemaker, A Gentleman* opens to the sounds of warring Romans conquering the ancient Britons. "*Maximinus and Dioclesian*" are named as the perpetrators of the violence to clarify that the conflict between Rome and Britain is no normal campaign of colonial expansion. British evangelization and conversion has preceded Rome's arrival on the island and now the "Barbarous Romans" put "to sword, and torture all, that beare the / Name of Christians" (B2v).[23] The reign of Diocletian is a pivotal period in the early church according to the *Golden*

---

[21] For more on how *Shoemaker* fits into this imaginary, see Lisa Hopkins, *Renaissance Drama on the Edge* (London: Routledge, 2016).

[22] Alison A. Chapman, "Whose Saint Crispin's Day Is It?: Shoemaking, Holiday Making, and the Politics of Memory in Early Modern England," *Renaissance Quarterly* 54 (2001): 1467–94.

[23] William Rowley, *A Merrie and Plesant comedy: Never before Printed, called A Shoo-maker a Gentleman* (London: John Okes, 1638). All subsequent in-text parenthetical citations come from this edition.

Legend as well as the *Book of Martyrs*. Foxe narrates that the "Tenth Persecution," under Diocletian is notable for the "most violent edictes and proclamations" that:

> insued a great persecution amongest the gouernoures of the Church, amongest whom many stoode manfullye, passing through many exceeding bytter tormentes, neither were ouercome therwith, being tormented and examined diuers of them diuersly: some scourged, al theyr bodies ouer with whips and scourges: some with racks rasynges of the flesh intollerable were cruciated: some one way, some an other way put to death.[24]

Known to both Catholics and Protestants as the period that produced many early church martyrs, the reign of Diocletian anchors the temporality of persecution in *A Shoemaker, A Gentleman*.

Jacobean audiences were well aware of the chronology of Britain's Christianization. For example, as Margreta de Grazia observes, Shakespeare's *King Lear* presents Albion BC for Albion AD audiences. The story is set on and about the landscape of England in the time before Christ for audiences who inhabit the same place in a temporally distinct England.[25] The specter of the resurrection separates Shakespeare's seventeenth-century readers and audiences from their pre-Christian ancestors. Those who suffer in *King Lear* and even do so in terms of a Christian repertoire of suffering—purgation, passion, *pietà*—"have no access to salvation history."[26] Rowley's play establishes its setting in Britain AD through the context of the persecution. The brother princes Crispin and Crispinian seek refuge with shoemakers because the native craftsmen are all secret Christians in the early years of the church. This dramatic version of the romance of Crispin and Crispinian creates a strong link between the common populations of ancient Britain and that of contemporary audiences in Jacobean England.

Sainthood emerges in episodes of miracles, conversion, and martyrdom in the play's linked subplots of Hugh and Winifred and Alban and Amphiabel. Rowley verifies the truth of Winifred's virginal sanctity through miraculous theatricality that draws from the conventions of the dumb show in *If You Know Not Me, You Know Nobody*. In *Shoemaker*, those conventions are divided and distributed over two separate scenes. Wearing a nun's black veil that is referred to as a "cloister habit," Winifred states she is resolute in her chastity and directs Amphiabel, her confessor, to observe "what Heaven hath done" and shows him St. Winifred's Well (C4r). The Well is notable as a monument that survived the Reformation and continued to host pilgrims during the Stuart era. Music plays as "*an* Angell *ascends out*

---

[24] Foxe 1570, 1:109.
[25] Margreta de Grazia, "*King Lear* in Albion BC," in *Medieval Shakespeare: Pasts and Presents*, eds. Ruth Morse, Helen Cooper, and Peter Holland (Cambridge: Cambridge University Press, 2013), 138–156.
[26] de Grazia, "King Lear in Albion BC," 156.

of the Well" and gives Amphiabel a "sign that holy Christians weare" (C4r). The angel also blesses the spring and recounts its healing powers. The miracle propels Amphiabel into action for the cause of Christianity. Prior to the miracle at the Well, the priest embraced secrecy and hiding. Afterwards, he resolves to leave Holywell and travel "straight . . . to the face of persecuting *Albon*" in Verulamium, the Roman city buried under the present Hertfordshire city of St. Alban's and named for the monastery dedicated to England's protomartyr (C4r). Once converted by Amphiabel, Alban receives the "Embleme of a Christian" that the Angel bestowed upon Amphiabel during the miracle at the well (D2v). The cross that Alban wears, "the daring Badge of Christianity," visually announces his conversion to Maximian (D3r). The Emperor rages and sends soldiers to Holywell after Amphiabel and Winifred, ordering them to "lay desolate the confines of that superstitious / Virgin, that with her sorcerous devotion works miracles, / By which she drawes Christians, faster than we can kill 'em" (D3rv). It is striking that the accusation of superstition for Winifred's traditional sanctity comes from the mouth of a pagan persecutor of Christians. Although Winifred's part in this stage adaptation of *The Gentle Craft* is relatively small, she acts as the catalyst for the victorious establishment of Christianity in ancient Britain. The tyrant's ire is not misdirected. The spread of Christianity across the map of Britain from the West in Wales to the East in Verulamium (St. Alban's) can be traced through the symbolic transfer of the stage property of the miraculous cross from the virgin's angel to Amphiabel to Alban.

Winifred performs a second miracle at the Well in a scene that cites both the dumb show in *If You Know Not Me, You Know Nobody* and the legend of St. Agnes. In citing the St. Agnes legend, Rowley's version of Winifred also responds to Marina's performance in the brothel by restoring the temporary sanctity of *Pericles* to a more permanent legacy of English sanctity. Winifred reiterates that she is "contract and wedded to Christ" and that angels sing "Chast Hallelujahs . . . to the celebration of" her "Virgin rights" (E3r–v). As soon as she proclaims that she is ready and willing to die in "the Militant Field of Martyrdom," Roman soldiers storm the stage (E3r). Holding "*a booke*," the virgin cautions them not to threaten her at the site of her miraculous Well: "tyrant, this place is hallowed ; doe not awake / the thunder, if it strike, the boult will fall downe / Perpendicular, and strike thee under mercy" (E4r). In spite of her warning, the officer in charge mocks her "Virgin water" and Winifred responds to their disbelief with outward proof. She declares "Doe, play with Lightning till it blasts thee" and instantly one of the officer's men is blind and raving "Guide me to the divill" (E4r). But the virgin intercedes on behalf of her blind persecutor with the miraculous speech act, "By helpe of heaven thus I thine eyes restore" and returns his eyesight (E4r).[27] Having

---

[27] Not only are these two miraculous episodes absent from St. Winifred's traditional life, but also they combine aspects of recognizable episodes from other virgin martyr legends. The first scene recalls

proved the power of Christianity over her Roman pagan adversaries, Winifred and Hugh are taken to Verulamium for execution, the site of Alban and Amphiabel's future death. This scene reveals that Rowley scripted a theatrical shorthand for the longhand version of the business with the book in Heywood's previous saint play. Elizabeth's apotropaic book in *If You Know Not Me, You Know Nobody* also appears in Winifred's hands even though she neither opens nor reads from it. It is a material sign associated with sanctity in the subplot of Winifred, Amphiabel, and Hugh. Although the book continues to anchor the virgin's sanctity through a discipline of holy reading it is as much an efficacious property that activates the miracle as it is a functional property for prayer.

In crafting the theatrical St. Winifred, Rowley defers to the authoritative version of theatrical sanctity, that is, Elizabeth in *If You Know Not Me, You Know Nobody*. Winifred is reconfigured from both her traditional *vita*, which continued to circulate in seventeenth-century recusant culture, and Deloney's more famous version of her life in *The Gentle Craft*, a prose collection. In Winifred's traditional life, a prince attempts rape, fails, decapitates her, and a well springs up from where her head falls.[28] A priest puts her head back on her body and she resurrects as the ground swallows her assailant to hell. Later, she founds a monastery and dies a holy death. In contrast to this out-of-order Celtic narrative that takes place in the Middle Ages, Deloney places his virgin in the ancient period and reorganizes her *vita* to fit the anticipated and more recognizable structure of virgin martyrdom wherein religious life precedes martyrdom.[29] However, Deloney also attacks traditional observances of religious life and emphasizes martyrdom as the central element of sanctity. After Winifred "received the Christian Faith" Deloney narrates that she "became so superstitious . . . wherefore forsaking all manner of earthly pomp, she lived a long time very poor . . . by the side of a most pleasant springing Well."[30] The description of Winifred's improvised monastic life of chastity, poverty, and prayer as "superstitious" separates Deloney's legend from traditional saints' lives. Rather than serve as an example of virtue and holy intercession for other Christians this post-Reformation tale explains hermitic virginity as the product of an excessive indulgence in piety. The term "superstitious" recategorizes her pursuit of holiness as papist. Deloney's inventive execution of Winifred and Hugh develops martyrological motifs that are absent elsewhere in *The Gentle Craft*. Winifred

---

the angelic apparition that validates St. Cecilia's claims to consecrated virginity in her legend, and the second scene borrows its smite-and-restore structure from the life of St. Agnes, when demons attack the young man who attempts to rape the saint in the brothel and God restores him to life through her sympathetic prayers.

[28] The basic narrative outline of Winifred's life, defense of virginity, death, resurrection, and monastic life derives from a twelfth-century Latin *vita* composed by Robert, Prior of Shrewsbury. See "Robert Pennant's *Life of St Winefride*," in *Two Mediaeval Lives of Saint Winefride*, trans. Ronald Pepin and Hugh Feiss (Toronto: Peregrina Publishing, 2000), 22.

[29] Thomas Deloney, *The Gentle Craft*, ed. Simon Barker (Farnham, UK: Ashgate, 2007), 14.

[30] Deloney, *The Gentle Craft*, 7.

is executed by bleeding. She is "pricked in every vain, the scarlet blood sprung out in plentifull sort, much like a precious fountain lately filled with Claret Wine."[31] In her dying, then, Winifred imitates both the holy well and Christ's crucifixion. Her blood, furthermore, becomes sacred in its reference to communion wine. She dies "like a Conduit suddenly drawn drie" and her blood is gathered in a cup, poisoned, and given to Hugh who also dies as a Christian.

In *A Shoemaker, A Gentleman*, Rowley retains Deloney's method of the death for the companionate martyrs but the sacrificial bleeding is made to more resemble the saints of medieval legendaries rather than the de-Catholicized saints of *The Gentle Craft*. The extended meditation on Winifred's bleeding in Deloney's prose text is absent. Instead, Rowley indulges traditional hagiography and continues to dramatize Winifred as *sponsa Christi*. The virgin, who possesses the power to bring down angels, sees a vision of them running "to meet and welcome / me unto the Land of blisse / Singing I have spunne a golden thred" as her life leaves her body (H4v–I1r). Whereas Deloney toiled to depict a post-Reformation martyrdom that included tropes of Christian sacrifice absent of miraculous conventions, Rowley scripted a generic virgin martyr's life and death as it was understood in the theatre.

Although Rowley invented Winifred's role in Amphiabel's conversion of Alban, much of the protomartyrs' story in *A Shoemaker, A Gentleman* is lifted directly and without revision from the pages of saints' lives. The gruesome details of Amphiabel's execution are announced by Maximian:

> This fiend Amphiabel, from whose damn'd teat
> He suck'd this poison, shall there be bound
> By a fixed stake, to which nail'd fast,
> The navel of his belly being open'd,
> Then with your sword prick him, and force him run
> About like a wheel, till he has spun his guts out:
> And that dispatch'd, saw off his traitorous head (H3v–H4r)

Unlike Winifred's altered death, this one reflects the description of Amphiabel's martyrdom in traditional hagiography.[32] Deloney's prose tale contains minor but very real declarations against "superstitious" religion and at least some of the modifications to his legends of the saints are a product of anti-Catholicism. Rowley's retention of Alban and Amphiabel's traditional *vita*, the insertion of miraculous virginity in the revised Winifred story, and the overall emphases on miracles and martyrdom at known sites of sanctity on English soil build on the precedent of

---

[31] Deloney, *The Gentle Craft*, 18.
[32] This detail appears in John Lydgate's *Life of Saint Alban and Amphiabel*, the *South English Legendary*, and the *Golden Legend*. In her edition of *Shoemaker*, Trudi Darby recognizes Rowley's source for the Alban-Amphiabel plot as Book IV of Holinshed's *Chronicles*. See William Rowley, *A Shoemaker, A Gentleman*, ed. Trudi Darby (London: Nick Hern, 2002), ix.

Heywood's play. The only heroic Christians to survive the Roman occupation are the brother princes, Crispin and Crispinian, who keep their identities hidden. At the play's end, they receive public honors in London, where it is revealed that Crispin secretly has married the daughter of Maximian and is named the next the leader of Roman Britain.[33] This finale veers from the traditional *vita* of the brother shoemaker saints, in which they are both celibate and martyred. Yet, the survival of Crispin and his heirs trace Christian futurity from Holywell and St. Albans to the Stuart present.

Hidden Hagiography in *Guy of Warwick* and *The Birth of Merlin*

A Shoemaker, A Gentleman reconfigures saints to suit the plot of that play, but all of those characters are based on established saints. Consultation with the *Golden Legend*, *The Kalendre of the New Legende of England*, Mirk's *Festial*, and other collections of saints' lives places Winifred and Hugh, Crispin and Crispinian, and Alban and Amphiabel in a larger context of English cults, *vitae*, and history. In contrast, Guy in *Guy of Warwick* and Anselm in *The Birth of Merlin* are created saints through the processes of both traditional and theatrical hagiography. As Thomas Heffernan expertly explains in his description of how Walter Daniel reported on the life and death of his fellow monk to compose the *Vita Sancti Aelredi*, the writer of saints' lives "is more interested in what his subject has in common with the sacred; thus, his prose eschews the particular for the ideal."[34] A subject is thus transformed into a dramatic saint through staging the life as *vita* just as a subject is transformed into a saint in prose or poetry through writing the life into *vita*. The legendary Guy of Warwick can be identified as a saint not through inclusion in the *Golden Legend* or in the liturgical calendar, but through a specific pattern of repentance and hermitic withdrawal, the ideal to which Heffernan refers. Guy becomes a saint through a similar set of gestures through which Amphiabel is established as a saint in the actual pages of devotional literature. The hermit Anselm of *The Birth of Merlin* is an invention of the playwright, but, like Guy, his acts identify him as a saint. In addition to these behavioral aspects of sanctity, the production of theatrical miracles provides verification of the truth of Guy and Anselm's sanctity.

---

[33] Another romanticized version of the Crispin and Crispinian legend appeared in the Cordwainers' pageant of 1613 in Wells on the occasion of Queen Anne's visit to the city. In that pageant, one of the brothers married St. Ursula. See James Stokes, "The Wells Cordwainers' show: New Evidence Concerning Guild Entertainments in Somerset," *Comparative Drama* 19 (1985–86): 332–46, and "Women and Mimesis in Medieval and Renaissance Somerset (and Beyond)," *Comparative Drama* 27 (1993): 176–96; and Gina M. Di Salvo, "Saints' Lives and Shoemakers' Holidays: The Gentle Craft and the Wells Cordwainers' Pageant of 1613," *Early Theatre* (2016): 119–38.

[34] Thomas Heffernan, *Sacred Biography: Saints and Their Biographers in the Middle Ages* (Oxford: Oxford University Press, 1988), 74.

The figure of Guy of Warwick first emerged in medieval English and French legends that merged the genres and tropes of romance and hagiography. Most versions place Guy in the pre-conquest kingdom of King Athelstan. There, he must prove his love for a lady and/or repent of his previous military conquests by journeying to Constantinople or Jerusalem to fight dragons, pagans, Saracens, or other mythic or ethno-religious populations that threaten Christendom. As Lee Manion argues, the Renaissance crusading tradition commemorates or adapts "the medieval ideal of a united Christendom to engage with early modern concerns about relations between Catholic and Reformed."[35] Manion, furthermore, argues that the postmedieval use of the crusading tradition comes with the ability to "'convert' the past by offering, inadvertently or intentionally, a medieval model for Christian cooperation."[36] Many English versions of the Guy of Warwick legend resemble the quest-driven travels of Arthurian knights or military saints like SS George, Christopher, or Eustace who crusade, battle, and suffer for the sake of Christianity. In the Jacobean dramatic version, as Guy journeys from England to the Holy Land and back, he increasingly performs like the martial saints rather than secular romance heroes. Indeed, it is during Guy's itinerant and episodic wandering that he transforms from a newlywed knight to a celibate hermit.

The play begins at Warwick Castle with King Athelstan and his retinue bidding farewell to Guy and his new bride, Phyllis. Unlike other versions of the legend, this one does not depict Guy's conquest of monsters and opposing knights to earn Phyllis's love. The conquest precedes the opening of the play and now Guy repents of it, telling his new wife that he has vowed to God, "never to lie by my fair Phillis side, / to eat, to drink, nor rest long in one place" until he has redeemed Jerusalem (133–4).[37] He exchanges his aristocratic clothing for a "Palmers Gown . . . Hat and Staff," that is, the "blessed Weeds of Pilgrimage," and embarks on his journey (160, 163). Thus outfitted, he leaves his newly pregnant wife in Warwick. Helen Cooper notes that "Guy's penitence is modelled particularly closely on the life of St. Alexis, who embarked on his life of penance on his wedding night," albeit before consummating the marriage.[38] The nonconsummation before martial wandering will be familiar to readers and audiences of *All's Well That Ends Well*. Like Alexis, Bertram ventures to "wars and never bed" with Helena whose own pilgrimage, bed trick, and quasi-Marian reappearance "with child" solves the marital conflict of the play (2.3.288, 5.3.358). The role of marital consummation as well as the presence of the miraculous places *Guy of Warwick* in the entanglement of hagiography

---

[35] Lee Manion, "The Crusading Romance in Early Modern England: Converting the Past in Berners's *Huon of Bordeaux* and Johnson's *Seven Champions of Christendom*," *Journal of Medieval and Early Modern Studies* 48, no. 3 (2018): 492.

[36] Manion, "The Crusading Romance," 492.

[37] *Guy of Warwick*, ed. Helen Moore, Malone Society Reprints (Manchester: Manchester University Press, 2007). All subsequent in-text parenthetical citations come from this edition.

[38] Cooper, *The English Romance in Time*, 94.

and romance that wanders between the legend of St. Alexis and the comedy of Shakespeare's play. Erotic, marital love distinguishes Guy from the celibate wanderers of hagiography, but the production of an heir emphasizes the importance of Christian futurity in England.

Supernatural presences enter the stage even before Guy achieves sainthood. Guy's journey from England is interrupted by an enchanter, who occupies the role of a devil character in this play. Not only does the enchanter attempt to stop his holy travel, but also his first appearance is accompanied with thunder and lightning, theatrical effects associated with the appearance of devils and pagan gods. Guy is liberated from his "hell bred slumber," by Oberon and a band of fairies who enter to musical accompaniment (443). In the Holy Land, Guy defends the Christian King of Jerusalem against the pagan Sultan of Babylon and then succeeds in converting his foe to Christianity. Afterwards, Guy wanders for twenty-one years before returning to England. At Winchester, as an old man, he vanquishes a giant pagan Dane and then returns to Warwick in the guise of a hermit. There, for nearly six more years, he occupies a cave, lives a penitential life of prayer and fasting, and receives charity from Phyllis, who does not recognize her husband.

In the final part of the play, Guy is tempted to break his vow to God. In overcoming the temptation, he imitates Christ and completes his journey from knight to saint. A week before his vow of disguised penitence is to expire and as he anticipates a reunion with his wife and son, an angel appears in his cave and announces, "Thou blessed Champion of the highest Heaven" that the "great Master sends thee word . . . that seven dayes being past thou sure shalt dye" (1350, 1352–3). In sadness, he considers revealing himself to Phyllis at once, but then resolves not to "break that vow of sanctity" (1374). A week later, the angel returns "to bear thy soul to Heaven," and leaves Guy to pray a lengthy and instructive final prayer concerning Christ's redemption of the "soul which sinful man, / hath forfeited to Satan, Death, and hell" (1421, 1449). While Guy is dying, his son and wife learn of his location in the cave and rush to him. His son is with him as he prays, "I come, I come, to thee sweet Christ I flye," but Phyllis enters just after his death (1525). After wandering for the full amount of penitential time, Guy dies within a short distance of the journey's end, that is, the reunification with his family at Warwick Castle. Typologically, he performs the role of Moses, albeit a Christian tragicomic one.[39]

---

[39] The 1661 title page of the play advertises it as "The Tragical History of Guy Earl of Warwick," but the 1620 (new style) Stationers' Register entry simply names it "A Play Called *the life and Death of GUY of Warwicke*" and attributes it to John Day and Thomas Dekker. Although other critics have wondered if the 1661 publication derives from an Elizabethan version, the water poet John Taylor reported attending a Guy of Warwick play at a London inn in 1618. Day and Dekker's initial collaboration on the play certainly could have occurred a decade before as the play's use of tragicomedy, English historical romance figures, and supernatural elements fits with the Jacobean era between *Pericles* and *The Birth of Merlin*. As Siobhan Keenan also notes, the 1661 play "is something of a generic 'hodgepodge', combining heroic adventure, comedy, tragedy, and romance in a manner akin to many early Elizabethan history plays and historical romances." "A Little Known Allusion to an Inn Performance in the Suburbs of Jacobean London," *Notes and Queries* (2003): 439.

He dies before reaching the promised reunion with his wife, but his soul ascends to heaven. The play closes as Guy's family and King Athelstan mourn Guy's death, but they recognize that "Heaven hath appointed this" (1580). In its Jacobean stage version, then, *Guy* sacralizes England as he returns to Warwick and lives out his life as a saint.

The Birth of Merlin also sacralizes the landscape through dramatizing monastic acts in a story of legendary heroes opposing foreign and pagan forces.[40] The main plot of the play involves the Britons—led by King Aurelius and then Uther Pendragon afterwards—fighting the invading Saxons. Ultimately, Uther Pendragon, King Arthur's father, triumphs over the Saxons. As in *Guy of Warwick* and *A Shoemaker, A Gentleman*, the subplots in *The Birth of Merlin* involve a holy hermit, vows of celibacy, and miracles across various geographic sites in England and Wales. The play also presents hierarchies and categories of good and evil, saints and devils, and miracles and magic. Although Merlin is the son of the Devil himself, the Welsh magician supports the Christian Britons against the pagan Saxons and the evil enchanter, Proximus. At the top of the hierarchy of marvel-making is Anselm the Hermit, who works miracles, counsels the Christians, and eventually becomes the Bishop of Winchester. Among Anselm's holy accomplishments is the conversion of two noble women and the establishment of convent life in England.

Anselm is an utter invention of *The Birth of Merlin*. While the name of the hermit links him to the famous Archbishop of Canterbury, his presence during the conflict of the Britons and the Saxons and his eventual seat at Winchester link him to St. Germain of Auxerre and St. Swithin, respectively. As reported by Matthew Paris, St. Germain arrived in mid-sixth-century England, venerated St. Alban, converted multitudes, and worked miracles on behalf of the Britons against the Picts and the Scots. To recall, St. Swithin was the ninth-century Bishop of Winchester whose cult grew under St. Dunstan's influence in the next century. During that time, Swithin's relics were moved within Winchester Cathedral, the local area enjoyed increased miracles, and his cult became associated with the expansion of English monasticism. The conflation of these various saints into the character of Anselm in *The Birth of Merlin* allows for the legendary acts and miraculous interventions of St. Germaine to be geographically linked with Winchester, a site of both sacred and royal authority. Not only was Winchester the resting place of St. Swithin's miraculous relics, but also it is the site of the mythic Arthurian round table at Winchester Castle, which Henry VIII had refurbished in 1522.

The ancient authority of the English church is established in this Arthurian play through the miracle-working of Anselm the Hermit. Not only have Anselm's prayers "o'rethrew / The pagan Host" during a battle between the Britons and

---

[40] Joanna Udall, *A Critical, Old-Spelling Edition of The Birth of Merlin (Q1662)* (London: Modern Humanities Research Association, 1991). All subsequent in-text parenthetical citations come from this edition.

the Saxons, but also the Saxons repeatedly curse Anselm for his Christianity (1.1.74–5). In doing so, the Saxons take on the role of the Roman and pagan persecutors in martyrdom or conquest legends. In an early court challenge, the pagan Proximus conjures spirits who appear in the guise of Hector and Achilles. The two ancient warriors "*manage their weapons to begin the Fight: and after some Charges, the Hermit steps between them, at which seeming amaz'd the spirits* [quake] *and tremble. Thunder within*" (SD 2.2.206). Like the saints of medieval legendaries and earlier saint plays, Anselm's miraculous disruption demonstrates the power of Christianity over pagan magic.

Anselm's holy acts extend to planting monastic life in ancient Britain. In a subplot involving two daughters of a noble Briton, the virtuously named Modesta and Constantia, Anselm counsels them to reject their promised suitors in favor of monastic life.[41] Anselm determines that Modesta is "in love" with "Religious Life" and "a Modest Virgin" (1.2.230, 234, 247). Therefore, he instructs her to direct her love toward heaven instead of marriage. Modesta later improvises a religious ceremony that cites St. Winifred's vows in *A Shoemaker, A Gentleman*. Before Anselm, Modesta vows her "chaste thoughts up to heaven" and then also convinces her sister, Constantia, to reject marriage for vowed virginity (3.2.5). Until the end of the play, when the Saxons have been "forc't to re-deliver / London and Winchester," the fate of the two vowed virgins is unclear (5.2.26–7). Only after the Britons have reclaimed their nation do the sisters' former suitors witness Modesta and Constantia "both enter the Monastery, / Secluded from the world and men for ever" (5.2.20–1). Munro observes that the play assumes that audiences are "unavoidably conscious of the way in which ... multiple historical and mythic narratives will end," that is, with the eventual conquering and division of Britain, and asks whether audiences will "align themselves with the soon-to-be-extinct British ... or do they identify with the incoming 'English' who figure as the "Saxon invaders"?[42] The subplot of Anselm and the holy virgins somewhat resolves this problem in offering the continuity of an ancient and native British Christianity. The tragicomic ending substitutes the wedding that traditionally ends a comedy for the vows of the nuns. Rather than a promise of English futurity based on fertility, Anselm's office as Bishop of Winchester and the sisters' permanent life as professed virgins links the ancient Britons to the English present through a tradition of monasteries and monastic cathedrals, such as the famous nunnery of Barking Abbey in London and the Priory of St. Swithin attached to Winchester Cathedral.

---

[41] Constantia is based on the elder brother of Aurelius and Uther Pendragon in Matthew Paris's version of the pre-Arthurian history. As Matthew Paris reports, Constans was given to "the church of Amphibalus, at Winchester" and became a monk. *The Flowers of History, Especially Such as Relate to the Affairs of Britain: B.C. 4004 to A. D. 1066*, trans. Charles Duke Yonge (Henry G. Bohn, 1853), Vol. 1, 210.

[42] "'Nemp your sexes!': Anachronistic Aesthetics in *Hengist, King of Kent* and the Jacobean 'Anglo-Saxon' Play," *Modern Philology* 111, no. 4 (2014): 734–61, 752

Theatregoers would have been familiar with religious ruins, especially those in and near London. Audiences of *Henry VIII* at Blackfriars watched an actor enact Katherine of Aragon's speech during the trial scene in the same location as the historic event actually occurred in the century prior. John Webster also harnessed the power of palimpsest location in the *Duchess of Malfi* (c.1612), which premiered at Blackfriars. In Act 5, Antonio gestures at "the ruins of an ancient abbey."[43] In performance, Antonio's lines both referred to the site of the Cardinal's palace while simultaneously excavating the memory of the theatre's past as a Dominican priory: "I do love these ancient ruins. / We never tread upon them, but we set / Our foot upon some reverend history" (5.3.9–11). As Alexandra Walsham, Peter Marshall, and Ceri Law observe, "The process of compelled forgetting" vis-à-vis Reformation iconoclasm "had the unforeseen effect of catalysing remembrance."[44] They go on to describe how "the ruins of religious houses, chapels, standing crosses, and other forms of Christian sculpture that littered the countryside remained a touchstone for recalling the medieval past and lamenting its loss."[45] The dissolution of the monasteries destroyed the shrines that held the relics of native saints in such places as Winchester Cathedral, Barking Abbey, and St. Albans. The loss of that material culture also severed the connection between story and site, memory and memorial. *The Birth of Merlin* does not reanimate the precise narratives of British saints, but it does recast hagiographical scenarios of early British Christianity onto the landscape of religious ruins. In doing so, it excavates a map of the nation determined not by administrative county but by veneration, pilgrimage, and prayer. Although the sites in these plays have been deconsecrated or dissolved, their continual dwelling, even as rubble, nonetheless materializes the geography of sainthood that first sacralized the land.

England and the Champions of Old Christendom

Tragicomedy, like the medieval legends of the saints, is a wandering genre. Indeed, the playwright John Kirke situated his play, *The Seven Champions of Christendom* (c.1635) in a metaphor of chorography because "it consists of many parts, not walking in one direct path, of *Comedy* or *Tragedy*, but having a larger field to trace" (A3v–A4r).[46] This larger field is the map of English and Welsh sanctity produced by the saints of the professional stage in the Jacobean and Caroline period. The saints journey across the ancient kingdoms of Britain or return to England after

---

[43] John Webster, *The Duchess of Malfi*, ed. John Russell Brown (Manchester: Manchester University Press, 1991), 5.3.2. All subsequent in-text parenthetical citations are from this version.
[44] *Memory and the English Reformation*, 24.
[45] *Memory and the English Reformation*, 24.
[46] John Kirke, *The seven champions of Christendome* (London: John Okes, 1638). All subsequent in-text parenthetical citations are from this version.

marking the boundaries between the ancient Christendom to which England has long belonged to and the rest of the world populated by heterodoxy, monsters, and non-Christians. As I conclude this exploration of itinerant sanctity and the forms they manifest on stage, I extend my examination of the saints who make up the old legend of England. Whether in traditional or de-sacralized form, these saints are not only able to materialize sacred space on home soil, but also to protect England against that otherworld occupied by the nation's religious enemies.

The use of saints in Stuart drama to revere and signify English nationhood stands in contrast to the earlier depiction of saints in Elizabethan drama. Before the Stuart period, saints were sometimes invoked in drama to represent England, but they do so without actual stage presence. For example, in Shakespeare's *Henry V* (c.1599), references to SS Crispin, George, and David measure the distance between England and Wales and the climactic battlefield at Agincourt. More to the point, these saints patronize the English cause against the French and ensure the rightful return of France to the king of England. But these saints do not materialize as characters and their acts and miracles are absent. As the Archbishop of Canterbury in the same play admits, their "miracles are ceased" (1.1.65). When Shakespeare does address the history of miraculous intervention by saints on English soil, he depicts the problem of fraudulent performance, something that I explored at the end of chapter 2. Saints may populate the English imagination of Shakespeare's history plays through their patronage, but their acts, appearances, and miracles are past. In *2 Henry VI* and *Henry V*, the status of native saints mirrors the post-Reformation landscape of disillusionment and absent presence. This absent presence is what Queen Elizabeth encounters in the *Entertainment at Harefield* when St. Swithin sends a letter in apology for the weather in 1602. By the late Elizabethan period, pageantry could welcome the epistolary presence of Swithin, but the late Bishop of Winchester did not appear before the queen as a character. It would not be until *The Birth of Merlin* premiered that a conflated bishop-saint of Winchester appeared alongside the Tudors' kingly predecessor, Uther Pendragon.

The turn from the ambiguous status of native saints in performance during the late Elizabethan period to their itinerant return in theatre during the Jacobean period also registers in the history of the Norwich St. George pageants. Because the Guild of St. George was not a religious fraternity, such as a chantry guild whose incorporation rested on praying for the souls of the dead, it was not dissolved during the Reformation.[47] Still, in 1559, the guild modified its annual event by excising all devotional or paradevotional elements and only retained the parading of the dragon. The Guild Book records that "it is fully condeceded and agreed that the ffeast nexte to be holden for the company and fellowshipp

---

[47] The Guild of St. George had been founded in 1385 and received a charter from Henry V in 1417. It was not dissolved until the eighteenth century. See Muriel C. McClendon, "A Moveable Feast: Saint George's Day Celebrations and Religious Change in Early Modern England," *Journal of British Studies* 38 (1999): 1–27.

of Saynt George for dyuerse cawses Weyed and considerid Ther shalbe neyther George nor Margett But for pastyme the dragon to com In and shew hym selff as in other yeares."[48] The records of the Guild of St. George imply that it would have been impolitic to parade George and Margaret through Norwich, at least in 1559. Unlike the religious fraternities who were compelled to sell their properties during their disbandment, the guild sold most of their properties related to the procession in 1550 even though it was not dissolved. Yet, the Norwich pageant continued through Elizabeth's reign and, like their modifications of earlier pageants, the records reflect upkeep and additions to the dragon and its bearers.[49] The continuation of this tradition even in modified form allowed for the eventual return of England's patron saint. St. George reappeared, "as part of the festivities intermittently between 1619 and 1632," however, he was now represented by a processional painted image rather than by a performer and the occasion was a Lord Mayor's Show rather than the pre-Reformation blend of civic and religious ritual on 23 April.[50]

A similar process of negotiated recovery of public hagiography occurred in London pageantry in the Jacobean period starting with the coronation of King James. In 1604, *The Magnificent Entertainment* by Dekker and Jonson featured SS Andrew and George meeting as the symbolic reunification of Scotland and England through the ascension of James. Afterward, Lord Mayor's Shows began to occasionally include patron saints. This era included St. Dunstan's appearance in a nonspeaking role in Anthony Munday's Goldsmiths' pageant in 1611 and St. Katherine appearing similarly mute in a Haberdashers' pageant authored by John Squire in 1620. In holding her sword and wheel on behalf of the London Haberdashers, St. Katherine, who remained in the English ecclesiastical calendar on 25 November, belonged to the old legend of England rather than to the new Counter-Reformation league of Catholic saints. In standing in silence on the streets of London in 1620, Katherine yet stood for England. By the time she started addressing mayors and London citizens in Thomas Heywood's pageants for the Haberdashers in the Caroline period in 1631, 1632, and 1637, the performance of ancient virgin martyrdom would be firmly established in the professional theatre, something I address in chapter 5.

The saints of the old legend of England that enact miracles, martyrdom, and monastic life in the subplots and episodes of romance also stand against the new-fangled heterodox saints of the Counter-Reformation. Shortly after *A Shoemaker, A Gentleman*, *Guy of Warwick*, and *The Birth of Merlin* celebrated the native saints of the soil, Thomas Middleton penned a scene involving a saint that symbolically depicts the foreign Catholic assault on English religious and political sovereignty.

---

[48] *REED: Norwich*, 47.
[49] The dragon acquired "A hoope of yron" in 1583, it was regularly repainted, and a Dutchman mended its wings with "an owld sheet," in 1584. *REED: Norwich*, 69–71.
[50] McClendon, "Moveable Feast," 22.

A Game at Chess was viewed by an estimated 7 percent of London in 1624 during the controversial marriage negotiations between England and Spain over the potential match between Prince Charles and the Spanish infanta.[51] These events were the first of a number of public scandals associated with Charles's courtship of Catholics in both romantic and political terms. At the beginning of Middleton's incendiary political drama, Ignatius Loyola appears with a Satanic vice character. The play presents an allegorical account of black Spanish chess pieces attempting to Catholicize the white English court through political intrigue and sexual violence. While much of the play relies on the oppositional dynamics of medieval morality plays—as well as the politics of an early modern ethno-racial binary—the only part of *A Game at Chess* that outright identifies characters as vice or devil-like characters is the Induction. The scene offers a key to the play's allegory with the late Spanish founder of the Jesuits and a snake-like companion, Error. The recently "sainted" Ignatius laments that while his "Sonnes and Heires" have "spread ouer the world" and "Couered the Earths face and made darke the Land," there is but a single "Angle of the World" that remains unconquered by the Jesuits (A3r). The priest wakes a supine and sleeping Error with a speech reminiscent of conjurors. He calls "vp *Error*, wake / Father of *Supererogation*, Rise / It is *Ignatius* calls thee *Loyola*" (A3v). Error wakes and tells Ignatius of his pleasing "Dreame, / A Vision" of their black order set against the white house of England in a game of chess (A3v). In England, there are saints, such as Polycarp, Cecilia, and Ursula, who Ignatius envies for their cults. These saints belong to the old legend. And then there are Roman Catholic saints, like Ignatius in Middleton's play, who represent the heterodox difference of foreign religious interference.

As the last "angle of the World" that remains uncorrupted, England anchors Christendom (A3r). Although St. George does not appear in *A Game at Chess*, it is clear that, as the patron saint of the old legend of England, he would surely protect England against the attack of the Spanish anti-saint. This function of St. George—as patron military protector of England—surfaces in the sprawling Caroline play *The Seven Champions of Christendom*. The play is a combination of Richard Johnson's 1596–97 prose narrative of the same name and the conventions of other early modern saint plays. The narrative follows St. George of England and his brother patron saints, David of Wales, Andrew of Scotland, Patrick of Ireland, James of Spain, Dennis of France, and Anthony of Italy. They crusade and battle monsters, witches, and pagans through a number of spectacular episodes across England,

---

[51] Thomas Middleton, *A game at chess* (London, 1625). All subsequent in-text parenthetical citations are from this version. Stephen Wittik writes that "the play attracted thirty thousand spectators, or a seventh of London's adult population, an unprecedented reception." See "Middleton's *A Game at Chess* and the Making of a Theatrical Public." *SEL* 55, no. 2 (2015): 423.

Europe, and the East.⁵² The play veers farther afield from traditional hagiography than any of the other tragicomedies. Removed from the tropes of hagiography and even embracing the martial and marital tropes of romance, these de-sanctified patrons of pre-Reformation Western Christianity nonetheless form an old map of Christendom that links the British representatives (George, Andrew, David, and Patrick) to their brothers in Spain, France, and Italy (James, Dennis, and Anthony). This band of brothers materializes a map of a mythic, heroic, and unified Christendom. In Sanok's work on fifteenth-century saints' lives and the English nation, she focuses on how writers rescaled saints across imaginative expanses, including geographical ones. Saints that formerly represented communities as small as a single monastery or as large as the Christian West were reshaped to fit England. Sanok writes that "where the regional cult of St. Wenefred, for example, or the institutional cult of St. Edith [of Wilton Abbey] scaled up from local to national, the pan-European cult of St. Ursula had to be scaled down to claim her as an English saint."⁵³ *The Seven Champions of Christendom* also experiments with scale. St. George reorients the map of Christendom so that it centers on England. Then, as he ventures with the patrons of Wales, Scotland, Ireland, France, Spain, and Italy, St. George gains dimension and scales up English Christianity so that it extends across a bloc of Atlantic nations.

In reorienting and rescaling the map of Christendom, *The Seven Champions of Christendom* completes an excavation of an old map of religious unification. The authority of the ancient temporality of the old legend contrasts with false or foreign saints of later ages. Indeed, the problem of legendary temporality and sainthood is first highlighted by Shakespeare in *All's Well That Ends Well*, a play that takes place in Spain, France, and Italy. On her pilgrimage along an ancient route from France to Santiago de Compostela, Helena asks, "Where do the palmers lodge?" and is told, "At the Saint Francis" (3.5.37–8). The landscape of Helena's wandering in the play includes both the shrine of St. James and the Franciscan refugio, that is, a site of the old legend and a site of foreign Catholicism, respectively. Notably, Helena— perhaps named for the saintly "mother of Constantine, who united Britain and Rome, the first English pilgrim"—continues to seek St. James but lodges with a widow instead of the friars.⁵⁴ As the national patrons of Spain, France, and Italy, it might seem that James, Dennis, and Anthony present a Catholic conflict to the patron saints of the British archipelago. However, under the leadership of St. George the brother patrons band together against the new saints of the

---

⁵² Lisa Hopkins considers the supernatural alongside the national in this play, along with Saint Patrick for Ireland and the Virgin Martyr in "Profit and Delight? Magic and the Dreams of a Nation," in *Magical Transformations on the Early Modern English Stage*, eds. Lisa Hopkins and Helen Ostovich (London: Routledge, 2014), 139–54.

⁵³ Sanok, *New Legends of England*, 245.

⁵⁴ Richard Wilson, "To Great Saint Jacques Bound: All's Well That Ends Well in Shakespeare's Spain," in *Sacred Text—Sacred Space: Architectural, Spiritual and Literary Convergences in England and Wales*, eds. Joseph Sterrett and Peter Thomas (Leiden: Brill, 2011), 104.

Counter-Reformation. Although they are not named in Kirke's play, these new saints are ones such as Ignatius Loyola, Joan of Arc, and Carlo Borromeo. Elsewhere in the culture and sometimes on stage, the new saints were ridiculed for their false claims to sanctity and, due to their association with Catholicism, also were associated with religious and military aggression against England. In contrast, the seven champions occupy the same hagiographical imaginary populated by the other saints encountered on Stuart stages and streets.

Reformation iconoclasm effected the anti-translation of the saints. When the reformers destroyed shrines and monuments, they destroyed the material culture of the old legend of England. The *vitae*, meaning, and myths of these saints were dislocated without new places to inhabit. Yet, the collective effect of the Jacobean and Caroline tragicomedies examined in this chapter is the imaginative re-placement of saints on the landscape of England and Wales. Toward the end of Michel de Certeau's essay, "Walking in the City," he reflects on the personal nature of spatial memory in urban environments, writing that, "memory is a sort of anti-museum: it is not localizable."[55] He goes on to explain that, "Places are fragmentary and inward-turning histories, pasts that others are not allowed to read."[56] This is a useful formulation inasmuch as it explains the opposite tendencies of the itinerant tragicomedies. The acts and travels of the saints are not a personal perambulation in a familiar neighborhood. Rather, the transformations of English and Welsh saints across a shared map of the mythical past produce a new memory of native sanctity of and through location. In this way, these tragicomedies participate in the future-oriented politics of imagining the landscape as a nation and restoring the saints of the ecclesiastical past to the early modern English present.

---

[55] Michel de Certeau, *The Practice of Everyday Life*, trans. Steven Rendall (Berkeley: University of California Press, 1984), 108.
[56] de Certeau, *The Practice of Everyday Life*, 108.

5
Devices of Virgin Martyrdom

How do you know that a saint is a saint? This is the central crux of the virgin martyr plays of the Stuart era, but it is not a new quandary brought about by the age of reform. In the late fourteenth century, Boccaccio took on the problem of knowing sanctity in the first tale of the *Decameron*. Set during the plague of 1348, eight young Florentines tell stories as they quarantine together for ten days. There is a spirit of competition among the storytellers, and they must meet thematic assignments for all the days except for the first, and so the entire compendium begins with a story that warns of sham sainthood. Ciappelletto, as he is known, is a man whose life is shot through with sin: fraud, lying, discord, murder, sodomy, gluttony. When he falls ill on a business trip, he cheats morality one last time by faking a solemn deathbed confession so that he can receive a decent burial. An "elderly friar whose life was holy and virtuous, well versed in the Scriptures" arrives and hears the confession recited by Ciappelletto.[1] Although the dying man has never confessed before, he tells the friar that he does so at least weekly and then admits to wrongdoing in nearly every category. But whereas Ciappelletto's sins are vast and ugly, the ones he describes during his deathbed performance are those of a holy man. For example, his actual gluttony is described as eating "enough for six" and drinking "like a fish," but to the friar he expresses remorse for indulgently guzzling water on fast days.[2] As a result, the unrepentant sinner is buried with great ceremony by the entire community of friars and his public reputation as a saint commences with a hagiographical sermon on the "most wonderful facts about his fasts, his virginity, his simple innocence and holiness," that is, his imitation of Christ.[3] When the Mass concludes, a crowd rips "the clothes off his body," which are received as relics, and then the people continue the set of social acts that turn a person into a saint: candle lighting, venerating, announcing miracles, and the performative uttering of "Saint Ciappelletto." It is a cynical tale, but one that highlights the general knowledge of how sainthood is enacted and sustained in a given society, something that appears frequently in medieval texts. Perhaps the least cynical account of the enaction of sainthood is found in Lollard confessions of faith. As Fiona Somerset has shown, these texts articulate "what to believe, what to say, how to feel, how to model oneself on holy predecessors and join them in anticipating

---

[1] Giovanni Boccaccio, *The Decameron*, ed. Jonathan Usher, trans. Guido Waldman (Oxford: Oxford University Press, 2008), 27–8.
[2] Boccaccio, *The Decameron*, 25.
[3] Boccaccio, *The Decameron*, 33.

or imitating Christ."[4] Like Ciappelletto, Lollards knew what specific and iterative actions legibly enact a social repertoire of sanctity.

The dramatic repertoire of sanctity is related to the social one in terms of its iterability and legibility, but it departs from it in terms of its representational hermeneutics. Actual saints present the confusion of seeming and being, something that the Jacobean and Caroline virgin martyr plays aim to solve through theatricality. *The Virgin Martyr* (1619) by Thomas Dekker and Philip Massinger represents a final innovation in the turn to theatrical sanctity in early modern drama. Along with the anonymous *Two Noble Ladies* (c.1619–22), *The Martyr'd Soldier* (c.1619–22) by Henry Shirley, and *Saint Patrick for Ireland* (1639) by James Shirley, the play sketches out the requirements of sanctity beyond the shores of England and Wales through a repertoire of virgin martyrdom. The virgin martyr plays build on the emphasis on virginity found in other saint plays, such as *If You Know Not Me, You Know Nobody*, *A Shoemaker, A Gentleman*, and *The Birth of Merlin*. These plays also make use of the collective set of theatrical conventions of sanctity, that is, angelic apparitions to musical accompaniment, books as apotropaic devices, and the miraculous—and often pyrotechnic—destruction of devils. Angels, demons, and their otherworldly theatricality saturate the stage. The sensory experience of the opposition between heaven and hell, and their respective creatures, is further augmented by the heightened role of soundscape. Celestial notes of "soft music" signal miraculous intervention against the rough cacophony of demonic interference. The use of music, whether instrumental or vocal, in these plays functions as a sign of supernatural presence or collision.

Unlike Elizabeth in *If You Know Not Me, You Know Nobody* and Winifred in *A Shoemaker, A Gentleman*, who embody political, cultural, and historical authority through their status as native virgin martyrs, the problem of knowing sanctity in the four plays addressed here is more difficult. All of the saints and their pagan tyrannical foes belong to ancient empires or kingdoms beyond England and Wales. Furthermore, during the period of the Reformation and Counter-Reformation, both the English and Roman Catholic churches claimed the early church and its martyrs as their own. Without the authoritative markers of established stage sainthood—English or Welsh, contra the papacy—sanctity needs more signification. The violent miracles of the virgin martyr plays, therefore, function as a sort of canonization in the theatre. These plays might seem "Catholic" in their aesthetics, but they do not reflect the anti-Protestant rhetoric featured in the assuredly Catholic parts of *St. Christopher*. The repertoire of virgin martyrdom enables the production of theatrical sanctity without adjudication by theology or religious confession. This is not Catholic sanctity, nor is it exactly Protestant sanctity. The plays addressed in this chapter rely on a formulaic—that is, generic—production of

---

[4] *Feeling Like Saints: Lollard Writings after Wyclif* (Ithaca: Cornell University Press, 2014), 153.

theatrical virgin martyrdom. In each of them, an event of rape and its miraculous avoidance functions as the primary signifier of sanctity.

The Advocates of Heaven and Hell

In addressing the various permutations of saints in early modern drama, I also have tracked the association of saints with spectacular theatricality and the development of a theatrical language for the staging of miracles. The virgin martyr plays follow the general patterns, conventions, and spectacles associated with previous saint plays. Many of those plays also emphasize chastity and virginity. The virgin martyr plays set themselves apart by adjudicating sanctity through rape and its miraculous avoidance. Whereas the performativity of sanctity in society is necessarily flexible as it moves across place and time, stage sanctity is much more static. As a dramatic repertoire, virgin martyrdom achieves recognizability through both general and precise repetition. Books, for example, appear frequently as stage properties in saint plays. Dorothy holds a book in *The Virgin Martyr* while Justina uses the same prop as an apotropaic instrument in *Two Noble Ladies*. The book is associated with sanctity, but it does not determine sainthood. The precise function of the device of the rape test is to determine sainthood. The virgin martyr plays present both a theatre of misogyny and a poetics dependent, not on God, but on the god of the machine.

The Virgin Martyr, Two Noble Ladies, The Martyr'd Soldier, and *Saint Patrick for Ireland* reflect the violent religious knowledge that characterizes earlier eras of virgin martyr narratives in England. Jocelyn Wogan-Browne identifies twelfth- and thirteenth-century Anglo-Norman hagiography as the period that developed particular meaning out of the violent collision between the virgin and her pagan tyrant, something that separates it from Old English *vitae*. In a saint's *passio*, "[t]orture as the pagan's mode of producing meaning is opposed and answered both by the virgin's own arguments and prayers and by God's production of miracles for the saint."[5] Similarly, Winstead shows how late thirteenth- and fourteenth-century Middle English legends, such as those found in the *South English Legendary*, "accentuated the differences between the saint and ordinary people, presenting her as a powerful intermediary with God, to be admired rather than imitated."[6] Later, in the fifteenth century, writers experimented with an emphasis on family life and Christian education in the lives of women saints, a strain of late medieval English hagiography that, according to Winstead, resurfaces in John Foxe's depiction of both ancient virgin martyrs and contemporary

---

[5] Jocelyn Wogan-Browne, *Saints' Lives and Women's Literary Culture, c. 1150–1300: Virginity and Its Authorizations* (Oxford: Oxford University Press, 2001), 107.
[6] *Virgin Martyrs*, 65.

Protestant martyrs.[7] The Stuart virgin martyr plays reject that more social and relational late medieval and Reformation model of virgin martyrdom for its extreme, super heroine predecessor. I am not arguing that the repertoire deployed by the virgin martyr plays deliberately modeled its characters on that earlier era of hagiography. Rather, the plays likely emerge out of a convergence of *Golden Legend*–style sanctity and seventeenth-century feminine dramatic sexuality. Questions of chastity, virginity, sexual loyalty, and seduction catalyze violence in Jacobean and Caroline tragedy and tragicomedy. In *Pericles*, which plays with the tropes of saints' lives rather than enacting them outright, Marina avoids rape through rhetorical finesse. In the decade after the premiere of *Pericles*, however, the dramatization of virgin martyrdom turned from ambiguity to adjudication.

The problem of knowing punctuates early modern drama. From the neurosis of *Hamlet* to the wax figures in *The Duchess of Malfi*, the theatre frequently dramatizes epistemological problems, especially around seeming, feigning, or performing in the representational (not performative) sense. For example, setting aside sanctity and martyrdom for a moment, the problem of knowing a virgin— an everyday one, that is, not a sanctified virgin—is a complex one. It is a problem staged at the Red Bull's indoor sister theatre, the Phoenix, around the same time as the debut of *Two Noble Ladies* and *The Martyr'd Soldier*. Act 4 of *The Changeling* (1622) by Thomas Middleton and William Rowley examines ways of determining sexual knowledge or lack thereof.[8] Having exchanged sex for murder, Beatrice-Joanna must feign her recently lost virginity to her new husband, Alsemero. There is neither a gynecological examination before nuptial consummation nor is a vial of pig's blood secretly spilled on the sheets after the act. Old tricks will not do. Rather, the bridegroom's gentleman-scholar closet of scientific experimentation provides a means of verification without relying on the hymen to witness to Beatrice-Joanna's virginity. With "seven hours to bedtime," the bride discovers the bridegroom's potions, one of which will reveal "whether a woman be a maid or not" (4.1.54, 4.1.41). Fortunately, her husband has labeled his experiments with directions: "Give the party you suspect the quantity of a spoonful of the water in glass M, which upon her that is a maid makes three several effects: 'twill make her incontinently gape, then fall into a sudden sneezing, last into a violent laughing; else dull, heavy, and lumpish'" (4.1.47–51). Beatrice-Joanna tests the experiment by drinking the potion along with her waiting woman. The maid reacts accordingly, but the bride is unaffected. When the bridegroom puts the bride to the test, she passes it by repeating the observed reactions of her maid and is pronounced, "Chaste as the breath of heaven" (4.2.150). However, when Alsemero later learns

---

[7] *Fifteenth-Century Lives*, 136–46.
[8] Thomas Middleton and William Rowley, "The Changeling," *Thomas Middleton: The Collected Works*, eds. Gary Taylor and John Lavagnino (Oxford: Oxford University Press, 2007). All subsequent in-text parenthetical citations from both this play and *The Revenger's Tragedy* are from this edition.

that "she's a whore," he curses "O cunning devils! / How should blind men know you from fair-faced saints?" (5.3.107, 108–9).

As Marjorie Garber observes, the "curious paradox of Alsemero's glass M is the fact that it produces, or is expected to produce, orgasmic effects in virgins, and not in women of sexual experience."[9] The problem with the business of glass M for the bridegroom-scientist is that it tests for sexual knowledge through the reaction of a woman who, as playgoers know from the paranoid misogyny of Jacobean revenge tragedy, can seem what she is not. English audiences have encountered this anxiety before. It drives the Marian gynecological exams in medieval biblical plays and produces the dramatic antagonism in *Measure for Measure* in which Angelo seems as religiously pure as Isabella actually is. The virginity test in *The Changeling* is not a spiritual test. It is only a physical test and, for that reason, it is easily faked. Scientific knowledge is undermined by "mimesis" when Beatrice-Joanna reenacts the performance of her actually maidenly maid.[10] Yet, for all the dissembling of purity and madness in *The Changeling*, the one spectacle that cannot be feigned is the ghost of Alonso who haunts the stage and substantiates the sin, crime, and guilt of his lascivious murderers. Men, blind or seeing, cannot know whores and devils from fair-faced saints if they rely on a woman's body to react to "physic." Alsemero's mistake is the same as Ciappelletto's confessor: both men relied on a show of virtue alone. This is why the virgin martyr plays of the same era posit that a saint is known, like a ghost, when the supernatural crashes the stage.

The theatricality of the virgin martyr plays perform a role similar to Alsemero, the scientific investigator of virginity. Yet, the threshold for verification in these plays is higher than that of the foolish husband who is satisfied in his quest for purity by a checklist of behaviors. In this sense, the device of rape is more akin to the processes of canonization in which a Devil's Advocate must scrutinize the integrity of the candidate for sainthood. The process of canonization became subject to increase regulation during the Middle Ages and, between the fifteenth and sixteenth centuries, was consolidated by Rome. Throughout the Middle Ages and then during the Counter-Reformation, the papacy worried about the standards and meaning of sainthood. In 1588, Sixtus V created the Congregation for the Rites and Ceremonies and, with it, further formalized the inquiries and processes related to canonization. While the Promoter of the Faith had played an official part in canonization proceedings since at least the thirteenth century, the agonistic, procedural role of the Devil's Advocate reconstituted itself in this period. Simon Ditchfield observes that "the intensely legalistic rather than theological cast imparted to canonization trials after 1588 represented a significant change of degree, engendering a thirst for written evidence and a rigour in its examination."[11]

---

[9] Marjorie Garber, *Symptoms of Culture* (New York: Routledge, 1998), 225.
[10] Garber, *Symptoms of Culture*, 229.
[11] Simon Ditchfield, "How Not to Be a Counter-Reformation Saint: The Attempted Canonization of Pope Gregory X, 1622–45," *Papers of the British School at Rome* 60 (1992): 383.

Not only is there a consideration of the acts of potential saints during their lives, but also a particular focus on the validity of reported miracles. The process of investigation is designed to ferret out the truth of the seeming saints, that is, the St. Ciapellettos. Although the role of the Devil's Advocate was discontinued in 1983 under John Paul II, doctors and physicists, among other professionals, might still be called upon by the Vatican to testify about the known causes of seemingly supernatural events so that the tribunal can determine whether an event seems or is a miracle.

Beginning in 1619, with *The Virgin Martyr*, the theatre devised its own rigorous process of determining sainthood through a trial of rape. The source narratives for the virgin martyr plays lack the explicit scenarios of sexual assault that are present in the lives of SS Agnes, Lucy, Anastasia, and Cecilia, among others. While the Agnes legend is by far the most well known, the genre of virgin martyrdom regularly included the motif of miraculous rape avoidance.[12] Lucy's tyrant condemns her to "the ribauldes of the toun" and tells them "to defoule her / and labour her so moche tyl that she be deed," but they are unable to accomplish the assault through protection of "the holy ghoost."[13] Anastasia's provost is unable to commit sexual violence because her prayers cause him to lose "hys wytte" so that "he embraced pottes pannes and the cawdrons" instead of her, something that will be familiar to readers of Hrotsvit's *Dulcitius*.[14] Forced to marry, the vowed virgin Cecilia reveals to her husband on her wedding night that "an aungel that loueth me / which euer kepeth my body whether I slepe or wake and yf he may fynde that ye touche my body by vylonye or foule and pollute loue / certeynly he shal anone slee you."[15] Instead of assaulting his bride, Valerian converts to Christianity and accepts a celibate marriage. In exchange, he receives a crown from an angel in a miraculous scene that resembles the grand finale of *The Virgin Martyr*, which I address in the next section.

The device of rape in these plays is the primary means through which Stuart theatre inherited medieval virgin martyr legends. To return to the metaphor of the canonization process, the devils who populate these plays force the theatre to take a position on the status of the saints. This innovation suspends the need for personal religious identification or prior knowledge of hagiographic tropes. As in the probing of the Virgin Mary and the torture of the eucharist in medieval drama, these plays produce proof in the face of doubt. Kathleen Coyne Kelly distinguishes between a test of virginity or an ordeal of chastity that occurs when "the subject's virginity is in doubt," whereas "a 'proof' of virginity" is an affirmation

---

[12] Gaspar suggests that *The Virgin Martyr* owes its rape avoidance to the St. Agnes legend. See Julia Gaspar, "The Sources of *The Virgin Martyr*," *The Review of English Studies* 42, no. 165 (1991): 17–19.
[13] Caxton, *Golden Legend*, lxxxxiii verso.
[14] Caxton, *Golden Legend*, lxxxxvii recto.
[15] Caxton, *Golden Legend*, ccclxxviii recto.

of fact."[16] Typically, proofs of sanctity occur through what Kelly identifies as the trope of "circumvented rape or near-rape" in hagiography, but these plays do not completely align with medieval literature.[17] The stage does not produce sanctity through faith but through doubt. These plays provide the device of rape as a test of virginity because sainthood *is* in doubt. The "proof" here is more legalistic than algebraic in that it is produced through the agon of heaven and hell. When devils, tyrants, and pagans attack the integrity of sanctity, the heavens respond—or not. The divine intervention or lack thereof delivers the verdict. Since the Elizabethan period, the theatre had been experimenting with ways to show truth within the boundaries of a dramatic world. Russ Leo identifies *The Murder of Gonazago*, the play-within-a-play in *Hamlet*, as a moment of meta-theorization in this regard. That is, Hamlet-as-producer "recognizes spectacle and stage-playing as ... absolutely crucial to discovery."[18] Along similar lines, the virgin martyr plays probe how to know sanctity as a matter of theatre.

Canonizing *The Virgin Martyr*

The Virgin Martyr by Dekker and Massinger adapts the legend of St. Dorothy, a fairly typical story of virgin martyrdom.[19] When a Roman tyrant demands that she profess paganism and sacrifice to the idols, she refuses. The tyrant sends for two apostate sisters to convert her. They fail, the saint reconverts them to Christianity, and the tyrant burns them at the stake. Dorothy is then tortured, imprisoned, and finally executed. She claims that, after her death, she will reside in a garden of roses and apples with Christ the bridegroom. The Roman official Theophilus mocks her by asking the saint to send flowers and fruit to him. After Dorothy's martyrdom, Christ, in the guise of a child, brings him roses and apples. Theophilus converts and is, too, martyred.

In adapting St. Dorothy into *The Virgin Martyr*, Dekker and Massinger retain scenarios and iconography that identify the saint and place her within new plots

---

[16] Kathleen Coyne Kelly, *Performing Virginity and Testing Chastity in the Middle Ages* (London: Routledge, 2002), 13
[17] Kelly, *Performing Virginity*, 42.
[18] Russ Leo, *Tragedy as Philosophy in the Reformation World* (Oxford: Oxford University Press, 2019), 158.
[19] Dorothy is absent from Jacobus de Voragine's original thirteenth-century *Legenda Aurea*, but she began to appear in Continental vernacular hagiography in the fourteenth century. The Dorothy legend first appeared in England in the fifteenth century in Osbern Bokenham's collection *Legendys of Hooly Wummen* and the anonymous *Gilte Legende*. Caxton, one of Dekker and Massinger's likely sources, drew his Dorothy from the *Gilte Legende* version. See Kirsten Wolf, "The Legend of Saint Dorothy: Medieval Vernacular Renderings and Their Latin Sources," *Analecta Bollandiana* 114 (1996): 41–72; Charlotte D'Evelyn, "Saints' Legends," in *A Manual of the Writings in Middle English, 1050–1500*, vol. 2, ed. J. Burke Severs (New Haven: Connecticut Academy of Arts and Sciences, 1970), 579–80. Julia Gaspar proposes that another source is the Kinsman brothers' English translation of Villegas's *Flos Sanctorum*. See Gaspar, "The Sources of *The Virgin Martyr*," 17–31.

of desire and Roman imperial conquest. The play includes an episode of apostate sisters, and the finale of the play includes a small child bearing fruit and flowers to an astonished Theophilus. Dekker and Massinger's additions to the Dorothy legend include the opposition between an angel and a devil, an instance of iconoclasm, a lovesick Roman, and a rape attempt. Dorothy, however, is not the Dorothy of medieval legends. Rather, she is The Virgin Martyr and the role she fulfills is a generic one. The deletions from and additions to the Dorothy legend could have produced roughly the same play with any number of other women saints, such as Katherine, Agnes, or Cecilia. Indeed, the saint's final lines before her execution imagine the circulation of her legend as a specific type of saint:

> Hereafter when my story shall be read,
> As they were present now, the hearers shall
> Say this of Dorothea with wet eyes.
> She liu'd a virgin and a virgin dyes.[20] (K2v)

In the scaffold speech, the protagonist declines to call herself Dorothy of Cappadocia. Nor is the play titled *The Tragedy of St. Dorothy*. Rather, the saint's own naming of herself as "a virgin" attempts to fix the meaning of her life and death as an iteration of dramatic sainthood. In doing so, *The Virgin Martyr* produces a type of play much more than it disseminates a particular *vita*.

Criticism concerning *The Virgin Martyr*, the most canonical of the non-Shakespearean plays addressed in this book, has shifted away from questions about the play's religious confession to a consideration of the play's dynamic depiction of conversion, liveliness, and theological reconciliation.[21] These approaches focus attention on the play's performance conventions and emphasize how the play's

---

[20] Thomas Dekker and Phillip Massinger, *The Virgin Martir A Tragedie* (London, 1622). All subsequent quotes are from this edition and cited parenthetically in-text.

[21] See especially, Nova Myhill, "Making Death a Miracle: Audience and the Genres of Martyrdom in Dekker and Massinger's *The Virgin Martyr*," *Early Theatre* 7, no. 2 (2004): 9–31; Jane Hwang Degenhardt, "Catholic Martyrdom in Dekker and Massinger's *The Virgin Martir* and the Early Modern Threat of 'Turning Turk,'" *ELH* 73 (2006): 83–117; Holly Crawford Pickett, "Dramatic Nostalgia and Spectacular Conversion in Dekker and Massinger's *The Virgin Martyr*," *SEL Studies in English Literature 1500–1900* 49, no. 2 (2009): 437–62; Jennifer Waldron, *Reformations of the Body: Idolatry, Sacrifice, and Early Modern Theater* (New York: Palgrave Macmillan, 2013); and Thomas J. Moretti, "Via Media Theatricality and Religious Fantasy in Thomas Dekker and Philip Massinger's *The Virgin Martyr* (1622)," *Renaissance Drama* 42, no. 2 (2014): 243–70. Louise George Clubb argues that the play promoted Catholicism through its similarity to Italian saint plays, see "*The Virgin Martyr* and the *Tragedia Sacra*," *Renaissance Drama* 7 (1964): 103–26. Gaspar rejects Clubb's conclusions, claiming, instead, that *The Virgin Martyr* aims to galvanize support for Bohemian Protestants. See "The Sources of *The Virgin Martyr*," 17–31, and *The Dragon and the Dove: The Plays of Thomas Dekker* (Oxford: Clarendon, 1990). Karen Bamford and Susannah Brietz Monta both agree that the play presents a pro-Protestant view, although Bamford generally views virgin martyrdom as the purview of Catholicism; see Bamford, *Sexual Violence on the Jacobean Stage* (New York: St. Martin's Press, 2000); Monta's conclusion, in part, rests on the fact that Dekker wrote "the rabidly anti-Catholic *The Whore of Babylon*." *Martyrdom and Literature in Early Modern England* (Cambridge: Cambridge University Press, 2005), 196. Theodora Jankowski reads the emphasis on virginity as a "Roman Catholic privileging of the estate" and that

presentation of sanctity draws attention to itself as theatre. The language of character roles, lines of business, dramatic genre, and stage blocking highlight the problem of knowing sanctity: Sapritius, the local Roman official, damns Dorothy "For playing thus the lying Sorceresse"; Theophilus describes her boasting of withstanding torture as "pageantry"; Sapritius's lovesick son, Antoninus, asks "what Tragedy then begins?" and, once Dorothy is in custody, she warns him not to "play the Ravisher"; her torturers announce they "are ready for the businesse"; Theophilus desires for his "selfe, thy hangman's part could play"; a witness characterizes Dorothy's execution as "her last tragicke scene"; and, Theophilus glosses her death "on this scaffold" as "thy first entrance into hell" (E2v, E4r, H4r, I3r, I4r, I4v, K1r). This vocabulary, along with the problem of how to unmask a pretender, recalls the lies of Ciappelletto's deathbed confession and Beatrice-Joanna's feigned virginity and ratchets it up a notch. Like the appearance of Alsemero's ghost, the supernatural occurrences in *The Virgin Martyr* divide the play between what seems and what inexplicably is.

The self-consciously theatrical language also draws attention to genre conventions. For the first few acts of the play, *The Virgin Martyr* hides the supernatural and, instead, presents a play of moral opposition. Initially, the angel and the devil figure as virtue and vice characters rather than the advocates of heaven and hell, respectively. Angelo, Dorothy's page, encourages her steadfast Christianity in the face of persecution, oversees her charitable work, and fills her with a "holy flame ... On wings of Cherubines" (D3v). Angelo's opposite is Harpax, who serves Sapritius, hates Dorothy, and avoids Angelo because when he encounters him, he "must sinke down" (E1r). The play offers hints of Angelo's and Harpax's supernatural collision, but it remains hidden until Dorothy's body is imperiled in Act 4. In this early part of the play, however, the opposition between virtue and vice extends to the contrast between saintly icon and pagan idol in two later scenes. At the end of Act 2, Angelo enters the stage, *"with a Booke and Taper lighted"* and gives both to Dorothy to hold (D1v). In medieval and Renaissance artwork, virgin martyrs frequently appear with books.[22] The tableau of the virgin martyr and her angelic companion remains on stage through forty-five lines of banal dialogue about prayers, good deeds, and angels. This image could easily accompany the "golden letters" of Dorothy's legend as an illustration in a collection of saints' lives (D3v).[23] It is a presentation of an icon of St. Dorothy and it is contrasted in the next act by the false worship and subsequent destruction of a Roman idol. The saint attacks paganism on the basis of unchaste idolatry, recategorizes Roman

---

the "challenge to Dorothea's virginity closely resembles Protestant attacks on Roman Catholic consecrated virginity and suggests a Catholic focus for the work"; see *Pure Resistance: Queer Virginity in Early Modern English Drama* (Philadelphia: University of Pennsylvania Press, 2000), 127.

[22] See Winstead, *Virgin Martyrs*, "The Politics of Reading," 147–80.

[23] Referencing the *Golden Legend*, Dorothy tells Angelo that "In golden letters downe ile set that day / Which gaue thee to me."

religious temples as "brothell houses rather," and rehearses the lascivious litany of mythology, beginning with "*Venus* whom you worship was a Whore" and "Your *Jupiter*, a loose adulterer, / Incestuous with his sister" (F3v, F4r). Theophilus's daughters join Dorothy in counterfeiting devotion as part of a pagan procession of a *"Priest With the Image of Iupiter, Incense and Censers"* (G1v). The Roman officials stand in awe of the sight of Dorothy's apparent rejection of Christianity. Then the daughters "*spit at the Image, / throw it downe, and spurne it*" (G2r). Exhorted by Harpax, Theophilus stabs them.[24] These opposites—Angelo and Harpax, Christian iconography and pagan idolatry—set the stage with the belligerents of virtue and vice, but do not yet produce spectacles of divine and demonic reactions. So far, God exists only in Dorothy's prayers. In the next act, the device of rape will draw out the *deus ex machina*.

The Virgin Martyr pivots from morality play to saint play when the miraculous enters the stage at the moment of the rape attempt. The earlier hints of supernatural collision between Angelo and Harpax explode in the second half of the play. Such theatrics are the answer to the question of Dorothy's sanctity. In Act 4, Sapritius attempts to unmake the virgin before her execution, in part, to destroy his son's infatuation with her. Given the diagnosis that Antoninus will "lose life if by a woman / He is not brought to bed," a desperate Sapritius identifies Dorothy as the antidote (H3r). The Roman storms the stage, *"dragging in* Dorothea *by the Haire, / Angelo attending"* and orders his son to "Break that enchanted Cave, enter, and rifle / The spoyles thy lust hunts after" (H3v, H3v-H4r). Dorothy cures Antoninus of his madness, but the threat of assault increases. Sapritius orders a guard to "fetch a slaue hither" in order to "Teach her ... to play the Whore" (H4v). As Dorothy's body remains a site of doubt, Dekker and Massinger introduce a new character to extract laughter and galvanize audience support for her. Sapritius demands to know the slave's origin:

> Slaue. From Brittaine.
> Sap. In the west Ocean.
> Sla. Yes.
> Sap. An Iland.
> Sla. Yes.
> Sap. I am fitted of all Nations.
> Our Roman swords ever conquer'd, none comes neere
> The Brittaine for true whoring: sirrah fellow,
> What would'st thou doe to gaine thy liberty? (H4v-I1r)

---

[24] As Theophilus kills his daughters, he expresses his rage as a "Furnace of wrath thrice hot already," a language of immolation that substitutes the actual execution at the stake that occurs in most *vitae* of Dorothy (G2v).

Desperate for freedom, the slave responds with a variety of feats, including fighting "naked with a Lyon," but when Sapritius charges him to "drag that Thing aside / And ravish her," the slave refuses with a virtuous speech:

> Sla. And ravish her ! is this your manly seruice,
> A Diuell scornes to doo't, tis for a beast,
> villaine, not a man, I am as yet
> But halfe a slaue, but when that worke is past,
> A damned whole one, a black vgly slaue,
> The slaue of all base slaues, doo't thy self Roman,
> Tis drudgery fit for thee. (I1r)

The Briton's honorable rejection of the tyrant's charge in favor of allegiance to Dorothy forges a link between ancient Christianity and the slave's national descendants who populate the London theatre. Although Dorothy is not British and the slave may not be a Christian, this pivotal moment associates ancient Britain with early church sainthood.

After the slave is dragged away, a third rape attempt occurs and this one finally pulls down proof from heaven. Dorothy prays to "That power supernall on whom waites my soule, / Is Captaine ore my chastity," a speech act that acknowledges her virginity as vowed and vocational (I1r). Angelo then effects a miracle:

> Sap. Call in ten slaves.
> Ang. They are come sir at your call.
> Sap. O Oh. *Falls downe.* (I1v)

Angelo's utterance is followed by Sapritius's sudden collapse, implying that the invisible "ten slaves" are creatures of supernatural punishment. After Antoninus begs the saint to "Forgive this wicked purpose of my Father," Dorothy prays "to those powers . . . he may recouer," and Sapritius stirs (I1v). Decrying her as a "witch," Sapritius sends her to her execution (I1v). This curse-and-restore miracle cites the St. Agnes legend as well as the second scene at St. Winifred's Well in *A Shoemaker, A Gentleman*. Again, Dorothy's sainthood is constructed on recognizable hagiographical moments to theatrical audiences rather than her own specific *vitae*.

Before the intervention of the *deus ex machina* settles the question of Dorothy's virginity, the supernatural elements of the play lie dormant. After that moment, however, the creatures and effects of heaven and hell are uncontainable, and they begin to drive the action of the play. Here, the theatre responds to the demands of the Devil's Advocate. The divine and demonic forces were cloaked in the oppositional dramaturgy of the morality play. Now activated, the sights and sounds of supernatural collision offer material proof for the cause of sainthood through the rest of Dorothy's martyrdom. With "Angelo *knee- / ling holds her fast*," the saint's prayers render her torturers ineffectual despite their exhaustive force of effort (13r). As she nears her death, Dorothy proclaims knowledge of an afterlife of heavenly fruit and flowers. Theophilus sardonically retorts, "pray send me some" (K1v). She promises that she will, and her companion undergoes a costume change that reveals his true nature. Invisible to all of the characters except for Dorothy and Harpax, the entrance of "Angelo *in the Angels habit*" and its subsequent effect on the devil substantiates the truth of the martyrdom (K1v). Harpax writhes in Angelo's presence and dumbfounds the Romans.

> Theo. What's the matter?
> Sap. This is prodigious, and confirmes her witchcrafte.
> Theo. *Harpax*, my *Harpax* speake.
> Har. I dare not stay,
>   Should I but heare her once more I were lost. (K1v)

With Harpax gone, the saint and her intercessor are able to effect the additional miracle of Antoninus's conversion. The sight of her execution catalyzes Antoninus's conversion which, as Pickett observes, "trades in a pagan paradigm of sacrifice for a spirituality based on ravishing vision."[25] Antoninus expresses religious skepticism due to Roman gods' "delight / in offerings of this kind," but he stops short of Christian conversion (I4r). Although, as Jennifer Waldron asserts, Dorothy "constantly redirects attempts to worship her toward Christ and God," the play repeatedly directs *our* attention to Dorothy's body and its marvelous effects.[26] In devotional literature, martyrdom is accompanied by the insistent catechizing that Christ, savior and lover, is the author of marvels. Such devotional edification is absent here. Dorothy and Angelo effect Antoninus's conversion through the affective phenomena of "a holy fire" within him (K2v). In his transformation from lovesick Roman to loving Christian, Antoninus is nonetheless sensationally connected to Dorothy. When "*her head* [is] *strucke off*," Antoninus also "*sinks*" (K2v). Although no headsman's axe has touched him, his soul also quits the stage with the saint's. Metaphysically bound to the only other Christian soul on the stage, Antoninus's miraculous death is a necessary outward sign. It distinguishes true conversion from feigned conversion, the very thing that Dorothy affected in her adoration of Jupiter.

The unexpected conversion of Theophilus concludes the play. Like Antoninus's conversion, it does not occur through rational sense but through supernatural

---

[25] Pickett, "Dramatic Nostalgia," 452.
[26] Waldron, *Reformations of the Body*, 200.

sensation. Thus far, Theophilus has resisted the effects of the miracles, including the *"Loud Musicke"* that fills the stage before Angelo's exit after the execution (K3r). Theophilus decries these celestial aftershocks as, "Illusions of the Divell" and retreats to his study to reinforce his disbelief through an anti-martyrological contemplative practice (K3r). In contrast to the holy book Dorothy held earlier in the play, Theophilus fortifies his soul with a "muster-booke of Hel-hounds" that blends martyrdom with *Titus Andronicus* (K3r). The book details how "A thousand wives with brats sucking their brests . . .Were minc'd and bak'd in Pies to feed starv'd Christians. / Ha, ha" (K3v). Theophilus's grotesque meditation is disrupted by Angelo's appearance to sudden *"Musicke"* with the promised *"Basket / fild with fruit / and flowers.* (K3v)" The Christianizing effects of Angelo's basket are signaled through yet another supernatural collision involving the devil. Harpax is compelled back to the stage to prevent Theophilus's transformation. In contrast to the cues of heavenly music, Harpax's diabolical laughter *"within"* grows *"lowder"* as it moves *"At one end," "At t'other end,"* and, finally, *"At the middle"* (K4v). Despite the distraction of the confounding racket, Theophilus eats of the divine fruit, which causes Harpax to reveal his true nature *"in a fear-full shape, fire flashing out of the study."* (L1r). Harpax's entrance as the devil amidst Theophilus's conversion mirrors Angelo's angelic revelation during the execution scene. The disguised supernatural characters are revealed as their human companions encounter peril and near metaphysical transformation. The angry pyrotechnics in this scene also recall the medieval stage devil who spurts mad fire after St. Paul's conversion in the Digby play, but Theophilus's response to Harpax cites Elizabethan invention. Using the imperative, "Avant," the man repeats the command used by St. Dunstan to de-conjure Asmoroth in *A Knack to Know A Knave* (L1r). However, due to the unconverted state of his soul, Theophilus's utterance is ineffectual and he must rely on *"A crosse of Flowers"* from the saintly fruit basket to repel Harpax (L1r). Theophilus then repents of his persecution "Of Dorothea, the holy Virgin Martyr" and proclaims Christianity to the astonishment of Diocletian and Maximian (L1v). Harpax enters at the very end to portray the defeat of hell as he *"falls downe"* once more (M1r).

The articulation of a repertoire of virgin martyrdom is most evident in *The Virgin Martyr*. Dekker and Massinger adapt parts of the St. Dorothy legend, appropriate and conflate general tropes of virgin martyrdom, and rely on the stage precedent of books, angels, demons, and music to stage miracles. The most identifiable part of the Dorothy legend—the appearance of a boy with apples and roses—becomes a more generalizable fruit basket and floral cross born by Angelo. The use of the cross as an apotropaic device cites the legend of St. Margaret, who makes the sign of the cross to defeat the dragon. In addition, the Christianizing effect of the cross appeared previously in *A Shoemaker, A Gentleman* when Winifred's angel gives the cross to Amphiabel who, in turn, converts Alban. Whereas in devotional hagiography, the apotropaic miracle was proof enough of the victory over the devil, the production of sanctity on stage requires a saturation of outward signs of supernatural collision and transformation.

The final show of sanctity in *The Virgin Martyr* reflects a history of stage devils along with the legend of St. Cecilia. Theophilus's execution concludes with the procession of a "Most-glorious Vision" featuring *"Dorothea in a white Robe, Crownes upon her robe, a / Crowne upon her head, lead in by the Angell, Antoninus / Caliste and Christeta following all in white, but lesse glorious, / the Angell with a Crowne for him* [Theophilus] (M1r). The crown of martyrdom is earned metaphorically at the moment of execution, but in the grand finale of *The Virgin Martyr* the martyrs' deaths are figured through actual coronation. Angelo proclaims victory as *"the divell / sinkes with / lightening."* (M1v).[27] Having incorporated all possible ingredients of previous saint plays—books, angels, demons, music—and reorganizing them around the proofs of virginity and sanctity that characterize subsequent virgin martyr plays, *The Virgin Martyr* thus concludes in a frenzy of marvels.

Discerning Virgins in *Two Noble Ladies*

The legend of SS Justina and Cyprian also occurs during the time of Diocletian, but it departs from the traditional structure of virgin martyrdom.[28] The magician Cyprian desires Justina, a Christian virgin of Antioch. Because Justina will never consent to sexual intimacy with Cyprian, he conjures devils to tempt her. When the first one proves too weak, he conjures another, and then the prince of the devils. Justina fends off each of them with the sign of the cross. The devil takes different forms, including a beautiful young man and a maiden, but each time Justina rejects demonic seduction. Finally, the devil casts a pestilence over Antioch and refuses to lift it until Justina consents to marry Cyprian. She refuses and the city turns against her, but eventually her prayers end the plague. Finally, Cyprian tires of the devil's inability to bend her to his sexual will and demands to know why the devil cannot overcome her. The devil tells him that God is more powerful than him, which causes Cyprian to convert and, eventually, he becomes the Bishop of Antioch. When their reputation reaches a Roman official, their shared martyrdom involves a cauldron of burning wax, pitch, and grease.

Instead of a series of failed attempts at seducing Justina through black magic, *Two Noble Ladies and the Converted Conjuror* depicts Cyprian's magic in a variety

---

[27] See chapter 2 for the demise of Castilliano in *The Devil and His Dame*. Other plays more generally depicted devils with fireworks and did not use pyrotechnics to indicate the divine defeat of demons. These plays include *If It Be Not Good, the Devil Is in It* by Thomas Dekker, *The Silver Age* by Thomas Heywood, and *Astrologaster* by John Melton (1620). See George Fullmer Reynolds, *The Staging of Elizabethan Plays at the Red Bull Theater, 1605–1625* (New York: Modern Language Association of America, 1940), 171–2.

[28] Justina and Cyprian's Middle English lives appear in the *South English Legendary*, the *Gilte Legende*, and the *Golden Legend*.

of situations, both comical and serious, and devotes only a single, extraordinary scene to his failed seduction of Justina and conversion to Christianity. In the stage iteration of the legend, Justina does not begin as a vowed virgin and, in a shocking departure from the genre of virgin martyrdom, even pursues marriage. Her consecration to Christ results from a need to strengthen her chastity against Cyprian's magic. The play ends before Justina and the converted Cyprian suffer martyrdom. In the place of an execution at the end of the "Trage=comicall Historie," an angel foretells of a future joint martyrdom in Antioch.[29]

Despite the differences in structure and conflict, both *The Virgin Martyr* and *Two Noble Ladies* operate within the same dramatic repertoire. Whereas Dorothy's sanctity materialized as part of an antagonistic relationship between Christian iconography and angelic miracles, on the one hand, and pagan idolatry and demonic defeat, on the other, *Two Noble Ladies* does not reproduce these neat sets of opposites. The adaptation of the Justina and Cyprian legend contains both tyrant and devil characters, but they are not a unified force of evil. Justina is condemned to death for professing Christianity by a tyrannical Caliph, but her main foe is Cyprian, a powerful magician who devises a magical rape plan. The source of his magic is a conjuring stick and knowledge gained through and represented by a set of books. Although Faustus's books and Prospero's book and stick offer stage precedents for Cyprian's properties, the play specifies different requirements for effecting magic. The magician's assistant, in fact, explains his master's practice at the beginning of *Two Noble Ladies* when he asks what would happen if the invading Egyptian army "should iuggle away your coniuring sticke, where are we then?" and decides to "hide . . . among your bookes / for there lies moste of your arte" (1.2.94–6). Scholarship is the means through which Cyprian holds knowledge of necromancy, but the stick activates his spells. Moreover, the stick differentiates necromantic books from other books on stage. As James Kearney argues, the book could act as a multidirectional agent of conversion. That is, "not all conversions are created equal. Christians of different confessional camps necessarily believed that many textual conversions were conversions to apostacy" or, like Dr. Faustus, to necromancy.[30] Eventually, an angel and prayer book counteract Cyprian's seductive magic, but the majority of the play features spectacles derived from Cyprian's dark arts. Angelic intervention only occurs in *Two Noble Ladies* at a specific moment that is consonant with the *deus ex machina* in *The Virgin Martyr*—when the body of the saint is imperiled by sexual assault.

---

[29] "Two Noble Ladies and the Converted Conjuror," British Library MS Egerton 1994, fol. 224v. All subsequent quotes will be cited parenthetically in-text and taken from *The Two Noble Ladies*, ed. Rebecca G. Rhoads (London: Malone Society Reprints, 1930). The play was never printed and, aside from the Malone Society edition, exists only in manuscript form. Having compared MS Edgerton 1994 to the published transcription, I quote here from the transcription.

[30] James Kearney *The Incarnate Text: Imagining the Book in Reformation England* (Philadelphia: University of Pennsylvania Press, 2009), 33.

Two Noble Ladies introduces the hierarchy of marvels before it stages Justina's evolution from a noble virgin to a virgin martyr. The early scenes of necromancy establish Cyprian's practice of the dark arts and his particular range of skills: he can suspend animation, materialize unseen secrets, and call up the devil to induce lust. The opposition between necromancy and divinity in the play emerges slowly because, although Cyprian's abilities are underpinned by a pact with the devil, his magic works along a continuum between virtue and vice. Cyprian's magic is first used to counteract the evil tyranny of the Sultan of Egypt. The Sultan demands that Cyprian and Lysander, a nobleman, help him find and kill his daughter, Miranda, who has fled the court to save herself from incest. Miranda figures as the second noble lady in the play. The Sultan ire and desire for his daughter is expressed in terms of grotesque mutilation. Echoing the justice of Roman persecution, the Sultan decrees that

> ... who ere findes Miranda
> disguise, and mangle her enticing face,
> seare vp her tempting breasts, teare wide her mouth,
> and slit her nose, that thus defac'd, my hate
> neither by loue nor pitty may abate. (2.1.552–6)

When Lysander defends Miranda's righteous flight, the Sultan orders his execution, but is prevented by Cyprian's magic: "The guard stands fixed, their / eyes rowling from the King / to Cyprian, and so too & fro" and the Sultan "beats them" (2.1.479–83). The tyrant attempts to "dissolue" Cyprian's "charme / and life together" (2.1.87–8). Cyprian casts another freezing spell that causes him to stand *"fixed in a posture of running at him with his / sword"* (2.1.88SD). Cyprian only releases the court from the spell once the Sultan promises to rescind his condemnation. The scene thus establishes that Cyprian's art can be used in the service of justice even as it underscores that the magician's strength derives from a combination of "hell and his arte" (2.1.548).

The immobility spell is followed by a revelation spell. Once Cyprian and Lysander quit the court, the magician uses his "arte" to oppose Egyptian tyranny for a second time. Although this is an act on the side of virtue, the conjuring operates in opposition to heaven. On the bank of the Euphrates, Cyprian's magic fills the stage with *"Thunder. Enter a Spirit, Like a souldier in armour / on his breast a sable sheild written on with Golden letters"* (3.3.1081–2). The writing on the shield reveals that Lysander is the kidnapped son of Antioch's last king and not an Egyptian prince. This necromantic spectacle is then upstaged by a greater marvel that begins with inexplicable "sound" of "heaun'ly harmonie." There are *"Recorders still. Enter an Angell shaped like a patriarch / vpon his breast a blew table full of silver letters, in his / right hand a red crossierstaffe, on his shoulders large wings"* (3.3.1099–105). The angel in this scene explains that divine power surpasses that of the magician's "deep caldean learning" of "magicke spells" and foretells that Cyprian "this learned heathen man / shall renounce Magicke, and turne Christian" (3.3.1012–13, 1120, 1010). Afterwards, Cyprian reveals that the miracle begins to work on him. Like Antoninus and Theophilus in *The Virgin Martyr*, conversion starts with sensation. Without renouncing his pagan practices, Cyprian nonetheless invites the angel to return and "Bring what thou wilt, thy presence is so full / of maiestie, that sure thou arte some god; / for I admire and tremble at thy sight" (3.3.1123–5).

Two Noble Ladies relies on a continual staging of marvels. Whereas the previous virgin martyr play contrasted miraculous intervention with the language of theatrical pretending, this play uses miracles to counter conjuring. It is a saint play that reverses the magical hierarchy of *The Devil and His Dame* inasmuch as the conjuring devil in that play overcame the formerly miracle-working prayers of St. Dunstan. The Jacobean and Caroline saint plays invite contests between seeming and being, and miracles and magic, but they do not reverse the hierarchy of the divine and the diabolical. There are comic moments involving devils, vice characters, and pagans in both the itinerant tragicomedies and the virgin martyr plays, but there are no parliaments of celebrating devils that, ironically, uphold the virtue of chastity.

A comic subplot establishes Cyprian's final trick. Although the first two demonstrations of Cyprian's art appear to be in the service of virtue, a third sequence workshops devilish vice. Cyprian conjures the devil, Cantharides, to aid a man in the seduction of a woman. Twice, "*Cantharides claws her*," a gesture that effects like an aphrodisiac. Through physical contact with the devil, the woman expresses sudden lust. The conjuring of Cantharides and the subsequent seduction reminds audiences that Cyprian's magic is maintained through his pact with the devil. Cyprian's rod and Cantharides' gestures not only form the theatrics of necromancy but also serve as efficacious tools of sorcery. No king or soldier can counteract Cyprian's conjuring. Only a show of divinity can outdo and, the angelic apparition foretells, undo demonic forces.

Yet, divine intervention on Justina's behalf is withheld until she has vowed virginity. The opening lines of the play are uttered by Justina begging, "O spare my life, seeke not a virgins bloud" as she flees an Antioch under siege by Egypt (1.1.1). Her speech is not efficacious, and she spends most of the play escaping rape, mutilation, and violent death. Justina is saved three times, by three species of intervention: human, magic, and miracle. Early in the play, three Syrian soldiers surround her in a secluded wood. As expected, she begs for death in order to prevent her rape and prays, "Help ye chaste pow'rs, help heau'n, help Angells, help" (1.4.265–70). No such angels appear. Instead, Miranda appears cross-dressed in armor to fight off Justina's rapists. Although Miranda is not an angel, she is a chaste power, having fled the court to avoid incest. An affinity based on chastity is established between the two women, even though Justina professes Christianity and Miranda does not. Their dedication to chastity is not a permanent dedication to celibacy but rather the transitional virginity of young women who seek virtuous marriages. When that chastity is imperiled, however, the women embrace death before dishonor. In court, Miranda tells her father that she agrees "with death, not with a fathers bed" just as Justina begs the soldiers for murder to prevent her rape (1.3.183).

That Justina is a noble virgin, but not a vowed one, is underscored by her betrothal to Clitophon, son of the Syrian Caliph. Clitophon welcomes the women to Syria, offers Justina safety, and takes Miranda, who remains disguised in male battle dress, as his attendant soldier. At first, Justina balks at Clitophon's profession of love for her, because of their religious difference, but when he offers to "turne Christian," she considers marriage because "To winne a soule to heau'n by yielding loue / may moue a virgin hart that has not vow'd / secluded chastitie" (1.4.328–31). In her reply, the virgin makes an important distinction between versions of Christian virginities. Justina distinguishes between the transitional state of a chaste woman and the perpetual one of nuns and virgin martyrs, respectively. As in *The Virgin Martyr*, the son chooses the Christian object of his affection over his father's religious and political patrimony. Perceiving his son "bewitch'd" by Justina, the Caliph pronounces "That name of Christian is thy doom of death" (3.1.893).[31] Justina cries out, "Is there no advocate? no intercession ? / are all about mee ministers of death?" (3.1.908–9). As in Justina's previous scene of peril, the virgin reveals her expectation for a miraculous intervention that never comes. This time, she receives rescue through necromancy. On the banks of the Euphrates, soldiers drag a "*bound*" Justina to the water's edge until spirits appear to fight off her executioners.

> *1. Souldier.* I am enforc'd I know not by what pow'r
> To hale her this way.
> *2. Souldier.* what strange noise is this?
> *1. Souldier.* dispatch, the tide swells high.
> *2. Souldier.* what feind is this?
> *1. Souldier.* what furie ceazes mee ?
> *2. Souldier.* Alas, I'm hurried headlong to the stream.
> *1. Souldier.* And so am I, wee both must drown and die.
>
> *Thunder.*
> *Enter 2. Tritons with silver trumpets*
> *The tritons ceaz the souldiers.*
>
> *The Tritons dragge them in sounding their trumpets.* (3.3.1149, 1164–71)

With cacophony, Cyprian's art storms the stage. This is the only intervention that Justina warrants according to the repertoire of virgin martyrdom. Although Justina professes Christianity, she is not saved from death through her faith. Her speech cannot call down the heavens to her aid. Only saints and angels can effect miracles

---

[31] The author(s) of *Two Noble Ladies* originally wrote "That name of Christian doomes thee, hatefull bitch," but revised to the line quoted here.

and, thus far, Justina is not sanctified. The rubric is the same in *Two Noble Ladies* as it is in *The Virgin Martyr*, wherein Dorothy's speech proves efficacious only after the verification of her metaphysical virginity.

The play has thus far portrayed Justina as a virgin and a Christian martyr, but not a virgin martyr, that special form of saint that receives angelic apparitions. When Cyprian first attempts to seduce her, she appeals to her status as "the trothplight wife of Clitophon" (4.5.1576). He counters by promising pleasures that can be wrought by magic, such as the ability to transform their "selues / in quaintest shapes to vary our delights" (4.5.1591–2). When he persists, Justina becomes a Virgin out of fear for her soul, professing that, "Heau'n has my vow, my life shall neuer bee / elder then my vnstain'd virginitie" (4.5.1619–22). She resolves that her faith is not strong enough to withstand Cyprian's necromantic advances by herself. Thus, Justina breaks her betrothal to Clitophon and becomes a bride of Christ.

A pivotal scene of Act 5 tries Justina's vow. The previous comic sub-plot with Cantharides established that Cyprian's "blacke arte" can "make" her "white thoughts like it" (4.5.1635–6). In plotting rape, furthermore, the conjuror recalls that his magic derives from the devil.

> ... hell shall force her
> to offer vp that Iewell of delight
> which miserlike she yet locks vp in coynesse.
> with greater heat she shall desire her rape
> then I haue done. Hells hookes she cannot scape. (4.5.1637–41)

As established earlier in the play, "Hells hookes,"—that is, Cantharides's clawing gesture—effect seduction and only divine force can intervene against Cyprian's art. But does Justina warrant a miracle? Cyprian demands to "see / this Christian saint," and "*Iustina is discovered in a chaire asleep, / in her hands a prayer book, divells about / her*" (5.2.1750–5). Justina is not the first woman to appear in this pose. Audiences previously encountered the posture of an immobile woman with a prayerbook in the exalted wife of Antonio in *The Revenger's Tragedy* (1606) by Middleton. After her rape by the son of a tyrant, she takes poison, and her discovered body is glossed by her Antonio and his friends: "That virtuous lady!" "Precedent for wives!" (1.4.6). Like the Roman wife Lucrece, her chastity is known through her suicide, and the point is further emphasized through the inclusion of two books:

> A prayer-book the pillow to her cheek;
> This was her rich confection; and another
> Placed in her right hand, with a leaf tucked up
> Pointing to these words;
> *Melius virtute mori, quam per dedecus vivere.*
> True and effectual it is indeed. (1.4.13–18)

This use of the two books combines the providence and piety associated with Elizabeth's book in the dumb show in *If You Know Not Me, You Know Nobody* with the ventriloquism of Ovid's *Metamorphoses* in Act 4 of *Titus Andronicus* in which Lavinia, without tongue or hands, proclaims her rape through pointing to the text of Philomel and Tereus. The Latin text Antonio's wife holds is stoic rather than Christian: "Better to die in virtue than to live with dishonour" (1.4.17N17). While the position of Justina's body recalls the problem of rape, she holds a single book, a prayerbook. The prayerbook signals to audiences that Justina's vow of virginity is true and that she—or God—will repel the assault and prove a saint.

The contest between Justina's claims to sanctity and Cyprian's magic commences with the magician calling for "ravishing notes to winne her maidenhead," which conjure "*Musick. A song.*" When the magician attempts physical contact with a "*Kisse*," she prays "Forbid it heau'n," "*looks in her booke, and the Spirits / fly from her* (5.2.1793–7). Cantharides, head devil, announces the truth of her sanctity, "Her prayers haue praevaild against our spells" (5.2.1799). The inviolate miracle, in turn, effects Cyprian's conversion. In Justina's traditional hagiography, the sign of the cross repeatedly performs the exorcism against the seductive demons. Here, the sanctifying and protective gesture is figured through the icon of theatrical sainthood, the book. Amazed by the force of Justina's prayers, Cyprian begs her to teach him "the sense and vse of this strong spell / call'd ffaith, that conquers all the pow'rs of hell" (5.2.1818–19). Justina instructs Cyprian to "take here this booke; call on that pow'rfull name," and "*The feinds roare and fly back*" (5.2.1845–7). When Cyprian accepts the book, Cantharides cries out, "wee are confounded" and spectacle confirms the defeat: "*Recorders. Enter the patriarch-like Angell / with his crossier staffe in one hand, and a book in / the other. / The Devills sinck roaring; a flame of fier riseth / after them*" (5.2.1854). Like *The Virgin Martyr*, this play, too, relies on increased pageantry to conclude the plot. The angel "*gives him the Booke*" and "*Toucheth his breast / with his crosse*" to effect conversion. Like Antoninus, Cyprian requires a miracle to transform desire for Justina into desire for Christ. The gesture seals Cyprian's conversion and he offers evidence of it by throwing "*his charmed rod, and … his books under the stage. a flame riseth,*" and embracing "sacred trueth alone," that is, "*The Angells booke*" (5.2.1899, 1901–2). With the conjurer thus converted, the angel directs Cyprian and his former conquest back to Antioch where they will "in Martyrdome / Mayntayne your faith" (5.2.1879–80).

Virgin Martyrdom without Virgins

Both *The Martyr'd Soldier* and *Saint Patrick for Ireland* participate in the repertoire of virgin martyrdom through a standard set of Christian protagonists, anti-Christian antagonists, miracles, and devices, including the device of rape, but neither of the plays depict or produce a virgin martyr. Instead, each play separately tests the limits of theatrical virgin martyrdom. Both plays use the device of rape to determine not only the status but also the exact requirements of sanctity. The device transforms from a frequent event in hagiography to a necessary trope of the saint play. In Katherine Gravdal's work on rape in medieval literature, she points out that while "the saint's martyrdom constitutes the apex" of the *vita* "there is a sexual plot particular to the female saints' legend" in the form of "rape, prostitution, seduction, and forced marriage."[32] In *The Martyr'd Soldier,* all of the "ingredients," to repeat Winstead's term, of theatrical sanctity appear, but they do not cohere around a virgin martyr. Instead, a Christian leader miraculously heals his foes, a knight is converted by angelic visitation, and a tyrant orders the rape of the knight's wife, Victoria. Other aspects of *imitatio Christi* are distributed to Victoria's male counterparts as her body alone bears the assault and the burden of miraculous proof.

The Martyr'd Soldier (c.1620–23) is a saint play set during the Arian persecution in North Africa. Henry Shirley based his play on Victor of Vita's fifth-century Latin *Historia persecutionis Africanae Provinciae, temporibus Geiserici et Hunirici regum Wandalorum.* Published by the English Catholic secret press in 1605, *The Memorable and Tragical History, of the Persecution in Africke: vnder Gensericke and Hvnricke, Arrian Kinges of the Vandals* details a unique persecution. The opposition is not between pagan rulers and Christian martyrs, but two sects of Christianity, the Arians and—from the perspective of the translation—the Catholics. A fourth-century theological doctrine, Arianism rejected the Trinitarian conception of God as three persons—Father, Son, and Holy Spirit—equitable in potency. Instead, Arianism posited that Christ the Son is subordinate to God the Father following the logic that the Father created the Son. Although most Eastern and Western sects of Christianity professed the Trinitarian Christology defined by the Nicene Creed in 325 CE, the Vandals brought Arianism with their invasion of the former Roman Empire in North Africa in 429 and began a program of forced conversion, exile, and violence on the Trinitarian population. Ralph Buckland, a Catholic priest who served the English mission from 1588 until his death in 1611, completed the translation.[33] Buckland's choice of text is obvious. The persecution of Vandal Trinitarians by a Vandal Arian king aided by an Arian ecclesiastical hierarchy is a typological precursor to the Protestant persecution of Catholics in England. In the preface, Buckland narrates that King Genseric demanded that all Vandal subjects profess Arianism, *"for conformity sake, to suffer themselues to be sprinckled with water of the Arrians handes, vnder certayne forme of wordes different from the Catholike manner."*[34] Buckland not only uses the term *Catholic* to describe the non-Arian Christians in his preface, but also renders the word

---

[32] Katherine Gravdal, *Ravishing Maidens: Writing Rape in Medieval French Literature and Law* (Philadelphia: University of Pennsylvania Press, 1991), 21, 22.

[33] *Oxford Dictionary of National Biography,* s.v. Ralph Buckland, by Peter Milward," accessed May 1, 2021. https://doi.org/10.1093/ref:odnb/3858

[34] Victor of Vita, *The memorable and tragical history, of the persecution in africke: Vnder gensericke and hunricke, arrian kinges of the vandals* ([England],1605), 7.

throughout his translation. *The Memorable and Tragical History, of the Persecution in Africke* is highly partisan. It documents the sanctity of the persecuted, admonishes the Arians for their violence, and addresses matters of doctrine throughout. In choosing the anachronistic terms "recusancy," and "Catholike" to describe the rejection of Arianism, Buckland's own Catholicism emerges in English.

Despite the perspective of the recusant translator, *The Martyr'd Soldier*'s use of its source text conforms to the shape of dramatic sanctity. The episodes of perseverance and persecution in Victor's fifth-century account do not reflect the workings of medieval English hagiography. *The Memorable and Tragical History, of the Persecution in Africke* lacks the miraculous interventions that offer outward signs of God's preference for the saints that are an anticipated and generic factor in devotional literature. For example, during the persecution of "sacred Virgins," Huneric, son and successor to Genseric, tortures the nuns with "firy-hot plates of yron and to their backe, belly, and paps; calling vpon them amidst thir paynes : confesse that your Bishoppes and Clergie-men lie by you . . . . But doing thus, he could by no meanes find any thing, where with to infame the Church of Christ."[35] In the hands of medieval English writers, the nuns' passions might be rendered as a back-and-forth with the tyrant, receiving increasingly grotesque tortures for each defiant speech and resulting miracle, but those elements are lacking here. Instead, there is suffering on behalf of Trinitarian Christianity and it is borne without miracles. These are typical tortures for female bodies in medieval saints' lives, but what is not typical is the absence of an angel or a miracle to make the fiery hot plates feel cool to the touch or the restoration of their burned off breasts. Furthermore, according to medieval English hagiography, virgin martyrs should not survive in mutilated form; their bodies should reflect eucharistic wholeness and the resurrected Christ. They are supposed to receive the crown of martyrdom in ecstasy like St. Katherine in baroque paintings and Dorothy at the end of *The Virgin Martyr*. They should not die like Anne Askew who, as reported by John Bale and John Foxe, could not walk to the stake due to her torture on the rack. Shirley took Buckland's translation of Victor's account and created stage hagiography from it through the instructions provided by the theatre, particularly *The Virgin Martyr*. Indeed, Shirley's liberal borrowing of scenarios, tropes, and staging from Dekker and Massinger's saint play walks a fine line between Jacobean repertory practice and fanfiction.

The Martyr'd Soldier opens to the Vandal King Genzerick on his deathbed asking for Christian martyrologies—not to prepare his soul for a godly death, but to allow him to die in contemplation of the murders, rapes, and mutilations he oversaw. Citing Theophilus's celebration of his work as a pagan persecutor of Christians at the end of *The Virgin Martyr*, Genzerick orders his assistants to "unclaspe that booke, / Turne o're that Monument of Martyrdomes : / Read there

---

[35] Victor of Vita, *The memorable and tragical history, of the persecution in africke*, 59.

how Genzerick h'as serv'd the gods, / And made their Altars drunke with Christians blood."[36] In contrast to the source text, the Vandal persecution in the play is not an intra-religious conflict concerning Trinitarian theology. Rather, the Vandal king is a pagan tyrant aligned with hell and modeled after Diocletian. Like his predecessors, Genzerick boasts of "Sacrifice to *Jupiter*" and "*Pallas*" and derives pornographic pleasure from the "virgins ravisht" (B2r, B2v). The play sets up the conflict of virgin martyrdom through the introduction of Genzerick's dying wish for "More, more, hang Mayden-heads, Christian Maiden-heads" (B2v). No Christian virgin or hellish devil materializes in this play, but the repertoire of virgin martyrdom does.

Miracles and angelic apparitions occur in *The Martyr'd Soldier* to mark sanctity and conversion. The Bishop Eugenius heals a "tortur'd wretch, whose sight was quite extinct" and now is "clearly restor'd againe" (C2r). Later, when Eugenius awaits execution in a jail "*loaden with many Irons, a Lampe burning by him*," an angel appears to "*soft musick; he astonisht & dazl'd*" and "*falls flat on the earth*" (E2v–E3r). The angel sings and leaves a note written in "golden Letters" (E3r).[37] The Vandal general, Bellizarius, is converted through sight and affect, like his disbelieving counterparts in previous plays, when he, too, is visited by an angel to "*Thunder*" and "*Musicke*" (C2v). He not only turns from a persecutor of Christians, but also his account of a dream vision of "a Garden / A Paradise ... the world contains not" converts his wife (D3v). The men bear torture, but the play demands proof of sanctity from Bellizarius's wife, Victoria, through the device of rape.

Unlike the virtuous British slave in *The Virgin Martyr*, two camel drivers in this play are all too willing to "mouse her," but after Victoria prays, "Guard me you heavens," the first "is struck made," and the second is "strucke / blinde" and deaf (H1r, H1v, H2r). Two willing slaves follow, but another miracle causes them to "*dance antiquely, and Exeunt*" (H2r). Victoria is later fed and healed in prison, in imitation of St. Katherine and then another extended rape attempt follows the St. Drusiana legend, a conflation noted by Karen Bamford.[38] Victoria hopes for death and "*two Angels about the bed*" take her life just before the assault is completed, and the tyrant kisses her cold corpse (I3v). One of the angels bids her "soule flye away : / Tyrant enjoy but a cold lumpe of clay" and introduces a new,

---

[36] Henry Shirley, *The martyr'd souldier* (London, 1638), B1v. All subsequent in-text parenthetical citations are from this edition.

[37] David Klausner finds that, in medieval drama, the use of vocal music is usually reserved for divine or heavenly interaction, whereas instrumental music represents its worldly opposite. For example, singing occurs in the York *Assumption of the Virgin* and the "Gloria" appears in the Chester play of the Shepherds. *The Martyr'd Soldier* is unique among early modern saint plays in replicating the medieval dramatic use of angelic singing. "Music in Drama," in *The Cambridge History of Medieval Music*, eds. Mark Everist and Thomas Forrest Kelly (Cambridge: Cambridge University Press, 2018), 506, 515.

[38] Bamford, *Sexual Violence*, 44, 45. For a more comprehensive discussion of torture and theatrical martyrdom, see Elizabeth Williamson, "Batter'd, Not Demolish'd: Staging the Tortured Body in *The Martyred Soldier*," *Medieval and Renaissance Drama in England* 26 (2013): 43–59.

potentially cacophonous and/or pyrotechnic, device of divine justice: "*A Thunderbolt strikes him*" (I4r). Although Victoria is a noble Christian wife and not a virgin who rejects all earthly suitors for Christ, she proves the necessary sanctity in the play according to the exacting standards of the device of rape.

Between the 1620s and the 1630s, the repertoire of virgin martyrdom comes to characterize the saint play. Neither *The Martyr'd Soldier* nor *Saint Patrick for Ireland* contain characters who fulfill virgin martyrdom. Instead, the repertoire is distributed across parts of these plays. The device of the rape test even makes its way into *The Seven Champions of Christendom*, which I addressed in chapter 4 as part of the old legend of England. At the very end of that Caroline play, St. George of England fights on the side of divine chastity—or at least a category of chastity determined by the marvelous avoidance of forced sexual contact. Three princesses "were supris'd / By a fierce savage and inhumane Monster, / And as his flaming Lust" pursued them, they turned into swans, but are unable to resume their human form (L3v). George offers a Christianized explanation of Leda and the Swan, catechizing that "heaven . . . to preserve / Their honors, chang'd their shapes" and that the swans can be "restore't agen" if they convert (L3v). The king agrees and "*The swans turne*" back into women as their father proclaims, "We all are Christians now" (L4r). In the original source tale by Johnson, six swan sisters are restored to their princess state, but Kirke's adaptation introduces George as both an evangelist and miracle-giver. Furthermore, in Johnson's version, not only does George attempt to rape a vowed virgin, but also he marries and begets sons. At the end of Kirke's play, in contrast, the former virtuous swans are transformed into Christian women and marry SS Andrew, Dennis, and Patrick. St. George, however, remains celibate and ready for his next quest "abroad for fame of Christendome" (L4r). Although the play mostly involves fighting monsters, it is clear that Kirke produced a saint play according to the repertoire of the virgin martyr plays: there is a devil character named "Tarpax," the seven patron saints learn of their destinies by reading off a heavenly tablet, and, most tellingly, the play cannot conclude until it throws in an episode involving miraculous rape avoidance. Even though *The Seven Champions of Christendom* does not feature virgin martyrs, it absorbs dramatic virgin martyrdom as part of its loose association with sainthood.

Like *The Martyr'd Soldier*, *Saint Patrick for Ireland* favors conformity to previous versions of theatrical sanctity.[39] Not only are confessional politics, polemics, and poetics largely absent in these plays, but the source tales' specific figures and

---

[39] Although Saint Patrick for Ireland debuted in Dublin and not at the Red Bull, James Shirley began his career at the Cockpit, the Red Bull's indoor sister theatre. See Lucy Munro for more on Shirley's connection to the repertory of the Red Bull saint plays. "Dublin Tragicomedy and London Stages," in *Early Modern Tragicomedy*, eds. Subha Mukherji and Raphael Lyne (Cambridge: D. S. Brewer, 2007), 175–92. See also Robert Lublin, "Shirley's Dublin Days: A Nervous Premiere of *St. Patrick for Ireland*," in *James Shirley and Early Modern Theatre: New Critical Perspectives*, ed. Barbara Ravelhofer (London: Routledge, 2016), 108–23.

narratives disappear as the characters emerge from assemblages of *vitae* reinterpreted through stage precedent. James Shirley's *Saint Patrick for Ireland* is another virgin martyr play without a virgin martyr.[40] The play depicts St. Patrick's return to Ireland as a miracle-working Christian missionary who is opposed by the necromantic theatrics of the native magician, Archimagus. The heroine of the play, Emeria, is the daughter of the pagan Irish king's "provost." That administrative title describes a stock villain in the legends of early church saints. It indicates that the pagans of Ireland in the play will respond to Christianity and virginity like the pagans of the Roman empire in saints' lives. Despite the formation of a scenario of virgin martyrdom, Emeria does not repeat the anticipated series of acts that fulfill the genre in the other plays. Instead, she offers a study in the requirements of theatrical sainthood through a failed proof of virginity.

Saint Patrick for Ireland introduces Emeria as a chaste and religious virgin. Through necromantic magic, the evil son of the king visits her in the guise of an Irish god that she hitherto fore has worshipped, but she rejects him when he comes, "To blesse thee with a rape" (3.2.128). Emeria, who prefers death to being "made so foule," faces a dilemma (3.2.135). Who or what can help her if her god is a rapist? Unlike the *Christian* virgins who reject pagan gods and receive miracles when their *passio* turns from debate and torture to sexual assault, Emeria is unable to bring down the heavens in her defense. She calls for aid, knowing that no *deus ex machina* will appear: "Oh help, some man; I dare not call upon / The gods, for they are wicked growne; oh help" (3.2.139–40). Her rapist carries her off stage and, "*The Devils rejoycing in a dance conclude the Act*" (E4r). Emeria's rape and partial religious transformation is notable, because when rape appears in medieval saints' lives and other saint plays, it is necessarily thwarted by a miracle. Why, then, is the assault of Emeria not interrupted? Why, moreover, does St. Patrick not appear and intervene with a miracle to prove the truth of Christianity, as he does elsewhere in the play? Emeria suffers, I argue, because her chastity, while exceptionally virtuous, is not exemplary virginity. Yet, the way in which Emeria and the entire play evoke a repertoire of virgin martyrdom complicates both the absence of miraculous interruption and her eventual and unprecedented transformation into a professed bride of Christ.

In crafting the virgin Emeria, Shirley created a character type and then named her after two converted sisters in Jocelyn of Furness's thirteenth-century *Life of St. Patrick*. In this *vita*, which was newly translated into English in 1625, Patrick visits his former master to convert him. The master commits suicide at the approach of the missionary, but his "two Daughters, were conuerted to the faith by Saint Patricke, and receaued the grace of Baptisme, wherein both were named

---

[40] John P. Turner, ed., *A Critical Edition of James Shirley's St. Patrick for Ireland* (New York: Garland Pub, 1979). All subsequent citations are in-text and parenthetical and come from this edition.

Emeria."[41] From that scant mention, Shirley stretched Emeria into a heroine who would both occupy and defy the established performance of virgin martyrdom. She begins the play as a pagan virgin, is transformed into a religion-less rape survivor, and, then, literally follows St. Patrick to become "Spouse to an eternall Bridegroome" who will "lay the sweet foundation of a rule" (5.3.8–10). Emeria fails to prove a virgin martyr, but eventually imitates St. Bridget.

The way in which the rape device functions in *The Virgin Martyr*, *Two Noble Ladies*, and *The Martyr'd Soldier* suggests that sainthood depends solely on the impossibly inviolate body of misogynist fantasy. As Munro writes, "the threat of sexual violence in the Red Bull saints' plays is thus part of a movement toward either conversion or martyrdom."[42] Yet, Emeria's rape and subsequent transformation into the first Irish nun, a professed *sponsa Christi*, ever so slightly revises the repertoire of sanctity. Emeria suffers rape because she is not Christian and, therefore, not a Virgin. That she lacks access to the mystical heavens of Christianity is why she calls for "some man" when she knows that her gods are devils. The rape device in *Saint Patrick for Ireland* is a violent instrument that gauges the state of Emeria's soul. The theatrical precedent for miraculous intervention hinges on consecrated rather than transitional Christian virginity. In *The Virgin Martyr*, Dorothy became efficacious only after divine intervention prevented her rape, thus validating the truth of her consecrated virginity. In *Two Noble Ladies*, the play withheld intervention until the Christian virgin Justina became a vowed Virgin. In *The Martyr'd Soldier*, the married noble woman, Victoria, receives intervention after her own conversion. The theatre tests out yet another scenario of sanctity in *Saint Patrick to Ireland*. It asks, What if the virgin is virtuous and rejects paganism, but is yet to become Christian? Is conversion necessary? And the play responds by withholding intervention to articulate the necessity of conversion. That the devils rejoice at Emeria's suffering makes her like the other saints, but that she survives rape is an external sign that she remains unchristened. Like the other virgin martyr plays, this one depicts the progress of feminine sanctity within obscene violence. Her rapist promises to "force thee into postures [that] shall / Make pleasure weep" and the court Bard adds to Emeria's trauma by performing "A lamentable ballad, of one lost / Her maiden-head," likely for the play to elicit shared laughter among the audience, an example of what Carissa Harris characterizes as "felawe masculinity" (3.2.143–4, 4.1.76–7).[43] The play finds ways to participate in the obscene pleasure that non-Christian characters (and, perhaps, audience members) derived from causing, watching, or recounting the comedy of assault, an aspect of English drama

---

[41] Jocelin, *The life of the glorious bishop S. Patrick apostle and primate of Ireland* (St. Omer, 1625).

[42] Munro, "Dublin Tragicomedy and London Stages," 186. See also, Alison Searle, "Conversion in James Shirley's St Patrick for Ireland," in *The Turn of the Soul: Representations of Religious Conversion in Early Modern Art and Literature*, eds. Lieke Stelling et al. (Leiden: Brill, 2012), 199–224.

[43] Carissa Harris, *Obscene Pedagogies: Transgressive Talk and Sexual Education in Late Medieval Britain* (Ithaca, NY: Cornell University Press, 2018), 26–66.

at least as old as the N-Town *Annunciation*. Still, *Saint Patrick for Ireland* takes an unprecedented position on the possibilities of feminine agency after sexual assault.

The play reproduces the repertoire of sanctity while also refusing to comply with the anticipated narrative of virgin martyrdom. It also offers an unexpected guidance on the concept of holy virginity. Emeria's rapist explicitly asks for her "Consent," which she refuses with the command, "Away" (3.2.129). This word not only repeats in the vernacular the Latin command "avaunt," but also it expresses that her soul rejects the advance. She confesses to her would-be fiancé that she remains "the shape" of herself, but lacks "the inward part," and tells him, "I am no virgin" (4.1.113, 4.1.143). Her noble suitor, who is also in a state of pre-conversion, nonetheless echoes St. Augustine in affirming the difference between consent and violence. He characterizes her rape as "monstrous sin" and counsels her that he will "think thee still a virgin, and thou art so" (4.1.152–3). At the end of the play, Patrick not only accepts Emeria as a convert, but also prophecies that "after [later] ages, with devotion / Shall praise," promising an indefinite veneration as the first *sponsa Christi* in Ireland (5.1.9–10). Emeria herself declares that her conversion, with its possibilities for transformation, "quieted the tempest in my soule, / And in this holy peace I must be happie" (5.3.6–7). Emeria's rape first acts as a measure of her soul, which proves not Christian, but then the trauma of the rape reorients her relationship to her native religion. On the one hand, it realizes the Patristic understanding of virginity which, as Suzanne Edwards emphasizes in her study of the "discourses of survival," is as a state that belongs to the Christian will rather than the body.[44] Indeed, there is little precedent for a failed proof of virginity followed by its eventual consecration by the will. On the other hand, the rape still participates in verifying the truth of Christianity inasmuch as it acts as a catalyst for Emeria's eventual conversion. Whereas the device of rape functions as a proof of sanctity in the first three plays, the late Caroline *Saint Patrick for Ireland* maintains the dramatic repertoire of sanctity while further refining the rubrics of theatrical sainthood.

Restoration Virgins

The afterlife of the saint play occurred in the Restoration era. Samuel Pepys reports watching *The Virgin Martyr* in 1661 and, again, in 1668. In addition, he attended an expanded version of *If You Know Not Me, You Know Nobody* in 1667.[45] In the early years of this new era of theatre—with female actors, two indoor companies,

---

[44] Suzanne M. Edwards, *Afterlives of Rape in Medieval Literature* (London: Palgrave Macmillan, 2016), 2.
[45] Pepys reviewed the 17 August 1667, performance of Heywood's play as "the most ridiculous that sure ever came upon stage, and endeed is merely a show . . . the play is merely a puppet-play acted by

and a proscenium arch and backdrops—two new plays featuring SS Cecilia and Katherine also appeared. These saints reflect the hagiographical motifs that circulated in the revivals. That is, Elizabeth's rhetorical skill in Heywood's play recalls Katherine's debate against philosophers in her *vita*, and Dorothy's melodic and angelic coronation pageant at the end of *The Virgin Martyr* draws on the angelic apparition in the Cecilia legend. In 1666, Matthew Medbourne, an actor for the Duke's company, completed *St. Cecily: Or, The Converted Twins*, and in 1669, John Dryden followed with *Tyranick Love*, the St. Katherine play with which I began this book's Introduction. These Restoration virgin martyr plays perform a severe adjustment to Jacobean and Caroline theatre's fascination with sexual knowledge even as they extend the formula of tragedy and virgin martyrdom. Angelic miracles confirm sainthood, but these plays dial back the extreme sexual violence. Rape is no longer used as a means of knowing or showing sainthood. The doubt that demands the *deus ex machina* in the virgin martyr plays is absent from Medbourne and Dryden's unique experiments with saints during this restored era of Stuart theatre.

As the first new virgin martyr play composed during the Restoration, *St. Cecily* reflects both the heroic style of its era and the growing English cultural interest in the patron saint of music.[46] Music does not appear in the saint's original *vita*, but Medbourne takes a cue from Renaissance portraiture, which frequently depicts Cecilia playing instruments, and reimagines the legend as a play with music. Cecilia's devotional life emerges in secluded organ practice, and her hymns affirm Christianity over Roman paganism. Valerian, her betrothed, worries that this "Superstition, mixt with a / Contmpt, of all our gods" will prove an obstacle to his pursuit of her, but his twin brother, Tibertius, assures him that all is "vanquish'd by powerful Love."[47] The virgin is unmoved. She asserts, "Heaven is my choice" over "carnal lust" (13). Nonetheless, Cecilia's parents arrange the marriage, and others conspire a bed trick for the wedding night. Earthly consummation does not come to pass. Cecilia speaks of her guardian angel and effects a miraculous change on both brothers. Valerian initially demands his marital right and describes Cecilia's angelic companion as "too much, / Beyond belief," before experiencing conversion

---

living puppets." *Diary of Samuel Pepys*, eds. Robert Latham and William Matthews, vol. 8 (Berkeley: University of California Press, 1970–83), 388.

[46] As a dramatist, Medbourne is best known for his translation of Moliere's *Tartuffe*, which premiered in London around 1669. His authorship of the play *St. Cecily* rests on his dedicatory epistle to Catherine, queen consort of Charles II, which precedes the text of the play in the 1666 quarto. See also Cheryl Wanko, "Medbourne, Matthew (bap. 1637?, d. 1680), Actor and Playwright," *Oxford Dictionary of National Biography*, September 23, 2004. https://www.oxforddnb.com/. St. Cecilia's Day celebrations began on November 22, 1683, and continue to the present day. In 1683, an ode by Christopher Fishburn was set to music by Henry Purcell and established a tradition of commissioning odes for the feast day. One of the more famous odes from the period is Dryden's "A Song for St. Cecilia's Day, 1687," which was set to a composition by Giovanni Battista Draghi.

[47] Matthew Medbourne, *St. Cecily: or, The Converted Twins* (London, 1666), 8. All subsequent in-text citations are from this edition.

through sensation: "a light's transfu'sd into my soul, / And a more powerfull fire has seiz'd upon / my now relenting heart" (42). A devil later attempts to reignite Valerian's former carnality through a "*Masque of Ladies, Devils & Satyrs*," but it disappears upon Cecilia's entrance. The saint, herself, serves an apotropaic function. Sainthood is further confirmed when the angel appears "*with two wreaths of flowers*" and hails the "Virgin, and your happy Spouse," as well as the converted Tiburtius (51). Shortly after, the Roman prefect Almachius orders their deaths. The officer who oversees the brothers' execution is infected with a holy madness and receives a vision of Valerian and Tiburtius with angels. Cecilia, who survives her attempted beheading, is joined by her guardian angel for three more days on earth to convert others. The play ends with two contrasting pageants: devils leading Almachius in chains to "*horrid Musick*" and angels and martyrs parading to "*Heavenly Musick*" (61).

Dryden's *Tyranick Love*, which might have been composed during a revival of *The Virgin Martyr*, similarly uses oppositional pageantry to set the precedent of supernatural intervention before the event of martyrdom occurs.[48] The play opens with Maximian and his officers discussing war, pagan prophecy, and the "Christian Princess to receive...doom" (5). Katherine soon debates the emperor's philosophers and converts the best one, but her "doom" is delayed because Maximian becomes infatuated with her. After Katherine rebukes him, a conjuror is engaged to "move her heart" (29). Two necromantic spirits "*descend in Clouds*" and attempt to seduce a sleeping Katherine "from mournful piety" (30, 32). Then, more spirits appear, and a pageant occurs: "*Amariel, / the Guardian-Angel of S. Catharine, descends to soft Musick, / with a flaming Sword. The Spirits crawl off the stage*" (33). The angel erases the seduction nightmare from Katherine's memory and ascends back to the heavens. An escape plan is devised by a new convert, but the saint refuses through the sort of theatrical-conscious language that appears throughout *The Virgin Martyr*: "I am plac'd, as on a Theater, / Where all my Acts to all mankind appear, / To imitate my constancy or fear" (43). As anticipated, Katherine does not submit to Maximian even after he unveils the device of her execution, and her angel, again, appears "*with a flaming sword, and strikes at the Wheel*" (55). Katherine goes to her death narrating the state of her soul as "all pure, a white, and Virgin mind" (56). Her sainthood is further affirmed by soldiers who report that "she seem'd by Bride-men led" to the place of execution and that "Just at the stroke / Aetherial musick" sounded, "a radiant light" crowned her, and a miracle of "fragrant scents" and a "Balmy mist" covered the site (58). They go on to explain that when "the Cloud withdrew" her severed head was gone (58).

---

[48] Charles E. Ward writes that *The Virgin Martyr* "was a stock play of Dryden's company," the King's Company, and that "during 1668 it was especially popular." See "Massinger and Dryden," *ELH* 2, no. 3 (1935): 263.

As with early modern saint plays, both *St. Cecily* and *Tyranick Love* include subplots, such as those involving other Christians, intrigues, and love affairs. In terms of the main plot of virgin martyrdom, however, these plays both use oppositional pageantry that revives and reworks the pageantry of *If You Know Not Me, You Know Nobody* and *The Virgin Martyr*. Yet, these plays are distinct from the earlier virgin martyr plays. Cecilia and Katherine do not carry books to signal to audiences that their sainthood is present and miracles are imminent. Nor, despite the bawdy violence of Restoration comedy, are the bodies of the saints studied in the crucible of sexual violence as part of the process of determining sainthood. In this new era, one that added King Charles the Martyr to the *BCP*, scenes of miracles appear by the midpoint of the play and then repeat at the event of martyrdom. The proof of the Jacobean and Caroline process of dramatic canonization is absent, as is the doubt that demands it.

The Device of Rape and the Stage of Miracles

The transformation of sanctity through the device of rape in Jacobean and Caroline drama is significant in how it understands sexual trauma as a stable and reliable site of knowledge production, distinguishes between transitional and saintly virginity, and redistributes sanctity from the body of a saint to an entire play. In every case, the virgin martyr plays reimagine medieval English hagiography by inserting and conflating the episodes and tropes of other saints' lives. Aspects of the St. Agnes legend are included in a much revised version of St. Winifred in *A Shoemaker, A Gentleman* as well as in the rape episode in *The Virgin Martyr*. The anonymous author of *Two Noble Ladies* completely invents the attempted necromantic rape of Justina by merging *Doctor Faustus* with St. Agnes. Although conflated iterations of saints' lives characterize hagiography in general, in the case of *Saint Patrick for Ireland*, the St. Agnes proof transformed from a ceremonial trial into a theatrical requirement of sexual trauma. These plays document a shift in the articulation and understanding of how sanctity could be known in a pluralistic society. They stage explicitly what medieval saints' lives accomplish implicitly. The virgin martyr plays come to emphasize trials of sexual violence over and above execution as a means of final sanctification.

In all of its variety, Middle English hagiography focused on the body and person of the saint to demonstrate both broad and particular truths of Christianity. In our few extant examples of medieval saint plays that took the form of drama, the protagonist saints demonstrate the necessary acts of sanctity. In the fifteenth-century Digby, *Mary Magdalene* and *The Conversion of Saint Paul*, the plots of the plays are unified by the episodes of the saints' lives. This sort of episodic unification, the very thing that Aristotle and neoclassical critics reject as bad drama, also characterizes other saint plays. After *The Virgin Martyr* and *Two Noble Ladies*, however, later playwrights took the stuff of hagiography and the theatrical repertoire of sanctity—the conventions involving books, angels, devils, music, and rape—and distributed them throughout *The Martyr'd Soldier* and *Saint Patrick for Ireland*. In both plays, conversion, professions of faith, persecution, torture, miracles, and martyrdoms occur, but the device of rape is assigned to Victoria and Emeria, respectively. At some point, virgin martyrdom became so bound up with the idea of sanctity in Stuart drama that the plays are predicated on it even when the plot does not contain or center on a virgin martyr. The effect in/as theatre is that *saint* comes to categorize a type of drama rather than a type of Christian.

The Jacobean and Caroline virgin martyr plays use rape as an epistemically reliable event. In doing so, these plays take all of the sexual violence and misogyny of medieval saints' lives and reduce them to an essential core that becomes virgin martyrdom for theatrical audiences. As rape becomes a feature of the virgin martyr plays, it becomes as anticipated as angelic appearances, prayer books, and pyrotechnics. Whereas medieval saints' lives and other devotional literature provided varieties of gender, sexuality, and virginity, these plays deny that multiplicity.[49] Rape functions as the necessary factor in the adjudication of theatrical sainthood. From Aristotle to Sidney, critics proscribe employing *deus ex machina* as dramatic conflict resolution. For this reason, critics have focused on sudden supernatural occurrences, such as angelic appearances and miraculous restorations, as exactly this sort of device. Leo's recent work examines how Protestant thinkers interpreted Aristotle's *Poetics* and the debate over spectacle in the theatre. One such case is Daniel Heinsius, a seventeenth-century Dutch thinker, who understood devices and *dei ex machinis* as a separate category from the drama. To men such as Heinsius, as Leo explains, when a dramatist "takes recourse to stage machinery—literally, to the device used to raise or lower the actor in the theater—they make use of a mechanical art, distinct from poetry."[50] This sort of neoclassical critique is useful in understanding miraculous intervention in the virgin martyr plays. If the *deux ex machina* is disparaged as "an easy, common, and generally artless way for a poet to resolve a plot, a magical or irrational solution to a problem of composition and causality," in humanist and neoclassical criticism because it hinders truth, then it becomes a necessary part of the composition of the plot to resolve the question of truth in saint plays.[51] The rape device removes from audiences the interpretative burden—and freedom—of identifying or knowing sainthood. As a theatrical rather than theological mechanism, the *deus ex machina* serves as the transcendental adjudicator of sainthood.

---

[49] See especially Anke Bernau, Sarah Salih, and Ruth Evans, eds. *Medieval Virginities* (Cardiff: University of Wales Press, 2003), Samantha Riches and Sarah Salih, eds. *Gender and Holiness: Men, Women, and Saints in Late Medieval Europe* (London: Routledge, 2002), and Sarah Salih, *Versions of Virginity in Late Medieval England* (Cambridge: Boydell and Brewer, 2001).
[50] Leo, *Tragedy as Philosophy*, 15.
[51] Leo, *Tragedy as Philosophy*, 196.

Epilogue: Look Up, Look Up

Theatre wants you to believe. Although theatre is frequently described as a medium that requires the "suspension of disbelief," it is probably more accurate to approach it as a medium that desires belief but will settle for faith. Richard Schechner argues that performances "can be either 'make-belief' or 'make-believe.'"[1] Whereas *make-belief* performances in everyday life, "create the very social realities they enact," *make-believe* performances emerge through conventions that "mark the boundaries between pretending and 'being real.'"[2] Yet, even though theatre is not "real," the pretending must offer something of the real. Theatre cannot be done *as if* because the *if* must be real even if there is no status change on the part of the participants. In drama, that *if* takes the form of accidental action, inaction, ambition, separation, sorrow, regret, seduction, betrayal, and misunderstanding, among other conflicts. From ancient to Renaissance to modern drama, the theatre stages these definitive challenges of human life on the same stage as oracles, ghosts, spirits, witches, and, even, angels. If we receive these supernatural characters or elements as metaphors or as whimsy, then the whole thing falls apart. But it is usually not a problem. The capacities of theatrical illusion offer us a lifeline to experience the *if*, including the supernatural *if*, as real.

Aristotle first gestured toward the theatrical encounter with the conditionally real in the *Poetics*. Drama, he asserts, "is a more philosophical and more serious thing than history" because the latter relates "things that have happened" whereas the former represents "things that may happen."[3] That *may* is another version of the *if*. Evidence and argument will induce responses of affirmation or denial in historical accounts of the Battle of Agincourt or the Battle of Yorktown, but it is the St. Crispin's Day speech and the death of the Duke of York in *Henry V* that cause us to experience comradery and loss and it is the "The Battle of Yorktown" in *Hamilton* that embeds the betrayal of an incomplete vision of freedom within a heroic pageant of an impossible victory. Drama is not interested in historical accuracy. It is interested in provoking something of the real through the *if* or the *may*. It is terrifying, thrilling, and transformative to receive an *if* or a *may*: If you fought a man at a crossroads, if you hesitate to avenge, if your lover is dying. Whether it

---

[1] Richard Schechner, *Performance Studies: An Introduction* (New York: Routledge, 2002), 42.
[2] Schechner, *Performance Studies*, 42–3.
[3] Aristotle, *Poetics*, trans. Richard Janko in *The Norton Anthology of Theory and Criticism*, ed. Vincent B. Leitch et al. (New York: W. W. Norton & Co., 2001), 97. [1451a–b]

The Renaissance of the Saints after Reform. Gina M. Di Salvo, Oxford University Press. © Gina M. Di Salvo (2023).
DOI: 10.1093/oso/9780192865915.003.0007

happened 2,000 years ago or two seconds ago, the difference between history and the theatre has to do with their divergent epistemologies, one bound to the rational and the other bound to illusion.

Theatrical illusion is an essential part of the *if* or the *may*. The theatre is not like the liturgy of the Christian church, but there are elements of the liturgy that are useful for understanding theatrical illusion and what theatre does and does not ask of us. For churches that profess a eucharistic theology of real presence, the liturgy is designed for coreligionists to affirm that theology through the repetition of practices and prayers, actions and utterances. What the liturgy doesn't do is ask adherents to affirm—and, therefore, offer the possibility of denial of—the eucharist through the ways that they sort out truth and falsehood elsewhere. The question, "Do you actually believe that the wafer is the body of Christ?" removes the ritual from one epistemology to another. Whether the query comes from the Inquisition or from a curious interlocutor, the question does not belong to the ritual itself. Sarah Beckwith distinguishes between the sacramental and the theatrical as "how we are present to each other" and "how we present ourselves to each other," respectively.[4] As I see it, the liturgy is full of ceremony but free from illusion and the theatre is full of illusion but free from (enactive) ceremony. Like the liturgy, theatre might put forth essential or existential matters of seeming, being, or becoming, but it does not outright ask about the actual in terms of the rational: Do you actually believe it's a battlefield? Do you actually believe it's an angel? The conventions and technologies of the theatre are essential ways of knowing. Therefore, when an angel descends on a wire, the angel is there. The function of the wire is not to "suspend our disbelief," but to suspend us in theatrical knowing.

From the earliest performances in the Middle Ages to the virgin martyr plays of the Stuart era, English theatre makers experimented with and perfected theatrical conventions to show sainthood. The performances of late fifteenth-century to early sixteenth-century East Anglia, which produced the N-Town Plays and the Digby plays, and Jacobean and Caroline London, which produced the majority of early modern saint plays, stand out in the historical record for their production of theatrical miracles. Certainly, early modern theatre makers inherited the conventions, techniques, and practices of that earlier period, but together the theatre of late fifteenth-century East Anglia and the theatre of Stuart London articulate two dominant ways of using miracles to mark sainthood. In the first way, angels arrive to signify that the subject has progressed to sanctity. For example, in the Digby *Mary Magdalene*, *If You Know Not Me, You Know Nobody*, and *Guy of Warwick*, Mary Magdalene, Elizabeth, and Guy all enact holy lives before their sainthood is achieved, but the apparition or entrance of heavenly creatures signifies the state of their soul. Elizabeth utters that she will die "both a Virgin and a Martyr" if she

---

[4] Sarah Beckwith, *Signifying God: Social Relation and Symbolic Act in the York Corpus Christi Plays* (Chicago: University of Chicago Press, 2001), xv.

does not survive her persecution, but until the angel appears in the dumb show, it is an utterance without effect. For Elizabeth to become an entry in the English dramatic legendary as virgin martyr, the angel is needed to communicate that the conflict between Elizabeth and her enemies operates on a supernatural plane. The second type of miracle, conversely, stages doubt as the antagonist of sainthood. This dynamic contest is what plays out in the N-Town Mary Play and the four virgin martyr plays addressed in chapter 5. When the doubting midwife's hand is shriveled at the nativity or the doubting onlooker is eviscerated at the Assumption, these punitive miracles are proof of the Virgin Mary's miraculous virginity. The question of doubt that operates through bodily assault—and its miraculous refutation—articulates not what sainthood is but how it is known. Jacobean and Caroline theatre extends the question of doubt through the device of rape. *Two Noble Ladies* and *Saint Patrick for Ireland*, especially, reiterate Christian conversion and perpetual virginity as prerequisites of sainthood, not guarantees. The matter of theatrical sainthood is settled when the drama of doubt is countered by the miraculous. The operational doubt of these plays is different than the sort of rational, empirical, or historical skepticism that occurs outside of the theatrical: Did Mary Magdalene's prayers actually overcome the pagan priest in Marseille? Did God actually intervene in Elizabeth's preservation? Did Justina's prayers actually repel the rape? Are there actually miracles? This sort of iconoclasm is not prohibited from the theatre, but it typically vanishes upon entry because the wires are showing. Because illusion is an epistemology born of stagecraft and the *if* or the *may*, it is not trickery.

As I conclude this book on saints and miracles in medieval and early modern theatre, I contemplate two nondramatic hagiographies that exclude illusion before turning to a millennial dramatic fantasy that revels in it. In the twelfth-century *Life of Christina of Markyate* and the late twentieth-century film *Breaking the Waves*, we encounter stories of sanctity that invite doubt and denial. Moreover, both the text and the film lack many of the conventions of showing sainthood that operate in medieval and early modern saint plays. In contrast, *Angels in America: A Gay Fantasia on National Themes* by Tony Kushner utilizes the miraculous theatricality of the saint plays. In its staging and stage directions, Kushner's two-part epic also recovers the capacity and necessity of illusion in the staging of miracles.

"An angel is a belief"

Throughout *The Renaissance of the Saints after Reform*, I have traced the production and recognition of sainthood in English theatre. But what happens when there is only doubt and no signal of sainthood? What happens if sainthood is played out in the absence of the miraculous? What happens when there is failure in the *vita sanctorum*? What looks to be failure in some stories of sainthood is resolved not through the miraculous but through perspective.

The twelfth-century *Life of Christina of Markyate* takes up the problem of hagiographic failure, detailing the consequences of hagiographic ideation without miraculous intervention. Prayer, devotion, and suffering occur, but when no miracles appear on behalf of Christina's steadfast faith, she must either escape or endure. The *Life* presents a remarkable collision between saints' lives and lived reality.[5] From our critical vantage point, Christina attempts to emulate saints and, in the Christian world of medieval England, things go dreadfully wrong. Enacting the role of countless other virgins, Christina privately consecrates herself to Christ. Unfortunately, her holy virginity does not prevent rape attempts. When she is just a girl, a priest attempts to assault her in his private rooms. She prays for divine aid, but nothing happens. As he nears her, she spots the locked latch on the door, runs for it, opens it, and escapes. Later, as a young woman, she encounters another obstacle to her consecrated life: holy matrimony. As in the story of St. Cecilia, her parents override her nonconsent, beat her, and see her married against her will. Despite the fact that her encounter with the priest demonstrated a failure of miraculous deliverance from sexual assault, she again attempts to improvise on the scenario of virgin martyrdom. Specifically, she attempts to reenact St. Cecilia's wedding night, but she fails to convince her husband, and an angel, despite Christina's steadfast belief, does not appear. She cannot convert him: the church grants him the right to her body. Once again, after praying in vain, Christina escapes rape through her own ingenuity, intelligence, and agency. Her husband quits the bridal chamber, but he is not defeated. He collects a group of men, from her family and his, who intend to hold down Christina so that he can rape his bride, thereby satisfying the secular and ecclesiastical consummation of the marriage. Christina hides behind an arras on the wall, dangling in the air while clutching a nail, until the men leave. She escapes and lives out her life as an anchoress, but it is a difficult life. Her virginity comes at a cost. For years, she remains hidden in the darkness of a small enclosure that, due to the inability to move or encounter sunlight, causes digestive issues and nosebleeds.

Now, many readers—medievalists aside—will wonder whether Christina's life contradicts the idea of a *life* because God did not intervene on her behalf with the priest, with the gang of men, or, even, in her tomblike chamber. From the postmodern vantage point, it appears that Christina suffers from genre confusion. That is, she thinks she exists in hagiography when she is actually in *Game of Thrones*, an unforgiving imaginary of misogynist fantasy and violent medievalism that leaves no space for the earnest pursuit of religious life. Yet, the exemplarity of her *Life* exists in her steadfastness to suffer corporally. She continues to live out

---

[5] The description of this *vita* is from *The Life of Christina of Markyate, a Twelfth-Century Recluse*, ed. and trans. C. H. Talbot (Oxford: Clarendon Press, 1987).

her life as she promised to Christ, and her miraculous rewards, as unspectacular as they might seem to us, are dreams and visions that confirm sainthood for ideal audiences. The *Life* expects that its readers, copiers, and hearers will be epistemologically aligned. The *Life* expects that the reader will know this particular version of twelfth-century English sainthood when they encounter it. The *Life* is not meant for us who detect failure because the world does not crack open into miracles the way it did for St. Cecilia.

"With wings and arms that can carry you"

What if the *Life of Christina of Markyate* were written for twentieth or twenty-first century audiences, audiences who have very different understandings of sainthood, and less incentive to believe? Lars von Trier's film *Breaking the Waves* (1996) provides one possible answer to this question. Even viewers familiar with saints' lives or those who maintain devotion to saints will deny the sanctity of the protagonist, Bess McNeil. *Breaking the Waves* begins with a wedding, ends with a funeral, and presents a shocking *vita* that delays any signal of sanctity until the very last moment. The viewer is meant to align with the rational over the hagiographical. Set in a small coastal village in Scotland, the film centers on Bess, a deeply—and disturbingly—religious woman who attempts to redeem her husband's life through undesirable sex with other men. During Bess's increasingly grotesque corporal suffering, her doctor documents her as an "immature unstable person, a person due to the trauma of her husband's illness gave way in an obsessive fashion to an exaggerated perverse form of sexuality."[6] Near the end of the film, her doctor revises his opinion somewhat, saying that Bess suffered "from being good." Throughout the film, we see both the psychosis and the goodness. We see what sainthood might actually look like when enacted by a human being before a hagiographer works their life into a *life*. The film presents a *vita* without miracles, and it is revolting. We encounter what Christina's *Life* might look like in our own time.

Until God tests Bess, she excels at being godly. As the film opens, church elders question Bess about her desire to marry Jan, a Danish oil rig worker who is not a member of their church. They ask, "What good have outsiders brought?" to which she replies, "Their music." Somehow, these men, strict Calvinists, consent to the wedding. The music Bess means is the 1970s rock music that plays between the film's chapters, but her response also alerts viewers to the stripped-down soundscape of her religion. At church services, the hymns are only sung a cappella. At the end of the wedding, an "outsider" guest, the sort that smokes and drinks, calls out to, "Ring the bells then!" In response, the camera pans up to the empty belfry

---

[6] Lars von Trier, dir., *Breaking the Waves* (Zentropa, 1996). All subsequent quotes are also from this source.

where the congregation's ancestors stripped them during a prior age of reform. The minister explains, "We do not need bells in our church to worship God." The fervent iconoclasm remains, and the congregation are serious about their godly austerity. They denounce members in church, practice shunning, and embrace a no-nonsense view of eternal destiny. At a funeral in the early part of the film, the minister pronounces to a wooden box entering the wet rocky earth, "you are a sinner and you deserve your place in hell." It is done matter-of-factly and without malice.

We are unsure of Bess. She is childlike and childish, and she will "give anything to anyone." And because of this, we are also unsure of Jan. When they consummate their marriage—against a wall in the bathroom of the church—Bess is not quite all there. Later, she giggles at the sight of her husband's genitals. But, she is happy afterward, and the honeymoon period changes her. In between their scenes of lovemaking, she says, "It's stupid only men can talk in the service," and tells Jan that she likes "church bells. Let's put them back again." Her new affective engagement with romantic intimacy emerges in a desire to emit sound. No women speak during church services, but Bess sustains dialogues with God when the church is empty. She prays on her knees, leaning against a pew, in her regular voice, and then God answers her in another voice that she channels. When Jan returns to sea after their honeymoon, Bess turns to near hysterics and prays, "I can't wait... won't you send him home?" When God asks, "are you sure what you want?" she affirms she does, and an explosion on the oil rig sends Jan home—paralyzed in the hospital.

Like Christina, Bess believes that prayers and suffering are efficacious. Jan does not understand the deep imaginative recesses of religion and, therefore, attempts to meet her belief by asking Bess to take lovers. He tells her that it "will keep me alive." In fact, he believes that lovemaking will help her "get on with life." Jan, the outsider, cannot know that his wife believes that a world of harsh sea life—in which the sea is the source of both life and death—is also a world of supernatural resources. Bess struggles to break her vow of marital chastity, but when Jan returns to surgery God tells Bess, "prove to me that you love him and then I'll let him live." Although viewers might have encountered Abraham and Isaac, Job, and—perhaps, in their college English courses—Chaucer's Griselda, Bess's absurd test of devotion dramatizes a collision between the typology of sanctity and lived reality.[7]

Bess's attempts to take lovers are her cross. As Theresa Coletti describes Bess, she is a "would-be mystic... whose sexual excesses are both penance and pathway to the miraculous."[8] She first tries to seduce Dr. Richardson, her husband's young

---

[7] Eileen A. Joy has considered *Breaking the Waves* alongside The Clerk's Tale in "Like Two Autistic Moonbeams Entering the Window of My Asylum: Chaucer's Griselda and Lars von Trier's Bess McNeill," *Postmedieval: A Journal of Medieval Cultural Studies* 2, no. 3 (2011): 316–28.

[8] *Mary Magdalene and the Drama of Saints*, 230.

and handsome doctor, but he refuses her and she is forced to find far less desirable men. Here, the film offers the twentieth-century version of the violent misogyny of virginity tests in Jacobean and Caroline drama. Bess first proves her devotion with a hand job for an older stranger on a public bus. She vomits afterward, but God then gives: Jan is taken off a respirator. When Bess asks God whether she is going to hell, he asks her, "whom do you want to save, yourself or Jan?" She chooses her husband and shows her dedication through a transfiguration of habit: crochet black tights, red vinyl hot shorts, earrings, makeup, and a presumptuous updo. The film cuts between another surgery—Jan's blood pressure dropping, electric shocks—and Bess on the back of a motorbike. Jan is raised from the dead as a stranger thrusts into Bess on the ground. Soon, she is excommunicated and tells an incredulous Dr. Richardson that "God gives everyone a talent" and that hers is belief. Her belief leads her to board a ship where one man slices open the back of her shirt with a knife and another beats her. She escapes and shows up in church, preaching, "You cannot be in love with a word. You can love another human being. That's perfection." Later, children cast stones at her as she teeters up a hill in high heels, pushing a bicycle toward the church that has barred her. Jan then betrays her by signing forms to commit her to a hospital. (Can you spot the Christ figure in this film?)

When Bess learns that Jan is dying, she returns to the sadistic ship as a final trial of devotion. On her way from the shore, she pleads, "Father, why aren't you with me?" and channels back "I am with you, Bess." Hours later, there is no memory of her serene face on the water. Instead, she returns scratched, full of wounds, a woman of sorrows. Moments before she flatlines, she mutters, "I thought he might be better now." She dies, confused and "so wrong." The medical examiners and the elders of the church echo her own judgment at the hospital inquest and at her funeral, respectively. But between the hospital adjudication and the religious one, Jan progresses from a wheelchair to crutches. At the funeral, the minister pronounces, "Bess McNeil, you are a sinner, and for your sins you are consigned to hell." The coffin is lowered, but the camera catches that sand flows out of it—but there is no miracle yet. The body has been taken by Jan and his band of outsiders. The men bury her at sea in the middle of the night and without invoking Christ. Jan's final embrace of Bess enacts a unique *pietà*, one of the actual groom and bride, not a metaphor. A crash is heard as her body breaks the waves. Hours later, the crew on the oil rig are thrown into confused amazement. The radar shows that "nothing is out there," but on deck a blinding and brilliant white light hits Jan, walking, with the sound of church bells ringing out over the water, and eventually there is a shot of church bells ringing up in the clouds. Importantly, the nonbelieving crew are the hearers of the music of the spheres. There are no angelic illusions in the film, but the final scene implies that Bess has been carried from the sea to the heavens.

If the *Life of Christina of Markyate* anticipates a shared audience perspective that recognizes sanctity in suffering and small miracles, then *Breaking the Waves* expects a skeptical perspective that denies sanctity at least until the introduction of the miracle at the very end. Jan's recovery becomes miraculous rather than medical at the moment of Bess's sonic apotheosis. While the film does not offer prior precedent of the supernatural, the noticeable absence of and desire for certain sounds alerts us to the miracle of the bells. The ringing of the bells reverses the meaning of Bess's suffering and death from "so wrong" to saintly and redemptive. Yet, what is difficult about the encounter with the miracle at the end of *Breaking the Waves* is not that it occurs without prior precedent, but that its wires do not show. Like the rest of the film, it is presented as an *is* rather than as an *if*. Having spent so much time judging Bess's actions via the rational—Do you actually believe that a woman can redeem her husband through sexual suffering and a violent death?—the miracle is observed but not experienced.

"If it lets you down, reject it"

Although I am both a theatre scholar and a theatre maker, it is my experience as a theatregoer that transformed my understanding of illusion and the miraculous. In 2016, I attended the Folger Consort production of the Towneley *Second Shepherd's Play*. The play occurs in two parts: a longer farcical episode of attempted sheep-stealing and a shorter nativity scene at the end. The miracle of the incarnation and the promise of redemption reconciles the crime through the merciful solemnity of the nativity. In this particular production, Mary even handed the Christ child over to the boy-shepherd Daw to cradle for a moment. As a dramatic text and vernacular theology, *The Second Shepherd's Play* invites ample opportunities to consider the plight of the poor shepherds, Mak and Gil's plan of slaughter, and the encounter with the incarnation. But in the production I saw, the angel simply stole the show. Standing on the upper gallery over the stage with her arms outstretched over golden wings and with her white gown floating far below her, the angel offered a focal and aural point of common beholding: we all looked up. As an audience, we were transfixed by the illusion. In staging this miracle through risk, virtuosity, and iconographic recognizability, the play—at least this particular production—provoked a fleeting feeling of awe in that moment of collective beholding. The awe was real. It was like *Angels in America*—or, rather, *Angels in America* captures something essential about the miracles that populate medieval and early modern drama.

In "Nine Notes Regarding the Angel," Tony Kushner reflects on two decades of production experiences of *Angels in America* and expands on the stage directions of the play. He insists, among other things, that for the scenes with the Angel to work, audiences must sustain a collective faith in the illusion. Though he does not describe it this way, Kushner's "Notes" recall the instructional nature of the *Quem quaeritis* trope in the *Regularis Concordia*. Just as the monks were obligated to conduct the drama of the three Marys and the angel according to specific directions, so, too, are theatre makers obligated to present the Angel in *Angels in America* in a serious manner. It is imperative that the Angel's "dignity and her unequivocally serious purpose are never—as in not for one single second!—compromised by schticky winking at the audience."[9] There ought to be comedy, fear, and amazement, but, Kushner warns, "there are dire consequences if this reality is parodied or traduced. . . . Once faith in the seriousness of what's onstage has been withdrawn, however briefly, it's unlikely to return fully" (317–18). The capacities of theatrical illusion in *Angels in America* and their relationship to medieval and early modern saint plays were initially brought to my attention in casual conversations. In explaining what this book is about to members of the theatre community, I have been met with responses—recognitions—that describe experiences of affective amazement at the sudden rapturous appearance of the Angel at the end of *Part One: Millenium Approaches*. Some of these anecdotes came from professional productions with expertly rigged circus infrastructure and others came from college productions without large budgets. Kushner's play also has been utilized by Holly Crawford Pickett to consider how "the potential for thorough amazement is not diminished by a play's acknowledgment of the theatrical means of that effect's creation."[10] Pickett suggests that the role of illusion in Jacobean and Caroline plays that feature angels "seems to heighten rather than diminish those messengers' powers to religiously transform their audiences."[11] What *Angels in America* foregrounds for me is not that the staging of miracles in medieval and early modern saint plays enacts or effects religious transformation but that religious knowledge can operate without necessarily factoring into the transformative or restorative experience provoked by theatrical illusion.

The angelic moments in the "Gay Fantasia on National Themes" recover an unprecious account of the miraculous in the saint plays of medieval and early modern England. The two-part play draws from an arsenal of theatrical conventions. There is a scene when Prior Walter, the abandoned and dying lover, is in drag, but the conventions of cross-gendered performance are mostly presented as unfabulous and unfantastic, such as in opening scene with a Hasidic rabbi played in seriousness by a woman actor (as called for in the script). Then there are the layers of closeted pretending and queer decoding. On top of that, the play represents

---

[9] Tony Kushner, *Angels in America: A Gay Fantasia on National Themes*. Revised and Complete Edition (New York: Theatre Communications Group, 2013), 317. All subsequent in-text parenthetical citations are from this edition.
[10] Holly Crawford Pickett, "Angels in England: Idolatry and Transformation at the Red Bull Playhouse," in *Thunder at the Playhouse: Proceedings from the Fourth Blackfriars Conference*, eds. Peter Kanelos and Matt Kozusko (Selingsgrove, PA: Susquehanna University Press, 2010), 193.
[11] Pickett, "Angels in England: Idolatry and Wonder at the Red Bull Playhouse," 194.

imagined conversations, ghosts, visits from departed ancestors, and, eventually, the Angel who crashes through the drama of AIDS and religious inheritance in Ronald Reagan's America. It is a play saturated in illusion even as it presents scenes of politicking, caretaking, and seducing. The "threshold of revelation" experienced in a shared valium trip and fever dream in *Part One: Millennium Approaches* becomes more real as a feather falls from the sky and a voice demands, "Look up, Look up!" (33 and 35). Later, the voice becomes more insistent and the marvels more disruptive. Kushner offers directions on the play's "moments of magic" as "fully imagined and realized, wonderful theatrical illusions—which means it's OK if the wires show, and maybe it's good that they do, but the magic should at the same time be thoroughly thrilling, fantastical, amazing" (313). The grand finale of *Part One: Millennium Approaches* features a very ill Prior experiencing an inexplicable erection—an "infallible barometer" of supernatural presence—as the set begins to quake and, then, fall apart (257). Then, "the Angel descends through the ceiling," and hails him, "Greetings, Prophet" (125). As in medieval and early modern saint plays, the feather, the voices, and, finally, the appearance, all validate the truth of an incredible scenario. In this case, Prior is not a saint but a prophet, and the Angel is real. Kushner describes the ending as "the Angel's *traumatic* entry" (emphasis mine, 311). He goes on to explain, "[a] membrane has broken; there is disarray and debris" in the Angel crashing through the stage (311).

In *Part Two: Perestroika*, the conflict between humanity and heaven takes on a more principal role. The Angel reveals that God abandoned heaven due to human progress. She delivers an "Anti-Migratory Epistle" to Prior and charges him to stop human progress. Humans must cease to move, create, and change, the very things that God created humans to do and that distinguish our species from the angels. Jewish and Mormon allusions and encounters with the divine occur throughout the entire epic. In *Part One: Millennium Approaches*, the closeted Mormon Republican Joe Pitt confesses to obsessively looking at a picture of Jacob wrestling with the angel when he was a child. After fiery alephs appear and the Angel flies into the "gay fantasia," the *if* and the *may* of biblical wrestling materializes in *Part Two: Perestroika*. Hannah Pitt, Joe's mother, instructs the WASP-y Prior in angelology from her own faith tradition, "An angel is belief. With wings and arms that can carry you. If it lets you down, reject it" (242). She is confident in the "scriptural precedent," of Jacob and the angel until the sounds of trumpets, drums, and thunder accompany the Angel's reappearance (242). Hannah screams and admits that she thought Prior's claims about angelic visitation were "metaphorical" (258). Despite their shared terror, Prior follows Hannah's instructions in how to manage the wrestling scenario. The rejection of the Angel is not a rejection of a delusional vision, the stuff of dreams, hallucinations, and hagiographical ideation. It is a real rejection of the real Angel's real demands. After Prior rejects the Angel's epistle and demands that she bless him, he then physically struggles with her, something that the 2017 National Theatre and 2018 Broadway productions staged spectacularly. In those productions, the Angel "flew" around by being hoisted by a choreographed crew of stagehands as well as two puppeteers on either side of her who flapped her giant wings. As Kushner notes, "Moments when the crew takes active part in the dramatic event should be staged—interesting to watch, specific and unapologetic" (319). In the wrestling scene, the crew hooked wires onto the actors and puppeteers in the middle of the fight. During their furious struggle, the Angel lifted Prior into the air with her in a frenzy of beating feathers as she tried to escape him. It was miraculous to behold. It was not only a miracle for those who are adherents of the religion of the play, but for all audiences. Kushner's play presents Judaism and Mormonism contending with an altered cosmology of eros and a theology of abandonment. Hardly anyone—if anyone—in the theatre will be an adherent of the new religion as it is imparted through the revelation of the play, but many in the audience will be adherents of theatrical illusion. We need not share in a faith tradition to have faith in the illusion. The gasps in the theatre tell us we are not alone in this, and the utterances of "Oh God" and "holy shit" may be as affirmative as an "amen" is elsewhere. Or, it may, in fact, be an "amen." This, I believe, is what operates in the staging of the miraculous through a millennium of performances between *Quem quaeritis* and the present.

The capacities of illusion that are most obvious in *Angels in America* have been operational in the staging of saints and miracles since at least the tenth century. Earlier in this Epilogue, I stated that the Christian liturgy is not like theatre. The *Quem quaeritis* trope of the Easter liturgy might seem to contradict that assertion, since the liturgical drama is both liturgy and theatre. However, that *both* does not mean that the epistemologies of theatre and religion are collapsed so much as they are *both operating*. The role of religion and illusion in *Angels in America* makes it easier to discern the sophistication of the introduction of the trope into the liturgy. The radically different nature of religion in *Angels in America*, along with its extensive but still normative use of theatrical illusion, foregrounds the extent to which religion in medieval and early modern saint plays operates alongside theatrical illusion. Rather than recounting the visit to the sepulchre as narrative telling, the *Quem quaeritis* trope utilizes illusion to make the miracle more present: the monks, in their usual liturgical vestments, are directed to perform the roles of the three Marys and the angel. The event does not entail an interruption of the liturgy (ceremony) for the staging of a play (illusion). Rather, the introduction of a bit of theatre into the liturgy occurs as part of the entire ceremonial observation of Easter. Theatrical illusion is present as a second way of experiencing the miracle. It is a momentary doubling up of epistemologies that align rather seamlessly: there *is* religious faith that the angel *was* there at the empty tomb and there *is* theatrical faith in the illusion that the angel *is* there at the empty tomb. The introduction of the trope innovated a type of miraculous theatre that, at least according to our archives, first operated within religious ceremony. But because theatrical illusion has its own epistemology, it can also operate without religious ceremony or even a homogenous religious culture. Mary Magdalene's explosive victory over the pagan priest of Marseille in late medieval East Anglia, the angelic apparition at St. Winifred's Well on the Red Bull stage in Jacobean London, and Prior's wrestling with the Angel at the Mark Taper Forum in Los Angeles in 1992 all offer experiences and recognitions of the miraculous. Religious knowledge or religious transformation can operate along with it—or not.

Because miracles on stage are illusions, they are not false. They can be badly executed, of course, but their theatrical quality already places them beyond the rational determination of the actual or the faked. Theatre excels in the faked so that audiences can be transformed through encounters with the incredible. The illusion that is accomplished through pulleys, smoke machines, and the right set of wings compels us to look up because the *if* and the *may* provoke enough of a sense of the miraculous that it is experienced as being real. Stage sanctity has the ability to outlive various ages of religious reform because illusion offers its own way of knowing—and showing—the miraculous. In the theatre or as theatre, sainthood does not depend on faith in the status of miracles but on faith in the staging of miracles.

Note to Appendices 1 and 2

Appendix 1 and appendix 2 began as part of the research organization of *The Renaissance of the Saints after Reform*. While both tables were initially prepared in support of the book, they are provided here for readers to offer more detail about the claims of chapter 1 and to offer research support to other students and scholars of medieval and early modern England.

Because these appendices are not intended as a comprehensive catalogue or bibliography, the references have been kept to a minimum. Most entries in appendix 1, "The Chronological Table of Saint Plays" offer a single reference. Two references are provided in the rare cases in which an extant text is available along with records of events or in which the records are split between two reference sources. The selection criteria for references in the table prioritizes: (1) extant texts, (2) comprehensive records, and (3) the most recent reference source. It is my hope that the references in appendix 1 will provide a useful starting point for future research by other scholars and, because of this, the table was updated as new resources—such as Records of Early English Drama Online and *British Drama, 1533–1642: A Catalogue* edited by Martin Wiggins and Catherine Richardson—became available even after the manuscript was completed. Extant texts are cited by either STC numbers or published editions. Comprehensive records prioritize REED over other sources. For the most recent reference source, I have prioritized works that include the most comprehensive list of records, texts, and other references. For example, appendix 1 cites Wiggins and Richardson's *Catalogue* and Davidson's "British Saint Play Records" instead of Anna J. Mill's *Medieaval Plays in Scotland* and various records in Malone Society Collections as both former reference resources cite the applicable portions both of the latter works. In chapter 1 and elsewhere in the book, I more regularly cite and quote from the records reproduced in Mill, MSC, and similar works. Very occasionally in the table, an article or monograph is offered as the reference, and that is because that source is the most recent work to either publish or reinterpret a text or record. The format for the reference entries in appendix 1 reflect the general abbreviations used throughout *The Renaissance of the Saints after Reform* or reflect abbreviated versions of entries in the general bibliography.

For the appendix 2, "Table of Saints in Liturgical Calendars" an STC number has been provided for each entry.

APPENDIX 1

Chronological Table of Saint Plays

Date	Saint/Martyr	Place	Event/Title	Reference
c.970	3 Marys (Mary Magdalene, Mary Jacobi, Mary Salome)	Winchester	*Visitatio Sepulchri/Quem Quaeritis*	REED: Kent
c.1080–1120	Katherine	n/a	Anglo-Norman *vita*	BSPR
c.1100–1120	Katherine	Dunstable	"ludum de Sancta Katerina"	BSPR
1170–1182	n/a	London	"repraesentationes miraculorum quae sancti confessores operati sunt"	BSPR
1196	3 Marys (Mary Magdalene, Mary Jacobi, Mary Salome), Peter, John the Evangelist	Eynsham, Oxfordshire	Resurrection play	DTRB
c.1250	Nicholas	n/a	"pleye"	BSPR
c.1260	3 Marys (Mary Magdalene, Mary Jacobi, Mary Salome)	Norwich	Easter play	DTRB
1283	Nicholas	Gloucester	"ludentibus miracula sancti Nicholai"	REED: CWG
1298	Magnus	London	Fishmongers' pageant for Edward I's victory	BSPR
1308–1391, intermittently	Thomas the Apostle	Lincoln	"Ludus de Sancto Thoma didimo"	REED: Lincolnshire
1317–1387, intermittently	3 Kings of Cologne	Lincoln	"Ludum trium Regum"	REED: Lincolnshire

Date	Characters	Location	Description	Source
1345	n/a	Carlisle	"quendam ludum" and "ludere quoddam miraculum" on the Eve of St. Peter ad Vincula	REED: CWG
1361	John the Baptist?	Long Wittenham, Berkshire	"die decollacionis Sancti Iohannis Baptisti quando ludus erat"	REED: Berkshire
1363–1376	3 Marys (Mary Magdalene, Mary Jacobi, Mary Salome)	Barking Abbey	Visitatio Sepulchri by Katherine of Sutton	DTRB
1376–1569	Virgin Mary, Elizabeth, Joseph, Simeon, Apostles, Mary Magdalene, John the Baptist, Joseph of Arimathea, Nicodemus, Michael, Mary Jacobi, Mary Salome, Gabriel,	York	Corpus Christi plays	Ed. Davidson (2011)/REED: York
1377–1539	Virgin Mary, Apostles, Mary Magdalene, John the Baptist	Beverley, Yorkshire	Corpus Christi pageants	DTRB
1385	Thomas Becket	Lynn, Norfolk	"ludentibus interludium Sancti Thome Martiris"	BSPR
1389	Virgin Mary, Joseph, Blaise	Lincoln	Procession	REED: Lincolnshire
1389	Elene (Helena)	Beverley, Yorkshire	Procession of the Guild of St. Elene	DTRB
1389	Virgin Mary, Simeon, Joseph	Beverley, Yorkshire	Candlemas pageant of the Guild of St. Mary	DTRB

Continued

Continued

Date	Saint/Martyr	Place	Event/Title	Reference
1392	John the Baptist	London	Pageant for Richard II at Temple Bar	BSPR
1392–1579	Anne, Gabriel, Joseph, 3 Marys (Mary Magdalene, Mary Jacobi, Mary Salome), Virgin Mary, Peter, Thomas of India, Simeon, Peter	Coventry	Corpus Christi plays	Eds. King and Davidson (2000)/ *REED: Coventry*
1393	Katherine	London	"the pley of seynt Katerine"	BSPR
c.1393–1543	Virgin Mary, Elizabeth (select years)	Lincoln	Christmas pageant of Annunciation (and Visitation)	*REED: Lincolnshire*
c.1395–1419	Virgin Mary, Apostles, Michael, Gabriel, 3 Marys (Mary Magdalene, Mary Jacobi, Mary Salome), Longinus, Nicodemus and Joseph of Arimathea, Veronica	Penryn, Cornwall	*Ordinalia*	Ed. Harris (1969)
c.1400	3 Marys (Mary Magdalene, Mary Jacobi, Mary Salome)	Dublin	*Visitatio Sepulchri*	*DTRB*
c.1400–1531	George, John the Evangelist, Luke	Ipswich	Corpus Christi pageants	BSPR
c.1400–1542	Eligius/Eloy, Virgin Mary, Thomas Becket	Ipswich	Corpus Christi pageants	BSPR
1407–1471	3 Marys (Mary Magdalene, Mary Jacobi, Mary Salome)	Wells	"iij marias ludentes nocte pasche"	*REED: Somerset*
1408–1409	Virgin Mary	Boxley, Kent	"ludentibus vnum miraculum de sancta Maria"	*REED: Kent*
1408–1550	George	Norwich	Annual pageant/riding sponsored by Guild of St. George	*DTRB*/*REED: Norwich*
1409	Agnes	Winchester	"pleye of synt agnes"	*REED: Hampshire*

c.1410–1411	Cuthbert	"miraculum Sci. Cuthberti"	Durham	Johnston, "Pleyes of Miracles" (2015)
1415	George, Apostles, Martyrs and Confessors	Entry of Henry V after Agincourt	London	DTRB
1422–1575	Gabriel, Virgin Mary, Joseph, Elizabeth, Apostles, Mary Magdalene, Mary Jacobi, Mary Salome, Longinus, Joseph of Arimathea, Nicodemus, John the Baptist, Michael	Plays	Chester	Eds. Lumiansky and Mills (1974 and 1986)/ REED: Chesire
c.1425	n/a	Dux Moraud fragment	East Anglia	NCPF
1427	Alban	Entry of John of Lancaster	London	DTRB
1427–1581	3 Kings of Cologne, Virgin Mary, John the Baptist	Corpus Christi pageants	Newcastle Upon Tyne	REED: Newcastle
c.1430	Clotilda	A Mumming at Windsor by John Lydgate	Windsor	Mummings and Entertainments, ed. Sponsler (2010)
1431	George	"St georges playes playd in chester"	Chester	REED: Chesire
1444–11459	n/a	"a pley vpon seynt lucy day, and for a pley vpon seynt Margarete day"	Southwark, Surrey	Collier, "The Churchwardens Accounts of St. Margaret's Southwark." (1847 & 1848)
1441	Holy Innocents	"saltantibus, cantantibus, et ludentibus"	St Mary's Abbey, Winchester	DTRB
1441–1442	Lawrence	"Ludus Sancti Laurencij"	Lincoln	REED: Lincolnshire

Continued

Continued

Date	Saint/Martyr	Place	Event/Title	Reference
1442–1526	3 Kings of Cologne, Virgin Mary, Joseph, Bride, Helen, Simeon	Aberdeen	Event on Candlemas	*DTRB*
1445	Margaret	London	Entry of Margaret of Anjou by John Lydgate	*Mummings and Entertainments*, ed. Sponsler (2010)
1445–1546	Virgin Mary, Katherine, Margaret, Gabriel, Apostles	Coventry	Corpus Christi procession	*REED: Coventry*
1446	James	York	"gilde sancti christofori quemdam ludum de sancto Iacobo Apostolo in sex paginis compilatum"	*REED: York*
1447	Susanna	Lincoln	"Ludus Sancti Susanni"	*REED: Lincolnshire*
c.1450	St. Thomas spear, St. Blasius' body, St. John the Baptist's coat, Four evangelists, St. Katherine's wheel, St. Andew's cross, St. Barbara's castle	Dundee	Procession	*DTRB*
c.1450–1520	3 Marys (Mary Magdalene, Mary Jacobi, Mary Salome), Joseph, Peter, John the Evangelist, Andrew	n/a (in the North)	Christ's Burial and Resurrection	*Digby Plays*
c.1450–1527	n/a	Norwich	"diuers disgisings and pageuntes as well of the liff and marterdams of diuers and many hooly sayntes"	*DTRB*
c.1450–1475	Virgin Mary, 3 Marys (Mary Magdalene, Mary Jacobi, Mary Salome), John the Baptist, 3 Kings of Cologne, Joseph of Arimathea, Longinus, Thomas	East Anglia	N-Town Plays	Ed. Sugano (2006)

c.1450–1500	3 Kings of Cologne, Virgin Mary, Joseph	*Y Tri Brenin o Gwlen* (*The Three Kings of Cologne*) attributed to Iolo Goch	Wales	Ed. and trans. Klausner and Baruch (2012)/*REED: Wales*
c.1450–c.1504	Meriasek, Silvester, Peter, Paul, Virgin Mary	*Beunans Meriasek* (*Life of Saint Meriasek*)	Cornwall	Ed. W. Stokes (1872)
c.1450–1576	Virgin Mary, Gabriel, Elizabeth, Joseph, 3 Kings of Cologne, Simeon, Apostles, John the Baptist, Mary Magdalene, Mary Jacobi, Mary Salome, Longinus, Joseph of Arimathea, Nicodemus,	The Towneley Plays	n/a	Ed. Epp (2018)
c.1451–1456	Michael	"Solemn Play…of the battle between St Michael and the Devil"	Spalding, Lincolnshire	*REED: Lincolnshire*
1452–1453	Robert of Sicily	"ludus de Kyng Robert of Cesill"	Lincoln	*REED: Lincolnshire*
c.1453–1460	Ke	*Beunans Ke* (*Life of St Ke*)	Cornwall	Eds. Thomas and Williams (2016)
1454–1455	James	"Ludus de Sancto Jacobo"	Lincoln	*REED: Lincolnshire*
1455/6	Denys	"ludum oreginale Sancti Dionisij"	York	*REED: York*
c.1455–1456	Clare	"ludus de Sancta Clara"	Lincoln	*REED: Lincolnshire*
1456	Edward the Confessor, John, Margaret	Entry for Queen Margaret	Coventry	*REED: Coventry*
1456–1534	George	"pley boke"	Lydd, Kent	*REED: Kent*
1459–1543	Virgin Mary	Assumption/Coronation pageant on Feast of St. Anne	Lincoln Cathedral	*REED: Lincolnshire*

Continued

Continued

Date	Saint/Martyr	Place	Event/Title	Reference
1461	George	Bristol	Pageant for Edward IV	*REED: Bristol*
1462	Nicholas	Glasgow	University "interludium" on the saint's translation	BSPR
1464	Paul, Elizabeth, Mary Cleophas	London Bridge	Coronation pageant for Elizabeth Woodville	*DTRB*
1467–1532	George	Leicester	Riding	BSPR
1469	Elizabeth, Virgin Mary and Gabriel	Norwich	Annunciation and Visitation pageant for Elizabeth Woodville	BSPR
1474	Edward the Confessor, George, 3 Kings of Cologne	Coventry	Entry for Prince Edward	*REED: Coventry*
c.1475–1500	George	Woodbridge, Suffolk	Geroge and the Dragon	*DTRB*
c.1475–1500	Lawrence	n/a	Ashmole Fragment	NCPF
c.1475–1525	Virgin Mary, Theophilus	Durham	"gamen" of Theophilus	NCPF
1478–1524	George	Salisbury	Riding	*DTRB*
1482–1483	George	Thame, Oxfordshire	"ye play cald Synt George"	BSPR
1485–1553	Eligius/Eloy	Perth	"playaris"	BSPR
1485–c.1534	Erasmus	Perth	"playaris"	BSPR
1486	Ethelbert, George, Virgin Mary	Hereford	Pageant for Henry VII	*REED: HereWor*
1486	Virgin Mary	Worcester	Whitsun pageant for Henry VII	*REED: HereWor*
1486	Virgin Mary	York	Assumption pageant for Henry VII	*REED: York*
1494	George	London	Pageant	*DTRB*

1488–1507	George, 3 Kings of Cologne	Lanark, Scotland	Corpus Christi pageants	*DTRB*
c.1488–1489	Fabine and Sabine	Thame, Oxfordshire	"ye box of ye play of Fabine & Sabine"	BSPR
1490/91	Katherine	Coventry	"A Play of St Katherine in the Little Parke"	*REED: Coventry*
1496	Christopher	Salisbury	Entry of Henry VII	*DTRB*
1498	George	Coventry	Entry of King Arthur	*REED: Coventry*
1498–1499	3 Kings of Cologne	Reading	"horssys for the kynges of colen on may day"	*REED: Berkshire*
1498–1566/7	George	Dublin	Annual pageant on St. George's Day and Corpus Christi	BSPR
1498–1569	Virgin Mary, Joseph, 3 Kings of Cologne, Apostles	Dublin	Corpus Christi pageants	*DTRB*
1499	Virgin Mary	Chester	"Storie of the Assumption of our Lady was played at the abbey gates" for Prince Arthur	*REED: Cheshire*
c.1500	Mary Magdalene	East Anglia	Digby *Mary Magdalene*	Ed. Coletti (2018)
c.1500	Paul	East Anglia	Digby *Conversion of Saint Paul*	*Digby Plays*
c.1500	Virgin Mary, Joseph	East Anglia	Digby *Candlemas Day and the Killing of the Children*	*Digby Plays*
1501	Katherine, Ursula	London Bridge	*Recypt of the Ladie Kateryne*	Ed. Kipling (1990)

Continued

Continued

Date	Saint/Martyr	Place	Event/Title	Reference
1501/2	3 Kings of Cologne	Canterbury	Pageant	*REED: Kent*
1502	Virgin Mary, Joseph, Gabriel	Edinburgh	Entry of Margaret Tudor	*DTRB*
c.1502–1558, not inclusive	George	York	"pagyant" and play in later years	*REED: York*
1503–c.1548	Katherine	Hereford	"Seinte keterina with Tres Tormenters" in Cappers' annual Corpus Christi procession	*REED: HereWor*
1504	Mary Magdalene	Taunton, Somerset	"Mary Magdalen play"	*REED: Somerset*
1504–1543	Thomas Becket	Canterbury	Annual pageant on Eve of Translation	*REED: Kent*
1505	Christian/Christine	Coventry	"Magnum ludum vocatum seynt christeans play"	*REED: Coventry*
1505	Thomas Becket	Mildenhall, Suffolk	"a play off Sent Thomas … in the hall yard"	BSPR
1506–1507	Mary Magdalene	Oxford	"scriptura lusi marie magdalene" at Magdalen College	*REED: Oxford*
1509	Edmund	Bury	"Saint Edmund's play"	Gibson, *The Theater of Devotion* (1989)
1510–1511	n/a	Newcastle Upon Tyne	Dragon procession for St. George's Day	*REED: Newcastle*
c.1510–1520	John the Evangelist	London	"saint jon euuangeliste *en* trelute"	BSPR
1511	George	Bassingbourn, Cambridgeshire	"the play of … of the holy martir seynt george"	*REED: Cambridgeshire*
1511	George	Ipswich	"the pageant of George"	*DTRB*

Year	Subject	Place	Description	Source
1511	Virgin Mary, 3 Kings of Cologne	Aberdeen	"padgeanes playit prattelie"	*DTRB*
1512	Blythe	London	Drapers' MSW pageant	*BSPR*
1512–1513	Virgin Mary	New Romney, Kent	"lusorum beate marie"	*REED: Kent*
1512–1538	Virgin Mary	London	Drapers' MSW pageant	*BSPR*
1515–1516	Virgin Mary	Chester	"the shepards play & the Assumption in St Iohns churchyard"	*REED: Cheshire*
c.1515–1516	Feliciana and Sabina	Shrewsbury	"ludum & demonstracionem Martiriorum feliciane et Sabine martirum"	*REED: Shropshire*
1517–1518	3 Kings of Cologne	Shrewsbury	"tres Reges colonie equitantibus in interludo"	*REED: Shropshire*
1519	Virgin Mary and Elizabeth	London	Skinners' MSW pageant of the Visitation	*BSPR*
1519	Thomas Becket	London	Skinners' MSW pageant "playing the Martyrdom of St. Thomas Becket"	*BSPR*
c.1519–1521	Christina	Bethersden	Three day "ludo beate Cristine"	*REED: Kent*
1520	Robert the Devil	Guines (France)	Performance	*DTRB*
1520–1537	Virgin Mary	Sutterton, Lincolnshire	Intermittent records for Assumption "play"	*REED: Lincolnshire*
1521	John the Baptist	London	MSW pageant	*BSPR*

Continued

Continued

Date	Saint/Martyr	Place	Event/Title	Reference
1521	Margaret and George	London	MSW pageant	DTRB
1521	John the Evangelist	London	Drapers' MSW pageant	BSPR
1522	George, John the Baptist, Edmund, Edward the Confessor, Dunstan, Thomas Becket, Erkenwald, Virgin Mary, Gabriel, and Michael	London	"the assumption of owr lady"	BSPR
1523	George, John the Baptist, Edmund, Edward the Confessor, Dunstan, Thomas Becket, Erkenwald, Virgin Mary, Gabriel, and Michael	London	Repeat of 1523	BSPR
1523	Lawrence	Dublin	"lyff of saincte larens playyde one the hoggen gren"	BSPR
1523	Swithin	Braintree, Essex	"A Play of St Swythyn acted in the church on a Wenesday"	BSPR
1523	Ursula	London	Drapers' MSW pageant	BSPR
1525	Andrew	Braintree, Essex	"There was a Play of St. Andrew acted in the Church"	BSPR
c.1525—1526	Katherine	Shrewsbury	"Saynt Kateryn is play"	REED: Shropshire
1527	Peter, Paul, James	Greenwich	Anti-Lutheran morality play by John Rightwise	Streitberger, Court Revels (1994)
1527	John of Bowre	Girimsby, Lincolnshire	"the play of holy John of bowre"	REED: Lincolnshire
1527	Martin	Colchester	"Seynt Martyns Pley"	BSPR
1528	Crispin and Crispianus, Virgin Mary, Joseph, Apostles	Dublin	Pageants	BSPR

Date	Saints	Location	Event	Source
c.1528–1547	George, Virgin Mary	Morebath, Devon	Annual pageant	REED: Devon
1529	John the Evangelist, Ursula	London	Drapers' MSW	BSPR
1529	Robert of Sicily	Chester	"play" or "Enterlude"	REED: Cheshire
1529	Ursula, John the Evangelist	London	Drapers' MSW pageants	DTRB
1530–1556	George, John the Evangelist, Lawrence, Martin, Virgin Mary, Nicholas, Sebastian, Stephen	Aberdeen	Corpus Christi procession	BSPR
c.1530–1565	Virgin Mary, Joseph, 3 Kings of Cologne, John the Baptist	Norwich	Biblical plays at Pentacost	DTRB
1532	Virgin Mary, Joseph, George, Thomas Becket	Canterbury	City Watch pageants	REED: Kent
1533	Anne, Virgin Mary, Mary Salome, Mary Cleophas, James, John the Baptist	London	*The noble tryumphaunt coronacyon of quene Anne* by John Leland and Nicholas Udall	STC 656
1534	Mary Magdalene, Peter	Reading	Resurrection play	Wiggins
1534	John the Baptist	n/a	*Vita divi Joannis Baptistae* by John Bale	Wiggins
1534	Christopher	London	Drapers' MSW pageant	BSPR
1534	Eustace	Braintree, Essex	"There was a play of Placy Dacy als St. Ewe Stacy"	BSPR
1535	John the Evangelist	London	Skinners' MSW pageant	BSPR

Continued

Continued

Date	Saint/Martyr	Place	Event/Title	Reference
1535	Virgin Mary, Elizabeth	London	Ironmongers' MSW pageant	BSPR
c.1535–1540	Thomas the Apostle	York	"a religious interlude of St. Thomas the Apostle"	REED: York
c.1536–1538	John the Baptist	n/a	*Vitam Dixi Joanis Baptisti* by John Bale	Happé, "The Protestant Adaptation of the Saint Play" (1986)
1536	George	Lostwithiel, Cornwall	"St Georges rideng"	REED: Dorset, Cornwall
1537	Augustine, Paul	n/a	*A Reverent Receiving of the Sacrament* by Thomas Wylley	Wiggins
1537	Thomas Becket	n/a	*De traditione Thomae Becketi* by John Bale	Wiggins
1538	John the Baptist	n/a	*The Chief Promises of God unto Man by all the Ages in the Old Law* by John Bale	STC 1305
1538	John the Baptist	n/a	*John Baptist's Preaching in the Wilderness* by John Bale	*The Complete Plays of John Bale*, ed. Happé (1985-86)
1538	Reference to the Virgin Mary	St. Andrews	Royal Entry of Mary of Guise	DTRB
1539	John the Baptist	n/a	*1 and 2 De baptismo et tentatione* by John Bale (lost)	Wiggins
1539	Virgin Mary	Holbeach, Lincolnshire	"marycart"	REED: Lincolnshire
1539–1540	John the Baptist	West Port, Dundee	*The Beheading of John the Baptist* by James Wedderburn (lost)	Wiggins
1539–1562	John the Baptist	Maldon, Essex	Pageant	DTRB

1540	Virgin Mary	London	Planned Drapers' LMS pageant	BSPR
1541	Margaret, Virgin Mary	London	Drapers' LMS pageant	BSPR
1541	Mary Magdalene, John the Evangelist, Peter, Thomas, Joseph Arimathaeus	Brasenose College, Oxford	*Christus redivivus* by Nicholas Grimald (lost)	Wiggins
1541–1548	Stephen or Alban?	n/a	*Protomartyr* by Nicholas Grimald (lost)	Wiggins
1541–1557	George	Stratford-Upon-Avon	Riding	*DTRB*
c.1551–1556	Michael	Spalding, Lincolnshire	"Solemn Play held in the Gore … written & directed by one Howson a prest"	REED: *Lincolnshire*
c.1542–1543	Thomas Becket	Canterbury	"pley"	REED: *Kent*
1545	Peter, Paul	Cambridge	*Pammachius* by Thomas Kirchmayer	White, "The *Pammachius* Affair at Christ's College, Cambridge, in 1545" (2007)
c.1545–1553	Virgin Mary, Apostles, 3 Marys (Mary Magdalene, Mary Jacobi, Mary Salome)	n/a	Fragment of the *Resurrection of Our Lord*	Eds. Wilson and Dobell (1912)
1546	John the Baptist	n/a	*Archipropheta* by Nicholas Grimald	Ed. Merill (1969)/Wiggins
1546–1558	George and Christopher	York	Riding and Play of George with Pageant of Christopher	REED: *York*
1547	Edward the Confessor, George	London	Coronation pageant for Edward VI	Wiggins

Continued

Continued

Date	Saint/Martyr	Place	Event/Title	Reference
1547	Athanasius	n/a	*Athanasius, sive Infamia* by Nicholas Grimald (lost)	Wiggins
1550	Paul, Peter, Raphael	n/a	*Free Will* by Thomas Hoby (lost)	Wiggins
c.1550	John the Evangelist	n/a	*Here begynneth the enterlude of Iohan the Euangelyst*	STC 14643
c.1550–1566	Mary Magdalene	n/a	*Life and Repentaunce of Mary Magdalene* by Lewis Wager	STC 24932
1553–1554	John the Baptist	London	Merchant Taylors' LMS pageant by Richard Mulcaster	Wiggins
1554	John the Baptist	London	Grocers' LMS pageant	Wiggins
1555	3 Marys (Mary Magdalene, Mary Jacobi, Mary Salome), Apostles, Simon	New Romney, Kent	Planned Pentecost play	REED: Kent
1555–1556	Rosmonus	Ashburton, Devon	Corpus Christi play	REED: Devon
1555–1556	Thomas Becket	Canterbury	"pley"	REED: Kent
1556	Mary, Raphael, Saul, Peter	Magdalene College, Oxford; Trinity College, Cambridge	*Christus triumphans* by John Foxe	Wiggins
1559	George, mabye John the Baptist	London	"there was a May-game … and a goodly pagant"	REED: Ecclesiastical London
1560	John the Baptist	New Romney, Kent	Crucifixion play at Whitsuntide	REED: Kent
1562–1563	Nicholas	Chelmsford, Essex	"play days"	DTRB

c.1562–1563	John the Baptist	Trinity College Cambridge and Bordeaux, France	*Baptistes, sive Calumnia* by George Buchanan	STC 3969/*PhilMus*
c.1565–1572	Peter, Paul	n/a	*Freewill* by Henry Cheke	STC 18419
1566	John the Evangelist's visions	Coventry	Royal Entry of Elizabeth I	REED: *Coventry*
1568	John the Baptist	London	Merchant Taylors' LMS pageant by Richard Mulcaster	MSC III/Wiggins
c.1570–1580	Michael	Herefordshire	*Processus Satanae*	MSC II.3/*LPD*
1577	Robert	Perth	"sanc tobertis play"	BSPR
1578	Ambrose	Clementina, Prague (English College)	*Ambrosia* by Edmund Campion	Ed. Simons (1970)
c.1580–1650	John the Evangelist, 3 Marys (Mary Magdalene, Mary Jacobi, Mary Salome), Michael	Kilkenny	Corpus Christi and Midsummer Plays	Fletcher, *Performance and Polity in Pre-Cromwellian Ireland* (2000)
1585	George	London	August event by the London Armourers' and Braisers' Company	A. Lancashire, *London Civic Theatre* (2002)
1587–1590	Winifred's Well	London	*John a Kent and John a Cumber* by Anthony Munday	Ed. Byrne (1923)
1588	English Knight of St. George; French Knight of St. Denis	London	*Suleiman and Perseda* attributed to Thomas Kyd	STC 22894

Continued

Continued

Date	Saint/Martyr	Place	Event/Title	Reference
c.1590–1600	Ethelbert	n/a	"Play of Oswald"	Greg, "A Dramatic Fragment" (1904)/*LPD*
c.1590–1600	Edward the Confessor	London	*Edmund Ironside*	Ed. Boswell (1927)
c.1591–1592	Joan of Arc	London	*1 Henry VI* by William Shakespeare	STC 2273
1592	Dunstan	London	*Knack to Know a Knave*	STC 15027
1594	Richard of Chichester	London	*Richad the Confessor* (lost)	*LPD*
c.1594	Alban?	London	*Warlamchester* (lost)	*LPD*
c.1594	Saints?	London	*Diocletian* (lost)	*LPD*
1598	Ursula?	London	*Conan, Prince of Cornwall* by Thomas Dekker and Michael Drayton (lost)	*LPD*
1599	Thomas Becket	St. Omers	*Brevis dialogismus in festi Sancti Thomae Cantuariensis Anglorum patroni*	Houliston, "*Breuis Dialogismus*" (1993)
c.1600	Dunstan	London	*The Devil and His Dame* by William Haughton	Wing G1580
c.1600–1629	Michael, Peter, Paul, John the Evangelist	n/a	*The History of Popish Purgatory* attributed to Robert Owen	Wiggins
c.1601–1623	George	n/a	*St. George for England* by William Smith (lost)	Wiggins
1602	Saints?	London	*Judas* by W. Bird, S. Rowley, W. Haughton (lost)	*LPD*
1602	Saints?	London	*Pontius Pilate* by Thomas Dekker (lost)	*LPD*
1602	Swithin	Harefield House, Essex	Entertainment at Harefield House by John Davies	Ed. Goldring et al. (2014)

c.1603–1625	Mary Magdalene?	n/a	"Mary Maudling" masque	Cutts, "Jacobean Masque and Stage Music" (1954)
1604	Andrew, George	London	*The Magnificent Entertainment* by Thomas Dekker and Ben Jonson	Ed. Dutton (1995)
c.1604	Elizabeth Tudor	London	*If You Know Not Me, You Know Nobody, Pt. 1* by Thomas Heywood	STC 13328
1607	George	Wells	Mercers' pageant	*REED: Somerset*
1609	Christopher	Yorkshire	Touring play of St. Christopher	Keenan, "The Simpsons Players of Jacobean Yorkshire and the Professional Stage" (2013)
1609	Andrew and George	London	*Campbell, or The Ironmonger's Fair Field* by Anthony Munday	STC 18265
1610	George	Chester	*Chester's Triumph* Richard Davies and Robert Amerie	STC 5118
1611	Dunstan	London	*Chryso-Thriambos* by Anthony Munday	STC 18267
1612	Thomas More	English College, Rome	*Thomas Morus*	*PhilMus*
1612	Saints, Virgin Mary	St. Omers	Comedy (lost)	Wiggins
1613	Joseph of Arimathea, Thomas Becket	English College, Rome	*Sanctus Thomas Cantuariensis*	*PhilMus*

Continued

Continued

Date	Saint/Martyr	Event/Title	Place	Reference
1613	Clement, Ursula, Crispin and Crispianus, George, John the Baptist, Clement	Guild pageants for Queen Anne	Wells	REED: Somerset
1614	Saint?	The She Saint by Robert Daborne (lost)	London	Wiggins
1616	Ignatius Loyola	Risus Anglicanus	Oxford or Cambridge	PhilMus
1617	Andrew, George in emblem	Entertainment	Holyrood, Scotland	Wiggins
1617	George, Andrew	Plays for King James	Edinburgh	DTRB
1618	Rochester, Thomas More	Roffensis	English College, Rome	PhilMus
c.1618	Hugh, Crispin and Crispianus, Winifred, Alban and Amphibalus	A Shoemaker, A Gentlemen by William Rowley	London	STC 21422
1619	Cuthbert, Neot	Aluredus by William Drury	English College, Douai	PhilMus
1619	Alban, Amphibalus, Stephen	Sanctus Albanus by Thomas Stillington (lost)	English College, Rome	Wiggins
1619	Dorothy	The Virgin Martyr by Thomas Dekker and Philip Massinger	London	STC 17644
c.1619–1622	Justina and Cyprian	Two Noble Ladies, and The Converted Conjuror	London	Ed. Rhoads (1930)
c.1619–1622	Saints	The Martyr'd Soldier by Henry Shirley	London	STC 22435
c.1620	Guy of Warwick	Guy, Earl of Warwick attributed to John Day and Thomas Dekker	London	Ed. Moore (2007)/LPD

1620	Edward the Confessor	English College, Douai	*Emma Angliae Regina ac matre Hardicanuti Regis* by Thomas Carleton (lost)	Wiggins
1620	Katherine	London	*Tres Irenes Trophoea* by John.Squire	STC 23120.5
1621	George	Chester	Planned civic pageant	REED: *Cheshire*
c.1622	Anselm	London	*The Birth of Merlin* by William Rowley	Wing R2096
1623	Guy of Warwick	St. Omers	*Guido Varvicensis*	Wiggins
1623	Vitus	St. Omers	*Vitus* by Joseph Simons	*PhilMus*
1623	Pelagius	St. Omers	*Sanctus Pelagius Martyr* by Joseph Simons	*PhilMus*
1623	Ignatius Loyola	Trinity College, Cambridge	*Loyola* by John Hackett	*PhilMus*
1624	Chad	St. Omers	*Mercia* by Joseph Simons	*PhilMus*
1624	Ignatius Loyola	London	*A Game at Chess* by Thomas Middleton	*Complete Works*, ed.Taylor and Lavagnino (2007)
1624	Paul Miki?	Grammar Class, St. Omers	*Paulus Japonensis* (lost)	LPD
1624	Alban?	n/a	*Tragedy of Saint Albans* by James Shirley (lost)	Wiggins

Continued

Continued

Date	Saint/Martyr	Place	Event/Title	Reference
c.1625	Francis Xavier	St. Omers	*Sanctus Fran Xaverius, sive Gloriae divinae zelus*	Takenaka/Burnett, *Jesuit Plays on Japan and English Recusancy* (1995)
1626	Damian	St. Omers	*Sanctus Damianus* by Joseph Simons	PhilMus
1628	Edward the Confessor	London	*Britannia's Honour* by Thomas Dekker	STC 6493
1631	Katherine	London	*London Jus Honorarium* by Thomas Heywood	STC 13351
1632	Katherine	London	*Londini Artium et Scientiarum Scaturirgo* by Thomas Heywood	STC 13347
1634	Virgin Mary	St. Omers	Play	Wiggins
c.1635	George, Andrew, Patrick, Denis, James, Anthony, David	London	*Seven Champions of Christendom* by John Kirke	STC 15014
1635	Peter, Paul, Raphael	n/a	New translation of *Freewill*	Wiggins
c.1635	Thomas Becket	English College, Douai	*Icon ecclesiastici*	PhilMus
1637	Katherine	London	*Londini Speculum* by Thomas Heywood	STC 13349
1639	Patrick	London	*Saint Patrick for Ireland* by James Shirley	STC 22455

1641	Austin?	London	*England's First Happiness, or the Life of St. Austin* (lost)	LPD
Pre-1642	George	Morpeth, Northumberland	St. Geroge Day's costuming at church	DTRB
1666	Cecilia	London	*St. Cecily, Or The Converted Twins* by Matthew Medbourne	Wing M1583B
1669	Katherine	London	*Tyrranick Love, or The Royal Martyr* by John Dryden	Wing D2393
1686	George	Bartholomew Fair	"Valiant St George and the Dragon, A Farce"	Van Lennep, Avery, and Scouten, eds. *The London Stage, 1660–1800, Part 1: 1660–1700* (1965)

APPENDIX 2

Table of Saints in Liturgical Calendars

Month	Saint/Feast	Mirk	Sarum Missal 1498 STC 16172	Goodly Primer 1535 STC 15988	Manual of Prayers 1539 STC 16010	Sarum Primer 1543 STC 16029	English Primer 1545 STC 16034	1547 Edwardian Primer STC 16048	1549 BCP STC 16274 Folger	BCP 1552 STC 16285	BCP 1553 STC 16288a	Sarum Primer in English and Latin 1558 STC 16082	BCP 1559 STC 16292a	BCP 1580 16307	BCP 1594 STC 16318
JANUARY															
	Circumcision (1)	x	x	x		x	x	x	x	x	x	x	x	x	x
	Octave of Stephen (2)		x	x		x						x			
	Octave of John the Evangelist (3)		x	x		x						x			
	Octave of Holy Innocents (4)		x	x		x						x			
	Octave Thomas Becket (5)		x	x											
	Simon Bishop (5)											x			
	Edward the Confessor (5)		x												
	Epiphany (6)	x	x	x	x	x	x	x	x	x	x	x	x	x	x
	Felix and January (7)			x		x						x			
	Lucian (8)		x	x		x						x	x	x	x
	Joyce (9)			x		x						x	x	x	x

Continued

Continued

Month	Saint/Feast	Mirk	Sarum Missal 1498 STC 16172	Goodly Primer 1535 STC 15988	Manual of Prayers 1539 STC 16010	Sarum Primer 1543 STC 16029	English Primer 1545 STC 16034	1547 Edwardian Primer STC 16048	1549 BCP STC 16274 Folger	BCP 1552 STC 16285	BCP 1553 STC 16288a	Sarum Primer in English and Latin 1558 STC 16082	BCP 1559 STC 16292a	BCP 1580 STC 16307	BCP 1594 STC 16318
	Paul the Hermit (10)			x		x						x			
	Arcadius (12)			x		x						x			
	Octave Epiphany (13)		x	x		x						x			
	Hilary (13)		x	x		x	x				x		x	x	x
	Felix (14)		x	x		x						x			
	Maurus (15)		x	x		x						x			
	Marcellus (16)		x	x		x						x			
	Anthony the Great (17)		x	x		x					x	x			
	Sulpicitius (17)		x												
	Prisca (18)		x	x		x						x		x	x
	Wulstan (19)		x	x		x						x			
	Fabian and Sebastian (20)		x	x		x	x	x			x	x	x	x	x
	Agnes (21)		x	x		x					x	x	x	x	x
	Vincent (22)		x	x		x	x				x	x	x	x	x
	Emerentiana (23)			x		x						x			
	Timothy (24)			x		x	x	x				x			
	Conversion of Paul (25)	x	x	x		x	x	x	x	x	x	x	x	x	x
	Projectus (25)		x												

Polycarp (26)			x		x		x			
Julian (27)		x	x			x	x			
Agnes (28)		x	x			x	x			
Valery			x			x	x			
Balthild (30)		x				x	x			
Saturn and Victor (31)						x	x			
FEBRUARY										
Bridget (1)		x	x			x	x			
Candlemas (2)	x	x	x	x	x	x	x			
Blase (3)		x	x		x	x	x	x	x	x
Gilbert (4)		x	x		x		x	x		
Agatha (5)		x	x		x	x	x	x	x	x
Vedast and Amand (6)		x					x	x		
Dorothy (6)						x				
Angule Bishop and Martyr (7)		x	x		x		x			
Paul the Bishop (8)			x		x		x			

Continued

Continued

Month	Saint/Feast	Mirk	Sarum Missal 1498 STC 16172	Goodly Primer 1535 STC 15988	Manual of Prayers 1539 STC 16010	Sarum Primer 1543 16029	English Primer 1545 STC 16034	1547 Edwardian Primer STC 16048	1549 BCP STC 16274 Folger	BCP 1552 STC 16285	BCP 1553 STC 16288a	Sarum Primer in English and Latin 1558 STC 16082	BCP 1559 STC 16292a	BCP 1580 16307	BCP 1594 STC 16318
	Apollonia (9)					x						x			
	Scholastica (10)		x	x		x						x			
	Translation of Frideswide (11)		x												
	Eufrasia (11)			x		x						x			
	Wulfran the Bishop (13)			x		x						x			
	Valentine (14)		x	x		x	x	x			x	x	x	x	x
	Faustin and Jovita (15)			x		x						x			
	Juliana (16)		x	x		x						x			
	Policron (17)			x		x						x			
	Simeon (18)			x		x						x			
	Sabine (19)			x		x						x			
	Mildred (20)			x		x					x	x			
	69 Martyrs (21)			x		x						x			
	Chair of Peter (22)		x	x		x						x			
	Matthias (24)	x	x	x	x	x	x	x	x	x	x	x	x	x	x
	Invention of Paul (25)			x		x						x			
	Nestor (26)			x		x						x			
	Augustine (Austin) of Canterbury (27)			x		x	x					x			

MARCH										
	David (1)	x				x	x			x
	Chad (2)	x				x	x	x	x	x
	Martin (3)					x	x			
	Adrian (4)				x	x				
	Eusebius of Cremona (5)					x				
	Victor and Victorine (6)					x	x			
	Perpetua and Felicity (7)	x				x		x	x	x
	Deposition of Felix (8)					x	x			
	40 Martyrs (9)					x	x			
	Agapite the Virgin (10)					x	x			
	Quirion and Candide (11)			x		x	x			
	Gregory (12)	x		x		x	x	x	x	x
	Theodora the Matron (13)			x		x	x			

Continued

Continued

Month	Saint/Feast	Mirk	Sarum Missal 1498 STC 16172	Goodly Primer 1535 STC 15988	Manual of Prayers 1539 STC 16010	Sarum Primer 1543 STC 16029	English Primer 1545 STC 16034	1547 Edwardian Primer STC 16048	1549 BCP STC 16274 Folger	BCP 1552 STC 16285	BCP 1553 STC 16288a	Sarum Primer in English and Latin 1558 STC 16082	BCP 1559 STC 16292a	BCP 1580 STC 16307	BCP 1594 STC 16318
	Longinus (15)			x		x						x			
	Hilary and Tacoam (16)			x		x						x			
	Patrick (17)		x	x		x						x			
	Edward King and Martyr (18)		x	x		x	x	x			x	x	x	x	x
	Joseph (19)			x		x	x					x			
	Alkmund (19)	x		x											
	Cuthbert (20)			x		x						x			
	Benedict (21)		x	x		x						x	x	x	x
	Epaphroditus (22)											x			
	Theodore (23)			x		x						x			
	Agapite the Martyr (24)			x		x						x			
	Annunciation (25)	x	x	x	x	x	x	x	x	x	x	x	x	x	x
	Castor (26)			x		x						x			
	Dorothy (28)			x		x						x			
	Victorinus (29)			x		x						x			
	Quirinus (30)			x		x						x			
	Aldelm (31)			x		x						x			

APRIL

Theodora the Virgin (1)		x			x		
Mary of Egypt (2)		x			x		
Richard of Chichester (3)	x	x			x	x	x
Ambrose (4)	x	x		x	x	x	x
Martinian and Martin (5)		x		x	x	x	x
Sixtus (6)		x			x		
Euphemia (7)		x			x		
Hegesippus and Felix of Burgundy (8)					x		
Perpetuus (9)		x			x		
7 Virgins (10)					x		

Continued

Continued

Month	Saint/Feast	Mirk	Sarum Missal 1498 STC 16172	Goodly Primer 1535 STC 15988	Manual of Prayers 1539 STC 16010	Sarum Primer 1543 STC 16029	English Primer 1545 STC 16034	1547 Edwardian Primer STC 16048	1549 BCP STC 16274 Folger	BCP 1552 STC 16285	BCP 1553 STC 16288a	Sarum Primer in English and Latin 1558 STC 16082	BCP 1559 STC 16292a	BCP 1580 STC 16307	BCP 1594 STC 16318
	Guthlac (11)			x		x						x			
	Tiburtius, Valerian, and Maximus (13)		x				x					x			
	Julian (13)			x		x									
	Tiburtius (14)											x			
	Oswald (15)			x		x						x			
	Isidore (16)			x		x	x					x			
	Anicete (17)			x		x						x			
	Eleuther (18)			x		x						x			
	Alphege (19)		x				x					x		x	x
	Victor (20)			x		x						x			
	Simeon (21)			x		x						x			
	Soter (22)			x		x						x			
	George (23)		x	x	x	x	x	x		x	x	x	x	x	x
	Wilfrid (24)			x		x						x			
	Mark (25)	x	x	x	x	x	x	x	x	x	x	x	x	x	x
	Cletus (26)			x		x						x			
	Anastasius (27)			x		x						x			
	Vitalis (28)		x									x			
	Peter of Milan			x		x						x			
	Deposition of Erkenwald (30)		x	x		x						x			
	Eustace (30)										x				

MAY

Philip and James (1)	x	x	x				x	x	x	x
Athanasius (2)		x	x	x			x			
Invention of the Cross (3)	x	x	x				x	x	x	x
Feast of the Coronation (4)							x			
Alexander, Eventius, and Theodulus (3)	x									
Goddard (5)			x				x		x	
John the Evangelist (6)	x	x					x	x	x	x
John Before the Latin Gate (6)	x	x	x	x			x			
John of Beverley (7)		x	x				x			

Continued

Continued

Month	Saint/Feast	Mirk	Sarum Missal 1498 STC 16172	Goodly Primer 1535 STC 15988	Manual of Prayers 1539 STC 16010	Sarum Primer 1543 STC 16029	English Primer 1545 STC 16034	1547 Edwardian Primer STC 16048	1549 BCP STC 16274 Folger	BCP 1552 STC 16285	BCP 1553 STC 16288a	Sarum Primer in English and Latin 1558 STC 16082	BCP 1559 STC 16292a	BCP 1580 STC 16307	BCP 1594 STC 16318
	Appearance of Michael (8)			x		x						x			
	Translation of Nicholas (9)		x	x		x						x			
	Gordian and Epimachus (10)		x	x		x						x			
	Anthony the Martyr (11)			x		x	x	x				x			
	Nereus, Achilleus, and Pancras (12)		x									x			
	Pancras (12)										x				
	Servatius (13)			x		x						x			
	Translation of Chad of Mercia (15)		x												
	Isidore (15)			x		x						x			
	Brendan (16)			x		x						x			
	Translation of Bernard (17)			x		x	x	x				x			
	Dioscorus (18)			x		x						x			
	Dunstan (19)		x	x		x						x	x	x	x

Bernardine (20)		x			
Helen (21)		x	x		x
Juliana (22)		x	x		x
Desiderius (23)			x		x
Translation of Francis (24)			x		x
Aldhelm (25)	x	x	x		x
Urban (25)					
Augustine (Austin) of Canterbury (26)	x	x	x	x	x
Bede (27)		x	x	x	x
Germain (28)	x	x	x		x
Corone (29)		x	x		x
Charles II					
Nativity (29)					

Continued

Continued

Month	Saint/Feast	Mirk	Sarum Missal 1498 STC 16172	Goodly Primer 1535 STC 15988	Manual of Prayers 1539 STC 16010	Sarum Primer 1543 STC 16029	English Primer 1545 STC 16034	1547 Edwardian Primer STC 16048	1549 BCP STC 16274 Folger	BCP 1552 STC 16285	BCP 1553 STC 16288a	Sarum Primer in English and Latin 1558 STC 16082	BCP 1559 STC 16292a	BCP 1580 STC 16307	BCP 1594 STC 16318
	Felix (30)					x						x			
	Petronilla (31)		x	x		x					x	x			
JUNE															
	Nicodemus (1)		x	x		x	x				x	x	x	x	x
	Marcellinus and Peter (2)		x	x		x						x			
	Erasmus (3)			x		x						x			
	Petroc (4)			x		x						x			
	Boniface (5)		x	x		x	x				x	x	x	x	x
	Mellon (6)			x		x						x			
	Translation of Wulstan (7)			x		x						x			
	Gildard and Medard (8)		x	x		x						x			
	Translation of Edmund the Martyr (9)		x	x		x						x			
	Primus and Felician (9)		x												
	Yue (10)			x		x						x			
	Barnabas (11)	x	x	x		x	x	x	x	x	x	x	x	x	x
	Basilides, Cyrinus, Nabor and Nazarius (12)		x	x		x						x			

Basil (14)	x	x		x	x			
Vitus, Modestus, and Crescentia (15)	x	x		x			x	
Cyricus and Julitta (16)	x							
Translation of Richard (16)	x	x		x			x	
Botulph (17)		x		x			x	
Marcus and Marcellianus (18)	x		x		x		x	
Gervase and Protase (19)	x			x			x	
Translation of Edward the Martyr (20)	x	x		x		x	x	x
Walburge (21)		x		x			x	x

Continued

Continued

Month	Saint/Feast	Mirk	Sarum Missal 1498 STC 16172	Goodly Primer 1535 STC 15988	Manual of Prayers 1539 STC 16010	Sarum Primer 1543 16029	English Primer 1545 STC 16034	1547 Edwardian Primer STC 16048	1549 BCP STC 16274 Folger	BCP 1552 STC 16285	BCP 1553 STC 16288a	Sarum Primer in English and Latin 1558 STC 16082	BCP 1559 STC 16292a	BCP 1580 16307	BCP 1594 STC 16318
	Winifred (21)	x													
	Alban (22)		x	x		x	x					x			
	Etheldreda (Audrey) (23)		x	x		x						x			
	Nativity of John the Baptist (24)	x	x	x	x	x	x	x	x	x	x	x	x	x	x
	Translation of Eligius (25)			x		x						x			
	John and Paul the Martyrs (26)		x	x		x						x			
	Crescens (27)			x		x						x			
	Leo (28)		x	x		x						x			
	Peter and Paul (29)	x	x	x	x	x	x	x	x	x	x	x	x	x	x
	Commemoration of Paul (30)		x	x		x						x			
JULY	Octave of John the Baptist (1)		x	x		x						x			
	Visitation of Mary (2)		x	x	x	x	x	x		x	x	x	x	x	x
	Translation of Thomas the Apostle (3)			x		x						x			

Translation of Martin (4)	x	x		x			
Zoe (5)		x	x				
Octave of Peter and Paul (6)	x	x	x				
Translation of Thomas of Canterbury (7)	x	x	x		x		
Candidy the Martyr (7)				x			
Relic Sunday	x						
Grimbald (8)		x	x		x		
Cyril (9)		x	x	x	x		
Seven Brothers (10)	x	x	x		x		
Translation of Benedict (11)	x	x	x		x		
Nabor and Felix (12)		x	x		x		

Continued

Continued

Month	Saint/Feast	Mirk	Sarum Missal 1498 STC 16172	Goodly Primer 1535 STC 15988	Manual of Prayers 1539 STC 16010	Sarum Primer 1543 16029	English Primer 1545 STC 16034	1547 Edwardian Primer STC 16048	1549 BCP STC 16274 Folger	BCP 1552 STC 16285	BCP 1553 STC 16288a	Sarum Primer in English and Latin 1558 STC 16082	BCP 1559 STC 16292a	BCP 1580 STC 16307	BCP 1594 STC 16318
	Privat (13)											x			
	Translation of Swithin (15)		x	x		x						x	x	x	x
	Translation of Osmund (16)		x	x		x						x			
	Kenelm (17)		x	x		x						x			
	Arnold (18)		x	x		x						x			
	Ruffin and Justin (19)			x		x						x			
	Margaret of Antioch (20)	x	x	x		x	x				x	x	x	x	x
	Praxedes (21)		x	x		x						x			
	Mary Magdalene (22)	x	x	x	x	x	x	x	x		x	x	x	x	x
	Apollinaris (23)		x	x		x						x			
	Christina (24)		x	x		x						x			
	James (25)	x	x	x	x		x	x	x	x	x	x	x	x	x
	Christopher (25)		x												
	Anne (26)	x	x	x		x	x	x			x	x	x	x	x
	Seven Sleepers (27)		x	x		x		x			x	x			
	Sampson (28)		x	x		x						x			

Felix, Simplicius et al (29)	x					x	
Abdon and Sennes (30)	x	x	x			x	
Germain (31)	x	x	x			x	
AUGUST							
Peter in Chains (1)	x						
Lammas (1)	x	x	x		x	x	x
Stephen (2)	x	x	x			x	
Invention of Stephen (3)	x	x	x			x	
Justin (4)		x				x	
Oswald (5)	x						
Transfiguration (6)	x	x	x	x		x	x
Sixtus et al (6)	x						
Name of Jesus (7)	x	x	x	x		x	x
Donatus (7)	x						

Continued

Continued

Month	Saint/Feast	Mirk	Sarum Missal 1498 STC 16172	Goodly Primer 1535 STC 15988	Manual of Prayers 1539 STC 16010	Sarum Primer 1543 16029	English Primer 1545 STC 16034	1547 Edwardian Primer STC 16048	1549 BCP STC 16274 Folger	BCP 1552 STC 16285	BCP 1553 STC 16288a	Sarum Primer in English and Latin 1558 STC 16082	BCP 1559 STC 16292a	BCP 1580 STC 16307	BCP 1594 STC 16318
	Cyriac (8)		x	x		x						x			
	Romanus (9)		x	x		x						x			
	Laurence (10)	x	x	x		x	x	x		x		x	x	x	x
	Tiburcius (11)		x	x		x						x			
	Clare (12)		x	x		x						x			
	Hippolytus (13)		x	x		x						x			
	Eusebius (14)		x	x		x						x			
	Assumption (15)	x	x	x	x	x	x	x			x	x			
	Octave of Laurence (17)		x	x		x						x			
	Eusebius (17)						x								
	Agapetus (18)		x	x		x						x			
	Magnus (19)		x	x		x						x			
	Lewis (20)			x		x						x			
	Bernard of Clairveux (21)		x	x		x					x	x			
	Octave of Assumption (22)		x	x		x						x			
	Timothy and Apollinaris (23)		x									x			

Bartholomew (24)	x	x	x		x	x	x	x	x
Lewis the King (25)		x	x				x		
Zephyrinus (26)		x	x				x		
Rufus (27)	x	x	x				x		
Augustine of Hippo (28)	x	x	x	x		x	x	x	x
Beheading of John the Baptist (29)	x	x	x	x			x	x	x
Felix and Adauctus (30)	x	x	x				x		
Cuthburge (31)	x	x	x				x		
SEPTEMBER									
Giles (1)	x	x	x	x			x	x	x
Chrysostom (1)			x	x					

Continued

Continued

Month	Saint/Feast	Mirk	Sarum Missal 1498 STC 16172	Goodly Primer 1535 STC 15988	Manual of Prayers 1539 STC 16010	Sarum Primer 1543 16029	English Primer 1545 STC 16034	1547 Edwardian Primer STC 16048	1549 BCP STC 16274 Folger	BCP 1552 STC 16285	BCP 1553 STC 16288a	Sarum Primer in English and Latin 1558 STC 16082	BCP 1559 STC 16292a	BCP 1580 16307	BCP 1594 STC 16318
	Anthony (2)			x		x						x			
	Translation of Cuthburt (4)		x	x		x						x			
	Bertin (5)		x	x		x						x			
	Eugenius (6)			x		x						x			
	Enarchus (7)											x			
	Nativity of Elizabeth I (7)													x	x
	Nativity of Mary (8)	x	x	x	x	x	x			x		x	x	x	x
	Gorgonius (9)		x	x		x						x			
	Silvius (10)			x		x						x			
	Protus and Hyacinth (11)		x				x	x				x			
	Marcian (12)			x		x						x			
	Maurilius (13)			x		x						x			
	Holy Cross (14)	x	x	x		x						x	x	x	x
	Cornelius and Cyprian (14)		x												
	Octave of Mary (15)		x	x											
	Edith (16)		x	x		x						x			

Lambert (17)		x	x			x		x
Victor and Corone (18)			x			x		
January (19)			x	x		x		
Eustace (20)			x	x		x		
Matthew (21)	x	x	x	x	x	x	x	x
Maurice (22)		x	x			x		
Thecla (23)		x	x			x		
Andoche (24)			x			x		
Cyprian and Justina (26)		x	x	x	x	x	x	x
Cosmas and Damian (27)		x	x			x		
Exuperius (28)						x		
Michael (29)	x	x	x	x	x	x	x	x
Jerome (30)		x	x	x	x		x	x

Continued

Continued

Month	Saint/Feast	Mirk	Sarum Missal 1498 STC 16172	Goodly Primer 1535 STC 15988	Manual of Prayers 1539 STC 16010	Sarum Primer 1543 STC 16029	English Primer 1545 STC 16034	1547 Edwardian Primer STC 16048	1549 BCP STC 16274 Folger	BCP 1552 STC 16285	BCP 1553 STC 16288a	Sarum Primer in English and Latin 1558 STC 16082	BCP 1559 STC 16292a	BCP 1580 STC 16307	BCP 1594 STC 16318
OCTOBER															
	Remy (1)		x	x		x						x	x	x	x
	Germanus, Vedast, Bavo (1)		x												
	Thomas de Cantilupe (2)		x												
	Leger (2)		x			x						x			
	Candidy the Martyr (7)					x						x			
	Francis (4)			x		x						x			
	Apolinaris (5)			x		x						x			
	Faith (6)		x	x		x					x	x	x	x	x
	Mark, Marcellus, and Apuleius (7)		x	x		x						x			
	Pelagia (8)			x		x						x			
	Dennis (9)		x			x	x					x	x	x	x
	Gereon (10)		x	x		x						x			
	Nicasius (11)		x	x		x		x				x			
	Wilfrid (12)			x		x						x			
	Translation of Edward the Confessor (13)		x	x		x	x				x	x	x	x	x
	Calixtus (14)		x			x									

Wulfran (15)		x	x					
Michael in the Mountain Tomb (16)		x		x				
Etheldreda (Audrey) (17)		x	x			x	x	x
Luke (18)	x	x	x	x	x	x	x	
Frideswide (19)		x	x					
Austrebert (20)			x					
Ursula (21)		x	x				x	x
Mary Salome (22)		x		x				
Romain (23)		x	x				x	x
Maglore (24)		x	x				x	
Crispin and Crispinian (25)		x	x			x	x	x

Continued

Continued

Month	Saint/Feast	Mirk	Sarum Missal 1498 STC 16172	Goodly Primer 1535 STC 15988	Manual of Prayers 1539 STC 16010	Sarum Primer 1543 16029	English Primer 1545 STC 16034	1547 Edwardian Primer STC 16048	1549 BCP STC 16274 Folger	BCP 1552 STC 16285	BCP 1553 STC 16288a	Sarum Primer in English and Latin 1558 STC 16082	BCP 1559 STC 16292a	BCP 1580 16307	BCP 1594 STC 16318
	John of Beverley (25)		x												
	Euaristus (26)			x		x						x			
	Simon and Jude (28)	x	x	x	x	x	x	x	x	x	x	x	x	x	x
	Narcissus (29)			x		x						x			
	Germain of Capua (30)			x		x						x			
	Quentin (31)		x	x		x						x			
NOVEMBER	All Saints (1)	x	x	x	x	x	x	x	x	x	x	x	x	x	x
	All Souls (2)	x	x	x		x	x	x				x			
	Eustace (3)		x	x											
	Winifred (3)		x	x								x			
	Amantius (4)			x		x						x			
	Leet (5)			x		x						x			
	Leonard (6)		x	x		x						x	x	x	
	Wilfrid (7)			x		x						x			
	Four Crowned Martyrs (8)		x			x		x				x			
	Theodore (9)		x	x		x					x	x			

Martin of Rome (10)	x			x				
Martin of Tours (Martlemas) (11)		x	x	x	x		x	x
Mennas (11)		x						
Patern of Sens (12)				x			x	
Brice (13)		x		x		x	x	
Translation of Erkenwald (14)		x	x	x			x	x
Machutus (Malo) (15)		x					x	x
Edmund of Abingdon (16)		x	x	x	x	x		
Hugh (17)		x	x		x		x	
Ini Regni Eliz (17)								x
Octave of Martin (18)		x	x	x		x		

Continued

Continued

Month	Saint/Feast	Mirk	Sarum Missal 1498 STC 16172	Goodly Primer 1535 STC 15988	Manual of Prayers 1539 STC 16010	Sarum Primer 1543 STC 16029	English Primer 1545 STC 16034	1547 Edwardian Primer STC 16048	1549 BCP STC 16274 Folger	BCP 1552 STC 16285	BCP 1553 STC 16288a	Sarum Primer in English and Latin 1558 STC 16082	BCP 1559 STC 16292a	BCP 1580 STC 16307	BCP 1594 STC 16318
	Elizabeth of Hungary (19)			x		x						x			
	Edmund King and Martyr (20)		x	x		x	x	x				x	x	x	x
	Presentation of Mary (21)					x						x			
	Cecilia (22)		x	x		x	x					x	x	x	
	Clement (23)		x	x		x	x			x		x	x	x	x
	Felicity (23)		x												
	Chrysogonus (24)		x	x		x						x			
	Katherine (25)	x	x	x		x	x	x			x	x	x	x	x
	Linus (26)		x			x						x			
	Agricole (27)			x		x						x			
	Rufus (28)			x		x						x			
	Saturnin (29)		x	x		x						x			
	Andrew (30)	x	x	x	x	x	x	x	x	x	x	x	x	x	x
DECEMBER	Eligius (1)					x						x			
	Libane (2)			x		x						x			
	Deposition of Osmund (3)		x	x		x					x	x			
	Barbara (4)			x		x						x			
	Sabas (5)			x		x						x			

Nicholas (6)		x		x		x	x		x	x
Octave of Andrew (7)		x		x		x				
Conception of Mary (8)	x	x		x		x	x		x	x
Eulalia (9)							x	x		
Cyprian the Abbot (10)		x		x			x			
Damasus (11)		x		x			x			
Lucy (13)		x		x	x		x	x	x	x
Odile (14)				x			x			
Valery (15)		x		x			x			
O Sapienta (16)(first of the Advent antiphons)	x	x		x	x		x	x	x	x
Lazarus (17)		x		x						
Gracian (18)		x		x			x			
Venetia (19)		x		x			x			

Continued

Continued

Month	Saint/Feast	Mirk	Sarum Missal 1498 STC 16172	Goodly Primer 1535 STC 15988	Manual of Prayers 1539 STC 16010	Sarum Primer 1543 16029	English Primer 1545 STC 16034	1547 Edwardian Primer STC 16048	1549 BCP STC 16274 Folger	BCP 1552 STC 16285	BCP 1553 STC 16288a	Sarum Primer in English and Latin 1558 STC 16082	BCP 1559 STC 16292a	BCP 1580 16307	BCP 1594 STC 16318
	Julian (20)			x		x						x			
	Thomas (21)	x	x		x	x	x	x	x	x	x	x	x	x	x
	30 Martyrs (22)			x		x						x			
	Victoria (23)			x		x						x			
	Nativity of Jesus (25)	x	x	x	x	x	x	x	x	x	x	x	x	x	x
	Stephen (26)	x	x	x	x	x	x	x	x	x	x	x	x	x	
	John (27)	x	x	x	x	x	x	x	x	x	x	x	x	x	
	Holy Innocents (28)	x	x	x	x	x	x	x	x	x	x	x	x	x	
	Thomas of Canterbury (29)	x	x	x								x			
	Translation of James (30)			x		x						x			
	Silvester (31)		x	x	x	x						x	x	x	x

Bibliography

Manuscripts

Bodleian MS Ashmole 750
Bodleian MS Digby 133
Bodleian MS Eng. Poet f. 2
Bodleian MS Laud Misc 108
British Library MS Egerton 1994
British Library MS Egerton 2623
National Library of Scotland Advocates MS 19.2.1 (accessed online https://auchinleck.nls.uk/)
TNA STAC 8/19/10
TNA STAC 8/12/11
TNA STAC 8/18/11

Digital Resources

British History Online (BHO)
Database of Early English Playbooks (DEEP)
Early English Books Online (EEBO)
Eighteenth Century Collections Online (ECCO)
English Short-Title Catalogue (ESTC)
Folger Digital Texts (Barbara Mowat et al., eds., *Shakespeare's Play, Sonnets, and Poems*, www.folgerdigitaltexts.org)
The Internet Archive (archive.org)
The Lost Plays Database
Oxford Dictionary of National Biography (ODNB)
The Philological Museum
Records of Early English Drama Online

> *REED: Berkshire*
> *REED: Cambridgeshire*
> *REED: Hampshire*

Primary

Aelred of Rievaulx. *The Mirror of Charity: The Speculum caritatis of St. Aelred of Rievaulx*. Trans. Geoffrey Webb and Adrian Walker. London, A.R. Mowbray, 1962.
Annals of English Drama, 975–1700. Edited by Alfred Harbage, Samuel Schoenbaum, and Sylvia Stoler Wagonheim. 3rd edition. London: Routledge, 1989.

Aristotle. *Poetics*. Trans. Richard Janko. In *The Norton Anthology of Theory and Criticism*. Edited by Vincent B. Leitch et al., 90–117. New York: W. W. Norton & Co., 2001.
Baillie, William M., ed. *A Choice Ternary of English Plays: Gratiae Theatrales (1662)* Binghamton, NY: Medieval & Renaissance Texts & Studies, 1984.
Baker, Donald C., John L Murphy, and Louis B. Hall, Jr., eds. *The Late Medieval Religious Plays of Bodleian MSS Digby 133 and e. Mus. 160.* EETS o.s. 283. Oxford: Oxford University Press, 1982.
Bale, John. *The Complete Plays of John Bale.* 2 Vols. Edited by Peter Happé. Cambridge: D. S. Brewer, 1985–86.
Bale, John. *The first two partes of the actes or vnchast examples of the Englysh votaryes.* London, 1551. STC 1273.5.
Bale, John. *King Johan.* London: Printed for the Malone Society by J. Johnson at the Oxford University Press, 1931.
Beard, Thomas. *A retractiue from the Romish religion.* London: William Stansby, 1616. STC 1658.
Beunans Meriasek. *The Life of Saint Meriasek, bishop and confessor. A Cornish drama.* Edited by Whitley Stokes and translated by Dominus Hadton. London: Trubner & Co., 1872.
Bewnans Ke: The Life of St Kea: A Critical Edition with Translation. Edited by Graham Thomas and Nicholas Williams. University of Exeter Press, 2016.
Boccaccio, Giovanni. *The Decameron.* Edited by Jonathan Usher. Trans. Guido Waldman. Oxford: Oxford University Press, 2008.
Bokenham, Osbern. *Legendys of Hooly Wummen.* Edited by Mary Sergeantson. EETS, o.s., 206. London: Oxford University Press, 1928. Reprint, New York: Kraus Reprints, 1971.
A Calendar of Dramatic Records in the Books of Livery Companies of London, 1485–1640. Edited by Jean Robertson and D. J. Gordon. Malone Society Collections. Vol. 3. Oxford, 1954.
Calendar of State Papers and Manuscripts Relating to English Affairs Existing in the Archives and Collections of Venice and in Other Libraries of Northern Italy 1158–1580. Edited by Rawdon Brown and G. Cavendish Bentinck. 7 vols. London: Eyre and Spottiswoode, 1890.
Calendar of State Papers Domestic: James I, 1611–18. Edited by Mary Anne Everett Green (London: Her Majesty's Stationery Office, 1858).
Campion, Edmund. *Ambrosia: A Neo-Latin Drama by Edmund Campion, S.J.* Translated and Edited by Joseph Simons. Assen: Van Gorcum & Co., 1970.
Catholic Church. *Missale secundum vsum in signis ecclesie Sarum.* London: Wynkyn de Worde, 1498.
Catholic Church. *Primer in English and Latin after Salisburye.* London: John Wayland, 1558. 16082.
Caxton, William, ed. *Legenda aurea sanctorum, sive, Lombardica historia.* By Jacobus de Voragine. London: William Caxton, 1483. STC 24873.
Caxton, William, ed. *Here begynneth the legende named in latyn legenda aurea, that is to say in englyshe the golden legende...* By Jacobus de Voragine. 2nd printing. Westminster: Wynkyn de Worde, 1493. STC 24875.
Chester Mystery Cycle. Edited by R. B. Lumiansky and David Mills. 2 Vols. EETS s.s. 3 and 9. London: Oxford University Press, 1974 and 1986.
A Chronicle of London, from 1089 to 1483. Edited by Edward Tyrell and Nicholas H. Nicolas. London: Longman, Rees, Orme, Brown, and Green, 1827.
Church of England. *A goodly prymer in englyshe.* London: William Marshall, 1535. STC 15988.
Church of England. *A manuall of prayers, or the prymer in Englyshe.* London: John Waylande: 1539. STC 16010.
Church of England. *A prymer in Englysh and latyn, after the vse of Sarum.* London: Thomas Petit, 1543. STC 16029.
Church of England. *The primer set furth by the Kinges maiestie [and] his clergie, to be taught lerned, and red: and none other to be vsed thorowout all his dominions.* London: Richard Grafton, 1547.
Church of England. *Book of common prayer.* London, 1549. STC 16271.
Church of England. *Book of common prayer.* London: Richard Grafton, 1549. STC 16274.
Church of England. *Book of common prayer.* London: Richard Grafton, 1552. STC 16285.
Church of England. *Book of common prayer.* London: Edward Whitchurch, 1553. STC16288a.
Church of England. *Book of common prayer.* London: Richard Jugge and John Cawood, 16292a.
Church of England. *Book of common prayer.* London: Christopher Barker, 1580. STC 16307.

Church of England. *Book of common prayer.* London: Christopher Barker, 1594. STC 16318.
Church of England. *Iniunccions geue by the most excellent prince, Edward the sixte.* London, 1547. STC 10090.3
Church of England. *Ininctions geuen by the Quenes Maiestie.* London, 1559. STC 10099.5.
Collections. Edited by W. W. Greg. Volume II, Part 3. Oxford: The Malone Society, 1931.
The Control and Censorship of Caroline Drama. Edited by N. W, Bawcutt. Oxford: Oxford University Press, 1996.
The Cornish Ordinalia: A Medieval Dramatic Trilogy. Edited by Markham Harris. Washington, D.C.: Catholic University of America Press, 1969.
A Critical Edition of James Shirley's St. Patrick for Ireland. Edited by John P. Turner. New York: Garland Pub, 1979.
A Critical, Old-Spelling Edition of The Birth of Merlin (Q1662). Edited by Joanna Udall. London: Modern Humanities Research Association, 1991.
Croxton Play of the Sacrament. Edited by John T. Sebastian. Kalamazoo: Medieval Institute Publications, 2012.
Customary of the Cathedral Priory Church of Norwich. Edited by J. B. L. Tolhurst. London: Henry Bradshaw Society, 1948.
Davies, Richard and Robert Amerie. *Chesters triumph in honor of her prince.* London: John Brown, 1610. STC 5118
de Villegas, Alonso. *Flos Sanctorum.* Saint-Omer, 1621. STC 24731b
de Villegas, Alfonso. *The Lives of the Saints.* Translated by Edward Kinesman. 2 vols. (English Recusant Literature, 1558–1640). London: The Scholar Press, 1977.
Dekker, Thomas. *Brittannia's Honor.* London: Nicholas Okes and John Norton, 1628. STC 6493.
Dekker, Thomas. *The Dramatic Works of Thomas Dekker.* Edited by Freson Bowers. 4 vols. Cambridge: Cambridge University Press, 1958.
Dekker, Thomas, and John Webster, *The famous history of Sir Thomas VVyat.* London: Thomas Archer, 1607. STC 653.
Dekker, Thomas and Ben Jonson. *The Magnificent Entertainment Given to King James.* In *Jacobean Civic Pageantry.* Edited by Richard Dutton. Keele: Keele University Press, 1995.
Dekker, Thomas, and Philip Massinger. *The virgin martir: a tragedie.* London: Thomas Jones, 1622. STC 17644.
Deloney, Thomas. *The Gentle Craft.* Edited by Simon Barker. Aldershot: Ashgate, 2007.
The Digby Mary Magdalene Play. Edited by Theresa Coletti. TEAMS Middle English Texts. Kalamazoo: Medieval Institute Publications, 2018.
Dorne, John. *Day-Book of John Dorne, Bookseller in Oxford, A.D. 1520.* In *Collectanea I. Part III.* Edited by F. Madan, 71–177. Oxford Historical Society. Oxford: Clarendon Press.
Dryden, John. *Tyrannick love, or The royal martyr. A tragedy.* London: H. Herringman, 1670. Wing D2393.
The Early South-English Legendary; or, the Lives of Saints. Edited by Carl Horstmann. MS Laud 108. EETS o.s. 87. Milkwood, NY: Kraus Reprint, 1987.
Edmund Ironside. Edited by Eleanore Boswell. Malone Society Reprints. Oxford: Oxford University Press, 1927.
Extracts from the Account Rolls of the Abbey of Durham. Edited by J. T. Fowler. 3 vols. Durham: Andrews, 1898–1901.
Four Romances of England: King Horn, Havelok the Dane, Bevis of Hampton, Athelston. Edited by Ronald B. Herzman, Graham Drake, and Eve Salisbury. Kalamazoo: Medieval Institute Publications, 1999.
Foxe, John. *Actes and monuments of these latter and perillous dayes.* Aldersgate: John Day, 1563. STC 11222.
Foxe, John *The ecclesiasticall history contaynyng the actes and monumentes of thynges passed in euery kynges tyme in this realme: especially in the Church of England.* Aldersgate: John Daye, 1570. STC 11223.

Foxe, John. *The first volume of the Ecclesiasticall History, contayning the Actes & Monuments of thinges passed in every kinges time, in this Realme, especially in the Churches of England*. London: John Daye, 1576. STC 11224.

Foxe, John *Actes and Monuments of matters most speciall and memorable, happenyng in the church, with an universal historie of the same*. Aldersgate: John Daye, 1583. STC 11225.

Gratiae theatrales, or, A choice ternary of English plays composed upon especial occasions by several ingenious persons. London: R.D., 1662. Wing G1580.

The Great Chronicle of London. Guild Hall MS 3313, fols. 275a–92b. Edited by Thomas, A. H. and I. D. Thornley. London: G. W. Jones, 1938.

Greene, Robert. *The honorable historie of frier Bacon, and frier Bongay*. London, 1594. STC 12267.

Gregory of Tours. *Life of the Fathers*. Trans. Edward James. Liverpool: Liverpool University Press, 1991.

Grimald, Nicholas. The Life and Poems of Nicholas Grimald. Edited by Le Roy Merill. Hamden: Archon Books, 1969.

Guy of Warwick. Edited by Helen Moore, Malone Society Reprints. Manchester: Manchester University Press, 2007.

Henslowe, Philip. *Henslowe's Diary*. 2nd edition. Edited by R. A. Foakes. Cambridge: Cambridge University Press, 2002.

Henslowe, Philip. *Henslowe's Diary*. Edited by W. W. Greg. Vol. 1. London: A. H. Bullen, 1904.

Here begynneth the enterlude of Iohan the Euangelyst. London: John Waley, ca.1550. STC 14643

Heywood, Thomas. *If you knovv not me, you know no bodie: or, The troubles of Queene Elizabeth*. London: Nathaniel Butter, 1605. STC 13328.

Heywood, Thomas. *Englands Elizabeth*. London: Philip Waterhouse, 1631. STC 13313.

Heywood, Thomas. *London ius honorarium*. London: Nicholas Okes, 1631. STC 13351.

Heywood, Thomas. *Londini artium & scientiarum scaturigo*. London: Nicholas Okes, 1632. STC 13347.

Heywood, Thomas. *Londini Speculum: or Londons Mirror*. London: John Okes, 1637. STC 13349.

Heywood, Thomas. *Thomas Heywood's Pageants: A Critical Edition*. Edited by David M. Bergeron. The Renaissance Imagination. Vol. 16. New York and London: Garland Publishing, 1986.

Horstmann, Carl, ed. *Altenglische Legenden, Neue Folge*. Heilbronn: Henniger,1881.

Hughes, Paul L. and James F. Larkin, C.S.V., eds., *Tudor Royal Proclamations, Vol. II: The Later Tudors (1553–1587)* New Haven, CT: Yale University Press, 1969.

Jacobus de Voragine. *The Golden Legend: Readings on the Saints*. Trans. William G. Ryan Princeton: Princeton University Press, 1993.

Jocelin. *The life of the glorious bishop S. Patrick apostle and primate of Ireland*. Saint-Omer, 1625. STC 14626.

John Nichols's The Progresses and Public Processions of Queen Elizabeth I: A New Edition of the Early Modern Sources. Edited by Elizabeth Goldring et. al. 5 vols. Oxford University Press, 2014.

The kalendre of the newe legende of Englande edited from Pynson's printed edition, 1516. Edited by Manfred Görlach. Heidelberg: Universitätsverlag C. Winter, 1994.

Kirke, John. *The seven champions of Christendome*. London: John Okes, 1638. STC 15014.

A Knack to Know a Knave. London: Richard Jones, 1592. STC 15027.

Kushner, Tony. *Angels in America: A Gay Fantasia on National Themes*. Revised and Complete Edition. New York: Theatre Communications Group, 2013.

Letters and Papers, Foreign and Domestic, Henry VIII. Vol. 4, 1524–1530. Edited by J. S. Brewer. Her Majesty's Stationery Office, London, 1875.

The Life of Christina of Markyate, a Twelfth-Century Recluse. Edited and trans. by C. H. Talbot Oxford: Clarendon Press, 1987.

The Lives of Women Saints of Our Contrie of England: also some other liues of holie women/written by some of the auncient fathers, c. 1610–15. Edited by Carl Horstmann. EETS o.s. 86. Milkwood, NY Kraus, 1987.

Ludus Coventriae or The Plaie Called Corpus Christi. Edited by K. S. Block. EETS e.s. 120. Oxford: Oxford University Press, 1922. Reprint 1960.

Lydgate, John. *The Minor Poems of John Lydgate, Edited from all Available MSS., with an Attempt to Establish the Lydgate Canon. Part 2: Secular Poems.* EETS o.s. 192. London: Oxford University Press, 1934. Reprint 1961.
Lydgate, John. *Saint Albon and Saint Amphibalus.* Edited by George F. Reinecke. New York: Garland, 1985.
Lydgate, John. *Mummings and Entertainments.* Edited by Claire Sponsler. Kalamazoo, MI: Medieval Institute Publications, 2010.
Machyn, Henry. *The Diary of Henry Machyn.* Edited by John Gough Nichols. London: Camden Soceity, 1848.
Marlowe, Christopher. *Doctor Faustus: A Two-Text Edition.* Edited by David Scott Kastan. New York: W. W. Norton, 2004.
Marlowe, Christopher. *The Tragical History of Dr. Faustus.* In *Renaissance Drama: An Anthology of Plays and Entertainments.* Edited by Arthur F. Kinney, 193–226. 2nd edition. Malden, MA: Wiley-Blackwell, 2005.
Medbourne, Matthew. *St. Cecily: or, The Converted Twins.* London, 1666. Wing M1583B.
Middleton, Thomas. *A game at chess.* London, 1625. STC 17884.
Middleton, Thomas. *Thomas Middleton: The Collected Works.* Edited by Gary Taylor and John Lavagnino. Oxford: Oxford University Press, 2007.
Mirk, John. *A Critical Edition of John Mirk's Festial: Edited from British Library MS Cotton Claudius A.II.* Edited by Susan Powell. 2 vols. EETS o.s. 334–5. Oxford: Oxford University Press, 2009–11.
The Monastic Agreement of the Monks and Nuns of the English Nation (Regularis Concordia). Edited and translated by Dom Thomas Symons. London: Thomas Nelson and Sons, Ltd., 1953.
Munday, Anthony. *Camp-bell, or the ironmongers faire feild.* London: Edward Allde, 1609. STC 18265.
Munday, Anthony. *Chruso-thriambos. The triumphes of GOLDE.* London: William Jaggard, 1611. STC 18267.
Munday, Anthony. *John a Kent and John a Cumber.* Edited by Muriel St. Clare Byrne. Oxford: Malone Society Reprint, 1923.
The N-Town Plays. Edited by Douglas Sugano. Kalamazoo: Medieval Institute Publications, 2006.
Non-Cycle Plays and Fragments. Edited by Norman Davis. EETS, s. s. 1. London: Oxford University Press, 1970.
The noble triumphant coronacyon of queen Anne. London: John Gough, 1533. STC 656.
Ordinale and Customary of the Benedictine Nuns of Barking Abbey. Edited by J. B. L. Tolhurst. London: Henry Bradshaw Society, 1926.
Paris, Matthew. *The Flowers of History, Especially Such as Relate to the Affairs of Britain: B.C. 4004 to A. D. 1066.* Trans. Charles Duke Yonge. Henry G. Bohn, 1853.
Paston Letters and Papers of the Fifteenth Century. Edited by Norman Davis. 3 vols. Oxford: Clarendon Press, 1971.
Pepys, Samuel. *Diary of Samuel Pepys.* Edited by Robert Latham and William Matthews. 11 vols. London, 1970–83.
The Receyt of the Ladie Kateryne. Edited by Gordan Kipling. EETS o.s. 296 Oxford: Oxford University Press, 1990.
Records of Early English Drama: Bristol. Edited by Mark C. Pilkinton. Toronto: University of Toronto Press, 1997.
Records of Early English Drama: Cheshire Including Chester. Edited by Elizabeth Baldwin, Lawrence M. Clopper, and David Mills. Toronto: University of Toronto Press, 2007.
Records of Early English Drama: Chester. Edited by Lawrence M. Clopper. Toronto: University of Toronto Press, 1979.
Records of Early English Drama: Coventry. Edited by R. W. Ingram. Toronto: University of Toronto Press, 1981.
Records of Early English Drama: Cumberland, Westmoreland, Gloucestershire. Edited by Audrey Douglas and Peter Greenfield. Toronto: University of Toronto Press, 1986.
Records of Early English Drama: Devon. Edited by John Wasson. Toronto: University of Toronto Press, 1986.

Records of Early English Drama: Dorset, Cornwall. Edited by Rosalind Cocklin Hayes, C. E. McGee, Sally L. Joyce, and Evelyn Newlyn. Toronto: University of Toronto Press, 1981.
Records of Early English Drama: Ecclesiastical London. Edited by Mary C. Erler. Toronto: University of Toronto Press, 2008.
Records of Early English Drama: Hereford and Worcestershire. Edited by David Klausner. Toronto: University of Toronto Press, 1990.
Records of Early English Drama: Kent: Diocese of Canterbury. Edited by James M. Gibson. 3 vols. Toronto: University of Toronto Press, 2002.
Records of Early English Drama: Lincolnshire. Edited by James Stokes. 2 vols. Toronto: University of Toronto Press, 2009.
Records of Early English Drama: Newcastle Upon Tyne. Edited by J. J. Anderson. Toronto: University of Toronto Press, 1982.
Records of Early English Drama: Norwich, 1540–1642. Edited by David Galloway. Toronto: University of Toronto Press, 1984.
Records of Early English Drama: Oxford. Edited by Elliott, Jr., John M. and Alan Nelson (university), Alexandra F. Johnston and Diana Wyatt (city). 2 vols. Toronto: University of Toronto Press, 2004.
Records of Early English Drama: Shropshire. Edited by J. Alan B. Sommerset. 2 vols. Toronto: University of Toronto Press, 1994.
Records of Early English Drama: *Somerset, including Bath.* Edited by James Stokes. (Toronto: University of Toronto Press, 1996).
Records of Early English Drama: York. Edited by Alexandra F. Johnston and Margaret Rogerson. 2 vols. (Toronto: University of Toronto Press, 1979).
Records of Plays and Players in Kent, 1450–1642. Edited by Giles E. Dawson. Malone Society Collections. Vol. 7. Oxford: Malone Society,1965.
Records of Plays and Players in Lincolnshire, 1300–1585. Edited by Stanley J. Kahrl. Malone Society Collections. Vol. 8. Oxford: Malone Society, 1974 for 1969.
Records of Plays and Players in Norfolk and Suffolk, 1330–1642. Edited by David Galloway and John Wasson. Malone Society Collections. Vol. 11. Oxford: Malone Society, 1980.
The Resurrection of Our Lord. Edited by J. Dover Wilson and Bertram Dobell. Oxford: Malone Society Reprints, 1912.
Rowley, William. *The birth of Merlin, or, The childe hath found his father.* London: Thomas Johnson, 1662. Wing R2096.
Rowley, William. *A Merrie and Plesant comedy: Never before Printed, called A Shoo-maker a Gentleman.* London: John Okes, 1638.
Rowley, William. A *Shoemaker, A Gentleman.* Edited by Trudi Darby. London: Nick Hern, 2002.
Rowley, Samuel. *VVhen you see me, you know mee.* London: Nathaniel Butter, 1605. STC 21417.
Shakespeare, William. *The Late, and Much Admired Play, Called Pericles, Prince of Tyre.* London: Henry Gosson, 1609. STC 22334.
Shakespeare, William. *Mr. William Shakespeare's Comedies, Histories, & Tragedies.* London, 1623. STC 2273.
Shakespeare, William. *Henry VI, Part 1.* Edited by Edward Burns. Arden Shakespeare Third Series. London: Arden Shakespeare, 2004.
Shirley, Henry. *The martyr'd soldier.* London: John Okes, 1638. STC 22435.
Shirley, James. *St. Patrick for Ireland.* London: Richard Whitaker, 1640. STC 22455.
The South English Legendary: edited from Corpus Christi College, Cambridge, MS. 145 and British Museum MS. Harley 2277, with variants from Bodley MS. Ashmole 43 and British Museum MS. Cotton Julius D. IX. EETS s. 235, 236, 244. Edited by Charlotte D'Evelyn and Anna J. Mill. 3 vols. London: Oxford University Press, 1956–59.
Squire, John. *Tres Irenes Trophaea. Or The Trymphs of Peace.* London: Nicholas Okes, 1620.
Stanzaic Guy of Warwick. Edited by Alison Wiggins. Kalamazoo: Medieval Institute Publications, 2004.

The Three Kings of Cologne. Edited and Translated by David Klausner and Benjamin Bruch. In *The Broadview Anthology of Medieval Drama*, 303-8. Edited by Christina M. Fitzgerald and John T. Sebastian. Peterborough, Ontario: Broadview Press, 2012.

The Thornton manuscript (Lincoln Cathedral Ms. 91), comp. Robert Thornton. Facsimile of the original manuscript printed by Derek Brewer and A.E.B. Owen. New York: British Book Centre, 1975.

The Townley Plays. Edited by Garrett Epp. TEAMS Kalamzoo: Medieval Institute Publications, 2018.

A Tretise of Miraclis Pleyinge. Edited by Clifford Davidson. Kalamazoo: Medieval Institute Publications, 1993.

Two Mediaeval Lives of Saint Winefride. Translated by Ronald Pepin and Hugh Feiss. Toronto: Peregrina, 2000.

The Two Noble Ladies. Edited by Rebecca G. Rhoads. London: Malone Society Reprints, 1930.

Victor of Vita. *The memorable and tragical history, of the persecution in africke: Vnder gensericke and hunricke, arrian kinges of the vandals.* [England],1605. STC 24714.

von Trier, Lars. *Breaking the Waves.* Zentropa, 1996.

Wager, Lewis. *A new enterlude, neuer before this tyme imprinted, entreating of the life and repentaunce of Marie Magdalene.* London: John Charlevvood, 1566. STC 24932.

Walter Daniel. *The Life of Aelred of Rievaulx.* Translated by F. M. Powicke with an introduction by Marsha Dutton. Kalamazoo, MI: Cistercian Publications, 1994.

Webster, John. *The Duchess of Malfi.* Edited by John Russell Brown. Manchester: Manchester University Press, 1991.

Wilkins, George, John Day, and William Rowley. *The trauailes of the three English brothers.* London: John Wright, 1607. STC 6417.

William Fitz Stephen. *Norman London.* Trans. H. E. Butler. New York: Italica Press, 1990.

Wilson, John. *The English Martyrologe.* Saint-Omer, 1608. STC 25771.

The Winchester Troper, from MSS. Of the Xth and XIth Centuries. With other Documents illustrating the History of Tropes in England and France. Edited by Walter Howard Frere. London: Henry Bradshaw Society, 1894.

The York Corpus Christi Plays. Edited by Clifford Davidson. TEAMS. Kalamazoo: Medieval Institute Publications, 2011.

Secondary

Anglo, Sydney. "The London Pageants for the Reception of Katherine of Aragon: November 1501." *Journal of the Warburg and Courtland Institutes* 26 (1963): 53-89.

Anglo, Sydney. *Spectacle, Pageantry, and Early Tudor Policy.* 2nd edition. Oxford: Clarendon, 1997.

Appleford, Amy. "Shakespeare's Katherine of Aragon: Last Medieval Queen, First Recusant Martyr." *Journal of Medieval and Early Modern Studies* 40 (2010): 149-72.

Arber, Edward, ed. *A Transcript of the Registers of the Company of Stationers of London: 1554–1640 A.D.* 5 vols. London: Priv. print, 1875-94.

Arber, Edward, ed. *A Transcript of the Registers of the Worshipful Company of the Stationers, from 1640–1708 A.D.* 3 vols. London: Stationers Company, 1913-14.

Arrell, Douglas. "*King Leir* at Gowthwaite Hall," *Medieval & Renaissance Drama in England* 25 (2012): 83-93.

Aston, Margaret. *England's Iconoclasts. Vol. One: Laws against Images.* Oxford: Clarendon Press, 1988.

Aston, Margaret. *Broken Idols of the English Reformation.* Cambridge: Cambridge University Press, 2015.

Badir, Patricia. *The Maudlin Impression: English Literary Images of Mary Magdalene, 1550–1700.* Notre Dame: University of Notre Dame Press, 2009.

Baker, Donald C. and John L. Murphy, "MS. Digby 133: Scribes, Dates, and Early History," *Research Opportunities in Renaissance Drama* 10 (1967): 153–66.

Bamford, Karen. *Sexual Violence on the Jacobean Stage.* New York: St. Martin's, 2000.

Bayer, Mark. "Staging Foxe at the Fortune and the Red Bull." *Renaissance and Reformation* 27 (2003): 61–94.
Bayer, Mark. *Theatre, Community, and Civic Engagement in Jacobean London*. Iowa City: University of Iowa Press, 2011.
Beckwith, Sarah. "Ritual, Church and Theatre: Medieval Dramas of the Sacramental Body." In *Culture and History, 1350–1600: Essays on English Communities, Identities, and Writing*. Edited by David Aers, 65–90. Detroit: Wayne State University Press, 1992.
Beckwith, Sarah. *Signifying God: Social Relation and Symbolic Act in the York Corpus Christi Plays*. Chicago: University of Chicago Press, 2001.
Beckwith, Sarah. "Stephen Greenblatt's Hamlet and the Forms of Oblivion." *Journal of Medieval and Early Modern Studies* 33 (2003): 261–80.
Beckwith, Sarah. *Shakespeare and the Grammar of Forgiveness*. Ithaca, NY: Cornell University Press, 2013.
Bergeron, David, ed. *Pageantry in the Shakespearean Theater*. Athens: University of Georgia Press, 1985.
Bernau, Anke, Sarah Salih, and Ruth Evans, eds. *Medieval Virginities*. Cardiff: University of Wales Press, 2003.
Berry, Philippa. *Of Chastity and Power: Elizabethan Literature and the Unmarried Queen*. London: Routledge, 1989.
Bevington, David M. *From Mankind to Marlowe: Growth of Structure in the Popular Drama of Tudor England*. Cambridge: Harvard University Press, 1962.
Bhasin, Christine Scippa. "Prostitutes, Nuns, Actresses: Breaking the Convent Wall in Seventeenth-Century Venice," *Theatre Journal* 66 (2014): 19–35.
Blackmore, Humphrey P. and Frank Stevens. The Festival Book of Salisbury, Published to Commemorate the Jubilee of the Museum. Salisbury: Bennett Bros., 1914.
Bloom, Gina, Anston Bosman, and William N. West, "Ophelia's Intertheatricality, or, How Performance is History," *Theatre Journal* 65 (2013): 165–82.
Brennan, Anne L. "Parish Play Accounts in Context: Interpreting the Bassingbourn St. George Play." *Research Opportunities in Renaissance Drama* 35 (1996): 55–72.
Brown, Carleton. "An Early Mention of a St. Nicholas Play in England." *Studies in Philology* 28 (1931): 594–601.
Brown, Peter. *The Cult of the Saints: Its Rise and Function in Latin Christianity*. Chicago: Chicago University Press, 1981.
Butterworth, Philip. "Late Medieval Performing Dragons." *The Yearbook of English Studies* 43 (2013): 318–42.
Caldwell, Edward, ed. *Documentary annals of the reformed Church of England, 1546–1716*. 2 vols. Oxford: Oxford University Press, 1844.
Chambers, E. K. *The Medieval Stage*. 2 vols. Oxford: Clarendon Press, 1903.
Chambers, E. K. *The Elizabethan Stage*. 4 vols. Oxford: Clarendon Press, 1923.
Chapman, Alison A. "Whose Saint Crispin's Day Is It?: Shoemaking, Holiday Making, and the Politics of Memory in Early Modern England." *Renaissance Quarterly* 54 (2001): 1467–94.
Chapman, Alison A. *Patrons and Patron Saints in Early Modern Literature*. London: Routledge, 2013.
Clark, Stuart. *Thinking with Demons: The Idea of Witchcraft in Early Modern Europe*. Oxford: Clarendon Press, 1997.
Clopper, Lawrence. "Miracula and The Tretise of Mirclis Pleyinge." *Speculum* 65 (1990): 878–905
Clopper, Lawrence. "*Communitas*: The Play of Saints in late Medieval and Tudor England." *Mediaevlia* 18 (1995): 81–109.
Clopper, Lawrence. "Why are There So Few Saint Plays?" *Early Theatre* 2 (1999): 107–12.
Clopper, Lawrence. *Drama, Play, and Game: English Festive Culture in the Medieval and Early Modern Period*. Chicago: University of Chicago Press, 2001.
Clubb, Louise George. "*The Virgin Martyr* and the *Tragedia Sacra*." *Renaissance Drama* 7 (1964): 103–16.
Coldewey, John. "The Digby Play and the Chelmsford Records," *Research Opportunities in Renaissance Drama* 18 (1975): 103–21.

Coletti, Theresa. "The Design of the Digby Play of *Mary Magdalene*." *Studies in Philology* 76 (1979): 313–33.

Coletti, Theresa. *Mary Magdalene and the Drama of Saints: Theater, Gender, and Religion in Late Medieval England*. Philadelphia: University of Pennsylvania Press, 2004.

Collier, John Payne. "The Churchwardens Accounts of St. Margaret's Southwark." *The British Magazine* 32 (1847): 481–96 and 33 (1848): 1–16.

Collins, Eleanor. "Repertory and Riot: The Relocation of Plays from the Red Bull to the Cockpit Stage." *Early Theatre* 13, no. 2 (2010): 132–49.

Cooper, Helen. *The English Romance in Time: Transforming Motifs from Geoffrey of Monmouth to the Death of Shakespeare*. Oxford: Oxford University Press, 2004.

Cowling, Jane. "A Fifteenth-Century Saint Play in Winchester: Some Problems of Interpretation." *Medieval and Renaissance Drama in England* 13 (2001): 19–33.

Cox, J. Charles. *Churchwardens' Accounts from the Fourteenth Century to the Close of the Seventeenth Century*. London: Methuen, 1913.

Cox, John D. *The Devil and the Sacred in English Drama, 1350–1642*. Cambridge: Cambridge University Press, 2001.

Cutts, John P. "Jacobean Masque and Stage Music." *Music & Letters* 35 (1954): 185–200.

Dailey, Alice. *The English Martyr from Reformation to Revolution*. Notre Dame: Notre Dame University Press, 2011.

Davidson, Clifford, ed. *The Saint Play in Medieval Europe*. Early Drama, Art, and Music Monograph Series 8. Kalamazoo, MI: Medieval Institute Publications, 1986.

Davidson, Clifford. "Saints in Play: English Theater and Saints' Lives." In *Saints: Studies in Hagiography*. Edited by Sandro Sticca, 145–60. Binghamton: Medieval and Renaissance Texts and Studies, 1996.

Davidson, Clifford. "British Saint Play Records: Coping with Ambiguity." *Early Theatre* 2 (1999): 97–106.

Davidson, Clifford. "British Saint Play Records." ScholarWorks at WMU, 2002. https://scholarworks.wmich.edu/early_drama/2/

Davis, Tracy C. "Nineteenth-Century Repertoire." *Nineteenth Century Theatre and Film* 36, no. 2 (2009): 6–28.

Davis, Tracy C. "How Do You Know a Mermaid When You See One? How Do You See a Mermaid When You Know One?" *Theatre Journal* 71 (2019): 257–87.

Dawson, Anthony. "Shakespeare and Secular Performance." In *Shakespeare and the Cultures of Performance*. Edited by Paul Yachnin and Patricia Badir, 83–97. New York: Ashgate, 2008.

D'Evelyn, Charlotte and Frances A. Foster. "Saints' Legends." In *A Manual of the Writings in Middle English, 1050–1500*. Edited by J. Burke Severs. 2: 410–40 and 556–635. New Haven, CT: Academy of Arts and Sciences, 1970.

de Certeau, Michel. *The Practice of Everyday Life*. Trans. Steven Rendall. Berkeley: University of California Press, 1984.

de Grazia, Margreta. "*King Lear* in Albion BC." In *Medieval Shakespeare: Pasts and Presents*. Edited by Ruth Morse, Helen Cooper, and Peter Holland, 138–56. Cambridge: Cambridge University Press, 2013.

Degenhardt, Jane Hwang. "Catholic Martyrdom in Dekker and Massinger's *The Virgin Martir* and the Early Modern Threat of 'Turning Turk.'" *ELH* 73 (2006): 83–117.

Degenhardt, Jane Hwang. *Islamic Conversion and Christian Resistance on the Early Modern Stage*. Edinburgh: Edinburgh University Press, 2010.

Dessen, Alan. *Johnson's Moral Comedy*. Evanston: Northwestern University Press, 1971.

Di Salvo, Gina M. "Saints' Lives and Shoemakers' Holidays: The Gentle Craft and the Wells Cordwainers' Pageant of 1613." *Early Theatre* 19 (2016): 119–38.

Di Salvo, Gina M. "'A Virgine and a Martyr both': The Turn to Hagiography in Heywood's Reformation History Play." *Renaissance and Reformation* 41 (2018): 133–67.

Diehl, Huston. *Staging Reform, Reforming the Stage: Protestantism and Popular Theater in Early Modern England*. Ithaca, NY: Cornell University Press, 1997.

Ditchfield, Simon. "How Not to Be a Counter-Reformation Saint: The Attempted Canonization of Pope Gregory X, 1622–45." *Papers of the British School at Rome* 60 (1992): 379–422.

Dodd, Charles. *Dodd's Church History of England, From the Commencement of the Sixteenth Century to the Revolution in 1688*. New York, 1841.

Doran, Susan. "Virginity, Divinity and Power: The Portraits of Elizabeth." In *The Myth of Elizabeth*. Edited by Susan Doran and Thomas S. Freeman, 171–99. New York: Palgrave Macmillan, 2003.

Dresvina, Juliana. *A Maid with a Dragon: The Cult of St. Margaret of Antioch in Medieval England*. Oxford: Oxford University Press, 2016.

Duffy, Eamon. *The Stripping of the Altars: Traditional Religion in England, c. 1400–1580*. New Haven: Yale University Press, 1992.

Duffy, Eamon. *The Voices of Morebath: Reformation and Rebellion in an English Village*. New Haven: Yale University Press, 2001.

Edwards, Suzanne M. *Afterlives of Rape in Medieval Literature*. London: Palgrave Macmillan, 2016.

Fenton, Kristen A. *Gender, Nation, and Conquest in the Works of William Malmesbury*. Suffolk, UK: Boydell & Brewer, 2012.

Fitzgerald, Christine M. *The Drama of Masculinity and Medieval English Guild Culture*. London: Palgrave Macmillan, 2007.

Fletcher, Alan J. Drama, Performance, and Polity in Pre-Cromwellian Ireland. Toronto: University of Toronto Press, 2000.

Ford, Judy Ann. *The Printing History of William Caxton's Golden Legend*. London: Routledge, 2020.

French, Katherine L. 'To Free Them from Binding': Women in the Late Medieval English Parish. *The Journal of Interdisciplinary History* 27 (1997): 387–412.

Garber, Marjorie. *Symptoms of Culture*. New York: Routledge, 1998.

Gasper, Julia. *The Dragon and the Dove: The Plays of Thomas Dekker*. Oxford: Clarendon Press, 1990.

Gasper, Julia. "The Sources of *The Virgin Martyr*." *Review of English Studies* 42 (1991): 17–31.

Gibson, Gail McMurray. *The Theater of Devotion: East Anglian Drama and Society in the Later Middle Ages*. Chicago: University of Chicago Press, 1989.

Giles, Kate. "Marking Time? A fifteenth-century liturgical calendar in the wall paintings of Pickering parish church, North Yorkshire." *Church Archaeology* 4 (2000): 42–51.

Giles, Kate. "Seeing and Believing: Visuality and Space in Pre-Modern England." *World Archaeology* 39 (2007): 105–21.

Gillen, Katherine. "Authorial Anxieties and Theatrical Instability in John Bale's Biblical Plays and Shakespeare and Wilkins' *Pericles, Prince of Tyre*." In *Stages of Engagement: Drama and Religion in Post Reformation England*. Edited by James D. Mardock and Kathryn R. McPherson, 154–80. Pittsburgh, PA: Duquesne University Press, 2014.

Gorlach, Manfred. *The South English Legendary, the Gilte Legende and Golden Legend*. Braunschweig: Institut fur Anglistik und Amerikanistik, 1972.

Grant, Teresa. "Drama Queen: Staging Elizabeth in *If You Know Not Me You Know Nobody*." In *The Myth of Elizabeth*. Edited by Susan Doran and Thomas S. Freeman, 120–42. New York, NY: Palgrave Macmillan, 2003.

Grantley, Darryll. *English Dramatic Interludes, 1300–1580: A Reference Guide*. Cambridge: Cambridge University Press, 2004.

Grantley, Darryll. "Saints and Miracles." In *The Cambridge Companion to Medieval English Theatre*. Edited by Richard Beadle and Alan J. Fletcher, 263–86. Cambridge: Cambridge University Press, 2011.

Gravdal, Katherine. *Ravishing Maidens: Writing Rape in Medieval French Literature and Law*. Philadelphia: University of Pennsylvania Press, 1991.

Greenblatt, Stephen. *Shakespearean Negotiations: The Circulation of Social Energy*. Berkeley: University of California Press, 1989.

Greenblatt, Stephen. *Hamlet in Purgatory*. Princeton: Princeton University Press, 2001.

Griffith, Eva. *A Jacobean Company and Its Playhouse: The Queen's Servants at The Red Bull Theatre, c.1605–1619*. Cambridge: Cambridge University Press, 2013.

Grindlay, Lilla. *Queen of Heaven: The Assumption and Coronation of the Virgin in Early Modern English Writing*. Notre Dame: Notre Dame University Press, 2009.

Groves, Beatrice. *Texts and Traditions: Religion in Shakespeare, 1592–1604*. Oxford: Oxford University Press, 2007.
Gurnis, Musa. *Mixed Faith, Shared Feeling: Theater in Post-Reformation London*. Philadelphia: University of Pennsylvania Press, 2018.
Guynn, Noah D. *Pure Filth: Ethics, Politics, and Religion in Early French Farce*. Philadelphia: University of Pennsylvania Press, 2019.
Hackett, Helen. *Virgin Mother, Maiden Queen: Elizabeth I and the Cult of the Virgin Mary*. New York: St. Martin's Press, 1995.
Happé, Peter. "The Protestant Adaptation of the Saint Play." In *The Saint Play in Medieval Europe*. Edited by Clifford Davidson, 205–40. Kalamazoo: Medieval Institute Publications, 1986.
Hardison, O. B. *Christian Rite and Christian Drama in the Middle Ages: Essays in the Origin and Early History of Modern Drama*. Baltimore: Johns Hopkins Press, 1969.
Harris, Carissa. *Obscene Pedagogies: Transgressive Talk and Sexual Education in Late Medieval Britain*. Ithaca: Cornell University Press, 2018.
Harris, Jonathan Gil. *Untimely Matter in the Time of Shakespeare*. Philadelphia: University of Pennsylvania Press, 2009.
Hart, F. Elizabeth. "'Great is Diana' of Shakespeare's Ephesus." *Studies in English Literature, 1500–1900* 43 (2003): 347–74.
Haskins, Charles Homer. *The Ancient Trade Guilds and Companies of Salisbury*. Salisbury: Bennett Bros., 1912.
Heffernan, Thomas J. *Sacred Biography: Saints and Their Biographers in the Middle Ages*. Oxford: Oxford University Press, 1988.
Hickerson, Megan. *Making Women Martyrs in Tudor England*. New York: Palgrave Macmillan, 2005.
Hill, Tracey. *Pageantry and Power: A Cultural History of the Early Modern Lord Mayor's Show, 1585–1639*. Manchester: Manchester University Press, 2011.
Hill-Vasquez, Heather. "The Possibilities of Performance: A Reformation Sponsorship for the Digby *Conversion of St. Paul*," *Research Opportunities in Renaissance Drama* 22 (1997): 2–20.
Hill-Vasquez, Heather. *Sacred Players: The Politics of Response in the Middle English Religious Drama*. Washington, D.C.: The Catholic University of America Press, 2007.
Hirschfeld, Heather. *The End of Satisfaction: Drama and Repentance in the Age of Shakespeare*. Ithaca: Cornell University Press, 2013.
Hopkins, Lisa. "Profit and Delight? Magic and the Dreams of a Nation." In *Magical Transformations on the Early Modern English Stage*. Edited by Lisa Hopkins and Helen Ostovich, 139–54. London: Routledge, 2014.
Hopkins, Lisa. *Renaissance Drama on the Edge*. London: Routledge, 2016.
Houliston, Victor. "*Breuis Dialogismus*," *ELR* 23 (1993): 382–427.
Jackson, Ken and Arthur Marotti. "The Turn to Religion in Early Modern English Studies," *Criticism* 46 (2004): 167–90.
Jankowski, Theodora A. *Pure Resistance: Queer Virginity in Early Modern English Drama*. Philadelphia: University of Pennsylvania Press, 2000.
Jenkins, Jacqueline and Katherine J. Lewis, eds. *St. Katherine of Alexandria: Texts and Contexts in Western Medieval*. Turnhout: Brepols, 2003.
Jensen, Phebe. "Recusancy, Festivity, and Community: The Simpsons at Gowlthwaite Hall," *Reformation* 6 (2002): 75–102.
Johnson, A. H. *The History of the Worshipful Company of the Drapers of London*. 5 vols. Oxford, 1914–22.
Johnston, Alexandra F. "Pleyes of Myracles." *English: Journal of the English Association* 64 (2015): 5–26.
Johnston, Bronwyn. "Who the Devils is in Charge? Mastery and the Faustian Pact on the Early Modern Stage." In *Magical Transformations on the Early Modern English Stage*. Edited by Lisa Hopkins and Helen Ostovich, 31–46. Farnham: Ashgate, 2014.Jones, David. "The Cult of St. Richard of Chichester in the Middle Ages." *Sussex Archaeological Collections* 121 (1983): 79–86.
Justice, Steven. "Did the Middle Ages Believe in their Miracles?" *Representations* 103 (2008):1-29.
Justice, Steven. "Eucharistic Miracle and Eucharistic Doubt." *JMEMS* 42 (2012): 307–32.
Kawachi, Yoshiko. *Calendar of English Renaissance Drama, 1558–1642*. New York: Garland, 1986.

Kearney, James. *The Incarnate Text: Imagining the Book in Reformation England.* Philadelphia: University of Pennsylvania Press, 2009.
Keenan, Siobhan. "A Little Known Allusion to an Inn Performance in the Suburbs of Jacobean London." *Notes and Queries* 50 (2003): 437–40.
Keenan, Siobhan. "The Simpsons Players of Jacobean Yorkshire and the Professional Stage." *Theatre Notebook* 67 (2013): 16–35.
Keene, Derek. Survey of Winchester. 2 vols. Oxford: Oxford University Press, 1985.
Kelly, Kathleen Coyne. *Performing Virginity and Testing Chastity in the Middle Ages.* London: Routledge, 2002.
King, John N. "The Godly Woman in Elizabethan Iconography." *Renaissance Quarterly* 38 (1985): 41–84.
King, John N. "Queen Elizabeth I: Representations of the Virgin Queen." *Renaissance Quarterly* 44 (1990): 30–74.
King, John N. *Foxe's* Book of Martyrs *and Early Modern Print Culture.* Cambridge: Cambridge University Press, 2006.
King, John N. and Christopher Highley, eds. *John Foxe and His World.* Aldershot: Ashgate, 2002.
King, Pamela M., and Clifford Davidson. *The Coventry Corpus Christi Plays.* Kalamazoo: Medieval Institute Publications, 2000.
Kipling, Gordon. "The London Pageants for Margaret of Anjou: A Medieval Script Restored." *Medieval English Theatre* 4 (1982): 1–27.
Klausner, David. "Music in Drama." In *The Cambridge History of Medieval Music.* Edited by Mark Everist and Thomas Forrest Kelly, 500–26. Cambridge: Cambridge University Press, 2018.
Knutson, Roslyn Lander. *Playing Companies and Commerce in Shakespeare's Time.* Cambridge: Cambridge University Press, 2001.
Kolkovich, Elizabeth Zeman. *The Elizabethan Country House Entertainment: Print, Performance, and Gender.* Cambridge: Cambridge University Press, 2016.
Lancashire, Anne. "London Craft Guild Records." *REED Newsletter* 3 (1978): 1–9.
Lancashire, Anne. London Civic Theatre: City, Drama, and Pageantry from Roman Times to 1558. Cambridge: Cambridge University Press, 2002.
Lancashire, Ian. *Dramatic Texts and Records of Britain: A Chronological Topography to 1558.* Toronto: University of Toronto Press, 1984.
Leo, Russ. *Tragedy as Philosophy in the Reformation World.* Oxford: Oxford University Press, 2019.
Lerer, Seth. "Medieval English Literature and the Idea of the Anthology." *PMLA* 118 (2003):1251–62.
Lewis, Katherine J. *The Cult of St. Katherine of Alexandria in Late Medieval England* Rochester: Boydell Press, 2000.
Light, Michelle. "Evidence of Sanctity: Record-keeping and the Canonization at the Turn of the 13th Century." *Archivaria* 60 (2006): 105–23.
Lin, Erika. "Popular Festivity and the Early Modern Stage: The Case of *George a Greene*," *Theatre Journal* 61 (2009): 271–97.
Loewenstein, David and Michael Witmore, eds. *Shakespeare and Early Modern Religion.* Cambridge: Cambridge University Press, 2015.
Lublin, Robert. "Shirley's Dublin Days: A Nervous Premiere of *St. Patrick for Ireland*." In *James Shirley and Early Modern Theatre: New Critical Perspectives.* Edited by Barbara Ravelhofer, 108–23. London: Routledge, 2016.
Lupton, Julia Reinhard. *Afterlives of the Saints: Hagiography, Typology, and Renaissance Literature.* Stanford, CA: Stanford University Press, 1996.
Lupton, Julia Reinhard. *Citizen-Saints: Shakespeare and Political Theology.* Chicago: University of Chicago Press, 2005.
Lupton, Julia Reinhard. "The Religious Turn (to Theory) in Shakespeare Studies." *English Language Notes* 44 (2006): 145–49.
Lupton, Julia Reinhard. *Shakespeare Dwelling: Designs for the Theater of Life.* Chicago: University of Chicago Press, 2018.
Maclean, Sally-Beth. "Saints on Stage: An Analytical Survey of Dramatic Records in the West of England." *Early Theatre* 2 (1999): 45–62.

Manion, Lee. "The Crusading Romance in Early Modern England: Converting the Past in Berners's *Huon of Bordeaux* and Johnson's *Seven Champions of Christendom*." *JMEMS* 48 (2018): 491–517.
Manley, Lawrence and Sally-Beth MacLean. *Lord Strange's Men and Their Plays*. New Haven: Yale University Press, 2014.
Mardock, James D. and Kathryn R. McPherson, eds. *Stages of Engagement: Drama and Religion in Post Reformation England*. Pittsburgh, PA: Duquesne University Press, 2014.
Marshall, Peter. "The Naming of Protestant England." *Past and Present* 214 (2012): 87–128.
McClendon, Muriel C. "A Moveable Feast: Saint George's Day Celebrations and Religious Change in Early Modern England." *Journal of British Studies* 38 (1999): 1–27.
McGee, C. E. and John C. Meagher. "Preliminary Checklist of Tudor and Stuart Entertainments: 1558–1603." *Research Opportunities in Renaissance Drama* 24 (1981): 51–155.
McInerney, Maud Burnett. *Eloquent Virgins from Thecla to Joan of Arc*. New York: Palgrave McMillian, 2003.
Mehl, Dieter. "The Late Queen on the Public Stage: Thomas Heywood's *If You Know Not Me You Know Nobody*, Parts I and II." In *Queen Elizabeth I: Past and Present*. Edited by Christa Jansohn, 153–71. Studien zur englischen Literatur Vol. 19. Lit Verlag: Munster, 2004.
Mill, Anna Jean. *Mediaeval Plays in Scotland*. 1927. Reprint, New York: Benjamin Blom, 1969.
Mill, Anna Jean. "The Perth Hammermen's Play: A Scottish Garden of Eden." *Scottish Historical Review* 49 (1970): 146–53.
Monta, Susannah Brietz. *Martyrdom and Literature in Early Modern England*. Cambridge: Cambridge University Press, 2005.
Montrose, Louis. *The Subject of Elizabeth: Authority, Gender, and Representation*. Chicago: University of Chicago Press, 2006.
Morant, Philip. *The History and Antiquities of the County of Essex. Compiled from the best and most ancient historians*. 2 vols. London: printed for T. Osborne; J. Whitson; S. Baker; L. Davis and C. Reymers; and B. White, 1768.
Moretti, Thomas J. "Via Media Theatricality and Religious Fantasy in Thomas Dekker and Philip Massinger's *The Virgin Martyr* (1622)." *Renaissance Drama* 42 (2014): 243–70.
Mueller, Janel. "The Saints." In *Cultural Reformations: Medieval and Renaissance in Literary History*. Edited by Brian Cummings and James Simpson, 166–87. Oxford: Oxford University Press, 2010.
Munro, Lucy. "Governing the Pen to the Capacity of the Stage: Reading the Red Bull and Clerkenwell." *Early Theatre* 9 (2006): 99–113.
Munro, Lucy. "Dublin Tragicomedy and London Stages." In *Early Modern Tragicomedy*. Edited by Subha Mukherji and Raphael Lyne, 175–92. Cambridge: D. S. Brewer, 2007.
Munro, Lucy. *Archaic Style in English Literature, 1590–1674*. Cambridge: Cambridge University Press, 2013.
Munro, Lucy. "'Nemp your sexes!': Anachronistic Aesthetics in *Hengist, King of Kent* and the Jacobean 'Anglo-Saxon' Play." *Modern Philology* 111 (2014): 734–61.
Murphy, John L. *Darkness and Devils: Exorcism and King Lear*. Athens: Ohio University Press, 1984.
Muse, Mary Grace Adkins. "The Genesis of Dramatic Satire against the Puritan, as Illustrated in *A Knack to Know a Knave*." *RES* 22, no. 86 (1946): 81–95.
Myhill, Nova. "Making Death a Miracle: Audience and Genres of Martyrdom in Dekker and Massinger's *The Virgin Martyr*." *Early Theatre* 7 (2004): 9–31.
Newman, Barbara. *Medieval Crossover: Reading the Secular against the Sacred*. Notre Dame: Notre Dame University Press, 2013.
North, Thomas. *A Chronicle of the Church of S. Martin in Leicester during the Reigns of Henry VIII, Edward VI, Mary and Elizabeth: with some account of its minor altars and ancient guilds*. London: Bell and Day, 1866.
O'Connell, Michael. *The Idolatrous Eye: Iconoclasm and Theater in Early-Modern England* Oxford: Oxford University Press, 2000.
Parish, Helen L. *Monks, Miracles and Magic: Reformation Representations of the Medieval Church*. London and New York: Routledge, 2005.
Parker, John. *Aesthetics of Antichrist: From Christian Drama to Christopher Marlowe*. Ithaca: Cornell University Press, 2007.

Parker, John. "Who's Afraid of Darwin? Revisiting Chambers and Hardison ... and Nietzsche." *JMEMS* 40 (2010): 7-35.
Parker, John. "Holy Adultery: Marriage in *The Comedy of Errors, The Merchant of Venice*, and *The Merry Wives of Windsor.*" In *The Oxford Handbook of Shakespearean Comedy*. Edited by Heather Hirschfeld, 489-503. Oxford: Oxford University Press, 2018.
Parks, George "Shakespeare's Map for *The Comedy of Errors.*" *The Journal of English and Germanic Philology* 39 (1940): 93-97.
Peacock, Edward, ed. *A List of the Roman Catholics in the County of York in 1604* (London, 1872).
Pfaff, Richard W. *The Liturgy in Medieval England: A History*. Cambridge: Cambridge University Press, 2009.
Pickett, Holly Crawford. "Dramatic Nostalgia and Spectacular Conversion in Dekker and Massinger's *The Virgin Martyr.*" *SEL* 49 (2009): 437-62.
Pickett, Holly Crawford. "Angels in England: Idolatry and Transformation at the Red Bull Playhouse." In *Thunder at the Playhouse: Proceedings from the Fourth Blackfriars Conference*. Edited by Peter Kanelos and Matt Kozusko, 175-99. Selingsgrove, PA: Susquehanna University Press, 2010.
Poole, Kristen. *Radical Religion from Shakespeare to Milton: Figures of Nonconformity in Early Modern England*. Cambridge: Cambridge University Press, 2000.
Prudlo, Donald S. *Certain Sainthood: Canonization and the Origins of Papal Infallibility in the Medieval Church*. Ithaca, NY: Cornell University Press, 2016.
Reynolds, George. *The Staging of Elizabethan Plays at the Red Bull Theater, 1605-1625*. New York: MLA, 1940.
Rhodes, J. T. "English Books of Martyrs and Saints of the Late Sixteenth and Early Seventeenth Centuries." *Recusant History* 22 (1994): 7-25.
Riches, Samantha and Sarah Salih, eds. *Gender and Holiness: Men, Women, and Saints in Late Medieval Europe*. London: Routledge, 2002.
Robinson, Marsha S. *Writing the Reformation: Actes and Monuments and the Jacobean History Play*. Aldershot: Ashgate, 2002.
Row-Heyveld, Lindsey. "'The lying'st knave in Christendom': The Development of Disability in the False Miracle of St. Alban's." *Disability Studies Quarterly* 29 (2009). https://dsq-sds.org/article/view/994/1178.
Rutter, Tom. "Repertory Studies: A Survey." *Shakespeare* 4 (2008): 336-50.
Ryan, Patrick. "Shakespeare's Joan and the Great Whore of Babylon." *Renaissance and Reformation* 28 (2004): 55-82.
Ryrie, Alec. "The Liturgical Commemoration of the English Reformation, 1534-1625." In *Memory and the English Reformation*, 422-38. Edited by Alexandra Walsham et al. Cambridge: Cambridge University Press, 2020.
Rochester, Joanne M. "Space and Staging in the Digby *Mary Magdalen* and *Pericles, Prince of Tyre.*" *Early Theatre* 13 (2010): 43-62.
Salih, Sarah. *Versions of Virginity in Late Medieval England*. Cambridge: Boydell and Brewer, 2001.
Salih, Sarah. "Staging Conversion: The Digby Saint Plays and The Book of Margery Kempe." In *Gender and Holiness: Men, Women and Saints in Late Medieval Europe*. Edited by Samantha J. E. Riches and Sarah Salih, 121-34. London: Routledge, 2002.
Sanok, Catherine. "Performing Feminine Sanctity in Late Medieval England: Parish Guilds, Saints' Plays, and the *Second Nun's Tale.*" *JMEMS* 32 (2002): 269-303.
Sanok, Catherine. *Her Life Historical: Exemplarity and Female Saints' Lives in Late Medieval England*. Philadelphia: University of Pennsylvania Press, 2007.
Sanok, Catherine. "Good King Henry and the Genealogy of Shakespeare's First History Plays." *JMEMS* 40 (2010): 37-63.
Sanok, Catherine. *New Legends of England: Forms of Community in Late Medieval Saints' Lives*. Philadelphia: University of Pennsylvania Press, 2018.
Schechner, Richard. *Performance Studies: An Introduction*. New York: Routledge, 2002.
Schmitt, Jean-Claude. *The Holy Greyhound: Guinefort, Healer of Children since the Thirteenth Century*. Trans. Martin Thom. Cambridge: Cambridge University Press, 1983.

Schreyer, Kurt. *Shakespeare's Medieval Craft: Remnants of the Mysteries on the London Stage* Ithaca: Cornell University Press, 2014.
Schwartz, Regina Mara. *Sacramental Poetics at the Dawn of Secularism: When God Left the World.* Stanford: Stanford University Press, 2008.
Schwyzer, Philip. "'Monuments of Our Indignation': John Milton and the Reception of Reformation Iconoclasm in the Seventeenth Century." In *Memory and the English Reformation*. Edited by Alexandra Walsham et al., 238–54. Cambridge: Cambridge University Press, 2020.
Scoville, Chester N. "The Hood and the Basket: Image and Word in the Digby *Conversion of St. Paul*." *Research Opportunities in Renaissance Drama* 41 (2002): 157–67.
Searle, Alison. "Conversion in James Shirley's St Patrick for Ireland." In *The Turn of the Soul: Representations of Religious Conversion in Early Modern Art and Literature*. Edited by Lieke Stelling et al., 199–224. Leiden: Brill, 2012.
Shagan, Ethan. *Popular Politics and the English Reformation*. Cambridge: Cambridge University Press, 2003.
Scherb, Victor I. "Frame Structure in *The Conversion of St. Paul*." *Comparative Drama* 26 (1992): 124–39.
Sheppard, Philippa. "The Puzzle or Pucelle or Pussel: Shakespeare's Joan of Arc Compared with Two Antecedents." In *Renaissance Medievalisms*. Edited by Konrad Eisenbichler, 191–209. Toronto: Centre for Reformation and Renaissance Studies, 2009.
Simpson, James. *Burning to Read: English Fundamentalism and Its Reformation Opponents*. Cambridge: Harvard University Press, 2007.
Simpson, James. "1534–1550s: Texts." In *The Cambridge Companion to Medieval English Mysticism*. Edited by Samuel Fanous and Vincent Gillespie, 249–64. Cambridge: Cambridge University Press, 2011.
Simpson, James. "The Reformation of Scholarship: A Reply to Debora Shuger." *JMEMS* 42, no. 2 (2012): 249–68.
Sofer, Andrew. *Dark Matter: Invisibility in Drama, Theater, and Performance*. Ann Arbor: University of Michigan Press, 2013.
Solberg, Emma Maggie. "A History of 'The Mysteries.'" *Early Theatre* 19, no. 1 (2016): 9–36.
Solberg, Emma Maggie. *Virgin Whore*. Ithaca, NY: Cornell University Press, 2018.
Somerset, Fiona. *Feeling Like Saints: Lollard Writings after Wyclif*. Ithaca: Cornell University Press, 2014.
Sponsler, Claire. "From Archive to Repertoire: *The Disguising at Hertford* and Performance Practices." In *Medieval Theatre Performance: Actors, Dancers, Automata and their Audiences*. Edited by Philip Butterworth and Katie Normington, 15–34. Cambridge: D.S. Brewer, 2017.
Steggle, Matthew. *Digital Humanities and the Lost Drama of Early Modern England: Ten Case Studies*. Farnham: Ashgate, 2015.
Stilma, Astrid. "Angels, Demons and Political Action in Two Early Jacobean History Plays," *Critical Survey* 23 (2011): 9–25.
Stokes, James. "The Wells Cordwainers' show: New Evidence Concerning Guild Entertainments in Somerset." *Comparative Drama* 19 (1985–86): 332–46.
Stokes, James. "Women and Mimesis in Medieval and Renaissance Somerset (and Beyond)." *Comparative Drama* 27 (1993): 176–96.
Stokes, James. "The Wells Shows of 1607" In *Festive Drama: Papers from the Sixth Triennial Colloquium of the International Society for the Study of Medieval Theatre: Lancaster, 13–19 July, 1989*. Edited by Meg Twycross, 145–56. St. Edmunds, Suffolk: D. S. Brewer, 1996.
Straznicky, Marta. "The Red Bull Repertory in Print, 1605–60." *Early Theatre* 9 (2006): 144–56.
Streitberger, W. R. *Court Revels, 1485–1559*. Toronto: Toronto University Press, 1994.
Strong, Roy C. *The Cult of Elizabeth: Elizabethan Portraiture and Pageantry*. London: Thames and Hudson, 1977.
Summit, Jennifer. *Memory's Library: Medieval Books in Early Modern England*. Chicago: University of Chicago Press, 2008.

Takenaka, Masahiro. *Jesuit Plays on Japan and English Recusancy: An Essay by Masahiro Takenaka with Editions and Translations by Charles Burnett*. Tokyo: The Renaissance Institute at Sophia University, 1995.

Taylor, Diana. *The Archive and the Repertoire: Performing Cultural Memories in the Americas*. Durham: Duke University Press, 2003.

Thomas, Catherine B. C. "The Miracle Play at Dunstable." *MLN* 32 (1917): 337–44.

Vauchez, Andre. *Sainthood in the Later Middle Ages*. Trans. Jean Birrell. Cambridge: Cambridge University Press, 1997.

Waldron, Jennifer. *Reformations of the Body: Idolatry, Sacrifice, and Early Modern Theater*. New York: Palgrave Macmillan, 2013.

Waller, Gary. *The Virgin Mary in Late Medieval and Early Modern English Literature and Popular Culture*. Cambridge: Cambridge University Press, 2012.

Walsh, Brian. *Unsettled Toleration: Religious Difference on the Shakespearean Stage*. Oxford: Oxford University Press, 2016.

Walsham, Alexandra. *The Reformation of the Landscape: Religion, Identity and Memory in Early Modern Britain and Ireland*. Oxford: Oxford University Press, 2011.

Walsham, Alexandra, Bronwyn Wallace, Ceri Law, and Brian Cummings, eds. *Memory and the English Reformation*. Cambridge: Cambridge University Press, 2020.

Ward, Charles E. "Massinger and Dryden." *ELH* 2 (1935): 263–66.

Wasson, John. "Corpus Christi Play and Pageants at Ipswich." *Research Opportunities in Renaissance Drama* 19 (1976): 99–108.

Wasson, John. "Secular Saint Plays of the Elizabethan Era." *The Saint Plays of Medieval Europe*. Edited Clifford Davidson, 241–60. Early Drama, Art, and Music Monograph Series 8. Kalamazoo, MI: Medieval Institute Publications, 1986.

Watkins, John. *Representing Elizabeth in Stuart England: Literature, History, Sovereignty*. Cambridge: Cambridge University Press, 2002.

Watson, Nicholas. "Censorship and Cultural Change in Late-Medieval England: Vernacular Theology, the Oxford Translation Debate, and Arundel's Constitutions of 1409." *Speculum* 70 (1995): 822–64.

Weinstein, Donald and Rudolph M. Bell. *Saints and Society: The Two Worlds of Western Christendom, 1000–1700*. Chicago: University of Chicago Press, 1982.

Westlake, Herbert F. *Parish Gilds of Mediaeval England*. London: Society for Promoting Christian Knowledge, 1919.

White, Paul Whitfield. *Theatre and Reformation: Protestantism, Patronage, and Playing in Tudor England*. Cambridge: Cambridge University Press, 1993.

White, Paul Whitfield. *Drama and Religion in English Provincial Society, 1485–1660*. Cambridge: Cambridge University Press, 2008.

Wickham, Glynne. "The Staging of Saint Plays in England." In *The Medieval Drama*. Edited by Sandro Sticco, 99–119. Albany: State University of New York Press, 1972.

Wiggins, Martin and Catherine Richardson, eds. *British Drama 1533–1642: A Catalogue* Oxford: Oxford University Press, 2012–19.

Williams, Deanne. "*Friar Bacon and Friar Bungay* and the Rhetoric of Temporality." In *Reading the Medieval in Early Modern England*. Edited by Gordon McMullan and David Matthews, 31–50. Cambridge: Cambridge University Press, 2007.

Williamson, Elizabeth. *The Materiality of Religion in Early Modern English Drama*. Farnham: Ashgate, 2009.

Williamson, Elizabeth. "'Batter'd, Not Demolish'd': Staging the Tortured Body in *The Martyred Soldier*." *Medieval and Renaissance Drama in England* 26 (2013): 43–59.

Wilson, Richard. "To Great Saint Jacques Bound: *All's Well That Ends Well* in Shakespeare's Spain." In *Sacred Text—Sacred Space: Architectural, Spiritual and Literary Convergences in England and Wales*. Edited by Joseph Sterrett and Peter Thomas, 97–121. Leiden: Brill, 2011.

Winstead, Karen A. *Virgin Martyrs: Legends of Sainthood in the Middle Ages*. Ithaca: Cornell University Press, 1997.

Winstead, Karen A. *John Capgrave's Fifteenth Century*. Philadelphia: University of Pennsylvania Press, 2007.

Winstead, Karen A. *Fifteenth-Century Lives: Writing Sainthood in England*. ReFormations: Medieval and Early Modern Series. Notre Dame: University of Notre Dame Press, 2020.
Withington, Robert. *English Pageantry: An Historical Outline*. 2 vols. Cambridge, 1918 and 1926; reprinted NY, 1963 and 1980.
Wittik, Stephen. "Middleton's *A Game at Chess* and the Making of a Theatrical Public." *SEL* 55, no. 2 (2015): 423–46.
Wogan-Browne, Jocelyn. *Saints' Lives and Women's Literary Culture: c.1150–1350: Virginity and Its Authorizations*. Oxford: Oxford University Press, 2001.
Wolf, Kirsten. "The Legend of Saint Dorothy: Medieval Vernacular Renderings and their Latin Sources." *Analecta Bollandiana* 114 (1996): 41–72.
Womack, Peter. "Shakespeare and the Sea of Stories." *JMEMS* 29 (1999): 169–87.
Wortham, B. Hale. "The Churchwardens Accounts of Bassingbourn." *The Antiquary* 7 (1883): 24–6.
Worthen, W. B. "Antigone's Bones." *TDR: The Drama Review* 52 (Fall 2008): 10–33.
Wright, Stephen. "The Durham Play of Mary and the Poor Knight: Sources and Analogues of a Lost English Miracle Play." *Comparative Drama* 17 (1983): 254–65.
Wright, Stephen K. "Is the Ashmole Fragment a Remnant of a Middle English Saint play?" *Neophilologus* 75 (1991): 139–49.
Wylie, J. H. *The Reign of Henry V*. 3 vols. Cambridge: Cambridge University Press, 1914–29.
Ziegler, Georgianna. "England's Savior: Elizabeth I in the Writings of Thomas Heywood." *Renaissance Papers* (1980): 29–37.
Ziegler, Georgianna, ed. *Elizabeth I, Then and Now*. Seattle: University of Washington Press, 2003.
Zlatar, Antonina Bevan. *Reformation Fictions: Polemical Protestant Dialogues in Elizabethan England*. Oxford: Oxford University Press, 2011.
Zysk, Jay. *Shadow and Substance: Eucharistic Controversy and English Drama across the Reformation Divide*. Notre Dame: Notre Dame University Press, 2017.
Zysk, Jay and Katherine Steele Brokaw, eds. *Sacred and Secular Transactions in the Age of Shakespeare*. Evanston: Northwestern University Press, 2019.

Index

Admiral's Men, Lord (company) 18, 106
Aberdeen 29n28, 32
Aelred of Rievaulx 13, 27, 126
Africa, North 157–158
Albion see Britain
angels 32n41, 41, 50, 66, 75, 77, 85, 87, 90, 97, 109, 124n27, 125, 165, 171
   theatrical characters 1, 3, 20, 27, 32, 35, 37, 38, 41–42, 70, 82, 93–98, 103, 105–106, 122–123, 128, 138, 142, 144–150, 156, 159, 160, 164, 165–166, 169–170, 175–179
   characters like 109
Anna/Anne of Denmark 4
Annunciation 35, 40, 76, 163
Antioch 117, 120, 150, 151, 156
anthologizing as literary practice 113–116
Antichrist 28, 49, 81
antisemitism 40, 42, 65, 69
antitheatricalism 27–28, 40, 100
Appleford, Amy 108
Apollonius of Tyre 38, 113, 120
Arianism 157–158
Aristotle 166–167, 169
Arrell, Douglas 101–102
Arthur (king) 34, 115, 116
Arthurian legend 115–116, 127, 129
Askew, Anne 158
assassination see murder
Assumption 34–35, 41–42, 71, 116, 159n37, 171
Aston, Margaret 6n12, 47, 52n122

Bale, John 48, 51
   Acts of the English Votaries 49, 50
   De Traditione de Thomas Becket, 48
   King Johan 94–96
   Temptation of Our Lord, The 96n47
Bamford, Karen 9n25, 144n21, 160
baptism 69, 87, 101, 107, 108, 157–158, 161
baroque 109
Barton, Elizabeth 75
Bassingbourn 22, 23, 33–34
Beckwith, Sarah 6n11, 7n17, 8–9, 40, 119, 169
Bedingfeld, Sir Henry 88, 92–93, 97–98
bed trick 64, 127, 165
Bible 83
   as stage property 82, 91–94, 99, 105–106

Genesis 39, 177
Exodus 128
Proverbs 93
Daniel 93n38
Jonah 120
Apocrypha 93n38
New Testament 52
Gospels 38, 111
Revelation 32
biblical plays 18, 28, 36–37, 39, 60, 70, 107, 141
   terminology of 26
   Chester 39–40, 81, 94n39, 159–37
   N-Town (Hegge) 39, 40, 41–42, 60, 81, 163, 169, 170
   Towneley (Wakefield) 26, 39, 175
   York 26, 39, 159n37
Blackfriars (theatre) 101, 106–107, 120, 131
blindness 59, 73, 123, 159
blood (stage) 35, 40
Bocaccio, Giovanni
   The Decameron 137–138
Bokenham, Osbern 15
   Legenda Aurea 49
   Legendys of Hooly Wummen 143n19
Boleyn, Anne 107, 109
books
   as stage properties 3, 20, 57, 67, 93, 123–124, 138, 145, 149, 151, 155–156, 159, 166, 167
   see also Bible, as stage property
   and devotional culture 91, 145
   and iconoclasm 47–49
   religious regulation of 47, 52, 54–55
   service and liturgical 47, 49, 105
Book of Common Prayer (*BCP*) 44, 51–56, 78
Braintree 29–30
Britain 12, 111–136, 147
Bristol 31
Brokaw, Katherine Steele 8
Buckland, Ralph
   Memorable and Tragical History of the Persecution in Afrike, The 157–158

Candlemas 46, 48, 49, 53, 100n55
canonization 20, 44n92, 55–56, 65, 138, 141–143
Canterbury 29, 35, 48
carnivalesque 22, 25–26, 27, 28, 30, 31, 114

Catherine of Braganza 164n46
Catholicism 3–4, 5, 12, 19, 26, 43, 44–45, 54, 57, 64, 79, 79–110, 113, 124, 134–136, 157–158
 attacks on 49, 74–76, 79, 82, 105, 125, 134–136
Catholic Reformation *see* Counter-Reformation
Caxton, William
 Golden Legend, The xiii, 15, 33n41, 46, 49–50, 57, 65, 85, 86, 87, 89, 90,102, 106, 117, 120, 122, 125n32, 142, 143n19, 145, 150n28
celibacy 20, 50, 115, 118, 125, 127, 128, 129, 142, 160 *see also* virginity
Chapman, Alison 9, 68n24, 121
Charles I 3, 54n130, 134, 166
Charles II 1, 54n130
Charles V 34–35, 71, 97
Chaucer, Geoffrey
 Canterbury Tales, The 60, 114, 115, 173
childbirth and pregnancy 38, 40, 41, 46, 76, 107, 119, 127, 176 *see also* futurity *and* nativity
chorus 65, 68, 101, 114
Church of England 22–23, 47–48, 51–54, 88, 104
Christmas 27, 28, 29, 35n60, 43, 100
Cicognini, Giacinto
 Saint Mary of Egypt 36
Clark, Stuart 64–65
clergy (theatrical character) 60, 67–68, 85, 87, 92, 93, 96, 98–99, 103–105, 107–108, 134 *see also* friar, hermit, monks, *and* nuns
Clopper, Lawrence 24, 25–26, 28, 30, 31n35, 35n60
Cockpit (theatre) 9–10, 160n39
Coletti, Theresa 11n31, 70n30, 81, 173
comedy 20, 36, 37, 39, 58, 64–65, 119, 128, 130, 131, 166
conjuration *see* magic
conversion 28n23, 93, 151, 157
 and saints' legends 31, 32, 58, 94n40, 102–103, 112, 115, 120, 129, 142, 150, 161
 in drama 36, 37–38, 40, 42, 69–70, 103, 105, 107, 112, 121–123, 128, 129, 143–144, 148–149, 153–156, 157, 159, 160, 162, 163, 164–165, 170
Cooper, Helen 115n7, 127
Cornwall 23n2, 25
Coronation of the Virgin 35, 109
Corpus Christi 22, 28, 29, 32, 48
Corpus Christi plays *see* biblical plays
costumes/costuming 28, 30, 67, 68, 95, 103–104, 108–109, 122, 127, 148, 150, 152–153, 175
Counter-Reformation 12, 83, 104, 109, 133, 135–136, 138, 141

Coventry 34
Cowling, Jane 29
Cox, John 60n7, 94, 96,
Cranmer, Thomas 51–52, 75, 108
cross
 as stage property 103, 105, 123, 149, 156
 sign of (gesture) 58–59, 87, 101–102, 120, 149, 150, 156
cross-dressing 12n34, 22, 75, 153, 176
Croxton *Play of the Sacrament* 8, 40
Crucifixion 8, 13, 39, 65, 125

dancing 28, 108–109, 159, 161
Daniel, Walter
 Vita Sancti Aelredi 13–14, 16, 126
Davis, Tracy 16–17
Davidson, Clifford 24, 25–26, 31n35, 36
Day, John, and Thomas Dekker
 Guy of Warwick, The Tragical History of 111, 126–129, 169
Day, John, William Rowley, and George Wilkins
 Travels of Three English Brothers, The 101
deafness 159
debate/disputation
 depiction in drama 86–87, 100, 104–106, 165
 in saints' legends 84, 86, 87n22, 164
 prohibition of 48, 100
de Certeau, Michel 136
de Grazia, Margreta 122
de Villegas, Alonso
 Flos Sanctorum 104
Dekker, Thomas
 If It Be Not Good, The Devil Is In It 150n27
 Shoemaker's Holiday 72
 Whore of Babylon, The 107
Dekker, Thomas, and Ben Jonson
 Magnificent Entertainment, The 34, 78, 114, 133
Dekker, Thomas, and Philip Massinger
 Virgin Martyr, The 38, 142–150, 151, 153, 154–155, 158, 159, 162, 164, 166, 167
Dekker, Thomas, and John Webster
 Famous History of Sir Thomas Wyatt, The 96–97
Deloney, Thomas
 Gentle Craft, The 121–126
devils 49–50, 96, 102–103, 129, 150
 theatrical characters 1, 3, 20, 37, 42, 60–71, 98, 105–106, 110, 112, 138, 148–150, 153, 155–156, 160, 161, 165, 167
 characters like 76, 91–95, 128, 134,
Diana (goddess) 116–119

Digby plays 57, 170
   Conversion of Saint Paul 23n2, 25n9, 69–70, 149, 166
   Killing of the Children 31
   Mary Magdalene 23, 25n9, 36–39, 43, 65, 70, 81, 95–96, 113, 120, 166, 169, 179
Diocletian 72, 82, 84, 121–122, 149, 150, 159
Diocletian (lost play) 72
disability *see* blindness, deafness, injury, *and* madness
Ditchfield, Simon 141
dragon 32, 33, 34, 71, 114, 127, 132–133, 149
dreams 65, 90, 134, 159, 172, 177 *see also* sleeping *and* visions
Drue, Thomas
   Duchess of Suffolk, The 96
Dryden, John
   Tyrranick Love 1, 20, 164, 165–166
dumbshow *see* pageantry, conventions of
Durham, 23n2, 26

East Anglia 23n2, 37, 169, 179
Easter 27, 29, 30, 31, 178
Edgar (king) 50, 59–61, 63
Edward VI 34, 49, 51–52, 78
   theatrical character 96–97
Edwards, Suzanne 163
Egerton, Alice and Thomas 77–78
Ellerbeck 103
Elizabeth I 2, 44–45, 53, 54n130, 55, 74, 76–78, 132
   theatrical character 3, 16, 19, 80–110, 124, 138, 164, 169–170
Elizabethan Settlement 46, 52–53, 55
Ember Days 114
Ephesus 117, 118, 119–120
Epiphany 27, 100n55
eucharist 40, 48, 61, 125, 142, 158, 170–171
Exeter 28
Eynsham 27

fairies 64, 67–68, 128,
festivity 22–36, 47, 67–68, 114, 120, 132–33
Fitz Stephen, William
   Description of London, A 27
Folger Consort 176
Ford, Judy Ann 15
Fortune (theatre) 9, 67
Foxe, John, 48, 51
   Book of Martyrs (Acts and Monuments) 50, 55, 73, 81–98, 122, 139–140
friar (theatrical character) 62, 93, 96, 98
futurity 38, 126, 128, 129, 130

Garber, Marjorie 141
Gardiner, Stephen (Bishop of Winchester) 85, 87, 92, 93, 96, 98–99, 108
Gentileschi, Artemisia 2, 4
ghost 65, 115, 141, 145, 139, 177
Gillen, Katherine 95–96
Gilte Legende 15n41, 49n107, 143n19, 150n28
Glastonbury 49, 58, 64
Globe (theatre) 39, 101, 120
Gloucester 26n12
Gouthwaite Hall 100
Gower, John 112, 114, 118–119
   Confessio Amantis 114–115, 120
Grantley, Darryll 36
Gravdal, Katherine 157
Greenblatt, Stephen 5–6
green man 103–106
Green, Robert
   Friar Bacon and Friar Bungay 62–63
Green, Robert, and Thomas Lodge
   Looking Glass for London, A 59, 94n42
Gregory of Tours 13
guilds 51–52
   Cordwainers (Wells) 126n33
   Drapers (London) 32
   Goldsmiths (London) 78, 133
   Haberdashers (London) 3–4, 133
   Hammermen (Perth) 29n28
   Mercers (Wells) 114
   St. George (Norwich) 33, 132–133
   SS Christopher and George 33 (York)
   Skinners (London) 32
gunpowder 30, 35 *see also* pyrotechnics
Gurnis, Musa 6–7
Guy of Warwick 115–116, 126–129, 169
Gwyn, Nell, 1

hagiography 10–11, 13–16, 46, 52, 70–71, 80–81, 84–8, 98, 102–104, 116, 126
Hardison, O. B. 7–8
Harefield 76–78, 132
Harris, Carissa 163
Harris, Jonathan Gil 17–18
Haughton, William
   Devil and His Dame, The (*Grim, The Collier of Croyden*) 57–59, 63–69, 70, 153
Heffernan, Thomas 13–14, 126
Hegel 97
hell 37, 42, 60, 61, 62, 64, 66, 67, 71, 105, 124, 128, 152, 155, 156, 173, 174
Henrietta-Maria 3–4
Henry V 33, 74, 132n47
Henry VI 73n35

INDEX

Henry VIII 22, 35n59, 47–49, 75, 129
   theatrical character 97, 107
Henslowe, Philip 9, 57, 64, 72,
Hereford 22, 28, 29, 45, 51, 52
hermit 32, 102, 103, 105, 112, 126–131
Herod (king) 18, 60
Heywood, Thomas
   England's Elizabeth 164n45
   If You Know Not Me, You Know Nobody 3, 70, 78, 80–110, 118, 120, 122, 123, 124, 138, 156, 163, 166, 169–170
   Londini Artium & Scientiarum Scaturigo 4, 133
   London Ius Honorarium 4, 133
   Londini Speculum 4, 133
   Silver Age, The 150n27
Hickerson, Megan 85
history play 19, 72–76, 94, 96–98, 128n39, 132,
Hocktide 30n31
Holy Innocents 22, 28, 31
Holy Rood Day 67, 68
Holywell 53, 72, 73, 121–126, 147, 179
Hopkins, Lisa 121n21, 135n52
Hrotsvit of Gandersheim
   Dulcitius 36, 142
hymen 41, 140, 141

iconoclasm 20, 44–45, 48–51, 52–53, 70, 106, 131, 136, 144, 145–146, 170, 172–173
iconography 2, 4, 31–32, 33, 66, 68, 70, 78, 91–96, 100, 133, 143, 145–146, 149–150, 164, 166, 175
idols/idolatry 84, 97, 104, 143, 145–146, 151, 159
illusion 20, 63, 168–179
imitatio Christi 13, 14, 16, 58, 87, 88, 89, 93, 110, 128, 137–138, 157, 174
injury 41, 73, 171
Ipswich 32
Ireland 113, 134–135, 161–163
islamophobia 32, 101, 128, 127, 151, 152, 152, 154

Jackson, Ken 5
Jacobus de Voragine
   Legenda Aurea 15, 143n19
James I 34, 78, 114, 133
Jensen, Phebe 104n78, 106
Jesus Christ 28, 37, 70, 85, 87, 89, 90n32, 95, 102, 103, 111, 123, 125, 128, 143, 157, 174, 175
Jerusalem 37, 41, 70, 119, 127, 128
Jews/Judaism 32, 40, 41, 42, 65, 69, 101, 176–178
   see also antisemitism

Jocelyn of Furness
   Life of St. Patrick 161–162
John of Salisbury 27
Johnson, Richard
   Seven Champions of Christendom 134, 160
Johnston, Alexandra 25–26,
Johnston, Bronwyn 66
Jonson, Ben 113
Jupiter (god) 146, 148, 159 *see also* iconoclasm *and* idolatry
Justice, Steven 40

Katherine of Aragon 24, 106–109, 110, 131
Kearney, James 93, 151
Keenan, Siobhan 101, 128n39
Kelly, Kathleen Coyne 142–143
Kent 97, 112, 121
King, John 91
King Leir 101–102
Kirke, John
   Seven Champions of Christendom 131, 160
Klausner, David 159n37
Knack to Know a Knave, A 57–63, 64, 65, 67, 68–69, 70–73, 76, 149
Kushner, Tony
   Angels in America 20, 170, 175–179

Lammas Day 52
Langland, John
   Piers Plowman 81
Law, Ceri 131
Lent 27, 48
Leo, Russ 143, 167–168
Lerer, Seth 116
Lichfield 27
Life of Christina of Markyate 170–172, 175
Lincoln 27, 35, 36, 51
liturgy 45–47, 51–53, 169, 178
liturgical calendar 2, 11, 18, 19, 22–23, 24, 27, 28, 31, 42–47, 51–56, 57, 72, 77, 78, 80, 110, 111, 114, 133
Lollardy 48, 137–138
London 4, 22, 23n2, 24, 27, 29, 32, 34n53, 35, 55, 57, 60n7, 64, 66, 71, 73, 78, 99, 100, 101n58, 109, 112, 114, 126, 128n39, 130, 131, 133, 134, 147, 169, 179
Loewenstein, David 6
ludus 25, 28, 30
Lupton, Julia Reinhard 5, 7, 9, 120
Lycia 102, 104
Lydd 23n2, 25n9

Lydgate, John 15
  Life of Alban and Amphibalus 125n32
  Margaret of Anjou's Entry into London, 1445 34n53

madness 37, 42, 65, 66, 123, 141, 146, 159, 165
Magi *see* Three Kings of Cologne
magic 58, 61–68, 73, 95, 105, 117, 130, 149, 150–156, 161
magician character 19, 58–68, 95, 105, 128, 129–130, 150–156, 161, 165
Manion, Lee 127
Mardi Gras *see* Shrove Tuesday
Margaret of Anjou 34
Marlowe, Christopher
  Doctor Faustus 42, 59, 60, 61, 62–63, 93, 94n32, 151, 166
Marotti, Arthur 5
marriage 8, 39–40, 59, 66–68, 86, 106, 107, 115, 116, 118, 126n33, 127, 129, 134, 151, 154, 160, 173
  celibacy in 41, 127, 142, 165
  forced 41, 64, 165, 157, 172
  interruption of 62, 116
  mystical 85, 90 *see also sponsa Christi*
  rejection of 1, 48, 84, 89, 50, 130, 155
Marseille 37–38, 119, 179
Marshall, Peter 6n12, 131
martyrdom 9, 13–14, 27, 29, 31, 32, 35, 37, 58, 80–100, 112, 116, 118, 122, 124, 148, 156, 157
  avoidance of 106–110
martyrology 44–45, 54, 83, 86, 88, 91, 110, 149, 159 *see also* Foxe, John
Mary I 3, 12, 79,
  theatrical character 82, 85–86, 96–99
Maximian, 1, 82, 121, 123, 125–126, 149, 165–166
Medbourne, Matthew
  St. Cecily: Or, The Converted Twins 164–165
Melton, John
  Astrologaster 150n27
Merlin 115, 116, 129 *see also* Birth of Merlin, The *under* Rowley
Middleton, Thomas
  Game at Chess, A 134–135
  Revenger's Tragedy, The 155–156
Middleton, Thomas, and William Rowley
  Changeling, The 140–141
miracles 13, 30, 49–50, 55n135, 78, 84–85, 87, 117, 142, 172, 174
  fake 40, 50–51, 52, 58, 73, 85, 137–138
  theatrical 3, 7, 8, 18, 20–21, 27, 32, 34, 36–42, 66–71, 93, 95, 103, 105, 108–109, 118, 122–24, 128, 130, 139, 146–150, 152–156, 159–160, 166–167, 169–170, 175–179
  absence of 158, 161–163, 164–166, 171 *see also* magic *and* witchcraft, accusation of
miracula 25–26
Miranda, Lin-Manuel
  Hamilton 168
Mirk, John
  Festial 46, 49, 50
monk (character) 57–68, 95–96
monasteries/monasticism 13–14, 25–28, 77, 118, 120, 123, 124, 129–131, 179
  dissolution of 8, 47, 49–52, 53, 55, 131, 136 *see also* St. Dunstan
monster 113, 127, 132, 134, 160
morality play, conventions of 37, 58, 59–61, 73–74, 90, 95–97, 105–106, 107–108, 134, 145, 146, 148
Morebath 33
Mormons/Mormonism 177–178
Moses 128
murder 35, 60, 61, 62, 67, 72, 95, 98, 137, 140, 143, 159
Muhammad 38 *see also* islamophobia
Mueller, Janel 14, 48
Munday, Anthony
  Chryso-thriambos 78, 133
  John a Kent, John a Cumber 72, 73
Munro, Lucy 10n28, 118–119, 130, 160n39, 162
Murphy, John 106
Muslim characters 32, 101, 128, 127, 151, 152, 152, 154 *see also* islamophobia
mystery plays *see* biblical plays
mythology 34, 36, 71, 116–119, 146, 148, 156, 159

nativity 29, 35, 39–41, 159n37, 170, 175 *see also* childbirth
Nidderdale 100–106
Newman, Barbara 10, 116,
Noah 39
Norwich 27, 33, 71, 132–33
Nova Legenda Anglie 42
nuns 28, 36, 50, 96–97, 101, 118, 122, 130–31, 154, 158, 162

Ovid 156

paganism, depiction of 7, 26, 38, 69, 87, 119, 146, 148, 151, 158–159, 164–165
  characters 31n35, 32, 89, 113, 119, 127, 128, 129–130, 134, 138, 153, 158–159, 160
  ceremony 38, 145–146

rejection of 84, 89, 143, 160–161; *see also* idolatry *and* iconoclasm
pageantry
  conventions of 5, 11, 22–36, 92, 98, 70–71, 120, 132
  coronation 34, 78, 99–100, 109, 112, 114, 133
  Lord Mayor's Show 3–4, 78, 112, 132–133
  Midsummer's Watch 22, 29, 31, 32, 33n45, 71
  royal 4, 24, 34, 71, 76–78, 126
  in drama 82, 90–94, 98–100, 107–109, 117, 165, 168
Pallas (god) 159 *see also* idolatry
papacy 47, 49, 55–56, 95, 96, 108, 141–142
Paris, Matthew 129, 130n41
Parish, Helen 48, 50–51, 58
Parker, John 7–8, 9, 119,
Parker, Matthew 54, 55
Parks, George 119
patron saints 2, 4–5, 9n25, 14, 22, 32–34, 51–52, 59, 63, 71, 74, 78, 97, 99, 111–113, 132–136, 164
penance/penitential/repentance 14, 37, 41, 50, 69, 70, 75, 95, 103, 108, 112, 120, 126–129, 137, 149
  absence of 60, 62, 63, 65, 137
  sacrament of 95, 137, 145
Pepys, Samuel 90n33, 163
performativity 3, 16, 61n9, 80, 137
periodization 1, 9–10, 20, 57, 68
Persia 101
Perth 29n28, 32
Phoenix (theatre) 10n23, 140
Pickett, Holly Crawford 6n11, 94n42, 144n21, 148, 176
pilgrim/pilgrimage 20, 32, 38n67, 52, 72, 73, 75, 101, 118, 119, 122, 127, 131, 135
playbooks, records of 25n9, 30, 101n58
Plautus 36
  Menaechmi 119
poison/potion 66, 67, 95, 125, 140–141, 155
Pole, Reginald (Cardinal) 98–99
procession 22, 29, 30n31, 32, 33, 74, 97, 98, 133
prophesy 49, 75, 163, 165, 177
Protestant Reformation *see* Reformation
Protestantism 40, 44–45, 53, 55–57, 69n26, 74–76, 79, 80–85, 91–98, 100, 110, 144n21
  attacks on 91, 105–106
purgatory 8, 33, 45, 47, 52, 95, 101, 132
Purification of the Virgin, Feast of the *see* Candlemas
Puritans/Puritanism 48, 60, 83
Pynson, Richard
  Kalendre of the Newe Legende of Englande 42–43, 49, 50

pyrotechnics 30, 35, 37, 38, 66, 69, 70, 103, 105, 128, 138, 149–150, 156, 160, 164

Quem quaeritis 22, 27, 176, 178
queerness 150, 176–178

rape 2, 20, 50, 84, 117, 124, 139–163, 166–167, 170, 171
recusancy 19, 82, 100–106, 158 *see also* Catholicism
Red Bull (theatre) 9, 10n28, 12, 80n1, 101, 140, 160n39, 162, 179,
Reformation 6, 47, 49–53, 83–100, 138
relics 14, 25, 45, 55, 77, 81, 129, 137 *see also* translation Reformation attacks on 51–53, 131
repertoire (theatrical) 11, 16–18, 61, 82, 96–97, 138–140, 149, 151, 156–163, 166–167, 169–170
resurrection 8, 27, 28, 37, 38n68, 65, 111, 122
Richard the Confessor (lost play) 72
Robin Hood 30n31, 31
Robinson, Marsha 83n6, 96,
Roman Empire 112, 120, 121, 123, 126, 157
romance 12n34, 18, 19, 31, 33, 38, 39, 71, 78, 95, 101–104, 111–136
Rome 1, 38, 45, 49, 58, 62
rosary 57, 65, 66, 101
Rose (theatre) 9, 67
Rowley, Samuel
  When You See Me, You Know Me 83, 94, 96–98
Rowley, William
  Birth of Merlin, The 126, 129–131, 132, 133, 138
  Shoemaker, A Gentleman A 7, 12, 20, 72, 111, 112, 120–126, 130, 133, 138, 147, 149–150, 166
Ryrie, Alec 54

sainthood/sanctity 2, 13–14, 50, 70, 78, 126, 137–138, 171–175
  and Reformation 43–44, 48, 50, 55–56, 110
  theatrical 4, 9, 16–17, 27, 36, 58–59, 70, 80–81, 85, 104, 122, 143–143, 166–167, 169–170, 178–179
St. Albans 73, 121–126, 131
St. Christopher (lost play) 100–106, 110, 138
St. Winifred's Well 121–126, 147, 179
saint play, history of 22–42, 59, 68–71, 114, 153, 169–170
saints
  Agatha 13, 84, 86
  Agnes 13, 29, 41, 52, 84–85, 89–90, 117, 123, 142, 147, 166

256 INDEX

saints (*Continued*)
  Alban and Amphibel (Amphibalus) 54n130, 55, 72, 73, 121–126, 129, 149–150
  Alexis 127–128
  Alphege 54
  Anastasia 142
  Andrew 30, 34, 78, 114, 133, 134–136, 160
  Anne 31, 36, 47 *see also* Digby *Killing of the Children*
  Anselm 129
  Anthony 134–136
  Augustine of Hippo 109, 163
  Austin (Augustine) of Canterbury 49, 54
  Bartholomew 31
  Bede 54n130, 55
  Boniface 55
  Bridget 54, 162
  Catherine of Siena 43
  Boromeo, Carlo (Cardinal) 136
  Cecilia 41, 84–85, 123n27, 134, 142, 150, 164–165, 172
  Chad (Caedda) of Mercia 54, 55
  Christopher 32, 100–106, 111, 127
  Clement 4, 31, 52
  Cleophas 111
  Crispin and Crispinian 4, 14, 43, 45–46, 47, 72, 121–126, 132
  Cuthbert 26
  David 54, 132, 134–136
  Dennis 134–136, 160
  Dorothy 90n32, 111, 139, 143–150, 162
  Drusiana 159
  Dunstan 35, 44, 45, 49–50, 54, 55, 57–72, 76, 77, 78, 129, 133, 149, 153
  Edith 50n110, 135
  Edmund (king and martyr) 35, 54, 71, 116
  Edmund of Abingdon 46
  Edward (king and martyr) 54
  Edward the Confessor 34, 35, 54, 56, 71, 77
  Elizabeth 35n60 *see also* Annunciation
  Enarchus 54n130
  Erasmus 29n28
  Erkenwald 35, 71
  Etheldreda (Audrey) of Ely 54, 55
  Eustace (Placidas) 30, 31, 127
  Feliciana 30n31
  Gabriel 35 *see also* Annunciation
  Genevieve 14
  George 4, 22, 23n2, 25n9, 29, 31, 33, 34, 35, 43, 46, 52, 71, 72, 74, 78, 97, 99, 114, 127, 132–136, 160
  Germain 129
  Gilbert of Sempringham 55
  Gregory the Great 47
  Guinefort (dog) 13, 14
  Helen 135
  Hugh 54n130, 72, 121–126
  Ignatius Loyola 134, 136
  James 23n2, 118, 134–136
  Joan of Arc 43–44, 74–75, 79, 136
  John the Baptist 4, 23n2, 29, 35, 50, 71
  John the Evangelist 23n2, 32, 34, 116
  John of Beverley 46, 47
  Joseph 39, 41
  Justina and Cyprian 139, 150–156, 162, 166
  Katherine of Alexandria 1–4, 22, 24, 29, 30, 31, 44n93, 52, 75, 76, 84–85, 90n32, 114, 116, 133, 159, 164
  Lawrence 23n2, 25n9, 29n28, 47
  Linus 47
  Lucy 142
  Margaret of Antioch 22, 33, 34, 47, 58–59, 71, 75, 76, 84, 87, 116, 120, 133, 149
  Marina 120
  Mary Magdalene 14, 22, 23n2, 25n9, 37–39, 47, 95–96, 111, 113, 116, 119, 120, 169, 179 *see also* Digby *Mary Magdalene*
  Mary of Egypt 36, 120
  Mary the Virgin 8, 34–35, 37, 39–40, 46, 71, 74–76, 82, 89, 92n36, 93, 97, 101, 107, 116, 118, 119, 127, 141, 142, 169–170, 175 *see also* Annunciation *and* Assumption
  Mellitus 55
  Meriasek 23n2, 25n9
  Michael 35, 75
  Nicholas 22, 26n12, 43, 114
  Pancras 43
  Patrick 8, 43, 134–136, 160, 161–163
  Paul 23n2, 25n9, 69, 120, 149 *see also* Digby *Conversion of Saint Paul*
  Peter 42
  Polycarp 134
  Radigund 74–75
  Richard of Chichester 56, 72
  Sabina 30n31
  Sebastian 29n28
  Stephen 29n28
  Swithin 29, 30, 55, 77, 129, 132
  Thais 120
  Theophilus 23n2
  Thomas Becket (Thomas of Canterbury) 29, 32, 35, 47–49, 71
  Thomas the Apostle 41
  Ursula 4, 116, 134, 135
  Wilifrida 50n110
  Winifred 15, 53, 72, 73, 121–126, 135, 147, 149–150, 166, 179

INDEX 257

Sanok, Catherine 4, 28–29, 72, 73n35, 111, 116, 135
Santiago de Compostela 118, 135
Saxons 112, 129–130
Schechner, Richard 169
Schreyer, Kurt 94
Schwyzer, Philip 44
Scotland 34, 113, 114, 133, 134–135, 173
secular/secularity 5, 8, 11, 17, 27, 28–29, 32, 42, 52, 71, 121, 173
seduction 50, 95, 104, 140, 150–156, 157, 165, 173–174
seven deadly sins 37, 95 *see also* morality play
sermon 33, 46, 49, 56, 137
sexual violence *see* rape
Shakespeare, John 53n127
Shakespeare, William
 All's Well That Ends Well 20, 118, 127, 135
 Comedy of Errors 119
 Hamlet 8, 39, 45, 57, 140, 143
 Henry V 46, 72, 78, 97, 114, 132, 168
 1 Henry VI 17, 43, 59, 72, 73–76, 79
 2 Henry VI 17, 59, 72, 73, 132
 3 Henry VI 17
 Henry VIII (with John Fletcher) 19, 72, 82, 106–110, 120, 131
 King Lear 8, 101–102, 122
 Measure for Measure 73, 141
 Pericles, Prince of Tyre (with George Wilkins) 19, 38n68, 72, 101–102, 112–120, 123, 128n39, 140
 Richard III 17, 18, 72, 73–74
 Tempest, The 151
 Titus Andronicus 149, 156
 Winter's Tale, The 73, 107
Shirley, Henry
 Martyr'd Soldier, The 138, 139, 140, 156–160, 162, 167
Shirley, James
 Saint Patrick for Ireland 14, 138, 156–157, 160–163, 166–167, 170
Shrewsbury 29, 30, 114
Shrove Tuesday 22, 27, 100n55
Simpsons, The (company) 100–106
sleeping 64, 65, 67, 93, 108–09, 118, 134, 155, 165 *see also* dreams
Sofer, Andrew 62
Solberg, Maggie 11n32, 25n8, 26, 39, 42, 75, 76
Somerset, Fiona 137–138
sorcery *see* magic *and* witchcraft, accusation of
sound effects/soundscape 38, 138, 149–150, 172–173, 174–175

music 20, 50, 66, 90n33, 93, 98, 108–109, 117, 118, 122, 123, 128, 138, 149–150, 156, 159, 164–165, 166, 167
 thunder 37, 65, 66, 68, 69, 76, 105, 123, 128, 130, 152, 154, 159, 160, 177
South English Legendary 15, 42, 49n106, 50n109, 102n65, 115, 125n32, 139, 150n28
Squire, John
 Tes Irenes Trophaea 3, 133
Spain/Spanish 64, 71, 86, 97, 101, 104, 109, 113, 134–135
Spenser, Edmund
 Faerie Queene, The 74–75
sponsa Christi 84, 89–90, 98, 123, 125, 155, 162, 163
Sponsler, Claire 24
sports 27, 30
Stanislavsky, Constantine 39
Stilma, Astrid 98
Summit, Jennifer 8, 45, 52–55, 112–113,
superstition/superstitious 7, 8, 44, 52, 53n126, 64, 66, 84, 93, 113, 123, 124, 125, 164
Sussex's Men (company) 72

Tarsus 116, 117–118, 119
Taylor, Diana 16–17
temporality 11, 22, 29, 43, 44, 51, 52, 94n39, 114, 121, 122, 124
Thomas Lord Cromwell 96
Three Kings of Cologne 30n31
torment/torture 2, 4, 13, 28, 29, 30, 32, 33, 34, 71, 84, 86–88, 90n32, 101, 104, 121, 122, 139, 143, 145, 148, 158–159, 167
tragicomedy 12n34, 19, 20, 111–136, 140, 153, 160n39,
translation of relics 29, 30, 35, 46, 47, 48, 54, 55, 77, 81, 83, 129, 136
transubstantiation *see* eucharist
Tretise of Miraclis Pleyinge 28
Tyndale, William 75
typology 9, 55, 111, 112, 117, 120, 128, 157, 174
tyrant character 1, 17–18, 82n5, 85–86, 96, 98, 121–123, 128, 139, 146, 151, 154, 159, 161, 165
Tyre 117–118, 120
Two Noble Ladies and The Converted Conjuror 138, 150–156, 162, 166, 170

Uther Pendragon 129, 130, 132

Vandals 157, 159
Venus (goddess) 146 *see also* iconoclasm
vernacular theology 81, 175

Veruliamium *see* St. Albans
Victor of Vita
   Historia Persecutionis Africanae Provinciae 157–158
virginity 41–42, 76, 82, 89, 107, 122–23, 130, 138, 140–141, 153–155, 162, 171
virgin martyrdom 4, 41, 55, 76, 80–100, 110, 116–117, 123–125, 137–167, 171
visions 31, 32, 49, 50, 75–76, 90, 107–109, 118, 125, 134, 150, 159, 165, 172 *see also* dreams
Vita Sancti Cristofori 103, 116
Von Trier, Lars
   Breaking the Waves 20, 170, 172–175

Wells 4, 114, 126n33
Wager, Lewis
   Life and Repentaunce of Mary Magdalene, The 23n2, 43, 94–96
Waldron, Jennifer 144n21, 148
Wales 53, 111, 112, 113, 115, 121–126, 129–136
Walsh, Brian 6–7, 83, 97
Walsham, Alexandra 6n12, 131
Warlamchester (lost play) 72
Warwick 112, 127–129
Watson, Nicholas 81
Webster, John
   Duchess of Malfi, The 131, 140

wedding *see* marriage
Westminster Abbey 34, 53, 107
White, Paul Whitfield 101, 104
Wiggins, Alison 115
Williamson, Elizabeth 100, 105, 159n38
Wilson, Robert
   Three Lords of London 94n42
Winchester 22, 27, 29, 77, 112, 128, 129–131, 132
Winstead, Karen 10n31, 15n43, 84, 111, 139, 145n22, 157
witchcraft, accusation of 66, 74–76, 117, 123, 145, 147, 148, 154
Witmore, Michael 6
Wogan-Browne, Jocelyn 84n8, 87n22, 139
Wolsey, Thomas (Cardinal) 107–109
Womack, Peter 94n40, 113n4, 131
Wycliffe, John 48 *see also* Lollardy *and* Tretise of Miraclis Pleyinge

York 23n2, 25n9, 33, 45
Yorkshire 100–106
Yorke, Sir John 100–106

Zlatar, Antonina Bevan 50
Zysk, Jay 7, 8, 10, 61n9